MANY THORNS,
Yet Still Roses

Breaking the Silence with our Story of Sibling Group Adoption

JESSIE GALLAHER

Chasing Kites
publishing

Many Thorns, Yet Still Roses.
Breaking the Silence with our Story of Sibling Group Adoption.

Published by: Chasing Kites Publishing. www.ChasingKitesPublishing.com
Edited by: Lorraine O'Connor Anglemier

ISBN-10 (Ebook):   0-9998437-1-0
ISBN-13 (Ebook):   978-0-9998437-0-3
ISBN-13 (Paperback): 978-0-9998437-1-0

Author/Book website:
http://www.chasingkites.com/authors/Jessie-Gallaher/

Printed in U.S.A.

CONTENTS

Dedication. v

Preface. ix

Chapter 1. In for a Ride 1

Chapter 2. Nothing Happens Unless First We Dream. 7

Chapter 3. Mission Bound 19

Chapter 4. Open Your Heart and Take Us In 29

Chapter 5. You Had Him at Hello 33

Chapter 6. Too Real, Too Fast 39

Chapter 7. Crash Course on Herding Cats 45

Chapter 8. Life Is Either a Daring Adventure, Or Nothing at All. . . . 51

Chapter 9. Tear It Down 55

Chapter 10. The Right Choice Often Isn't Easy 65

Chapter 11. Step on Up, Folks. 75

Chapter 12. Assigned Seats 89

Chapter 13. Costumes, Candy and Chaos, Oh My!. 95

Chapter 14. Things Change All the Time. 107

Chapter 15. Challenges Make Life Interesting 123

Chapter 16. In a Rut, Searching for a Groove. 133

Chapter 17. Strong People Ask for Help 141

Chapter 18. When Two Worlds Collide 151

Chapter 19. Ah, Poop. 163

Chapter 20. Patience and Progress 177

Chapter 21. A Jumbo Roll of Red Tape 187

Chapter 22. Calling for Backup 195

Chapter 23. The Secret to Happiness is Low Expectations 205

Chapter 24. Strive for Progress, not Perfection 219

Chapter 25. A Picture is Worth One Thousand Words 231

Chapter 26. Believe It or Not 239

Chapter 27. Speed Dial 249

Chapter 28. Full Circle 259

Chapter 29. Adoption Day 273

Chapter 30. May Your Adventures Bring You Closer Together 279

Chapter 31. Poking the Bear 291

Chapter 32. Alone in a Crowd. 303

Chapter 33. Life's a Beach. 319

Chapter 34. Seeing the Light 333

Chapter 35. Brought Together by God. 349

Epilogue 357

Thank You. 363

Acknowledgments 365

About the Author 367

DEDICATION

To my husband: You saw how the expectation of silence impacted me, and encouraged me to tell all. Thank you for your support in this process, your love for our family, and your willingness to listen to me read each chapter aloud, for nearly two years! This is for you.

To my children: You have inspired me to dig deeper in faith than I ever thought possible. Thank you for trusting me with your story, and choosing to call me *"Mom."* I love you all! This is for you.

To the children waiting on God's timing and placement, as well as the families who answer the call: I hope that our story builds compassion in those who surround you, so that you may feel supported and loved on your journeys. Most of all, this is for you!

One night a man dreamed he was walking along the beach with the Lord. As scenes of his life flashed before him, he noticed that there were two sets of footprints in the sand. He also noticed at his saddest, lowest times, there was only one set of footprints. This bothered the man and he asked the Lord, *"Did you not promise that if I gave my heart to you that you'd be with me all the way? Then, why is there only one set of footprints during my most troublesome times?"*

The Lord replied, *"My precious child, I love you and would never forsake you. During those times of trial and suffering when you see only one set of footprints, it was then I carried you."*

PREFACE

I did worry about the potential for backlash against my being so brutally honest about our first year as a family. However, keeping that in mind, I still feel God's urge for me to share our story. There are too many families silently struggling through the chaos of family-transitioning with hopes for something better.

To be clear, I believe the struggle is understandable, as some variation of it is present with all forms of parenting. It's the part about doing it alone that doesn't sit well with me, and I believe that sharing the context of our experiences will help others to relate to each other on a deeper level. Though my children gave their blessing in sharing our story, I'm choosing to use pseudonyms for their privacy.

Of course, not all adoptions look like ours. Adoption journeys can have more or less chaos than ours did, as can the journeys of natural families. This is simply *our* story.

CHAPTER 1

IN FOR A RIDE

It was almost lunchtime on a hot and muggy Thursday, which was the typical weather outside Savannah, Georgia. My youngest boy, Caisen, and I had picked up my oldest two kids, Faith and Brandon, from the summer camp where they'd spent the morning. The four of us drove straight home, knowing we had an hour or so before leaving to pick up my two middle boys from a different summer camp.

I wasn't expecting an easy summer of getting all five of them to and from their various church and sports camps, but it was worth it for others to fuel the faith in my young brood's hearts. It would have been easier if my husband, Jordan, could've split the duties, but his long hours at work left me to be the ringleader of our circus.

Once home, we ate lunch. The kids didn't always agree on food, but everyone liked a good, old-fashioned PB&J with veggie straws. While we ate, Faith and Brandon told Caisen about the horses they'd fed, the fish they'd seen but failed to catch, and the small pool they played a game of water-basketball in.

"Sounds like you had fun, but I'm curious to hear what you learned at camp," I said.

"We don't really learn things there. That's not what camp is for," replied Brandon.

"Are you sure, Brandon?" I asked. *"I assume there was a lesson taught through the fun."*

"Actually," Faith cut in, *"we learned that it's important to memorize God's words, so that we'll have them when we need them."*

I liked the message and silently lifted a prayer that Brandon would take in the guidance.

With only a few bites left, Brandon asked if he could play with his iPod, which I knew was dangerous. He was either going to pitch a fit for not getting to play it, pitch a fit while playing it, or pitch a fit when play time ended. I gave permission, hoping to get a few minutes of peace, maybe more.

Faith and Caisen decided to color at the dining room table.

While washing our plates, I got a call from the camp where my boys, Henry and Clay, were. The director told me Henry had fallen off the cargo net and bit his lip. He also mentioned something about Henry getting elbowed and stepped on, but assured me that the lip was the only area of concern, though not warranting my picking him up early. I hoped his lip could close up before football camp later that night, or Jordan would have to take everyone else home from football camp while Henry and I went to the Emergency Room.

Though I understood it might be fine, I still called Jordan to let him know of the potential need for him later.

"I'll do my best," he answered.

I never doubted he'd give his best, but I knew the Army often claimed Jordan at the exact times I wanted him, and the Army typically won those battles. Don't get me wrong: when it was possible, Jordan got permission to join us. It just wasn't always possible, and certainly couldn't be guaranteed in advance. This was one of the many joys of being an Army wife.

Add this to the joys of being the primary caregiver of five active kiddos, and you see why I learned to embrace change and frequently adapt. I felt such blessing when days went as planned, which almost never happened.

When the timing was right, I gave Brandon a ten-minute warning for turning over his iPod, so we could pick up the other two kids. He said, *"Ok Mommy. I won't pitch a fit."*

I gave Brandon a five-minute warning. He said, *"Ok Mommy. I won't pitch a fit."*

I gave Brandon a two-minute warning. He said, *"Ok Mommy. I won't pitch a fit."*

"It's time to go, everyone. Load up," I said.

Brandon, my gangly, blonde pre-teen flopped off the couch screaming, *"You didn't even give me a warning. You're a terrible parent!"* While on the floor, he performed his signature move, which we referred to as his alligator roll, because his aggressive rolls back and forth across the floor looked much like an alligator attempting to kill. Some call the alligator's strong maneuver a death roll, which also felt fitting. He demonstrated this several times before throwing his iPod at me, all while still yelling.

I asked him to put his shoes on, and he refused. *"I'll only get ready to go if I get five more minutes, since you didn't tell me it was almost time."*

"I did tell you," I said, *"and we don't have five minutes. Put your shoes on, and get in the car."*

He kept rolling, kicking at the end table next to the couch.

"Faith and Caisen, please get in the car," I said, as I discreetly grabbed the shoes that Brandon had no interest in putting on. *"Brandon, I'm not going to have an injured Henry waiting on a late mom. Not over an iPod. Let's go."*

I got in our large black SUV, which we often referred to as our "big-rig," with his shoes behind my back. I acted like I was going to leave him at home, wishing I could, hoping he'd take the bait.

Thankfully, he followed us out the front door. He kicked the garage door a few times until I was in the driver's seat, then he banged on my window. I ignored him, knowing that my participation, by arguing or even agreeing, would only make things worse.

He pounded on the hood of our big-rig as he made his way around to the passenger side. He opened the back door and climbed in, but didn't close the door. I knew the reason. He wasn't preparing to leave with us. He just wanted to scream his insults directly into my ear.

Once Brandon was fully inside the car, I hit the gas enough to quickly hit the brakes, causing the door to shut itself. Child safety locks did the rest, allowing me to calmly say, *"Buckle up."*

Brandon put his seatbelt on, likely out of habit, which I took as a sign I could start making my way through the neighborhood. Without missing a beat, he shouted, *"You wouldn't even let me get my shoes, you're terrible!"*

Let him? I flat out told him to get his shoes, just like I gave a countdown. He was impossible.

I handed him his shoes, and he wasted no time in throwing them back at me. He didn't like solutions. He continued screaming, *"You're not a good mom. You're the worst mom there is."*

We turned onto the main highway between our house and the church where the day camp was being held. The highway didn't have a shoulder or many side streets. When the timing couldn't be worse, Brandon screamed, *"I don't care what you say, I'm going home to play my iPod!"* before unbuckling himself and attempting to climb into the front seat, where Faith was sitting, to get out the passenger door.

I didn't know he could still shock me, but he did.

I wedged my right arm against the front passenger seat, attempting to keep Brandon out of Faith's lap. I looked for a place to stop, hesitant to believe it would help. If I'd found a spot, I knew he'd push until he got through my arm-wall and out the door. I could picture him barreling his way down the highway, barefoot, with his hands over his face. He had no awareness of danger. Keeping the car moving was not safe, but it was safer than stopping while he was enraged.

We were two miles from our exit when he got over the top of my arm, grabbed Faith's handle and got the door cracked open. My heart skipped a few beats as Faith gasped and yanked it closed. It took solid effort from both Faith and me to get Brandon's scrawny self back into the middle row of seats.

I didn't know what to do. I thought maybe I could call 911 and ask to be escorted to a safe parking spot, but it would burn whatever small bridge I had been building between Brandon and me.

Or, maybe I could discretely flag a passing patrol car, so Brandon wouldn't know it was me who alerted the authorities to our unstable situation. I was willing to accept the ticket for having an unbuckled minor, if it meant I'd have some help, but no marked police cars came into view.

I couldn't find a solution because there wasn't one. Nothing was going to fix our problem because Brandon wouldn't grow through the experience. He wasn't interested in growth. He was impossible.

Brandon pushed forward a second time, with more determination. Faith and I fought hard to limit his attempt to another door-cracking, which was better than a wide-open door. The close calls were killing me.

Caisen didn't seem to notice what was happening, which was a blessing. However, I knew he'd notice a crash, or worse, he'd notice if Brandon pushed Faith or himself out the door. I couldn't let that happen but felt powerless to prevent it.

After being defeated two times, Brandon slammed himself into a seat in the middle row, shifting his attention back to my failures as a parent. He grabbed his seatbelt and slammed the buckle against the window several times as he screamed at me, *"You can't even make me put on my seatbelt. You're useless. You can't do anything right!"*

Part of me agreed. I felt like a failure. I knew I wasn't the cause for his rage, but I also wasn't able to fix him, no matter how much I tried. It was impossible.

Brandon continued to yell at me the last few minutes before I pulled into the church parking lot, where the camp was being held, but I couldn't let him distract me. I had another problem to focus on. I realized I couldn't safely leave Brandon unsupervised in the car, and I needed to sign out Henry and Clay.

I sweat a few bullets before remembering that the camp director called me about Henry's incident, which meant his number was in my recent call log.

I dialed the number, shared a watered-down version of my predicament, and asked if it was possible for him to facilitate a curbside pickup. It wasn't the first time I had to ask for an exception because of Brandon, and it wasn't getting any less embarrassing.

Brandon heard my special request and lost his mind. *"No, you can go in. I'm fine. I'm not doing anything wrong,"* with tears in his eyes. He didn't want me to think he was the reason I needed Henry and Clay escorted out to me, even though he was the reason. This told me he cared what I thought, but not enough to be respectful or obedient in the first place.

He then buckled himself and said, *"See, I'm being good. We can go in."*

The kid was impossible, but at least he was buckled, in time for me to park the car.

By that point in our foster/adoption journey, we were well aware that Brandon could be triggered by almost anything, and that almost ALL feelings would lead him to rage. He didn't know how to be anything but upset and seemed to seek reasons to be angry. We had maintained hope that we could help him develop better coping skills, but the process was stunted. Sadly, Brandon had not been set up to succeed in life. While trying to be compassionate toward him, we also had to consider the needs and quirks of four other children. Heck, Jordan and I had to consider our needs as well. You see, it's a complicated life we live, with many crucial memories and experiences necessary to show how we got here. To best explain our journey, I need to go back to the beginning. Don't you worry, though. I promise we'll run back into this moment, later.

CHAPTER 2

NOTHING HAPPENS UNLESS FIRST WE DREAM

I learned at a young age that family is complicated. I'm not talking about the typical frustrating stuff, like when you have family members you wouldn't choose as friends, but you're stuck together anyway. Also, I'm not referring to the messiness that divorce and remarriage brings, though that is part of my childhood story. While those are both challenging situations, the level of dysfunction I'm talking about is worse. I'm talking about children who are forcibly removed from their birth parents because at best, their parents can't keep them safe, and at worst, their parents are the danger themselves. These kids end up in foster care, where they wait for whatever comes next, whether it is to be reunified with their birth parents, or put up for adoption.

The first time I heard about foster care, I was in the fifth grade. I saw how the baggage of an unfair world weighed on my friend. I didn't know the details, but I knew she wasn't like the other ten-year-old kids. But then again, neither was I. She seemed to have a hard time making friends, and people liked to tease me about the gap in my front two teeth more than they liked to play wall ball with me, even though I was really good at wall ball. With this going for us, she and I made a good team.

Life was hard for my friend, but it was also really hard on me when she moved away from our school district without any warning. I still don't know what happened to her or where she ended up, but I sure do remember her red hair, and I believe I always will.

As the years rolled by, I often reflected over the possibilities. I wondered if she was ever reunited with her birth parents. Or, did she have to experience the pain of letting go of them forever? I wondered if she ever became available for adoption. And if so, did anyone ever choose her? Or, did she stay in foster care until she was 18, only to be sent out into the world all alone. The only thing I know for sure is that it wasn't fair that she would have to experience any version of that nightmare. It wasn't fair to her, or to all the other kids who've been failed by the people who were supposed to protect them.

When I got into middle school, my cousin was welcomed into our family as a baby. Her birth parents released their daughter into the hearts and home of my aunt and uncle. Truthfully, I couldn't imagine my life without my cousin, and I know my aunt and uncle feel the same. Comparing this new circumstance with the one of my friend, I wondered what caused one parent to do so poorly by their child, and speculated why the other chose to give their baby up for adoption at birth.

I'm not sure of the exact date and time, but I know it was during adolescence that I decided I would one day have an adoption story of my own. I would be there to right some of the wrongs done to a child in need. I was certain of it.

Of course, it would have to be at a much later date, because, like many other kids in middle school and high school, I had other more immediate needs to tend to, like volleyball practice, nail painting, and comparing boy-crushes with my girlfriends. So, adoption was put on my list of lifetime must-dos, located in my special, secret diary, along with my dreams to adventure outside my home state of Oregon, go on tour as a rock star, become a neurosurgeon, go to the Olympics, and cure cancer. Though I didn't stay on track with all of my childhood goals, the ones that mattered most remained on the list.

In 2002, I met Jordan. I was sixteen, and he was eighteen. We were both pole-vaulters (it's the track and field event where you run with a really long stick and use it to fling yourself up as high into the air as you can) who competed for rival high schools. That was back when we were young, with the world at our fingertips. Although now, at thirty-two and thirty-four, I'd like to believe that we are still young.

When Jordan and I met, we had some amazing friends in common, which made it impossible to get rid of each other, though I tried. Truthfully, no one was able to get on my nerves like Jordan could. I thought he was rude, selfish, and immature. For six years, he spread rumors about me, discouraged other guys from pursuing me, and showed his crush on me by pulling my hair and pushing me. He was basically a child. He wouldn't let up. He was worse than an annoying little brother, and I already had one of those.

In those six years, I finished high school as a valedictorian and went on to complete my Bachelor's degree, Summa Cum Laude. I even earned a couple of NAIA National Championship Titles in the women's pole vault and set a new school record. I was focused. Those years of my life were full of travel and adventure. And, I'd like to say I could steer clear of Jordan while I trained and competed, but I couldn't. We ran into each other at many meets, and at functions with our mutual friends, which made it easy to know that Jordan graduated high school as a top-notch athlete, gave college a good effort for a while, but then chose to work in a warehouse while he coached high school football and track and field.

After I graduated from college, I kept training and traveling while also working in student management at a local alternative-style high school. Life was going great for me, and I didn't feel even the littlest bit tempted to go on a date with Jordan, though he continued to ask. And I saw him regularly enough to be reminded I wasn't interested. There was no absence to make my heart grow fonder.

I can honestly say I didn't see the day coming where I'd agree to date him, but it came.

It was May of 2008, and we were twenty-two and twenty-four. We had been hanging out with friends, but there was a moment where it was just he and I together. I can still hear his sincere tone as he said, *"I'm sorry for the way I've been treating you. I'm going to lighten up because I can't risk losing you as a friend."*

The next night, I accepted an invite to watch a movie at his place, though I don't remember which one. We did more chatting than movie watching. I do remember he picked up Little Caesar's five-dollar pizzas, and I brought over fresh strawberry shakes. By the end of the night, it felt like we'd just had a pleasant date, even though I didn't go into it thinking it was a date at all. But it was clear to me; something had changed in this man. For the first time in years, when he leaned in to give me a kiss goodbye, I didn't turn away.

After a week or so, it was obvious to us both that something was going on between us. Jordan seemed happy about it, and I was genuinely surprised that I felt the same. I never would have guessed the day would come, and I assumed our friends and family would agree. I was wrong. In fact, I was disappointed when we revealed the news of our relationship and heard, *"It's about time," "Duh,"* and *"Figured as much"* in response.

We had learned a lot about each other over the many years we'd been in each other's lives, but there was still a lot to figure out through dating. While conducting the could-you-be-the-one interrogation process, we slyly asked each other all of the important questions, careful to not come across too strong. Faith, as it should be, was one of the early topics. Thankfully, we had the same views there. Christianity was important to each of us. We had separately worked through different denominations and eventually both landed at a big non-denominational church. Jordan loved the music, and I loved the charming pastor.

We also talked about future plans, dreams, and of course, the logistics of what life would look like. This was one of my favorite questions from Jordan: *"If we ever got married, would my four-wheeler still be mine, or would it be ours?"*

Ours. Definitely.

The time came to ask Jordan about adoption. I was nervous. What would I do if he were against it? Would that be a deal breaker? Was it even appropriate to ask him to consider such a big life choice this early in our relationship? Finally, I got up the courage to ask as we were washing dishes after eating spaghetti for dinner.

"So, out of curiosity, have you ever thought about adopting?" I asked.

My heart was pounding, and I immediately felt like I'd asked wrong. I mean, I didn't lead into it or anything. I just blurted it out.

"That's funny," he said, *"I'm sure most people first ask if their partner has thought about having kids at all, not just adoption."*

"Well, have you thought about kids?" I asked, thinking it just got more awkward.

"Yes, actually, and I've always wanted to adopt. Probably a boy, but maybe a girl."

I wasn't sure if I was more surprised or relieved, but I felt both.

Jordan went on to tell me about a boy he knew when he was younger who didn't have it so good. The boy's parents divorced, and didn't have much time or attention for the boy, who ended up bouncing back and forth between his mom's and his grandma's houses. The kid hung out at Jordan's house quite a bit and didn't have the best things to say about what was going on around him. Jordan said that the kid deserved a better home life and that he intended to be that better-life option for some kid, someday.

Also, one of Jordan's brothers came into the family through infant adoption, but Jordan said that just seemed normal to him. He was more motivated to adopt a child looking for a better home.

Based on what I knew of Jordan before this conversation, I never would have imagined that this would be his answer. It blew my mind. He truly was my other half. And, as we continued to talk about our life's ambitions, we found more similarities in our dreams and bucket lists.

Within a month of our starting to date, Jordan revealed that he'd always wanted to go back to college to complete his degree and signed himself up for classes. I was really proud of him for working so hard to earn something that he obviously valued, and I knew he'd stick with it.

After only four months of dating, Jordan proposed to me, at the base of a waterfall we had just hiked to. He looked so nervous while we sat on a large log, which made sense once he rolled off of his rear end and onto his knee. After I said, *"Yes,"* he smiled and said, *"I promised myself that if I ever got a chance to put a ring on your finger that I'd take it."*

Turns out, he spent six years knowing he wanted to marry me, but I spent that same amount of time wanting to marry anyone other than him. On August 14th, 2009, he won. He always did. It would be good to point out that Jordan is known for being both stubborn and persistent. Also loyal, hardworking, spontaneous, and, did I mention persistent? Seriously. There was no changing his mind once it had been made. And as we said, *"I will,"* I was very excited over the adventure we'd live out together.

A few short months into our marriage, Jordan shared yet another dream with me, about wanting to serve his country as an officer in the United States Army. His youngest brother, Jacob, was also working towards becoming an officer in the Army, and his older brother, Jayce, had served many years in the Marines. He was proud of them both and had hopes for himself, too. He specifically talked about wanting to wear our flag on his shoulder. I tearfully told him I'd be proud to walk that walk with him, once he had the four-year degree required for officers.

We leaned on each other while we prepared for our Army adventure. Well, mostly he leaned on me. He loaded up on credits and joined the track team to earn scholarship money. It took a couple of years, but he completed his goal of earning his degree and exceeded his expectations by becoming an NAIA Pole Vault All-American.

After graduation, he said, *"I didn't think I had it in me to graduate until you said you believed in me. Thank you."*

My heart melted.

Jordan took his Oath of Enlistment in February of 2011. He was then sent three thousand miles away, to Ft. Benning, Georgia to complete several months of trainings called Basic Training and Officer Candidate School.

The first night he was gone was the toughest. Our home didn't feel the same without him. Thankfully, my best friend Reagan stayed with me. We'd been friends since the first grade, getting closer and closer as the years rolled on. We watched *Zombieland* that night, cried, and ate popcorn. Lots of popcorn.

I stayed in Oregon with our blonde Labradoodle, named Butter, and two calico cats, named Perry and Violet. I still worked at the high school. I was really passionate about my position because it allowed me to mentor young kids who were making poor choices. I knew it wasn't the time to adopt just yet, so it felt like a great substitute.

Jordan and I spent nine months apart, though I flew out to visit him on five separate weekend passes. The separation was hard, but the handwritten letters we exchanged made it better.

I sent Jordan a letter every day he was gone, and sometimes twice. I didn't want him to feel lonely or forgotten. I even included pictures, almost daily. I sent pictures of some of our adventures as a couple, pictures of Reagan and me out living life, and pictures of myself doing daily things. I just wanted him to feel included. Sadly, though, I didn't get a letter from him for three weeks. And I didn't know why. Until that first letter came.

He explained to me that the soldiers didn't get mail privileges right away because they were working through other things. When they finally got mail call, Jordan had twenty or more letters from me. Apparently, they had a system where they had to do pushups to receive each letter, and extra pushups for any envelopes that were colored, or had stickers on the outside. Since all of my letters came from a stationery set of coordinating envelopes and cards, Jordan had many pushups to do. But he wrote that he would have done double if it meant getting a letter from me.

As much as he said he'd do double, he also asked that I get a stack of white envelopes and share the rules with anyone who asked for his mailing address.

This is how Jordan finished out that first letter:

"Anyways, Jessie, I love you so so so so so so so so so so so so so so so much. I've never missed someone so much in my life. It feels as though I am missing a part of my mind and heart being here. That sounded weird, but basically, I think I am now realizing how much I need you, and how thankful I am to be in your life. You are a warrior, Jessie. You sacrifice so much for others! God really created a special angel, and somehow, I was/ am lucky enough to be with you. I love you and miss you so much. You

are my driving force here and it is helping push me every minute. You are special, and I am so thankful for you. I love you. -Jordan."

As much as I hated waking up alone, cooking meals for one, and not being able to call or text freely, those letters actually had me feeling lucky to experience the separation. Each day that I found a letter in the mailbox was like having my birthday, Christmas, and anniversary all at once.

Unlike Jordan, I easily found blessings through that phase because there was no one yelling at me to wake up super early, screaming at me to do extra push ups all day, inspecting my bed-making skills, or telling me how and when to eat. I mean, there were some friends and family members who spoke out against our choice to become an Army family, but those challenges were small compared to Jordan's day-to-day activities.

When it was time to book my airfare to go see him for the first time, I was overwhelmed by so many feelings. What if he built me up so much over the months, and I didn't measure up when he actually got to see me again? Would either of us need time to ease back into our physical relationship or will we pick up as a married couple? Was he feeling the same butterflies I am? Was he thinking about seeing me or more excited to graduate from Basic Training, which was only his first necessary course?

Reagan opted to go to Ft. Benning with me. She was going to keep me company so I didn't drive myself crazy with anticipation, and she would also meet some of Jordan's new Army buddies. Reagan, who was the maid-of-honor in our wedding, had grown to be an important person to Jordan, too. He took it upon himself to be her wingman while he was gone. He talked about her with single soldiers. Only the ones he deemed worthy, of course. He showed them pictures that Reagan was in. He even did investigative work, asking about backgrounds and future intentions.

Thanks to Jordan's efforts, Reagan had some butterflies of her own about the trip.

In preparation for leaving, I got my hair cut. I donated a twelve-inch long braid to a company that makes wigs for children with different diseases that cause hair loss. As proud as I was of the donation, I was also upset with myself for making such a drastic change so soon before seeing my hubby.

I began panicking over whether or not he'd like the new look or if I would know how to style it cute, since I hadn't had hair that short in years. Granted, it was still below my shoulders, but only by a couple of inches. Reagan reminded me that my hair was still technically considered long, but it didn't feel long anymore.

To complete my new look, Reagan also took me shopping to get new outfits for family day, where I would first see Jordan, and for the Basic Training graduation ceremony.

"Ah, Jess, it fits you perfectly. Black and white, which is all you wear, but a little dressier than usual," Reagan said about both of the outfits we picked out.

Before we knew it, it was time to fly out.

Reagan and I were in our hotel room getting ready to go to the family day ceremony. We were sharing the mirror while doing our hair and makeup, and talking about Reagan's love life. Reagan said that if she found someone she was interested in, she would need to date him for five years before considering marriage, to be sure he was right for her. I giggled as I told her to keep her mind open. I said that if she spent years searching for the *"this-is-the-one"* feeling, and hadn't found it yet, she probably wasn't going to find it.

I know; that was great advice coming from a person who knew a man for six years before accepting his proposal to date. Technically speaking, though, we didn't spend much time actually dating before the *"we-just-knew"* feeling hit us.

We took a step back from the mirror, to make sure we were ready.

I was simple and classic in my wardrobe. My black shorts were a satin-like material with a small cuff at the bottom. The white top was unlike any I'd bought before. The back came high, and so did the front, and those pieces met close to my neckline, which required me to wear a strapless bra because the tops of my shoulders were bare. There were some details in the smooth white design that gave it a feminine touch. The black sandals and long, black, beaded necklace tied the look together perfectly.

Reagan wore a cute black dress. Of course, she did. She always wore dresses.

We drove through the main gate at Ft. Benning. It was surreal, as neither of us had been to an active military installation before. We didn't have military ID's, so it was a good thing we had already stopped to register as guests before arriving to the soldier with the outstretched hand.

We handed him our driver's licenses and our guest registration, and he gave us back a map with some decent directions to the training area we were headed to.

We made our way through post, which is another name for an Army installation, observing how much it looked like a regular community. I mean, a regular community with Army tanks, trucks, and soldiers everywhere. But, there were also stores, restaurants, and regular-looking buildings.

As we pulled into the correct parking lot, my heart began pounding. I was sweating, and my butterflies grew.

We found seats in the outdoor, yet covered, space set up for the ceremony.

The soldiers marched out in a tight formation, calling out their steps. They stopped in perfect rows and columns.

A man spoke to us all, something about how proud we should be of our soldiers and how they had earned a fabulous afternoon with their loved ones. At least, I think that's what he was saying. I wasn't paying as much attention as I probably should have. I was just waiting for him to say something like *"dismissed."*

When we were finally released, I stood up, anxious to finally get my arms around my man.

I stood. I waited. I waited some more. I stood on my chair to get a better view. I was a combination of confused and frustrated and listened in as Reagan asked a couple soldiers if they knew where Jordan went. The crowd started to thin. And still, no Jordan.

Just as I thought about crying, I saw my husband walking toward me, from a nearby building, with three big, green Army bags in tow.

He dropped his bags to give me a great, big hug. The kind of hug where my feet were no longer on the ground. As he set me back down, I asked where he had been.

"I wanted to beat the masses into the barracks to get my bags, so that we could get out of here," he said. *"Oh, and by the way, I told a couple of people we could give them a ride to the hotel, since they are staying at the same one."*

And, wouldn't you know, one of those men made an impression on Reagan. His name was David. He was also from Oregon, and Jordan had already told me that he thought they'd be perfect together.

With how casually Jordan spoke while holding my hand, I realized the answer to one of my questions. He was the same; I was the same; and we were married. No easing in. We were just going to pick back up. It felt so normal to be near him. I had never felt more thankful for normalcy in my life. And in case I didn't find that feeling on my own, Jordan struck up a conversation about kids.

He asked, *"Do you still think about adoption?"*

"I do."

"When we get to our first duty station, I want to start talking about the different options. I'm sure it's going to be a long process, so I want to get it started."

He didn't need to tell me twice. I was ready.

The next day was a whirlwind. I wore another black and white outfit, and Reagan wore another dress to the graduation ceremony. We tried to be touristy for a bit. However, we all knew what was coming. And when the time came, we exchanged goodbyes.

I visited four more times over the next six months, sometimes with Reagan, but also solo, with the last visit being exceptionally special. I flew out ahead of Reagan and accompanied David on a trip to a jeweler... Eek! As much as I hated keeping secrets from Reagan, I loved being in on it!

Reagan arrived just in time for us to get all gussied up for our first military ball. In fact, getting dolled up in Georgia together had become my new favorite activity with Reagan. There was always so much anticipation, vulnerability, and excitement.

I wore a floor-length, black ball gown with a plunging neckline. The black felt normal, but the ample cleavage was new for me. Jordan seemed to approve.

Reagan's dress was an empire waisted, purple gown with beaded details. It fit her perfectly.

The night of the ball was incredible. There were many toasts, constant laughing, and a lot of dancing. And, in front of the entire party, David proposed to Reagan. It was beautiful. And, she said, *"Yes."*

And as I'd predicted, it most definitely did not take her five years to consider marriage with this man. It only took a handful of days together, and a few months of letters, with some phone calls mixed in.

That weekend we also enjoyed a commissioning ceremony, where our soldiers' parents joined us in watching Jordan and David recite the Oath of Office, as they were officially awarded the title, *"Second Lieutenant in the US Army."* I was so proud of my husband for the way he tackled his dreams.

He wanted me and got me. He wanted a Bachelor's degree and earned it. He wanted to serve his country and worked so hard to make it happen. The only dream he had left was the one I shared--of answering a child's prayer for a loving family.

We all traveled back to Oregon. Jordan and I had two weeks for visiting before reporting to our next home, at Ft. Leonard Wood, Missouri. We saw friends and family. We watched football. We appeared in Reagan and David's wedding, as a Matron of Honor and a Groomsman. We hiked in the

Columbia Gorge and visited Multnomah Falls, where Jordan had proposed three years prior. We ate out. We packed.

At the end of our two weeks, we said goodbye to friends, family, and the state of Oregon. Jordan and David each had one more course to complete before receiving job assignments, but this course allowed for spouses to move with their soldiers. Reagan and David hit the road for Ft. Sill, Oklahoma, and we moved to Ft. Leonard Wood, Missouri. We knew we'd only be there for a few months, which meant our temporary location wasn't the place to launch our adoption plans, but it was the last stop before planting roots, somewhere.

After a few months of living in the Army's temporary lodging, which is Army code for a very small box in a hotel on the installation, we learned our home would be built at Ft. Stewart, Georgia.

CHAPTER 3

MISSION BOUND

When we got to Ft. Stewart, Georgia, we knew we'd be there a few years. We got busy setting up our new life. Jordan reported to his unit. I got a job on a research team where I worked with soldiers who had PTSD and/or depression. We bought a German Shepherd puppy and named her Cinder bringing the count to two cats and two dogs.

We explored our new rural territory and all the local beaches. We got ourselves familiar with Savannah, which was our closest city. We quickly fell in love with our surroundings--namely the quaint streets and the mossy oak trees that framed our view no matter which direction we looked. We found our new church, which was a large non-denominational Christian church with an incredible band and relatable pastor.

Once set, we actively prayed over what direction we should take the whole adoption thing.

You might not know this, but there are many adoption options. So many options. There are different ages and numbers of children and places where you can adopt both domestically and internationally. And, of course, there are pros and cons with each. We openly talked with friends and family about those different options. The responses were varied.

For example, Reagan knew how long we had been waiting to move forward with our adoption story, so she was happy for us. The topic wasn't a surprise for her.

Some of our new friends and acquaintances in Georgia were confused, not understanding why we would choose adoption, no matter which route. We found that most people we talked to assumed that infertility was the only reason to consider adoption, so our excitement threw them off. In fact, one friend admitted she didn't know if she was supposed to say, *"Congratulations,"* or *"I'm sorry,"* when we told her about our intentions.

Just about everyone in this category came around after hearing how passionate we were about adopting.

There were also some who were disappointed. Our parents started in this category--sad that they wouldn't get to experience the *"typical path"* of gaining grandchildren through us. We heard their concerns that Jordan and I would miss out on seeing what our own DNA would produce and some of the happy moments that biological parents experience through parenting children who had not been previously hurt. The concerns were valid.

However, like many others, their language needed some work, because it's not right to refer to biological kids as *"real kids"* or to imply that adoptive parents don't have kids of their *"own."* All kids are real, and all children in a family count, no matter their origin. However, we had plenty of time to work on verbiage throughout the process.

Once my mom accepted that our minds were made up, she backed us. Completely. It must have been hard for her to let go of the image of being in the delivery room or swaddling a newborn, but she did it.

Jordan's parents weren't prepared to come around as quickly, at least not in the way we were hoping. They wanted us to also try to give them biological grandchildren and to consider adopting a baby over an older child. They brought one of their five kids into the family through an infant adoption and had always been openly thankful for their chosen son, proving that they did approve of adoption; they just didn't understand our motivation for it.

Despite the heavy content of our talks with Jordan's parents, the fact that we were communicating was great because it showed that they were willing to listen to us and truly were interested in learning our motivations for adopting. We were hopeful that by the time we put a kid in front of them that they would have come fully on board, which seemed probable.

Less tolerant, though, were the many people who had strong opinions over which adoption option was best. It was somewhat overwhelming. Some would say we needed to adopt internationally because those kids are starving compared to the domestic kids who at least had food and water. At the same time, some people told us that as Americans, we had an obligation to keep our money in our own country, and it's stupid that some people spend the large fees required to adopt internationally when there are so many children locally.

I was surprised by how many people had opinions on how to adopt. Particularly those who were not even considering adoption.

Hey, I think I see a soapbox. I'm going to stand on it for a minute:

Mic-check. One-two-three. Ok. So, if you have ever adopted, have thought of adopting, want to adopt, eat food, rescued a dog or a turtle, are a human, have an Aunt named Fanny or an Uncle named Bob, or know a single person who meets any one of the aforementioned criteria, then I call upon you to actively dissuade all negative projections regarding which route of adoption is best. Yes, it is now your responsibility to step in and offer support or encouragement if you see someone adoption-path-shaming. Yes, that's a thing.

Just so you are prepared, please know there are millions of ways to illustrate that we all make choices, based on experiences, preferences, and, for people of faith, interpretations of God's message. I choose to explain like this: Adoption isn't like trucks or football teams, where it's ok or even enjoyable to project your favorites with authority. It's more like career paths and running shoes, where you just support everyone in picking the ones that fit them best. Trust me, you can't squeeze just anyone into your favorite shoes. Let them pick their own. In the end, adoption is a really hard thing that results in the sharing of someone's love with a child. There is NO wrong in that. As long as we are all doing our best, then there should be no judgment. Only support. Ok, stepping off the soapbox. Back to the journey.

Regardless of everyone's responses, the whole thing was starting to feel more real as we talked about our plans more freely. And then the time came to turn our words into actions.

We looked at waiting children in Africa. No rhyme or reason. It's just where we felt God led us to look. So, we pursued it. We knew it would be expensive. We knew it would be difficult considering the cultural and language barriers, but there were kids in need, and we were on a mission.

We found two brothers who moved us deeply. We had started doing the necessary paperwork and addressing the concerns of those who questioned our sanity.

First, *"Do they even speak English?"*

"Well, in the area of Ethiopia where they live, the people speak a local language that isn't directly translatable. So, they'd work to learn a relatable mainstream language; we'd learn bits of that language; and we'd eventually guide them into English. Oh, and we'd make do with picture books while we all are learning."

Their eyes would glaze over, so I'd recap with, *"No. They don't speak English."*

Then, *"How will they learn our customs? Do they even know how to use toilets?"*

"Funny you should ask. I just read a blog entry from a woman who was watching her husband try to explain by gesture to their adopted son from overseas how to use the toilet, specifically, what the toilet paper was for, when to stand, how to sit, and that the flush wasn't scary. Also, they had to introduce the boy and his sister to silverware, which was a very messy lesson to teach."

Shortly after we started hearing, *"We're praying for your boys,"* Jordan was interviewed, along with other Lieutenants, to see who should take charge of a platoon set for a deployment to Afghanistan. And, Jordan was picked.

There were highs and lows around this new adventure called *"deployment."* The lows, of course, were the separation, the danger, and the fact that the two boys wouldn't be coming home to us. However, Jordan was hand selected to lead soldiers. He felt it was a great honor, and I was so proud of my man. We accepted the challenge, put our faith in God, and focused on the positives.

While Jordan was gone, I leaned heavily on my mom and two closest friends and talked to Jordan's mom regularly as well.

Thankfully, when we moved to Georgia, Reagan and David moved to Ft. Bragg, North Carolina, only four hours away. When I wasn't working, I was spending as much time as I could with them. Especially after Reagan shared that she was pregnant. I didn't want to miss out on painting the baby's room and buying onesies. Besides, we didn't know how long we would be living close enough to see each other in short trips, so I wanted to make the best of it.

I also made sure to distract myself with adventures like kayaking, ziplining, trying new restaurants, and working hard to arrange a once-in-a-lifetime trip on a military hopper flight over to visit my sister-in-law in Germany while her husband, Jordan's brother, was also deployed.

Basically, I lived my life as fully as I could, while also making it clear to whomever I was visiting or chatting with that if the phone rang with a weird-cadenced number, I was going to answer, no matter what. I was taking no chance in missing whatever small opportunities I had to chat with my hubby. And as Jordan and I continued to navigate the challenges of deployment, we hoped God would provide guidance as to what our next family-planning steps should be. We were thinking maybe God used this deployment to deter us from the boys we'd watched and considered He might have something different in mind for us. Which, of course, He did.

While attending an event at our church, I felt moved. It was a 1950's themed function with games and activities which concluded with guest speakers sharing with us some details about sex trafficking in the area, specifically concerning preteen girls.

About a week later, I got a call from Jordan and shared the information with him.

"Jordan, did you know that Savannah has a big sex trafficking problem because it's a big port city? Ships, interstates, and planes all come through, making it an easy place for snatching and exporting young girls."

"I hadn't really thought about it, but that makes sense," he said.

"What do you think about looking into the foster system around here when you get back? Maybe we could prevent a young girl from falling into the wrong hands."

"You know," he said, *"that actually sounds good. It sounds tough, too."*

"Yeah, really tough. Older kids in foster care have many layers of hurt. I mean, love isn't usually the reason a kid sits in foster care."

Jordan responded, *"There's emotional scars of what brought them to foster care, scars from their time in foster care. There might be difficulties from past drug or alcohol abuse. Plus, neglect causes damage in the brain, especially during developmental years."*

"On top of that, there are the hurt feelings of being perceived as unwanted or unworthy. That would do a real number on any human!"

"If it was easy, everyone would do it. Well, not really. Many people would still choose not to. But, think of the impact we could have on the kid we find. Or worse, think of what would happen to the kid if we didn't find him. Or her. I think it's worth looking into," he said.

"I agree," I told him, *"and I think that we'd have a lot to offer a kid in need of healthy adult relationships. I'm picturing a kid from the school I worked at, and I felt like I made a difference for her."*

"Maybe you could call around and do some research on how to start a foster care adoption, so we'll be ready?"

And just like that, the decision was made. We were going to take a child out of foster care.

We didn't yet know what baggage our child would bring with him or her, but we knew there would be plenty of it. How could there not be? Anyway, our compassion cords were tugged. We knew it would be tough; it isn't for the faint of hearts. However, there were kids in need and we were on a mission.

Of course, there were some naysayers. People Jordan worked with said the kid would probably burn our house down. My mom said we'd have to be careful in selecting because we had animals in the house. Jordan's mom wanted us to look at the youngest kids possible and asked us to think about having our own kids first.

None of that deterred us. We responded to their concerns as best we could and stayed strong in our decision. We just felt that God shifted our attention to the foster care system for a reason. God knew, even then, who would join our family. And, we agreed, we'd need to be open and honest with each other throughout the process to make sure that we didn't get into something greater than we could handle.

So, we were surviving the deployment and the separation that comes with it. At the same time, we were working to help our social network understand and accept our new plan. We were working through some of our own fears and doubts while establishing our list of things needed for our next steps. We thought we had a handle on things when our plan was brought into question once again.

Someone asked us to consider adopting their unborn baby. I thought it was going to be a tougher decision than it was because we love babies, and we love to be of help. However, we recalled that there are more waiting parents than there are available babies. Therefore, we knew someone out there wanted and was praying for this baby. We didn't want to snatch that joy from an awaiting parent. At the same time, there are more children waiting in foster care than there are willing parents. Those kids were counting on us. Harder to place kids were out there, needing us. After thinking it through, we simply felt reaffirmed in our previous decision.

Again, not everyone agreed. It felt like our moms were trying to nicely say we were tossing away treasure for trash. We were well aware that we were stepping off the beaten path with our decision, but it was our choice to make. No one was going to force us to wear their favorite shoes, buy their favorite truck, or adopt their favorite kid. Stubborn-Man and I had made up our minds. At this point, we were only waiting for Jordan to return from his deployment, so that we could attend the foster care/adoption orientation because there were kids in need and we were on a mission.

Oh, wait a second. You thought that was the last big bump before jumping in? Really? Things could be that simple? I wish. There's always one more obstacle after you make a big decision. I believe it's God's way of testing conviction, and this particular test of His was the most challenging.

Toward the end of Jordan's deployment, he was in an accident. Well, it doesn't feel right to call it an accident since it was done intentionally. A suicide bomber rode a bike into the middle of a gathering of soldiers, including Jordan. The bomber was a teenager wearing an explosive vest, and Jordan was standing closest to him as he detonated. Jordan, along with other soldiers, and against his own desires, had to be taken to a rehabilitation center to make sure his healing got started in the right direction. He maintained a mostly mad attitude throughout his three-week long stay at the rehabilitation center, so I'm grateful to his caring comrades who ensured he couldn't fib his way out early, though he tried. He was persistent about it, but that was no surprise.

I worried about the impact of Jordan's Traumatic Brain Injury (TBI), and whether it would change our plans to adopt, but I also knew that worrying wouldn't help. I was 7,500 miles away from him, trying not to make assumptions based on the frustrations I heard coming through the phone. I felt so helpless and far away as I waited for him to get home.

Time kept rolling, and I kept drifting back into worry. One morning, as I was sitting in my cold office, letting my worry get out of control, God offered me a distraction. I got my much-anticipated call from Reagan requesting I hit the road for North Carolina and head straight to the labor and delivery department. It was September 13th, and I excitedly made the drive. Reagan did an awesome job and welcomed her healthy and happy baby into the world on September 14th, and I was just so happy to be a part of it. I enjoyed some major bonding time with little Jack, holding him while eating pizza and watching my favorite football team, the Oregon Ducks, play and win a game. However, I had to say goodbye after lunch on September 15th because my other long-awaited phone call came through. Jordan was on his way home and would be arriving in only a few hours.

As I drove home, I marveled at how perfectly Reagan's pregnancy lined up with Jordan's deployment dates. Reagan found out she was pregnant just after Jordan left, and Jack was born the day before Jordan got home. It was the perfect distraction for me, pairing the excitement of her journey with the worry over Jordan's travels.

I pulled into our driveway, but I left the garage door down so that I could hang Welcome Home banners on it. There were two--one from me and one from his parents. I got showered quickly and put on a knee length navy blue dress with red heels and a pearl bracelet. I made a final check in the mirror before racing to the installation in time for the Welcome Home ceremony.

Again, I stood in a crowd surrounded by other people who had already found their soldier, waiting for mine to show up. And when he did, I wrapped my arms around him as tight as I could. He lifted me off the ground and everything was perfect.

Jordan's reintegration upon coming home was a little rough. But, by the grace of God, his physical injuries were minor, and the trauma to his noggin was on the path toward recovery. And, against my expectations, Stubborn-Man was adamant that it was still time to get this adoption-thing rolling.

This was his reasoning: *"Life's unpredictable, Jess, and you need to make your move on the things that matter when you have the chance."* That left us with just one question left to answer--which of the two paths for adopting out of foster care would we walk?

The first option is foster-to-adopting. In this arrangement, you foster first, and you're asked to adopt IF a child placed with you becomes eligible for adoption. This path is risky because not all kids become eligible for adoption. In fact, many are reunited with their birth parents, in which case, you'd have to say goodbye. However, IF you do get the option with a child in your care, then you have already put effort into your relationship.

The second option is adoption-only which is when you adopt from the pool of children who have already gone through a legal process called Termination of Parental Rights (TPR) where birth parents' rights are legally severed by a judge, making them eligible for adoption. This path doesn't come with the same risk as foster-to-adopt, but you have to wait until the birth parents are legally out of the picture to move forward.

As an Army family, we knew our stay in Georgia was temporary. We didn't have the time to wait on kids who may or may not become available. That, and we wanted to be a solution for kids who were already waiting. Therefore, we picked the adoption-only plan and started sprinting. We sprinted. And sprinted. And grabbed some water, then sprinted some more. This meant we were filling out forms after forms, and then some more forms. We attended mandatory classes. We participated in a mandatory home study that took several meetings. We got some furniture for our spare room. It took about twelve months of sprinting to a finish line that was repeatedly picked up and moved. I'm telling you, we didn't waste any time, and it still took what felt like forever.

The wait took its toll on me. I cried on Thanksgiving because I had a kid out there somewhere not knowing my love. I cried on Christmas because I had a kid out there somewhere who didn't know we were fighting to get through the red tape. I cried on Mother's Day because I had a kid out there somewhere who didn't even know I existed. Heck, I even cried on a random Saturday as we walked down the aisles of Home Depot. It wasn't a light tear up. It was a full river sob. I felt so helpless. And poor Jordan, all he could do was hold me, nod at passersby, and forgive me for getting snot all over him.

Looking on the bright side, I appreciated that Jordan and I had time to enjoy each other after his deployment, to work on ourselves, and to prep everyone else in our lives. When we could finally see that the real finish line was coming, we went on one last trip as a family of two to clear our minds in anticipation of the end of the world as we knew it, um, I mean, the next chapter in our lives.

Our trip was relaxing. We hiked each day to a new waterfall; we camped and roasted marshmallows; and we took in the quiet. After so much sprinting, we really just enjoyed each other's company and overdosed on nature. I'm thankful for the memories we were able to make in the time between starting the process and becoming approved to adopt out of the foster care system.

Forced positive prospective aside, I hated that horrible long and slow process. Didn't the agency know that we had KIDS out there waiting on us?

Oh, whoops, did I say KIDS? As in plural? Oh, that's right. When Jordan came home, he also bumped the number up to two. Then, at some point along the really long and slow process, it went up to a possibility of three. About that time, we were invited to attend an annual adoption convention in Atlanta, Georgia on the 14th of August, which just happened to be our fifth wedding anniversary. We thought it would be cool to go to an event to pick out our kids on our special date. If nothing else, kid shopping would be a unique way to celebrate an anniversary.

CHAPTER 4

OPEN YOUR HEART AND TAKE US IN

I t was our fifth wedding anniversary, and it certainly was not like any of the others. First of all, this was only the second anniversary we were able to spend together thanks to Army trainings and deployments. However, even if we had been together every August 14th to celebrate our anniversary, we certainly wouldn't have spent the day at a convention picking out children. This August 14th was extra special.

We got on the road early for our four-hour trip to Atlanta, and we were feeling eerily calm. Thankfully by this time, just about everyone either supported us or had learned to accept our path. To help with the learning, Stubborn-Man had broadcasted a strongly worded statement indicating we were on a rough road, and we wouldn't be making time for those who made it rougher, which seemed to quiet the naysayers. Many people wished us luck and wished us a Happy Anniversary.

When we arrived at the convention, we didn't know exactly what to expect. All we had been told was that the Department of Family and Children's Services (DFCS) case workers from each of the counties in Georgia would be there showcasing all of the adoption-eligible kids. Flyers were made up to represent each child and also for all the perspective parents. Our flyer had a picture from our last trip together, with our dogs in front of a waterfall. The flyer also listed our hobbies, jobs, and the adoption circumstances we were open to. It said we were seeking a sibling group of two to three kids, ranging in age from ten to sixteen. We picked this age range knowing that older kids were less often selected and deserved the chance to be considered. Let me tell you. This made us a hot commodity, as there were many kids in this range and not many adults seeking them. We walked into the presentation room, which looked a lot like a high school science fair.

The booths were set up with bi-fold and tri-fold presentation boards. As promised, every county in the state was represented, and they were on missions to get their children adopted. People were calling us by name, LOUDLY, from all directions. Apparently, it's odd to request older kids and sibling groups and particularly odd to consider them both. This combination certainly made us popular.

I might be exaggerating a little when I say that the caseworkers were stuffing their kids' flyers into my shirt and purse, but I'm not stretching it by far. They were desperate to get our eyes on their kids, and, they were all certain that each of their kids would be a perfect fit for us. So much so, that I was wondering if they had actually read our flyer to see what we were comfortable with, or if they were only scanning it for the essentials they sought for their kids. Essentials like being alive, having food, and providing a space to call home.

Again, our flyer had our dogs on it, a German Shepherd and a Labradoodle. And, to be clear, our puppies were our babies. So, we gasped when one caseworker approached us to say, *"Look at these two boys. They are a little out of your age range, but not by much. And I see you have dogs. The younger boy only bit the dog in their foster home once."*

Another lady said, *"I know you're looking for a sibling group, but this kid is just so sweet and kind, and could really use the influence of a strong, disciplined Army man."*

Speaking of the Army, we had specified that we were an Army family that moved regularly, as most Army families do. One caseworker hunted us down to say, *"This kid is so special and dear to me. I know you move frequently, but I'm sure the doctor would sign off for him to be moved, especially if you guys assure him you would seek the necessary resources in each place to help him. He isn't the most stable, but I really think you're a good fit."* Really? How could we have been a good fit if our lifestyle was unsafe for him?

If nothing else, I quickly learned the lesson that one does not go to an adoption convention seeking perfection. At best, you are looking for the child whose baggage you are willing and able to help carry, knowing that there is and will be baggage. But, these caseworkers were like used car salesmen. They didn't seem to see the kids' baggage or the details of our story. But, they sure were trying to make the sale. And, they wouldn't take *"No"* for an answer. I'm not certain, but I think I remember someone trying to give us an all-expenses paid vacation, a new car, and their left arm, if only we would just take a closer look at their favorite child. Not really, but it was intense.

Our caseworker, Maggie, who was actually the fourth caseworker we'd been assigned to, thanks to the high turnover rate in the field, was also there scoping out the options. We touched bases with her while we were hiding from the mob of crazed used kid salesmen. We took a moment to catch our breath as we went over the stack of flyers she had collected on our behalf. Most of them were sibling groups of two, including the one where the younger brother bit the dog. She also had a sibling group of five in there. Yes, FIVE. A sibling group of five--ages eleven, ten, eight, six and four. Someone assured her they were the perfect fit for us. But then again, so was the medically unstable kid who would need a doctor's note to move with us.

We looked at each flyer with an open heart and an open mind including the one for the fantastic five. There was no picture because their court date to terminate parental rights was still just around the corner, and you can't share pictures until after a judge legally severs kids from parents. However, the write up was intriguing. Jordan and I paused on it, and we had a little dialogue exchange that went something like this:

Jordan: We couldn't take five.

Me: Definitely not. Where would they all sleep?

Jordan: Exactly! We couldn't even fit in one car!

Me: Oh my gosh, think of the food bill!

Jordan: We'd never get to eat out again!

Me: Poor kids.

So, we did what any couple would do after agreeing against the five. We went back into the madhouse to talk to their caseworker.

When we asked for additional information, she, of course, told us the kids were angels who were seeking adventure. She said they would probably grow up and go on tour as rock stars, or become neurosurgeons, or go to the Olympics, or cure cancer. The perfect sales pitch.

Also, she informed us that the oldest was a girl, followed by four boys, just as Jordan's oldest sibling was a girl, who was followed by four boys. They ranged in age from four to eleven, which was much younger than we were looking for. There were five of them, which was double what we were looking for. They hadn't gotten through TPR yet (that court process I mentioned), which means we'd need to do the work to switch to foster-to-adopt and accept the risk that comes with it. Ugh. However, as the caseworker pointed out, they were perfect for us. Ha!

We recognized that they weren't at all who we were looking for. But, there was one upsetting detail we couldn't shake. These five kids had been in foster care for over three years, and, wait for it, they were separated. Not only from their birth parents, but also from each other.

When we were walking out, I asked Jordan which of the options stood out. Focusing on the fact that Jordan's mind was never easily swayed, I was expecting him to bring up one of the many two-to-three kid options, or possibly even one of the single kids. I mean, it was the plan we came in with, right? Wrong.

Just like they say, *"If you want to make God laugh, tell him your plans!"*

So, Jordan looked at me and said, *"I think we're meant to take on the five. It's not fair that they are separated."* I felt sure God was behind the shift in Jordan. I couldn't think of any other reason that Stubborn-Man would be so quickly moved to make such a drastic change in his plan.

I sighed, hung my head and agreed. *"I was scared you'd say that. And I felt it too."*

If God had only moved one of us, I'm sure we would have tried to bargain our way out of it. But God spoke to us both. And we knew better than to argue with Him.

CHAPTER 5

YOU HAD HIM AT HELLO

W e had worked hard to get our friends and families on board with our choice to adopt older children before we went to the conference. And, they had mostly come around to accept the path we were walking. However, we hadn't prepared them for the possibilities that we ourselves didn't know to consider. Therefore, those who initially took the most convincing found our update fairly difficult to digest. Thankfully, some of the phone calls we made as we drove the four hours home went well. The call to my mother was one of my favorites.

Me: So, mom, let me read you this flyer. Yadda yadda yadda, stuff about the five, yadda.

Mom: Wait. What? There are five? Which ones are you adopting?

Me: The five.

Mom: All five? Are you crazy?

Me: Probably.

Pause.

Me: Mom?

Mom: Hold on, I'm having a real *"Sound of Music"* moment.

Both of us: A lot of laughing.

When I called Reagan, it took her a minute to believe that I wasn't pranking her. Then, she got overwhelmed for us. My predictably realistic best friend was right; it was a really, really big deal.

Along the drive home, we shared the news with a few other key players and received varied reactions. However, the most consistent responses were, *"Are you joking?"* and *"You've lost your minds."* Sometimes the tone was playful, and other times it was upset. More than once we had to say, *"Yes, we're serious."*

Eventually the shock wore off and we started a to-do list. We would need a new vehicle because a five seat '99 Toyota 4Runner certainly wouldn't do the trick. We would need two sets of bunk beds to get the four boys in one room. We would need lots of toothbrushes, underwear, backpacks, socks, deodorant, and, um, wait, *"We still don't even know what they look like! This is crazy!"* a car seat, two booster seats, kids' plates/cups/bowls, school information, *"WOW, it's a good thing my research project came to an end. I don't think I'll be taking a new position! At least not until we get the kids and have a better picture as to what life will look like,"* pre-K information, shoes, jackets, *"I wonder what size they wear,"* kids' toothpaste, definitely need more floss, bedroom furnishings, *"My head hurts,"* and so on and so forth. Then it hit me. Much of it we couldn't begin tackling because we first needed to learn interests, styles and sizes. It was a crazy feeling. So much to do, yet needing to wait.

And, of course, all this was flying through our minds, as we were still aware of the risk.

The kids had not yet been made legally eligible for adoption, and the case workers had not yet exchanged the necessary information to determine whether or not we would actually be deemed a match. So, we had a lot on our minds, a lot to talk about, and a to-do-list that could only grow.

All weekend long we thought and prayed over a group of kids we'd never met. Then, first thing Monday morning, we called our caseworker and told her we were interested in the sibling group of five. When we disclosed our *"choice"* to take five kids out of foster care, otherwise known as our break with sanity, she laughed at us. Laughter was beginning to feel normal. So were the tears, but then we also felt God was reassuring us that this was His plan.

Anyway, she told us she only kept the flyers that she thought we would consider, and this family didn't make her final cut, so she needed us to send her the contact info from our copy of the kids' flyer.

She walked us through the requirements for shifting into the foster-to-adopt category and reminded us of the risks, again.

The process for getting shifted into the foster-to-adopt category proved to be interesting. The adoption side required that there be a fire extinguisher in the home, and the fire marshal suggested it not be in the kitchen. He said most fires start in the kitchen, and you shouldn't have to go into the fire to get the extinguisher. Rather, you should have it someplace near the kitchen. However, foster care requirements stated the extinguisher needed to be in the kitchen. So, we had two, one in the kitchen and one out.

We had to draw an evacuation map and post copies in all of the doorways. I actually like how ours turned out. I wasn't artistic, but my couches looked like couches and my rugs looked like rugs. I felt proud. It certainly drew attention from visitors. I'm sure it was the mere fact that we had evacuation signs, but I told myself it was because they were impressed by my attention to detail.

We needed to pack an emergency kit to include blankets, cans of food, can opener (even though our canned food had the easy-pop lids), weather radio, matches, emergency plan write-ups, flashlights, batteries, etc.

All of this was in addition to providing our CPR/First Aid certifications and our foster training certificates. We quickly finished all of the requirements and then received a response from the kids' caseworker.

My heart stopped when I received the first email containing specific details. I was scared, and nervous, and excited. I was sitting in my kitchen, and I called Jordan at work.

"I'm ready, Jess. Read it to me."

"Are you sure? Because I know you'll be hooked if we look. Last chance to change your mind."

"What are you talking about? If there's something really bad, I could still pull back."

"You said you could look at puppies and still walk away, but I got stuck with a puppy to train. I'm just saying that I think opening the email and reading their story is close to commitment. Are you sure? Are you ready?"

"Yes. Let's read it."

I took a deep breath and clicked to open the document.

The packet was nearly four years old and pertained to the oldest sibling, Faith, though the family history and the section about their living circumstances seemed general. For the first time, I read each kid's first name, and their birthdates. Faith shared a birthday with my biological Dad. And just like that, I was committed.

We learned that Faith was eleven; Brandon was ten; Henry was now nine; Clarence was six; and Caisen was just barely four. Henry had turned nine shortly after the convention. I felt guilty and sad that we missed his birthday.

Jordan reminded me that we had no way of doing it any differently.

We read that the kids went into foster care in early April of 2011, which is about the time their birth parents landed themselves in jail, which is where they were both still residing.

35

Next, we read some of the circumstances that brought the kids into care. Faith and her siblings were born with drugs and alcohol in their systems, and then they experienced some severe neglect. For Faith, the neglect lasted eight years until she was placed into foster care. I couldn't know the details of her personal struggles, but I was certain there would be some challenging habits, tendencies, and world views to work through. How could there not be?

We read that there were cockroaches in the home; there was no door on the bathroom; and the kids were eating dog food. We read that Faith had been held back to repeat Kindergarten due to missing too much school. And, we read that upon arriving at the kids' home, Child Services found the youngest child, Caisen, who was only eight months old at the time. Alone. In the car. Strapped in his car seat. Without any way of knowing how long he'd been left there.

I couldn't help but pray aloud, *"Dear God, please don't let them remember all of these terrible details"* although I was well aware that the kids probably remembered much more than had been observed or documented by the adults who filled out the reports.

Our determination deepened. These kids had been through far too much hardship and needed someone to make it stop. These kids needed to be loved.

A couple of days later, the caseworkers scheduled a meeting for us to drive to the kids' county, six and a half hours away. It was called a staffing meeting, where all of the involved adults would come to the table to go over details. If any of the workers felt that we were not a good fit as potential parents, then additional work would need to be done to meet standards, or we'd have to move on to another family option. Our meeting was scheduled for September 22nd.

We were told that if the staffing went well, we would be allowed to meet the children that day and set up the transition schedule for day trips, weekend visits, and move-in dates.

The meeting was overwhelming. We were being evaluated. Even though the three caseworkers all smiled, I could feel their judgment. But I knew it was for a good cause. So, I smiled back and worked through the slim packets of information in front of each of us.

It was disappointing to see how many sections in their packets were left blank. The only way for the state to gain much of the background information is through parental disclosure. However, not all parents cooperate when their children are removed; therefore, the information about them can be limited.

In this case, the birth parents, who were not married, had drug addictions that influenced their decision-making and parenting skills. They were still serving sentences in jail, and the kids had not even seen their birth parents since they entered foster care.

We looked at the psychological evaluations that had been completed nearly four years prior! We had already gone over Faith's when it came by email, so we flipped past the family sections over to the area where each kid was evaluated individually.

Most of the information was outdated. Three and a half years is a long time in the life of a child. Obviously, the kid who was eight months old would be presenting differently as a four-year-old. The only present details the caseworkers were able to share were the ages and genders, which we'd already learned. Also, we learned the kids' current grades in school, and one of the boys had ADHD.

We were told about the kids' placement timeline--who they lived with, and for how long before being moved again. There were a few foster homes and also one placement with the maternal grandparents that was supposed to lead to adoption, but didn't. I would have liked more information about that, but there wasn't any. When that placement failed, the kids were placed back into general foster care. However, at that time, they had to be separated.

Instead of focusing on the list of things we hadn't learned, we chose to believe that we would gain more current and relevant information through interactions with the kids. And, over time we figured they'd share the scoop regarding their pasts.

Lastly, we learned that the TPR date was scheduled for October 15th, a month later than had been hinted to us at the convention. Which meant that we'd be developing relationships with these kids for a full month, including purchasing the items required for their visits, before knowing whether or not we could keep them. It was a risk that we had initially chosen to avoid, but was now necessary if these kids were meant to be ours.

The caseworkers explained to us that parents are only entitled to a window of twelve months to work on a reunification plan. If they don't prove ready to receive their children in that time, then they could file an appeal for an additional three months. However, they were not guaranteed any time beyond the total of fifteen months.

These kids had already been in care exceeding fifteen months, so no more time was guaranteed. Additionally, the birth parents were still unable to provide for them because they were still in jail. Therefore, the caseworkers felt fairly confident that TPR would be granted. Obviously, they could make no promises.

As the meeting was preparing to conclude, and we were supposed to go meet the kids, one of the ladies posed an objection to us as potential parents.

She looked at one of the other ladies and said, *"I don't feel like Jordan is committed. He's not engaging in this at all. I don't feel comfortable introducing them to the kids if they are still on the fence. It wouldn't be fair to the kids if they decide to back out."*

Personally, I felt this was just a tactic to intimidate on-the-fence couples into committing quickly, before they have had time to process. This seemingly protective approach was surprising after the desperate approach we received at the adoption convention. And, I could see that Jordan wasn't on the fence. To me, his clenched jaw and crossed arms were helping him hold in his complaints over how long it was taking for them to share little information with us.

Jordan looked directly at the woman and said, *"You don't know me well enough to interpret why I've remained quiet. And, I don't really know what you're expecting. It's not like I can ask you any questions because you don't have the answers. I'm not here for small talk; I'm here to meet my kids."*

I stepped in to buffer Jordan's bluntness with a little something like, *"What he means to say is, um, you had him at hello."*

CHAPTER 6

TOO REAL, TOO FAST

W e rode with our caseworker over to the local McDonald's to meet our kids for dinner. Quite the first meeting venue, don't you think? It was supposed to be less awkward than bringing the kids in to the office to sit around a big conference table.

We got there first. We were sitting in the dining area, waiting. And it wasn't an easy wait. We hadn't seen pictures of our kids-to-be, and neither had our caseworker, so we didn't know what to look for. And, the kids were separated, which meant they wouldn't be showing up all at once. That left us creepily staring down every single child who walked through the door, wondering if they would be ours. Several came through that were not ours. We gazed directly at each of them with soft smiles. They all glared back at us. Talk about awkward.

After ten or fifteen minutes, a man walked in with two boys who didn't glare back at us. They acted like they were also looking for someone they wouldn't recognize. Yup, they were two of ours. The boys stared blankly at us as their foster dad arranged for our caseworker to take responsibility for them because he had somewhere else to be.

As he left, the kids shyly said, *"Hello,"* and after asking, we learned they were ten-year-old Brandon and nine-year-old Henry. They were clean, nicely dressed, and were sporting fresh haircuts. Brandon looked at us with blonde hair, beaver teeth, the skinniest, knobbiest knees I'd ever seen, and bright blue eyes. Henry was looking through some eyes much like my own--greenish-blueish-greyish. He had cute freckles and was a little thicker than gangly Brandon. They didn't wait long before they asked if they could go play, and it seemed like the best option. Two down, three to go.

The next two kids to join our party came in with looks of anticipation, similar to the first two. They were eleven-year-old Faith and six-year-old Clarence, or Clay for short. They gave us a shy nod before taking off to meet their brothers in the kids' place. We were able to get an ok look at them as they went by. Sadly, they were both due for a shower. Clay was missing a large chunk of hair off the top of his head, and his shorts were too big. He had the biggest and brightest blue eyes I'd ever seen and puffy cheeks! Faith had a bright green fabric belt tied on and eyes that matched Henry's and my own. Her greasy hair was just below her shoulders and light brown in color. Heartstrings were tugged, for sure.

Lastly, Little Man came through like a storm. Four-year-old Caisen didn't notice us at all. He just darted to the playroom. I couldn't even tell you if he had eyes by how quickly he flew by! Turns out, he hadn't seen any of his siblings in about eight months, so that's where his focus was. Totally understandable.

We watched through the glass for a few minutes, unsure of what to do. It was interesting to watch them interact. It was a lot like watching a pinball machine, but with five balls going at once. And as if that wasn't complicated enough, one of the boys started crawling up the outside of the play struc-ture, and then his brothers tried to follow him. It got crazy in there. We assumed they were just excited to see each other.

We saw an opportunity to join them when a couple of the kids had just come out of the slide and hadn't dived back in yet. Clay came up to us and stood toe-to-toe with Jordan. Literally, their toes were touching. He looked waaaay up to Jordan and asked, *"So, are you my new dad?"* Jordan told Clay that's what we were working toward. Clay responded, *"So, can I go home with you?"*

By this time, we were seeing him more closely. The hair surrounding his chop-spot was overgrown; he was missing teeth, had sideways teeth, and had silver teeth. He had some extra weight packed on him. And he had a desperate, needy look on his face. I knew right then that this pathetic little chunk was meant to be mine! Partly because something about him reminded me of my little brother, which I'm sure my brother takes as a fabulous compliment after the description I just gave. However, I mostly felt for him because I could see all over him how much he wanted to be loved. He was exactly the child we had been praying for.

Then, the kid turned on a dime and sprinted back to the play structure. He attempted to jump onto the landing and dive through the doorway, but failed. Big time. His toe caught the landing, and he buckled down on him-self. He lost his balance and fell backward down the two steps. Yup. This kid was definitely meant to be ours.

The food was brought to us. Mind you, we were not ring leading this circus. We were there to watch, so watch is what we did. We watched as the kids filled not one, not two, not seven, but about eighty-four refills of soda and sweet tea. We watched them fight over the toys. We watched them break all of the posted rules. We heard them all yelling to and at each other with mouths full of food.

Brandon seemed to be the biggest voice in the crowd, shouting, *"He got more fries than me!" "You got pop? I want pop!"* and *"I'm not sitting by him, he's messy!"*

He wasn't wrong about the other boys being messy, but he wasn't much better. They were all desperately scarfing. Maybe they were just in a hurry to get back to playing?

We also heard little Caisen calling out and found that he had a southern drawl! It was adorable! Especially when he called for his sister, *"Fay-ith."* And, I could finally see that his eyes were blue.

We asked the kids a few questions. Faith talked like a baby, but indicated she would like to play sports. All the boys jumped in to say they also wanted to play. SCORE! Jordan and I were hoping they'd be as interested in sports as we were.

After eating, Faith went back in to play. Brandon asked Jordan for his phone as the boys interrogated us about the things they deemed important. *"What gaming systems do you have?" "What games do you have?" "Why don't you have other games?" "Are you really in the Army?' "Have you killed people?"* etc.

Brandon downloaded himself a couple of apps, and Henry tried to snatch the phone from Brandon. Brandon smacked Henry. Henry teared up in frustration. I handed Henry my phone. Over the next few minutes, they were both calling and Face-Timing people, opening every single app on the phones, taking pictures, and downloading games in between grabbing and snatching.

Clay, who had been sitting there fairly quietly, asked, *"Can I have a turn?"* with the most pathetic look I'd ever seen. We gave Henry and Brandon a heads up before requesting they rotate the phones. One phone moved to Caisen and the other to Clay. Clay asked me to find a game for him, and I handed it back to him as it was downloading. He sat there patiently.

Time went by, and Henry grabbed the phone from Clay claiming that it was his turn again, and Clay just dropped his head and sighed, *"I didn't even get to play it yet."* I was watching, and he truthfully hadn't played anything. He was still waiting for it to download. I asked that it be handed back to Clay, and it was. At this point, Brandon took the phone back from Caisen. Caisen, Brandon and Henry were squished so tightly together as they watched the screen like hawks.

I wanted to break it up a bit, so I challenged Clay. *"Hey, Clay, let me see how fast you can go through the entire maze and get back here to me. I'll time you. Ready, set, go!"* He made it in twenty-two seconds.

Henry wanted a turn. He made it in nineteen seconds.

Caisen went next, and he didn't come back.

Brandon was still glued to Jordan's phone, so Jordan said he needed it back and encouraged Brandon to take a turn. He made it through in seventeen seconds.

Clay, in a soft voice, asked, *"Can I try again?"* He got it in twenty seconds, and cried! Have I mentioned that this kid is totally pathetic? He said, *"I'm not good at anything!"* I tried to reassure him. I pointed out that he improved on his own first time, and I told him that I was proud of his efforts. He sniffled, and then he asked if he could hold the phone to time Brandon, who was ready for his next turn.

Brandon got sixteen seconds. Clay cried again.

At this point, Faith and Caisen re-emerged. Faith now had her bright green fabric belt tied around her head with Caisen on her shoulders. Clay saw this and walked right up to Jordan again and asked, *"Can I go on your shoulders?"* Jordan turned him around and picked him up. Clay landed on Jordan's shoulders and immediately seized in fear. It didn't help that Jordan is six foot, two inches. The kid was way up there. He squeezed tightly on to Jordan's head. Jordan tried to lift him to get him down, but Clay wouldn't loosen his grip; they were now fused together. He was up there and wasn't coming down.

Clay started hyperventilating, so I tried to distract him a bit. I picked up my phone and asked to take a picture. His smile came on strong, but he didn't relax a single muscle. This moment, this exact moment, stood out amongst all of the others in this meeting. My pathetic chunk of a kid was scared out of his mind, clearly had never been up on shoulders like that before, but wanted love and attention so badly that he would endure the fear for it. This kid.

It was about time for everyone to go their separate ways, so we asked to get a group picture before they scattered. Our family-to-be squeezed in tight on the landing that had earlier tripped up Clay. We said our goodbyes and told them we'd see them again on Saturday, just a few days later.

We got in the car to start our six-and-a-half-hour drive toward home. We were recapping the visit. Again, we were with our caseworker, Maggie, a super cute and proper lady. She wore a knee length skirt and heels, with a long necklace and eye-catching earrings. I guessed that she didn't have much chaos like this in her life, as she seemed to be getting dizzy and seeing stars, restating that she thought we were crazy. In between her comments about the mayhem, she also brought up how much each of the kids looked like us. It was true. There were many similarities, like hairlines, hair and eye colors, and big smiles! It felt like confirmation that God was in control, and knew what He was doing.

Our conversation went on. The highlights included Faith's baby-talk, Brandon's attempt at climbing the outside of the play structure, Henry's pop guzzling, Clay's, um, everything, and Caisen's accent. Also, their sports interests and need for dental work came up. It was a really big, overwhelming, exhausting day!

I opened my pictures to go back over the whirlwind that had just taken place. We had only taken a few. But, there were certainly more than a few on the camera roll! The kids had taken some pictures of each other, some pictures of us, and some selfies. Clay's silly-face selfie made my day. What a pathetic kid. Heart-melted.

CHAPTER 7

CRASH COURSE ON HERDING CATS

O ur next visit was set up differently. We were scheduled to pick up our rental minivan at zero-dark-thirty, drive six and a half hours to a park to collect the kids, have them for the day, drop them off before dinner, hit the long road back, return the minivan, and eventually get home. Test-driving children is quite the process.

We had the freedom to use the time in the middle however we wanted, so we did what anyone in our situation would do. We searched the Internet the day before for an activity. We found a farm with a corn maze, hayride, and hot dogs. Sounded great. Added bonus, it was only forty-five minutes from the pick-up/drop-off park so we wouldn't have to waste too much time in commuting. Speaking of commuting, I was totally ready to rock it in the rental minivan. Soccer mom for a day, woot-woot! At the same time, I was hoping that our hunt for a more permanent family rig would produce some viable options soon.

We arrived at the park to pick up the kids. Caisen was the only one who got there before we did. When we came walking up, he ran to Jordan and grabbed onto his leg. His foster mom gasped and explained that she was surprised because he wasn't even that comfortable with her husband. Caisen asked for a shoulder ride and chose to stay up there for some time. Good thing he was just a tiny tot. They told us he was four, but I've never seen a four-year-old that small. In fact, all the three-year-old kids I'd known were bigger than he was. But that was ok, it just added to his little cuteness! That, and his little Under Armour ball cap. Again, cuteness!

The foster family caring for Faith and Clay were away for the weekend, so the kids stayed with Brandon and Henry's foster family the night before. It was really sweet when their van pulled up and all four kids got out. They immediately split up. Brandon went straight to the playground, yelling, *"Hi Miss Jessie. Hi Mr. Jordan!"* as he ran past. Brandon's bright yellow shirt brought out his light blonde hair and tan.

Henry ran to us to show us the little Army stuffed bear he got that was, *"just like Mr. Jordan."* Henry's hair was a little darker than I had remembered. He asked me to hold his bear while he went to play.

Faith and Clay walked over to us as Henry sprinted away. Clay came in for a big, long, heart-melting hug and then said, *"Hello."* These two had a totally different look to them this time 'round. Faith's hair was still a little wet from her shower. She wore a pink, foofy, glittery skirt and matching shirt, with intentionally mismatched socks. Thankfully, her skirt had some shorts attached underneath because the next thing she did was go hang upside down on the monkey bars!

Clay was sporting a new look, too. His hair was gelled up, which helped to camouflage the still missing hair-chunk. It didn't do anything to help with the big gash on his forehead, though.

He said he was trying to fly, but apparently couldn't. He said it in a way that showed he was totally surprised when it didn't work out. This kid. Cracking me up from the beginning. He was wearing a WWE shirt and some blue plaid shorts. Again, rocking those big baby blue eyes.

We didn't yet have a car seat or two boosters, so we borrowed them from the foster families. Jordan lost two out of three in rock, paper, scissors, so he went to install the seats while I talked a little with Brandon and Henry's foster dad.

I could tell right away that he was a great man. His wife, too. They put a lot of effort into the kids, and you could see how deeply they cared. Not just for the ones placed with them but also for the extra two kids they took in the night before so that they could participate in our day trip.

Jordan wasn't gone long, and got back to the conversation at the perfect time.

The foster dad kept his eye on the kids as he offered us this advice: *"If you find yourselves in a situation where you can't find Brandon, you should start looking up."* Yes, up. *"Up on top of the play structures, up the walls, up the poles. Anywhere up."*

As soon as he finished his sentence, he shifted to yell to Brandon to get off an awning.

I leaned toward Jordan and whispered, *"Does this mean that Brandon's climbing up the outside of the play place at McDonald's was fairly typical behavior and not just a result of the excitement?"*

The boys' foster dad also urged us to be clear with our expectations and directions because the kids wouldn't guess them on their own. Truthfully, I felt much better having someone who actually knew the kids sharing information with me. It was comforting. He also gave me his and his wife's cell phone numbers, just in case.

When it was time, we rounded up the kids and hit the road. The first thing I heard was, *"Can I have your phone?"* Jordan said no, because he was using it for directions. I let them have mine, but it didn't last long. Sharing is caring, and there wasn't much of either between the back seats. I asked for it back and justified it by saying I needed to save the battery for pictures, which was true.

I asked if they had any questions for us. They said, *"No."* I giggled a little. Really?

"We are practically strangers, attempting to become your parents, and there's nothing you want to know about us?"

"Nope." Their standards were low.

I asked them their favorite colors, subjects, animals, if they had ever had pets, and what they wanted to be when they grew up. I just kept asking away to keep their attention off the phone and off of whacking each other. It mostly worked. I asked them how old they thought Jordan was. They guessed eighty-nine. I asked how old they thought I was and they guessed sixteen. I win!

We pulled into the parking lot. Before opening the doors, we went over the rules. Clear expectations, just like the foster dad said. The three rules we outlined were to stay together, hold hands through the parking lot, and no screaming. There was an echo of *"Yes, sir"* and *"Yes, ma'am,"* leading us to believe it was going to work out just fine.

We opened the doors, and they took off like cockroaches in light. Jordan tracked down Caisen and tossed him up on his shoulders. Faith and Clay were walking in the wrong direction, so I called to them, and then actually had to run after them. Brandon and Henry thought it was funny as they were sneaking in between cars. Yeah. Real funny.

I bought the tickets and applied the wristbands. We were at the beginning of the large corn maze. We, again, went over the rules. It helped that they were the same rules painted on all of the farm's signs. Emphasizing, no running and stay with your party. They all agreed, *"Yes sir, yes ma'am."* Then, they took off in a dead sprint into the three different entryways! I shouted, *"No running!"* To which they replied, *"We won't,"* as they were. I accepted it was going to be a long day.

Jordan and I separated in an attempt to wrangle them in. I was getting dirty looks and under-breath scolds from people because our kids were cutting through the corn. It was embarrassing. *"Stay on the path,"* was met with, *"I am,"* when they weren't! *"Walking please,"* also got the response, *"I am,"* when they weren't. *"Stop,"* was met with, *"I will,"* which earned, *"Now please,"* which got *"I did,"* but they didn't.

Brandon and Henry were the hardest to keep tabs on. Caisen, Clay, and Faith floated to and from. Whichever kid was next to me didn't want me to seek the other kids. They wanted to walk backward in front of me to maintain a direct-eye-contact conversation. I was thinking, *"I have a kid climbing up an old, creaky, wooden tower that has a 'stay off' sign on it, and you want me to stop and talk to you about the weed you just pulled?"* The kid jumped off the tower and resumed running. At least he was back on the ground, right?

As we were wandering through the maze, Jordan called me to say that Caisen needed to go potty, so I was on my own with the other four, but I only had two. So, while Faith talked to me in fluent baby talk about the Barbie collection she used to have that was left at a previous placement, Clay talked to me about how to develop his flying skills, and I simultaneously used my new-mom sonar to seek the others. Eventually, Jordan called to say he was back in the maze and was also on the hunt. We were trying to sweep through the whole thing, but it was hard when the kids we were seeking weren't staying on the path.

Eventually, Jordan and I made it out two different exits. We each had two kids. You'd think I would have had Faith and Clay, but no. I found Henry. Then lost Clay. Jordan had Caisen and Clay. We were still missing one. I said, *"Everyone, stay here with Jordan, I'll go find Brandon."* They all said, *"Ok,"* then they all ran back into the maze to look for Brandon. I dropped my head as I entered the maze for round two of the round up.

We did, at some point, make it out of that maze-trap on to the hayride. We sat against the back of the flatbed that was being pulled behind a tractor. First and foremost, the guide called out, *"Hands and feet in at all times!"* So, of course, every two point seven seconds we had another kid hanging over the edge. I'm sure the tour guide got tired of having to repeat, *"Ma'am, please keep your kids in the trailer,"* and *"Ma'am, please get control of your kids,"* every thirty seconds, but there wasn't a whole lot more I could do! There was no controlling them. I just wanted to cry and apologize, but I stayed at it.

"Henry, get your foot in please." "Faith, your hand." "Caisen, sit down please." "Henry, your foot again." "Caisen, get your foot in please." "Henry, now your hand." "Henry, have a seat." "Caisen, your hand." "Henry, your foot again."

You might be wondering why we didn't have to talk to Clay or Brandon at this point. That's easy to answer. They were sleeping. Clay fell asleep in Jordan's lap. He was propped in between Jordan's legs, back-to-chest style. His legs were wide open and outstretched in front of him. His head was hung down and to the side. His arms were flopped over Jordan's legs. He looked dead. Or, drunk. Either way, he was totally passed out. Brandon was sitting in a little ball. Feet-on-seat, knees tucked in, arms around knees, face on knees/forearms.

The pig races were next. Oh my gosh! The giggling that came out of the kids was music to my ears. Of course, they kept trying to climb over the railing and on to the track, but that's normal, right? They were trying to reach for the pigs as they went by, even though the intercom direction repeatedly announced not to. Aside from the stress of having *"the disobedient kids,"* it really was nice to see them laughing and giggling as innocent as could be!

It was time to feed the little busy-bees, so Jordan took them over to the really big inflatable trampoline while I went to order. *"Seven hot dogs, seven bags of potato chips. How much are the bottled waters? What? Three dollars and fifty cents, each? I'll take four."* I grabbed mustard and ketchup packages, napkins, napkins and more napkins. When I waved Jordan and the kids over, they came like a stampede.

They shoved each other around trying to get their *"favorite"* spots. I found that *"favorite"* meant anything that someone else had. I instructed Caisen and Clay to share a water bottle, Henry and Brandon to do the same, Faith was handed her own, and Jordan and I would share the fourth. Caisen took a drink and half of his hotdog was left inside the bottle. GAG! I mean, I knew they were disgusting eaters, but this took it to a whole new level. New directions. Clay and Henry share, Faith and Brandon share, Jordan and I share, and Caisen could have his food-filled bottle all to himself.

Lastly, we went to go feed some animals, which went mostly well, aside from Brandon trying to feed the one animal they were told not to. They shoved and pushed in front of other kids. They hung over the rails and into the pigpens. And they had all scattered to different exhibits. Apparently staying together just wasn't going to happen. The excitement of spending time with each other after so long apart wore off quickly! They were like repellent to each other.

Caisen, the youngest boy, fed one of the messier pigs that slobbered all over his hand. He screamed that the pig tried to eat his whole hand off. He shrieked, *"He tried to bite me! He wanted to eat me! That pig is mean!"* Faith tried to grab him, but he wasn't used to having her around and wanted nothing to do with her. I grabbed him, and it felt nice to be able to calm him down. I also had to soothe a crying Faith because her feelings were hurt that Caisen wouldn't let her pick him up and care for him. *"Faith, I saw you were trying to help. I appreciate that. I will let you know when I need help. Otherwise, it's ok for you to be a kid."*

Once she felt better, I turned my attention back to Caisen who had snot all over his face and shirt. It took a few minutes, but he calmed down.

We went back over to the bounce pad, but it didn't last long. The kids got reprimanded by the staff too many times for trying to launch people off and for flipping. Seemed like the right time to load back up in the minivan.

When we got to the park, they played for a few minutes before the first set of foster parents showed up to take four of the kids. We waited for a good twenty minutes with Caisen before being able to get a hold of the case worker, who then contacted his foster mom, who passed on the message that she miscalculated the time. It ended up that we had an extra hour with mini-man alone. It was much easier being two-on-one than it was two vs. five!

As we said our final goodbyes, the weight of the challenge we were taking on hit. It wasn't going to be just a really long day. There were going to be a lot of really long days.

We eventually made it back across the state of Georgia, said goodbye to the minivan, and drove home. We crawled straight into bed and passed out. Shoes on, without brushing our teeth. There was a weak *"go-team"* high five, a small kiss goodnight, and we were down for the count.

CHAPTER 8

LIFE IS EITHER A DARING ADVENTURE, OR NOTHING AT ALL

W e survived the initial meeting at McDonalds. No sweat. We survived the day trip to the farm. A little sweat. Our next step with these kids was to have them over to our house. It would be too easy to have them all come and go together, so a complicated transport schedule was put in place. On this particular day, Saturday, October 25th, all five were scheduled to come over. Three kids were on day passes, which boiled down to about five hours with us after allowing for the lengthy travel to and from our house. The other two kids had booked a nine-day stay, to cover their entire fall break. Good thing I wasn't working anymore!

Just to make sure things hit the desired level of crazy, the three kids on single day passes were scheduled to come back the following Friday. The plan was for us to keep all five kids until Sunday, and then they would all go back together. We had to brace ourselves for this nine-day marathon, especially the last three days.

Saturday morning, we did a final scan of the house. As required by foster regulations, outlet covers were in, locks were on doors that needed them, locks were off doors that couldn't have them, fire evacuation plans were clearly posted in every doorway, fire extinguishers were in their assigned locations, and our emergency bin was filled with a week's supply of canned foods, a can opener, a weather radio, a case of water, blankets for the entire family, batteries, and matches.

Since those details were already complete, we spent our time making sure the two sets of bunk beds were erect and stable, the nightlights were in, there was plenty of toilet paper, the sheets and comforters were spread, the remote controls had batteries, the groceries were bought, and other such things. We didn't need to check on anything vehicle-related because we knew we were going to be stranded for the entire first day. We couldn't fit our whole group in either of our cars. We were still shopping for a larger replacement vehicle, but we hadn't found the right one yet.

Once we made it through our final check, we sat down and waited. And waited. And waited. I had to change my shirt because I had pitted out. I was nervous. I took the dogs outside to run off some of their energy. I came back in. I waited some more. I got a text that they were lost and running late. I gave directions, and shortly after, they made their appearance.

From the moment everyone arrived, the wheels fell off the wagon, so to speak.

As I was trying to corral the kids, the driver told me that they were terrible. She said they kept unbuckling and climbing around and were messing with everything, including tearing apart her granddaughter's doll. I was anxious to get involved with the kids, and I wasn't sure what she wanted me to do about it, so I just apologized and asked if there was anything else I needed to know. Of course, I may have teared up a bit. It wasn't exactly what I wanted to hear, as I was about to begin my own battle with them. It was a total non-boost!

Into the house we all went. There were kids cycling through the bathroom and kids fighting over who was riding the dogs. First of all, my dogs weren't made for riding. The German Shepherd, Cinder, piddled. It was the first time that had happened in the entire three years we'd had her, and she had been around plenty of children. Butter, the Labradoodle, tried to be a good sport. I mean, she lets kids crawl on her and pull her eyelashes all the time, but only for so long before she taps out. I think she finally went and hid about the eightieth time Caisen jumped onto her from the couch, where each time she fell flat to the ground.

They found the cats. Henry tried to make Violet stay in a box so he could pet her. She didn't want to be in the box. Then, Perry was dragged down the hall. He wasn't a fan of his treatment either. The cats quickly chose to go hide with the dogs. I tried to stay in between the small people and the animals, because I didn't want an animal to get defensive and go after a child, or run away. I used a lot of redirection and distraction tactics like, *"Hey, what's that over there?"*

We let the kids play with the Xbox Connect. Bad idea. They weren't doing well taking turns, so we opened a few other games too. We had two kids playing Connect with Jordan in the living room and three kids playing a Ninja Turtle Superhero game in the dining room. There was a lot of shuffling back and forth between the two rooms. And everywhere else in the house, if I'm being honest. And there were no walking feet in my house. At all.

The kids kept disappearing into the bedrooms and bathrooms. We found them hiding in closets, under the desk, and on the second and third rows of the bookshelves. Of course, the books were then on the floor. The kids were under the covers, under the beds, and under laundry baskets. All this was happening in between turns of the games that were going on. I'm telling you, these kids were totally bonkers. And I can promise you; it wasn't due to lack of direction and reminders.

At one point, Jordan made a quip about the lack-of-informational meeting, where they told us that they were all typical, healthy children, with the exception of the one of who had ADHD. Just one kid and just one diagnosis. Yeah right!

Next, we found a couple of them launching themselves off of the top bunks and trying to land on the dresser. I was extra surprised to see scaredy-cat Clay making the jump, since he had reportedly learned he couldn't fly the weekend prior.

Speaking of Clay, he still had that same chunk of hair missing! It had been nine days since we had first seen it, it wasn't even new at that point, and it STILL wasn't fixed! Poor kid! For his sake, I couldn't wait until the TPR hearing, so that there was no longer a need to seek permission for haircuts. This kid was in serious need of a new hairdo!

After a delicious lunch of macaroni and cheese with apples, we decided to take our clown parade outside. We thought it would be less chaotic. Wrong again. They climbed around, under, and on Jordan's truck. They were jumping off the wall of the bed and aiming to land on each other WWE style. Jordan snatched little Caisen out of the air, as he was plunging head first toward the driveway. Caisen didn't even seem to recognize that anything had gone wrong with his jump.

We pulled out some balls. Henry kicked a soccer ball over the neighbors' fence. Clay got hit with a football and cried. Caisen went running after the rolling ball, towards the street. Jordan snatched Caisen before he jumped off the curb. At that time, Brandon noticed that the overhang of our roof was near the back of the truck and worked his way up to climb higher. Jordan tossed me the four-year-old, quickly reached out and snatched the ten-year-old out of the air, mid-jump, and then quickly gave me a *"this is insane"* look.

It was clear you couldn't take your eyes off these kids. The only problem, though, was that our four eyes couldn't always cover five scattered kids efficiently. We had to work together and talk a lot. *"I've got this one." "Grab that one." "Do you have eyes on him?" "Where's the other one?" "Give him to me." "Go get that one." "I've got this one."* "If nothing else, Jordan and I sure were getting good with communication and trust. We were allies in a new war!

The transport person came back to collect the three kids who were on day passes. We took a group photo in front of the house before loading up the kiddos. We said bye-bye to Brandon, Henry, and Caisen. The hugs and kisses goodbye were sweet, but the idea of three fewer screamers and runners was appealing.

We went out to dinner as a family of four. Just as we had observed before, these kids were extremely sloppy, messy, gross eaters. We made mental notes that we'd need more work on table manners. Regardless, the meal was much more enjoyable when we weren't drastically outnumbered!

We drove back home and got ready for bed. I checked on the bathroom to make sure there was still enough toilet paper, and found that at least one of our boys, possibly more, left some pee-spray for us. Clearly someone had either gotten distracted and spun around, or was excited and playing with their stream. Either way, I learned how gross little boys could be.

Clay was a little uncomfortable about sleeping in the boys' room alone, so I asked Faith to sleep in there with him until the rest of the boys came back. Solved that problem! We survived the day, and we were looking forward to the week. But we needed some sleep first!

CHAPTER 9

TEAR IT DOWN

We had six days of highs, lows, and gotta-get-'er-dones. The highest priority must-do was to lock in a bigger family vehicle option. Thankfully, a family donated one that had great potential, but then we got practical. The donated rig had very high mileage on it, and we had my 4Runner as a trade in. We thought about it, and we decided that trading in the donated rig along with mine would get us a great launch into a longer-term reliable rig. We had no reason to believe we'd have the additional trade-in boost later.

We located a Certified Used Yukon XL that would work for us, but the dealership needed a couple days to transport it in for us. When it arrived, we went in as a family of four to pick it up. It was uncomfortable making the purchase before the TPR court date, since we didn't know if the kids would be made legally available for adoption. But, the rest of the kids would be back in just a few days. We knew we needed to dive in with our faith in God, so that's what we did.

I took a picture of Jordan sitting with Clay in the finance office, filling out the necessary paperwork. Clay was wearing Jordan's Army hat and Oakley sunglasses, and they both sported ear-to-ear smiles as we got ourselves a large, black SUV. It was the perfect vehicle to fit a family of seven, plus our big dogs and baggage. We were officially a big-rig family, traveling in style! Just in time, too, because we had a big week ahead of us!

Jordan worked during the week, so we made use of the time we shared with him. We took the kids to the beach. Jordan buried Clay while Faith wrote sweet notes in the sand. We went to see Boxtrolls, their very first movie theater experience. We painted pottery. Clay painted a football piggy bank and Faith painted a fairy. We hung out at the house, watched classic Disney movies they hadn't seen before, colored, played Twister, and had fun preparing meals together. There were plenty of opportunities to see their smiles.

We also got to see their tears. In conversations with these two, all kinds of things came up. Clay said he didn't remember his birth parents, but he remembered that he had eaten dog food when there wasn't anything else around. He was only two when he first went into foster care, yet he remembered the dog food.

When Faith chimed in, she said that I reminded her of her mommy.

I asked how, and she said, *"I don't know. I don't remember much about her, but she was probably nice, probably pretty, and probably kind, like you."*

It was sweet of Faith to compliment me like that, but I was sad she was missing memories of her earlier years.

Clay cried a lot throughout the week. He colored outside the lines of a squirrel picture and cried. He tripped, fell down, and cried. He forgot what he was saying mid-sentence and cried. Faith spoke to him sharply a couple of times, about getting details wrong in a story, and he cried. His tears were not private or postponed. They were immediate. His little chin would quiver, and the tears would squirt out. Such a pathetic little guy. I felt so deeply for him!

Faith also cried a lot, but in a different way. If I asked her to put something away that she had forgotten, she'd disappear to her closet and cry. If she were asked to apologize for a rude comment to Clay, she'd disappear and cry. If I gave Jordan or Clay a hug, she'd disappear and cry. In the follow-up conversations, on the floor of her closet, I learned she was scared I wouldn't love her if she made too many mistakes. She was trying so hard to earn love and was truly hurt each time she thought she had blown it. If only she knew that NO KID should EVER have to EARN love!

Two things were certain. These two kids were fragile, and these two kids really needed some focused love and attention. As much as I'd like to say it was the best thing watching them fall asleep in our arms in the middle of the day, it was the opposite. No kid should be craving love this badly.

As we ate our last dinner as a family of four, I noticed a feeling of sadness. I didn't want our small family time to end. Don't get me wrong; I was happy to welcome our other three boys back, but I was feeling so connected to Faith and Clay, and I really wanted to keep developing our relationships. *"It's ok,"* I told myself *"we'll have years of time to grow together, as long as TPR goes through."* Yeah, that uncertainty about the upcoming court date was a hard thing to have hovering over us, but we kept praying it would come together.

We watched Cinderella while we waited for the three missing boys to arrive. We knew it would be late because they planned to start the six-and-a-half-hour drive after school. They crossed the line of late into early, finally arriving about half past midnight, not the least bit tired. We cycled the kids through brushing their teeth and getting their jammies on. We tucked the four boys into the boys' room, and tucked Faith into her room, for her first night alone.

After kissing her goodnight, we attempted to leave her room, and she fell apart in panic. Not just a little. She hyperventilated and sobbed. She was terrified. She had a nightlight, the door was open, and our room was just across the hall. No matter. She couldn't handle being alone. And what better time to receive this information than at one o'clock in the morning.

I sat on her bedroom floor, waiting for her to fall asleep. However, she was anxious over the idea of my leaving, so she wasn't really trying to sleep. I lay down. Time kept rolling on. At one point, I thought she was asleep, so I attempted to get up. Her ninja senses alerted her, and she panicked all over again. I played it off like I was just adjusting my position. I think she bought it because she lay back down. The tossing and turning resumed. Another eternity passed, and I just lay there, longing for my bed. I tried again. Strike two! I waited another forever before trying again. By this time, it was just shy of three o'clock in the morning. I moved so slowly and silently, I could have been passed by a stampede of snails scooting through molasses! And I made it! I tiptoed to my room, then to my bed, and snuck under the covers.

I'd like to say that the kids were so wiped out by their late night that they slept in, but that would be a lie. The first woke up about six o'clock in the morning, and all were wide awake by seven. It didn't take long to realize that the little cranky-monsters could have used more sleep, but there wasn't anything we could do about it now. So, breakfast was the next best thing.

We sat around the table. I recognized then that I would never be able to take the dining table's leaf out again. Big-family problems. We had placemats, bowls, spoons, and napkins on the table. We pulled out a few different options of cereal for them to choose from, poured the cereal and the milk, and watched the show begin. I was amazed at all the splashes and spatters going every which-way. We kept reminding the kids that we were all in the same room, and there was no need to yell. You'd think maybe just one of them would have learned to slow down and chew with their mouth closed. But no. They were all messy. And they all acted starved. In fact, they all demanded that they needed seconds. And thirds.

With a full mouth, Clay said, *"That's a weird clock,"* pointing to the piece on the wall. It was a collage of black numbers, with white hands.

"That's my favorite decoration in the entire house," I responded, as all of the kids looked up to see what we were talking about. *"It was a gift from my Aunt Anne. I think of her every time I look at it."*

"It's a cool clock," said Brandon. *"I like the numbers."*

"Me too," I said.

Then Brandon looked at Clay and called him a fat slob. Henry agreed. They both laughed at him.

I admit; Clay had a messier mess going on, but not enough to justify being called names. These were some of the first intentionally and directly rude behaviors we'd observed in them.

"Let's be nice to each other," I said, hoping they would redirect easily. They did.

They all resumed smacking, chomping, yelling, singing, and crying with their mouths full. When they started fighting over the cereal boxes for fourths, even though two of them were clearly so stuffed that they looked uncomfortable sitting in their chairs, I stepped in to redirect them.

We lured them from the table by turning on the TV, so that we could clean up the breakfast mess. If the dogs weren't so scared of the kids, I'm sure they would have loved to help clean the floor! But no, it was left to me.

In the next room, the kids didn't sit still well. They were cranky and whiny, thanks to no sleep. I pulled out some toy sets to redirect the bad attitudes, and it got rambunctious quickly.

The game was cops and robbers, and we had all kinds of plastic props: badges, batons, whistles, handcuffs, etc. The teams kept changing, the jail kept moving, and the game kept getting louder and louder. There was a lot of hiding, laughing, running, crying, yelling, arguing, more running, crying, more laughing; it felt like we were burning through the day. Yay! Unfortunately, time wasn't moving nearly as fast as we were. It was mid-morning when the most epic and thrilling game of cops and robbers abruptly came to an end. Mostly because the kids didn't want to stop beating each other up with batons. There are only so many times you can tell them to stop hurting each other before you have to be the bad guy who says Game Over.

The kids asked if they could play Super Mario Bros on the Nintendo Wii. We let them play four-player, swapping the controllers around so that all five could play. There is nothing that could have prepared us for how badly this was going to go. Well, that's not true. Full disclosure regarding the kids' behaviors would have helped. Either way, our adoption journey was about to take a real nosedive...

The kids were loud and physical. More than we would have liked, but not enough for us to be truly concerned. That is, not until Brandon got upset because things weren't going his way. He screamed at anyone who went anywhere near a mushroom or firepower without his permission. And, he would never give permission. Even if he already had firepower, he still wouldn't let anyone else have it! At first, he was just yelling at and shoving his siblings. Then, he whacked them with his remote and cried and screamed. When he first hurt Henry, who seemed to get hit more than the others, we asked Brandon to calm down. He always said, *"Oh, yes sir,"* or *"Oh, yes ma'am,"* but couldn't get a hold of himself.

We told Brandon he wouldn't be allowed to play anymore if he hit again. *"Oh, I won't,"* he said. And then he did. We asked him to hand over his remote. He reacted worse than any kid I had ever seen, including kids in their terrible two's and terrible three's. Before I divulge the details, remember that our relationship with this child was still brand, spanking new, having only seen him for an hour at McDonald's, a few hours at the farm, and a few hours when he came on his quick day pass the previous weekend. We had been told he had ADHD, and he had some medicine to help with that. We were prepared for ADHD, but ADHD is not the only problem we saw.

Immediately after we requested the remote, he went boneless, which is to say his body went limp as he fell to the floor. He flopped onto the ground and did some alligator rolls, while crying and screaming, *"That's not fair! It's his fault! If he didn't get in my way, I wouldn't need to hit him! It's his fault! He shouldn't get to play!"*

Poor Henry. I hadn't learned much about their background or history yet, but I knew enough to know that it wasn't Henry's fault that Brandon hit him. Brandon did not need to hit him, though he claimed he did. It was surprising to see this in a ten-year-old. I was caught completely off-guard by it. And it was only beginning.

I asked Brandon to come out of the living room with me, thinking it would help to remove him from the situation. That was a big NO! He put his back flat against the hall wall and was donkey-kicking the wall straight behind him with all his might. At the same time, he was smashing his head backwards against the wall. As a result, he didn't just put a hole in the wall, but he knocked the entire wallboard off the corner bracing.

In case you are wondering, the answer is no. He didn't stop there.

Jordan joined me in the hall. We were in disbelief. Brandon seemed so *"normal"* before. Who was this kid?

In response to Brandon's meltdown, Clay cried, as usual. Henry looked guilty and sorry, even though he hadn't done anything wrong. Faith sat there with a blank look, and Caisen carried on like nothing was happening. It was so odd, and it helped me to understand this wasn't the first time Brandon had lost control like this. Considering they hadn't spent much time together recently, this behavior must have tracked deep into their history. But no one told us?

I asked Jordan to stay with the other kids because they were going to need support through this too. I assured him I could handle Brandon, though I wasn't sure how.

I tried talking to Brandon. He wouldn't even acknowledge me. I tried calling the caseworker. No answer. I tried calling the foster dad. No answer. I tried calling the foster mom. No answer. I tried calling our agency. No answer. I hadn't yet been given the emergency lines because they were just on a visit. We were on our own. I was concerned about not having insurance information in case we needed to make a hospital run. In that moment, I felt unprepared and overwhelmed. It was hard to believe there was no one we could call, besides the police, but I REALLY didn't want to do that.

Then I remembered one more resource, my mom. When she answered, I said, *"The kid is screaming and yelling, and hitting walls. I don't have anyone else to call. Any ideas?"*

"Your brother used to throw big tantrums, too," she said. *"Have you tried a time out, or Tabasco sauce on the tongue? Or, tell him he'll miss out on something later today if he doesn't calm down."*

I didn't have the time to explain right then, but I knew I wouldn't be getting an answer from her. Brandon was not like my brother, and I didn't see any of her suggestions making much of an impact.

Since it was clear that help wouldn't be coming, I got creative. I'd ask Brandon to go with me to get lunch. If I could distract him, and maybe get him to leave the house with me in our new family rig, maybe he'd forget the game and simmer down. Maybe some one-on-one time would help? But, I was still in my pajamas. I quickly ran to change. And by quick, I mean, jammies came off, and I threw on some jeans and a sweatshirt. It was a judgment call; I needed to skip the bra, shirt and underwear. I didn't have time for luxuries. My new kid was bashing his head on a wall and tearing down the hallway.

I raced back to him and asked if he'd accompany me. I wanted him to feel special over picking what we'd eat. It didn't work. He banged harder, then stormed into the boys' room, wedged himself in between the end of one of the bunk beds and the wall, and resumed the kicking and head-banging combo, though this time the kicking was from a seated position and aimed at the bunk bed in front of him, while his head repeatedly struck the wall behind him. I tried to talk him through it. I tried to understand the problem. I tried to encourage him to take a deep breath. I asked him to place a pillow behind his head. Nothing was working.

Honestly, I wasn't even sure he could hear me. Or if he knew I was there, because he was screaming so loud. And not only that, he had his arms crossed over his face. He just kept yelling about how it wasn't fair and how it was all Henry's fault. Thankfully, I got an answer when he took his first shoe off and threw it at me. So, yeah, he knew I was there. Then the second shoe came. Now he was kicking in only socks, and I was praying that his feet wouldn't go through the footboard and his head wouldn't go through the wall. What could I do if they did? I had no one to call.

Jordan came in after a while to say we were all going to go get lunch. *"Time for our first family trip in the new car. Brandon, are you hungry?"* It didn't work the way he hoped. Brandon kept screaming and kicking, so Jordan got in the car with the rest of the family.

I pleaded with him, *"Brandon, please trust me. It's going to be ok. You need lunch; I'm sure you're hungry. Come on Brandon, can we get you some lunch?"*

I'm not exactly sure how long the rest of the family had been waiting for us, but I guess it was good practice for all the waiting that was to come in this new life. They apparently decided to test out the DVD system in the rig. I only know this because they were a good way into the movie Finding Nemo when I was finally able to talk Brandon into putting his shoes back on and getting into the SUV.

I climbed into the front passenger seat. I couldn't feel relief because I knew that our journey was just beginning. Jordan and I had matching *"what did we get ourselves into"* looks on our faces. Throughout the drive, Brandon continued grunting, but wasn't as loud as he had been.

Henry played with the window buttons. Jordan locked the windows. Henry kept playing with the buttons. Jordan asked him to leave the buttons alone, to which Henry replied, *"I'm not playing with the buttons."* Yet, the clicking continued. Again, Jordan asked him to stop, but Henry again denied doing it. I turned back toward him with a puzzled look on my face. I asked him to look at his hand, still on the window button. He said *"oh,"* and moved his hand. A few minutes later, he was back to clicking.

I made a mental note, *"We need to turn on the child safety locks when we stop next."*

As if that wasn't enough conflict for our first full-day with the full-family, we got another dose of it when we pulled into McDonald's. Inside, there was no line. We walked up to the counter as a family. I said, *"All right everyone, when it's your turn, tell me if you want chicken nuggets or cheeseburger, Gogurt or apple slices, and milk or water."*

I planned to go from oldest to youngest, so I asked Faith for her choices. She stared blankly at me. I asked Brandon what he wanted; he grunted and crossed his arms back over his face. I asked Henry what he wanted. He asked how many chicken nuggets came in the kid's meal. I said four and he said he'd think about it. At this point, the cashier was annoyed and a couple people had gotten in line behind us. I asked Clay. He said cheeseburger. GREAT! At least one kid was ready! *"Gogurt or apple slices?"* He said he wanted French fries. *"It comes with fries. Do you want Gogurt or apple slices to go with it?"* He picked Gogurt. Then he asked for Coke. I reminded him the choices were milk or water. He picked milk.

I looked at Caisen, and he just shrugged his shoulders. I looked at Jordan, who had been helping Henry with his decision, and he shrugged his shoulders too. He didn't know how to fix our problem.

The couple behind me groaned. I was embarrassed to be the mom who had no clue, and I had no idea how to make it better. And no one around us knew our story, so they just treated me like the problem.

I went back to Faith. *"Nuggets or Burger?"*

She said, *"Um, burger?"*

I didn't ask her if she was asking me about burgers or stating she'd like a burger. *"Gogurt or apples?"*

She mumbled something that sounded like *"shirt."* It rhymed with the end of Gogurt, so I ordered Gogurt. I then said, *"And I'll just get milk for everyone."* Henry then cried. He wanted Sweet Tea, which wasn't even an option!

The looks were getting worse. The cashier rolled his eyes in response to the man behind us sighing obnoxiously. I just wanted to say, *"I'm so sorry. I just barely met these kids, they're clearly broken, and I'm doing my best!"* But I didn't. I kept trying to get through the torture. I touched back with Henry. Chicken nuggets was the final decision, with honey mustard and Gogurt. Eventually I got orders out of Caisen and Brandon. One was nuggets with barbeque sauce, the other was a cheeseburger. One was Gogurt. The other asked for French fries. *"Yes, it comes with fries AND your choice of Gogurt or apples,"* and the choice ended up being apples. Then I just quickly threw in the two adult meals as quick as I could with a *"Please get me out of here"* look on my face, and tone.

As I walked away, the same man said, *"About time"* from under his breath. I felt bad. But I wasn't sure what I could have done differently. And I wasn't sure exactly what I felt bad about. What I did know, however, is that I wasn't feeling much support or encouragement on my first really tough day, as these conflicts put the other chaotic days to shame. In fact, I felt like a terrible new mom, as confirmed by the onlookers. I kept thinking, *"How will we get through this?"*

We took the kids to an inflatable park to burn off some of their cranky, irritated energy. It was expensive, but we planned to spend a significant amount of time inside which would make it worth it.

Caisen played in the little kid bounce house; Brandon joined and made it too bouncy for the little kids. Henry and Clay were tossing a ball around; Brandon took it. Faith was going up and down the slides in her own la-la-land, and Brandon came barreling by so she yelled at him to leave her alone. Then, Brandon got a teammate. Some kid with his hair in his eyes, who also picked on our other kids.

Henry came up to Jordan and me, crying about a giant spit wad on the front of his shirt, a loogie- soaked spot on the back of his shirt, and the final straw, spit on his face! Yes, he was spit on three different times. Since I had seen my kids were prone to letting things get out of control, I suspected he had done something to instigate or to escalate the situation. He assured me he had not. He said, *"That kid spit on me, three times!"* while pointing directly at long-bangs kid.

The mother of the other kid overheard Henry's exclamation and grabbed her kid, something I could not do because of the foster care rules, and said, *"Why did you spit on him?"* I was waiting to hear what Henry had done, certain it was coming, but the kid didn't respond. She asked, *"Did he spit on you?"* and the boy said NO. Wahoo! Henry didn't spit back! In that moment, I thought there might be hope for these kids after all.

The mother made her son apologize to Henry as she apologized to me. It was wonderful to be the gracious, not-embarrassed parent.

Then Brandon and Henry fought again, so it was about time to go, after only having been there forty-five minutes. The day sure was dragging.

The rest of the day was filled with more bickering, arguing, messy eating, yelling, and running. Their energy seemed never-ending. Eventually we got them to bed. Well, all except Faith. She required a battle-buddy for THREE HOURS before she finally fell asleep! At which point, I was beyond exhausted, and ready for bed.

Morning came way too soon. We began the day at level ninety crazy. I just kept counting down the minutes until we could drop them off at that same local McDonald's, as it had become the new pick-up/drop-off destination. Their transport met us there. We gave hugs and kisses goodbye. We confirmed we'd see them all at the courthouse for TPR on Wednesday. Yes, the big, anxiously-awaited day was just around the corner. They drove off, and Jordan and I sat there in wide-eyed wonder.

CHAPTER 10

THE RIGHT CHOICE OFTEN ISN'T EASY

I f it wasn't three o'clock in the morning, I would have been ecstatic. Oh, who am I kidding? I was ecstatic even at three o'clock. It was court day! I showered and dried my hair the night before, so that I could get a few more minutes before rising. When the alarm buzzed, I got up, brushed my teeth, put on deodorant, put on sweat pants and a t-shirt, grabbed my dress and some heels for court, and climbed in the car. I looked over at Jordan in the driver's seat, and he seemed to have accomplished the same tasks. Well, he also grabbed our water bottles. We were ready. I'm telling you, that super long drive was getting old! Old, but worth it.

We weren't sure what to expect, other than a tug-of-war between three lawyers and a judge. One lawyer would represent the State of Georgia, one represented the birth parents, and the third specifically represented the kids. I also knew the birth parents would be there, as it was a hearing regarding their rights to the kids. The kids would also be there, and I didn't know who the kids would go to for hugs first, the birth parents or us. It was a hard thing to think about.

I had been asked to testify, which I had never done before. I didn't know if the kids would see us as against their birth parents, or as a second set of parents who loved them. I wasn't told what I would be asked, but I knew I would be on the stand in front of the couple who maintained the rights to the children with whom I had been developing relationships.

We first drove to the Department of Family and Children's Services (DFCS) building, to meet up with the kids' caseworker. Upon entering, we asked her to point us towards the bathrooms, so we could get changed into our court attire.

I put on a conservative, knee length, black dress and some low black heels. My blonde hair was down, just below my shoulders, and I had applied enough make-up to look in the mirror and see my refreshed self again; it had been awhile since I saw anything other than a hot mess looking back at me.

I walked out of the ladies' room to find Jordan looking extremely handsome in his Army dress uniform. His smile seemed bigger and his green eyes seemed to sparkle as he wore his wrinkle free, custom fit black jacket, with First Lieutenant bars on his shoulders, and a perfectly tied half Windsor. His blonde hair was freshly cut, to ensure he remained within Army regulations. His shoes were shined, pants were pressed, and awards were straight.

The Purple Heart Medal caught my eye, and I suppressed a tear as I quickly reflected on how lucky I was to still have my best friend.

We climbed back in our car and followed the kids' case worker to the courthouse, and my mind raced as we parked and walked up to the big, brick building -- Are the birth parents already inside? Have the kids arrived? Are the kids feeling anxious or worried? What do the birth parents look like?

We walked through metal detectors at the entrance, which helped to ensure we felt the weight of what we were about to experience. We walked with the caseworker to a sitting area outside of the courtroom where our case would be heard, and we were approached by a woman who introduced herself as the lawyer representing the state of Georgia.

She started right into business, *"This type of court hearing (TPR) usually takes several days' worth of court appearances because of the importance of the decision, so I'll do my best to get you called before the end of the day, so that you don't have to come back out."*

Jordan quickly turned to me and said, *"You'll come back out, right? Even if I can't get off work?"*

"Of course," I replied to Jordan. There wasn't a doubt in my mind about being present for the entire duration. And I looked back at the lawyer to say, *"I'll be here, regardless."*

She continued, *"Wonderful, that takes a little pressure off of me. Today, we'll start by calling the birth mom to the stand, and we'll spend a while working through details with her. Then, the birth dad. We'll call you next. Then the judge will decide how he wants to hear from the kids. Lastly, we'll hear from the Guardian ad Litem about what he thinks is best for the kids. And that's about it."*

Just when I thought I had stored all the information I thought I would need, she remembered one last detail, *"I almost forgot, this judge, after gathering all of the information, usually takes four-to-six months to make a ruling, so we'll keep in touch to let you know what the answer ends up being. I'll see you in there."* And she headed into the courtroom.

That was not the timeline we had been led to expect, and I was beyond disappointed.

The stress of knowing how long this uncertain process would take was compounded by the realization that the Army was only keeping us in Georgia for another twelve-to-fifteen months. A prolonged legal process was going to eat up our timeline. Not to mention, we were already prepping for the kids to move in with us, which meant we would be deepening our relationships, not knowing whether or not they would actually become eligible for adoption. If we had to move before they were eligible, we wouldn't be able to take them with us, and the goodbye would be heartbreaking.

The overwhelming feeling was that we had been manipulated. Those used-kid-salesmen sure were good at their jobs, downplaying each huge step! However, when it came down to it, we knew these were the kids God chose for us, so the only direction to go was forward, with fairly guarded hearts.

The kids began to arrive. Henry and Brandon first, then Caisen, then Faith, and Clay. And every one of them came to us for hugs. Whether they missed their birth parents or not, I was reaffirmed with each embrace that we had places in the kids' hearts. Once all five kids were present, the kids' caseworker gathered the kids and took them to a different room, while we waited with a growing group of people for the large courtroom doors to open.

The caseworker came back and said they'd made the decision that the kids would not be allowed in the court room, or permitted to interact with the birth parents. The justification given to us was that it wasn't right for the kids to see the birth parents in their jumpsuits and hand/foot cuffs. I couldn't help but feel sad for the kids, as I'm sure they hoped to see their birthparents. However, the reasoning made sense. In fact, I wasn't sure I was prepared to see the orange getups either.

I also felt sad for whoever drew the short straw and was watching the kids. I knew from personal experience that it wouldn't be relaxing, but maybe the poor soul would gain a good story or two to share with loved ones afterwards.

While our wait continued, we did some chatting. Jordan asked Henry and Brandon's foster parents, *"Do you have any secrets about how to calm Brandon down when he's in a meltdown?"*

"Really?" exclaimed their foster dad, *"You saw a fit already? We didn't see our first big fit until about three-months in. He must really trust you."*

I chuckled at the idea that our miserable experience was a good sign. I thought a honeymoon period sounded good, but we clearly weren't getting one of those.

He continued, *"Oh, and the answer is no. I don't have any tips for you. Other than to stick with clear expectations."*

I had no chuckles for that.

We moved into the courtroom. We sat behind the kids' caseworkers and in front of the foster families. There were many other people present, waiting for cases of their own. The judge called our case first, but when the lawyer told him that it was to determine TPR, the judge decided to hear the quicker cases first. As a couple of cases opened and closed, I made some observations.

The birth parents were chained in place near the doorway by the judge's bench, and I was trying to look at them without rudely staring. She had a hard look about her. Her light brunette hair was down, framing her stern facial expression. There was no hint of a smile, and no twinkle in her eye, as though the weight on her shoulders had suffocated any happiness right out of her. And he didn't look any softer. Truthfully, neither one of them looked as I had pictured them, but I could see some resemblances between them and the kids.

When it was finally time, my heart raced. Birth mom was called to the stand, where she was questioned by her lawyer for about an hour. We heard about the sexual abuse she suffered earlier in life, how young she was when she first left home, the extent of her drug usage, her criminal activity, her failures regarding the kids, and her plans for the future. As much as I felt for the kids who had suffered through her bad choices, I was also sympathetic to this woman for what she had endured.

It was apparent through her entire testimony that she was intelligent, she'd had a hard life, and she'd grown into a hard, tough person. I was impressed by her quick-witted responses, the precision of her words, and her ability to detect the traps that the state's lawyer was setting up. She was also defensive, though I probably would have been, too.

As it progressed, I felt she either had denial issues, or she was just trying to convince the judge that her actions weren't as bad as everyone else made them out to sound. Either way, when a person is trying to downplay drug and alcohol use during pregnancy, roach-infested living arrangements, and repeat criminal activity, it doesn't project that they've come to terms with their choices, taken responsibility, or intended to behave differently in the future. Speaking of the future, hers was knocking at the door. We learned she had a release date planned for the following day, another detail that had not been shared with us.

However, toward the end of birth mom's testimony, we learned that her release plan had some holes in it. When the state's lawyer asked about it, she gradually changed her answers, and by the end, she acted like she didn't owe the lawyer any explanations.

"I applied to a couple of halfway houses, but I'm not sure which one I'll go to," she answered.

"Do any of them allow participants to bring their children with them?"

"I don't know," she replied, *"I didn't ask."*

"Is there anyone who could watch the kids for you while you work a program, so that they can be removed from general foster care?"

"No."

"So, your plan would be for the kids to stay in foster care for however long it takes for you to get a job, get a place to stay, and build a life where you could provide for them? Do you have a guess as to how long it will take?"

"I don't know," she said, with a raised eyebrow that implied she didn't like the questions, or she just didn't care what the lawyer thought about her plan.

She was excused from the stand soon after, and left me with the feeling she didn't have any remorse for her past actions, or any intention of changing.

I tried to put myself in her shoes. It was tough. I didn't believe she was meant to live life this way. I saw potential in her, and I was sad that things had gone so wrong. Certainly, her choices couldn't be overlooked or excused. However, that didn't stop me from recognizing that the trauma she experienced as a child probably impacted her in a way that could not be undone, at least without any kind of treatment or therapy. And, I couldn't help but realize how much harder it would be for her to work through recovery with five emotionally burdened kids at home. I didn't see a life of happiness in her future with the kids, or in the kids' future with her.

The birth dad was called to the stand next, and other than being older with greying hair, he didn't have many distinguishing features. He wasn't tall or short. He wasn't skinny or fat. His testimony was not at all like the birth mom's. I didn't see any reason his life went off the tracks, other than he decided to give drugs a try when he was thirteen and never gave them up. He had two previous marriages, with children, who he was no longer involved with. And, he *"never found the right time"* to get divorced from his second wife, so the entire fourteen years he had been with birth mom, he was technically still married to another woman. I couldn't figure out what birth mom saw in him. He didn't come across as the brightest, most charming, or most motivated of individuals. Or, maybe he just didn't care to present himself any better for the sake of the kids.

It was also brought up that he hadn't even been writing the kids while he was in jail and didn't indicate he was all that interested in maintaining a relationship with them. And, as with birth mom, he confirmed there was no one in his life who could care for the kids while he completed his jail sentence, confirming that the only options for the kids were to continue sitting in foster care, or be released for the possibility of adoption. He didn't seem to be all that concerned over which way it went.

It was my turn next. I was so nervous. I didn't want to make enemies of the birth parents, and I didn't want to say anything that the kids might hear later and use to decide it was my fault they were severed from their birth parents. I was also scared their lawyer might have something hurtful up her sleeve in an attempt to smear us. I felt so much pressure to perform, but was given no script or guidance in advance. It was very intimidating.

Thankfully, the state's lawyer started with a few easy inquiries, like my name. She also asked how long we'd been married, where we lived, what our lives looked like, about our time with the kids, and what our intentions were for the kids.

While asking about our intentions, she opened the door for me to talk about the resources we had lined up, the difficulties we'd already observed with the kids, and our plans for addressing those challenges. Her questions were open-ended, and I used the freedom to speak in a way that both disarmed the birth mom and painted a clear picture for the judge.

For the birth mom, I tried to be as sensitive as possible. I spoke carefully, recognizing that this was not the life she had planned. I knew that insults from me had no place, nor would it help to make obvious comparisons between our intentions and her abilities. I didn't need to put her down to build myself up. I wasn't there to *"take her kids,"* but to love five kids who so desperately needed it. I shared my hopes for each of them, the difficult road ahead, and the resources I had in mind to assist us.

For the judge, I was clear that these kids were living an unacceptable life of being separated from each other. I advocated that the children needed a better option than just sitting in Foster Care for additional months, or years. And, I reaffirmed we were not only willing, but able to take on the challenge. I did, however, indicate we were on a timeline because we knew we'd be moving sometime within the next year.

While I spoke, much of the hard, stern expression had slipped off of the birth mom's face. By the time birth mom's lawyer stood up to take her turn questioning me, she divulged that she only had one question for me: *"How do you feel about future contact with the birth parents?"*

My answer was simple: *"I won't force the kids to participate in a relationship with their birth parents, but I won't prevent it, either. My parents divorced when I was young, and my mom and stepdad, whom I call dad, raised me. I didn't see my birth dad, whom I also call dad, as frequently as I would have liked, and it hurt. I won't deny the kids the opportunity if they wish to reach out in the future, as long as it is safe, appropriate, and with the respect and understanding that Jordan and I are the parents."*

"I have no more questions," she said, so I was told I could go back to my seat next to Jordan.

The judge left the room to go chat with the kids privately and was gone a good twenty to thirty minutes. During this time, the birth parents were ushered to a different location, I'm not sure where, as the lawyers convened. The case workers, foster parents, guardian ad litem, Jordan and I sat there, talking about football, of all things. The lawyers stayed in their pow-wow the entire time the judge was gone, with the exception of the state's lawyer coming over to us to confirm our stance on future contact. We weren't sure where the conversation was going, but the lawyer seemed hopeful.

As the judge and birth parents came back in, the foster parents all left to take the kids back to school. We stepped out into the hall to say goodbye and reminded the kids that we would see them all in just a couple of days. We got back into the courtroom as the judge began to explain that his time with the kids was both chaotic and entertaining. Apparently one of the kids tried to climb up the bookshelf. The kids all indicated that they liked us, we were nice, we had gaming consoles and video games, and they liked our food. They didn't want to be in foster care anymore and said that they'd like to live with us. Of course, we weren't in the room to hear these conversations, but it's how the judge summarized what he'd heard.

The next person called was the guardian ad litem, who said, *"Taking on these five kids is a significant challenge, and I'm not certain that a capable, willing couple will come forward in the future, should the birth parents be given another chance and fail."* He also said, *"It's hard on kids to be separated from their siblings, but often necessary in order to get them placed in foster homes and forever families, and this might be their only chance to be adopted together."* Then he was done. Short and sweet.

As tears flowed down birth mom's face, the lawyers asked to approach the bench.

Then, the judge addressed the courtroom, *"I have been a judge, seeing cases like this, for over twenty-six years. These kinds of cases are hard because you want to do what is best for the kids, while respecting the birth parents' rights and wishes. I have to say, that in the entire time I have been working in this capacity, I have never made this kind of ruling from the bench. I like to maintain the birth parents' rights while I watch to see how an adoptive placement works, because you just never know what's going to happen."*

My heart told me I should start crying, but my brain said I needed to continue listening.

"The answer has never been as clear as it is right now. The only chance these kids have of overcoming their circumstances and to live successful, happy adult lives is to be with Jessie and Jordan."

Just as I thought it couldn't get any better, he went on to say, *"Birth parents have six months to appeal this court's ruling, but I was just made aware that they are waiving their right to appeal."*

The judge continued speaking, but my head was reeling. I was surprised the birth parents made the difficult, selfless, decision to let go of the kids, considering how just a couple of hours earlier, birth mom seemed to feel entitled to them. It must have been an incredibly difficult decision. And, their willingness to remove themselves as an obstacle relieved so much stress. Many future months of worry had just been put to rest.

I tuned back in and heard the judge ask if he could clone us because he knew many more kids in need of parents like us. Everyone, myself included, giggled. Then, court was adjourned. The judge left and the birth parents were escorted away, and I was just sitting there, stunned.

The state's lawyer approached us and said that I gave the best testimony she had ever heard, asked if I was sure I hadn't done it before, and said that I should offer a class to help others prepare. Her compliment served as a cherry on top of the wonderful news we had just received. Our kids were deemed eligible for adoption. And, with TPR under our belts, we were well on our way!

I made my way over to the kids' caseworker and asked, *"How do we go about scheduling the meeting to change us over to an adoptive placement, now that TPR has been granted?"*

"It's going to be at least several months before the court's paperwork becomes available to us. In the meantime, we'll get the kids moved in under a standard foster placement."

Several months? Another detail that had not been made clear earlier. At least we knew what the paperwork would say though. And we now had a clearer picture of what we needed in order to finalize the adoption - paperwork from this court hearing so we could switch over to adoptive placement and six months of having the kids in our home. Once those two things were completed, we could initiate the legal process of adoption. Simple, right?

We had a celebratory lunch with the caseworker and foster parents. Brandon and Henry's foster mom shared that she had been trying to teach the boys how important hugs were and helped them practice. She seemed genuinely happy for the kids and also sad to say goodbye. Clay and Faith's foster mom seemed a little standoffish with her body language. I thought she might be shy and perhaps preferred to talk to the people she knew better. No matter. All in all, the day went far better than we could have hoped for.

CHAPTER 11

STEP ON UP, FOLKS

O ne of the grey clouds above our heads blew away when the birth parents were legally out of the picture, making the kids eligible for adoption. We continued with our transitional move-in schedule. We had plenty of Army time left in Georgia to get through the required six months of living with the kids before finalizing our adoption, and we were deepening our relationships with them.

As planned, all five kids came back to us two days after court. Three of the kids would be with us for a Friday-through-Sunday weekend, while the remaining two kids would stay with us for their Fall Break, with the understanding that I would drive them back to their foster home Wednesday night.

We were excited and anxious to talk to the kids about how they felt after TPR was granted and also about their thoughts of joining our family, permanently. As much as I knew they were already attaching to us, I was still nervous that any number of them might object.

The kids got to our house late at night, again. We quickly worked through hellos, hugs and kisses, got everyone's teeth brushed and jammies on, and then gave everyone goodnight hugs and kisses. I read everyone a fifteen-minute Disney nighttime story based on the movie Cars, out of a book I had bought earlier that day. Jordan sat on Caisen's bottom bunk with Clay and Caisen tucked under his arms. Henry and Brandon laid on their top bunk beds, leaning over. I sat on the floor, with Faith using my thigh as a pillow. I may or may not have used her forehead as a bookstand for a bit. The kids settled down by the end of the story.

Jordan helped move Clay over onto his own bottom bunk when the reading concluded and everyone got tucked in. I took my place on Faith's floor.

The next morning was just as crazy as our previous mornings. Kids were running and screaming, despite constant reminders to use walking feet and quiet voices. The kids ate breakfast as messily as ever. However, this time, the dogs got brave and came in to eat cereal scraps off the floor and chairs, and even crept in close enough to lick a spoon that was swinging to-and-fro.

When the food was gone, the playing resumed, and I kept an extra watchful eye on Brandon.

We took the kids to a park for an hour to burn some energy before lunch. It was a good choice, even though the kids didn't play super well together. They chose to play tag, but they supplemented *"tagging"* with shoving, pushing, punching, and kicking. They yelled at each other, cried, and tried to deny being *"tagged"* to avoid being *"it."* I'd never seen kids ruin a classic game of tag like this.

Next was freeze tag. Again, unnecessary roughness and major cheating took place. After a child was frozen, they'd just wait for the *"it"* kid to turn around, then they'd take off running again. It really wasn't fair. We worked hard as referees, but the game was still failing. That's when Jordan and I realized we weren't going to be able to conduct this circus from the outside.

So, I became *"it."* We played for what seemed like forever! There was no extra fighting, because the kids weren't on opposing teams and therefore had no reason to run near each other. I was chasing after each of them, and I was the only one tagging, hoping they would eventually find the fun in the game. And, maybe even learn through my modeling that light touches by the *"it"* person are both acceptable and encouraged.

Jordan and I also tried to model that it's fun to be chased down, and being tagged isn't actually defeat. It's all part of the fun of the game. When I ran out of steam, I traded places with Jordan, and he became the *"it"* man. We went back and forth a couple of times before we were pooped and decided to head home for lunch.

Pizza was the day's menu selection. It didn't last long, as the kids didn't really take the time to chew. They just shoveled it in as they kept loudly chatting away. I understood that this was just their style, but I wasn't getting used to it.

We put the TV on for an episode of Spongebob Squarepants. After so much running and chasing, then enduring lunch, I was due for a few minutes of down time before our next big adventure. But, there were no minutes to spare. I cleaned up the kitchen mess and got them ready to head back out.

We loaded up and took the kids to a local Seafood Festival. We figured the kids would have a blast, and we would make some memories. We walked through the craft booths. Caisen was on Jordan's shoulders, which made it easy to keep track of at least one kid. When we got a little further into the fairgrounds, we saw the ticket booth for the rides. We got each of the kids a ride-bracelet.

The first ride we came to was like a ferris wheel, except the seats were inside cages that individually rotated. I really didn't think anyone, other than Brandon, was going to enjoy it, but they all begged to climb aboard. Caisen was too short, so he waited with Jordan and me.

Henry tried to go on with Brandon, to which I gave a big-ol' *"oh-no-no!"*

"Why not?" exclaimed Henry.

"Well, Henry, Brandon is more of a daredevil type, and you are a safety-first kind of kid. I don't think you'd enjoy that match up, at all. Please, trust me on this."

He was clearly upset, but they all complied. Henry and Clay rode together while Faith was assigned a seat next to Brandon.

The ride began and Henry and Clay quickly learned they were in too deep! Their heads were tucked in, their fists were tightly clenched on the handles, they were keeping their individual movement to an absolute minimum, and their screaming conveyed some serious panic.

Faith was also screaming with her head tucked, but that's because she was stuck in a cage with a crazy boy. Brandon was having the time of his life, doing his best to keep the cage rocking and rolling. Poor Faith.

When it came time to exit, Clay and Henry climbed out, their knuckles still white. They told us that they were terrified. I said, *"Hey Henry, aren't you glad I didn't let you ride with Brandon?"* as I pointed up to the cage where Faith was still trapped inside, as Brandon was laughing an evil laugh.

Henry's eyes got wide, and he slowly and deliberately nodded his head.

Victory! I had just proved I had his best interests in mind and that I was trustworthy. Not that I could say the same for Faith, who legitimately could have lost trust in me forever!

They went on many more rides: big slides, carousels, racetracks, looping rides, spinning rides, and dropping rides. There were many laughs and screams. When they were rided-out, we told each kid that they could choose two games to play.

Clay picked his game first, a typical carnival game where three heavy pins stand stacked, and your challenge is to knock the three pins over with a single throw of a ball. He wanted to use both of his games here, so he was given two balls. Clay threw his first ball, missed, and cried. Brandon pushed in, saying how easy it would be, and told Clay that he would win the game for him. Clay handed over his second ball, and Brandon took the shot. Brandon also missed, which made Clay cry more and gave Brandon a reason to yell and kick dirt.

We continued to walk through the fairgrounds, looking for the games the kids wanted to play. As we walked, we let the kids know that the games were set up for them to lose, and we encouraged them to do their best, without the expectation of winning. We covered the whole *"focus on the fun of playing"* thing.

We stopped at the basketball booth with the deceiving oval hoop for Jordan to take an attempt. As he was squaring off, the kids kept trying to climb on top of the half wall. The looks we were getting were not kind. I kept pulling kids off, as Jordan took his shot. He won. He's such a stud.

Next, we came to the balloon-popping dart game. All the kids decided to use their tickets here, aside from Clay, who had already spent his. And yes, Clay had a breakdown, claiming the pinball game should have counted as Brandon's turn instead of his because Brandon was the one who completed the turn. However, Clay was the one who handed Brandon the ball.

Henry took his first try and did not win. The tears began as he waited for his second turn. We reminded him that it was meant to be fun, and the games weren't set up fair because the companies wouldn't make money if they created games that everyone won. The message wasn't going over well.

Faith tried next, another sad loss.

Then Caisen, more tears.

We encouraged them to try something else, but they begged to continue with their promised games at this particular booth.

Next, Brandon went. Winner, winner! He picked out a bright orange teddy bear, looking so happy and proud as he rubbed it in his crying siblings' faces.

More tears from Henry.

Faith's head hung low.

Caisen cried harder.

Brandon lost on his final turn and went from zero to one hundred in no time flat. He kicked the ground and swung his arms while screaming, *"The game wasn't fair. The balloon moved. They cheated. I should have won. I hate the carnival."*

We decided to leave, to get Brandon out of public. I anticipated some backlash from the other kids, but we got the opposite. They seized the opportunity to be shining stars in comparison to Brandon. While he screamed, they snuggled up, trying to hold our hands, ride our shoulders and backs, and thank us for the fun day.

As we walked out of the carnival, down the road, and toward the parking lot, I reassumed my position of supporting and encouraging Brandon, hoping to speak some logic into him.

I reminded him that he had won a teddy bear, and to that he said, *"So what?"*

I built him up with, *"Nobody else won a stuffy. You did great."*

He again said, *"So what?"* with his arms crossed over his face, as he wandered back and forth into the street. I kept pulling him back, afraid he'd get hit by a car. He seemed to have major blinders on, ignoring anything he saw or heard that wasn't connected to the carnival game.

It was overwhelming to me, and obviously for him, too. I couldn't understand why someone would focus on the loss of one game instead of the victory of another. I couldn't understand why someone would let one minute of disappointment cancel out an entire afternoon of excitement and fun. And, I couldn't understand why the disappointment would translate into such a meltdown. I mean, no one likes to lose, but his response was over the top! Still, as much as I couldn't understand this child's issue, and as much as I was both embarrassed and overwhelmed, I knew one thing for sure. This kid needed love, support and help in a desperate way!

The night went on. Bedtime came and everyone went to sleep, except for me. I had to sit on Faith's floor for another three hours. I wasn't loving this routine, but I certainly felt for her. Her panic was so real, her circumstances were so sad, and she needed to feel love and support.

Not just Faith. Clay was so pathetic; he needed someone to love and support him. Henry needed it too. And so did Caisen. These poor kids. And, certainly Brandon did too. They were totally kicking our butts, but they were kids in need and we were still on a mission!

The next morning, Jordan roughhoused with the three younger kids, while I did a volcano science experiment with the older two. We were committed to the kids, but we were also counting down the minutes to drop three of them off at McDonald's. Not because we wanted to say goodbye or quit on them, but because we recognized the marathon-like quality of our journey, and knew any possibility of success would require us to make use of whatever breaks we were given.

Truth be told, I was feeling nervous about the day where they'd come to stay with us for good, without any more breaks. However, there wasn't time in our survival mode to stop and consider that fast-approaching reality, even though we felt it coming.

After saying goodbye to Faith, Clay and Caisen, we enjoyed our night of two-on-two by taking Henry and Brandon to see The Book of Life, their first theater experience. They thought it was the coolest thing!

Brandon bit his fingernails the entire time, even with reminders to stop eating his poor fingers. Henry kept folding the chair up and down. And up. And down. Dude just can't help it!

After the movie, we ate dinner at an old restaurant in downtown Savannah, called The Pirate's House, where pirates walked through and told us the tales of the restaurant's many ghosts. The kids were so impressed, making it a great close to the weekend.

Monday morning came, and Jordan had a regular work week. The odds went from being five vs. two to two by myself. Easy peasy, right?

I decided to take the boys to the beach. They had never been before. Henry played with the window buttons and door handle the whole way. He removed his hand every time he was asked. But, it always found its way back quickly.

The boys ran straight into the waves while I sat in the sun and watched. I took it in for a few minutes, before calling Reagan.

"They're playing in the water and I can see smiles. It's probably best that I can't hear what they're saying because it would probably ruin my moment, but right now I feel like a normal mom watching her normal kids."

"I'm so happy for you, Jess," she said. *"You deserve a normal moment. Take it in."*

The boys came out of the water and began playing in the sand.

"That's my sand!" Brandon screamed at Henry, loud enough for me to hear against the wind, as Henry shoveled handfuls of sand into a mound.

"But I was here first," Henry shrieked.

"Well, the moment's over. Gotta go," I said to Reagan as I started walking towards the boys.

Brandon drew a big circle in the sand, around the pile Henry had gathered, and shoved Henry out while saying, *"This is my space, and you need to find someplace else to go!"*

They clawed at each other, demanding their individual rights to the special sand, that looked just like all of the other sand around us.

I stepped in the middle, scared that Brandon would pitch a fit if I didn't handle things just right. I knew it would go badly to ask Brandon to leave Henry alone, but it also wouldn't be fair to kick Henry out, so I tried something else. I asked Henry to come look at something with me, leaving Brandon with the perfect space.

Henry and I walked away from the water, where the sand was drier. He helped me dig the hole that I would soon bury him in. We dug while we talked about the beach, the festival, and the time that I saved him from Brandon on the crazy ferris wheel ride. I was actually having a nice time talking with Henry. We would have talked longer, but Brandon came over to crash the party.

Brandon talked, not to me or to Henry, but just filling the space. He seemed determined that there not be any quiet.

"We're at the beach," he said, *"and there is sand."*

"Yes, that's true," I said, wondering if there would be a question or a point to his ramblings.

I thought he might be jealous of the conversation Henry and I were having, and wanted to participate, but didn't have anything to talk about. So, he just talked to talk.

As soon as I finished with Henry, I got to work digging a hole for Brandon, at a much faster pace than I had used on the first hole, and I put my sunglasses on Henry as he waited. Brandon had no sand-manners, and I was impressed by how well Henry accepted the resulting sand in his face.

When the hole was dug, I happily buried Brandon and took pictures. My sugar cookie babies unearthed themselves and came after me as they pretended to be zombies. I felt relief when they zombie-walked after me, instead of each other. Brandon caught me first, thank goodness, or he may have flipped out. I hated the pressure I felt to tend to Brandon, but I hated his meltdowns more.

We left the beach with just enough time to go home, clean up, and leave again for an Army function. Jordan's company was hosting an event for families to come together, enjoy activities, share a meal, and mingle. Events like these happen regularly, but this would be our first time bringing children with us.

The kids seemed very excited to see Jordan at work and to check out the inflatable play houses, laser tag, and roller skating. I, on the other hand, was nervous that Brandon might cause a scene, or embarrass Jordan in front of his soldiers, so we talked in the car about what *"best behavior"* looks like, and how military families are expected to follow certain rules at these functions. They seemed eager to represent Jordan well, and I tried to be hopeful.

They climbed in the inflatable houses. It didn't last long, due to a combination of *"this is boring"* and *"they are scaring the other kids."* They were scaring me, too, with how rambunctious they were getting inside, so we moved over to roller skating. The kids told us they were champion skaters. Not in those exact words, but they sure did paint the picture that it was a regular activity. Once they had skates on and tried to stand up, we realized that they had never actually roller skated before.

"But I thought about it," Brandon said, as though it was the same thing.

We weren't skating at an actual skating rink. We were in a large gym where the kids had no half wall or railing to hold onto. Therefore, impromptu skating lessons commenced. Henry got Jordan, and Brandon got me. Brandon must have run over my flip-flop-exposed toes a hundred times! But, he was determined, and I wasn't going to stand in his way. Well, technically my toes were in his way. But, I wasn't going to hold him back. I knew his frustration threshold was small, and I didn't want to test it.

We took a food break after their first skating lesson. We walked through the buffet lines and loaded the kids up with the dishes they selected. Henry selected significantly more than Brandon, which didn't surprise me.

As we sat to eat, there was an announcement that the laser tag room was going to be starting up soon.

Brandon ate about two and a half bites before saying he was full, and then he begged to go play laser tag. Henry, on the other hand, scarfed all of his food, and started offering to eat Brandon's.

"I'd like you to eat a little more, Brandon. This is dinner, and you asked for everything on your plate."

"But this food sucks! It tastes terrible," he said, as he shoved his plate away.

I looked to Henry next, and said, *"You've had plenty. Brandon will be done in a moment, and you guys can go play."*

I should mention, we weren't at a table alone. We sat with two other families, whose eyes were fixed on us.

It took some negotiating, but both boys survived. Brandon got through his food, while Henry stared at him, drooling. Then, both boys received permission for laser tag.

My pulse quickened, and I said a quick prayer, *"Lord, Brandon is going into the laser tag room, with other kids, without Jordan or me. Please let him navigate this experience without causing trouble."*

I mingled with a few Army wives while I waited on the boys. Each conversation started the same way: *"What a blessing! Do they know how lucky they are? Do they appreciate everything you're doing for them?"*

I made a mistake with the first spouse I spoke to, by sharing some of the challenges we'd already faced.

"Don't forget, you asked for this," is how she responded.

I didn't think I was complaining, but I think it came across that way, so I changed my approach for the conversations that followed. I hid my nerves and tucked our struggles away.

The result was this, *"Maybe one day they'll feel gratitude, but today's goal is for them to feel safe."* And, if I got my way, the other kids in laser tag would feel safe, too.

My prayer was not answered the way I had hoped.

A child came out of the laser tag room pointing at Brandon while loudly asking, *"Who are this boy's parents?"*

With a heavy sigh, I stepped forward. He walked right up to me and said, *"He kicked me in the private area. He is not a nice boy."*

We knew this boy's parents. I apologized to them and then turned to Brandon, who was causing a scene in front of Jordan's work crew.

He loudly explained his point of view, *"It was his fault because he wouldn't let my team win!"*

I took him to the side and reminded him that we were at Jordan's workplace, and that his behavior mattered. I asked if he would apologize, and he said, *"No, because it was his fault!"*

"Apologizing for your part in the fight does not mean you were the only one who had made a mistake, or that the other boy didn't do anything wrong. It just means that you recognize you could have handled things differently. It means you see that your choice to kick the other boy was not the best possible choice," I said. *"So please apologize to the other boy for choosing to kick him. It's the right thing to do."*

After a few more loud, embarrassing exclamations, and some awkward grunting and flailing, Brandon finally grunted a terrible apology to the other boy. We knew we weren't going to get anything better out of him, so we apologized to the other parents again, and figured it was a good time to leave.

Since we had met Jordan there, I asked if Jordan would drive the boys home so that I might catch my breath with a few minutes to myself. He agreed and we traded keys.

As I was pulling through the parking lot toward the exit, the other boy and his family came walking out of the building. When the other boy's mom got near the truck, I rolled my window down.

"Kids are complicated. You should take the long way home and maybe stop for ice cream. You deserve it," she said.

I appreciated her words. Then, as she walked away, her son approached the window and said, *"You need to teach your son some manners. He's not a nice boy."*

I smiled, said thank you, and rolled the window up. In the quiet of Jordan's truck, the tears rolled down my cheeks, and not because of disappointment in Brandon. I understood that he had experienced a rotten life, and had developed some inappropriate behaviors along the way. The challenge ahead of me was becoming clearer. It wasn't going to be easy. And even though some people would offer kind words, the majority of onlookers were never going to understand, or even try to.

When I got home, Brandon was in full fit, determined to convince the world it wasn't his fault that he kicked the kid. We weren't even arguing with him, but he kept it going. And going. When he ran out of steam, it was well after bedtime. We tucked him in and said goodnight.

Cue more tears, mostly due to exhaustion and stress. This kid was going to be tricky, and I had two more days before my next refresh!

Tuesday was a day of errands. I asked the boys to help me stock up on kid supplies, like shampoo, body wash, toothpaste, and hooded towels, telling them I needed their input to get their favorite types. We went to the PX, which is a store on a military installation with goods similar to a Walmart or Target, where Henry and Brandon saw child-sized soldier outfits. They begged to have them. I asked if that's what they wanted to wear for Halloween, and they both did. They were so excited about Halloween, that I made a commitment to do my best to ensure they would actually get to celebrate it.

I called the caseworker to adjust the current travel schedule, which had them driving to us during the time of trick-or-treating. As I talked on the phone, we continued shopping. We grabbed towels, new toothbrushes, some movies, some puzzles, and a few other items. I didn't stay on the phone for long, though, because I quickly realized that the kids needed five hundred and seventy-six percent of my attention, but the case worker agreed to contact the foster parents and transport individuals to see if we could work something out where the kids leave early enough to come trick-or-treat with us, or leave late enough to do it before the drive.

We continued with our errands. As much as I loved getting things done, it was also tough because Henry grabbed every single thing he saw, whether it was of interest to him or not. When he wasn't grabbing, he was casually dragging his hand along the shelves, or lying on the ground to get a better look under the bottom shelves. This kid was absent-mindedly fidgety.

We finished our to-do list and called Jordan. Sadly, Jordan wasn't able to join us for dinner, so we just stopped at Zaxby's, which is a fast food restaurant known for its fried chicken, on our way home.

We ordered our food and sat in a rounded booth in the corner of the restaurant. When Henry decided he was done with his french fries, he closed the box and put it in the kid's meal bag. A few moments later, Brandon wanted to see if Henry's bag had a toy because his didn't. Zaxby's isn't a toy place, I told him, but he stuck his hand in anyway. He came up with a little ketchup on his hands. And, without pause, he wiped the ketchup on Henry.

I said, *"Brandon, why would you wipe your ketchup on Henry?"*

"It's Henry's ketchup!" he responded. *"So, he should have to clean it up. Not me!"*

Henry looked at me blankly, wondering if I was going to accept Brandon's logic.

"And who do you think is going to be cleaning Henry's shirt? Couldn't you have just wiped it on the napkin in front of you?"

Brandon's emotions took over, drawing looks from other customers. *"It's not my fault! It's his ketchup. It's his fault! I didn't do anything!"* he yelled as he shoved the tray off of the table. *"It's not my fault!"* He shoved the table away from the booth, into the walkway, which captured the attention of those who had been trying to ignore us previously.

I calmly asked him to take a deep breath and think it through with me, to help him see that the problem was actually small. I prayed God would inspire my words and help them to reach Brandon. However, there were no words that would help with this kid. There was no quick fix. He was mentally stuck and needed to let the fit pass. So, I was essentially stuck too.

I did my best to avoid eye contact with the surrounding people glaring at us. I was trying my best to do what was right for this kid. And for the kid next to him, who I had move to the booth behind me. I apologized to the employees who were clearly not happy with the mess he was making. I felt terrible for the other eaters who were staring in disbelief. I was in disbelief, too.

Brandon soon began to push the segments of the booth apart. I didn't even know that they could be shoved apart like that. At one point, he tossed his shoes, while he was still doing his best to push the booth pieces apart.

I just kept thinking that some of these people had probably seen terrible two's before, maybe terrible three's. Those kinds of fits couldn't be all that much different, I thought. Except for the fact that Brandon wasn't two or three, and I couldn't pick him up and carry him away, and he was big enough to dismantle furniture. But, other than that, I felt that this had to look normal. Right? NOPE!

In the meantime, Henry kept asking questions and sharing his thoughts about life.

"Who started Zaxby's? I bet it was a chicken farmer. I really like eating chicken, but I don't think I could be a chicken farmer. I'd rather just buy my chicken from Zaxby's. Or the store."

It's like he didn't even notice that I was in the middle of addressing a crisis. And, his feelings seemed hurt that I wasn't focused on chicken-talk. I felt sad that he was sad and also because he wouldn't give me space to work with Brandon. It was miserable.

Eventually Brandon agreed to move to the car. He didn't calm down, but he decided that he, like Henry and I, wanted to leave. Brandon walked out without his shoes, so I grabbed the sneakers and handed them to him as he climbed in the car. He didn't put the shoes on, and he wouldn't buckle, so we were stuck. I had Henry move to the front seat while waiting for Brandon to calm down.

We turned the car on to circulate air, and I asked Henry what kind of music he'd like to listen to. Brandon didn't like that I was paying attention to Henry instead of him, so he threw a shoe at Henry, who was pushing all the front seat buttons.

Henry opened the sunroof.

Brandon threw his other shoe.

Henry got the seat warmer on.

Clay's booster seat came flying forward.

Henry found the buttons that moved the seat forward and backward.

I broke and exclaimed, *"That is enough!"*

Brandon didn't agree, so he turned sideways in the seat and kicked at the windows. In his socks. As hard as he could. And, he was punching the seats, kicking the window and door, pushing all of the backseat buttons, and screaming at the top of his lungs.

I had no idea what to do, and I wondered, *"Why was this behavior never mentioned to us?"* I was unprepared for this. I knew he needed love and support, but he didn't seem to hear me or recognize that I was there. He was just exploding. All the while, Henry was giggling about changing the air temperatures.

Eventually, the fit ran its course, and he asked to play a game on my phone. Now, I knew I couldn't offer rewards after undesirable behaviors. I also didn't want to drag fits out any longer than necessary. So, I learned to compromise.

"No, you cannot have my phone. But, if you stay calm and collected for the whole drive home, then I'll let you two watch a little TV before bedtime."

He accepted, and we drove home. It was our last night together, and the next day was going to be a long one. I was tasked with driving the boys all the way back to their foster parents' home.

The morning was bumpy, but we got on the road close to our target time. We split up the six-and-a-half-hour drive with a stop at the zoo. It was their first zoo experience. I only had to say *"walking feet"* about a billion times, and they always said that they were walking, even though they weren't. They were awfully nice as they remained out of compliance. Even though they climbed on fences, went off paths, and ran often, I still found joy in watching their faces light up at each exhibit, especially when they saw the gorillas. They stuck their fingers up the statue-gorilla's nose, and I felt proud. I had a picture of myself doing the same thing!

We made it to our destination, and their foster parents invited me in to chat. They were nice and supportive, and offered me a soda for my drive home.

I said my goodbyes and reminded the boys they'd be coming back only two days later.

When I hit the road, I felt as though I had just been dropped out of a tornado.

CHAPTER 12

ASSIGNED SEATS

I t was Friday, October 24th, and all five kids were coming to us for a weekend. Just the weekend. Only two nights. Easy peasy. We were refreshed and ready for whatever obstacles the kids were bringing with them.

Friday night was a now typical whirlwind. They stormed in late, hyper, and rambunctious. They used attitude. They complained as they got their jammies on and brushed their teeth. We wrangled them all into their appropriate beds, which is much easier said than done. We pulled out a book. By the end, they were ready to sleep. Well, all except Faith. This time, Faith made me a bed on the carpet. It was cute. I was a little hesitant because I didn't want her thinking this would be a permanent solution, but, I was sleepy, and the pillow was just so soft. So, I indulged. And when the timing was right, I snuck off to bed. Could we really be getting the hang of things?

The next morning, bowls of cereal were split between kids' mouths and dogs' mouths via the floor, followed by the typical crazy playing. You know, the kind where I wonder what things were going to break, and if the cats and dogs would survive. When it was time, we packed lunches and hit the road.

We thought surprise tickets to Disney on Ice would be a hit, and we loaded them in the car without telling them exactly where we were going. However, thirty minutes into Brandon's fit, we decided to just call off the surprise and tell them. Brandon struggled with surprises, which was a good lesson to learn.

He then got mad that we told him. Brandon struggled without surprises, which was also a good lesson to learn.

"I'm sorry for making it a surprise and for sharing the surprise. Next time we'll just tell you up front." I thought it would help to hear that I wasn't blaming him, but instead I was taking responsibility for the situation. I was wrong.

"Wait, I can like surprises! I will like them! I will!"

I thought we were learning things about this kid's triggers, but we weren't. It didn't matter what we did or did not do, because everything was a struggle for him, which was our new understanding.

After *"I promise I'll like surprises"* wore off, his approach changed to *"What? Why do we have to go to that? That sounds dumb. I won't even like it! Why do we have to go?"*

We'd resolved one issue, and he'd pick another. Maybe his fits weren't necessarily about anything in particular, but about the timing? When the timing was right, he grasped onto anything to be upset about, and couldn't stop until he ran out of steam. But I didn't count it as a lesson learned, because everything else I thought was indicative of a pattern proved to be inconsistent.

Whether we were figuring him out or not, we still had five kids loaded in our large, family vehicle headed to Disney on Ice. We got there. Brandon's arms were still crossed over his forehead as we walked, so Jordan led the way with Caisen on his shoulders and Clay's hand in his own. I held Henry's hand and Brandon's sweatshirt hood. Faith walked in the middle. At least we had our family walk figured out!

We walked through the doors, and the *"gimmies"* began. It didn't matter that Henry was looking at toys rated for three and older; he wanted them. It didn't matter that Clay was looking at a girl's toy; he wanted it. It didn't matter that Faith was holding a toddler-sized princess dress; she wanted it. Caisen wasn't even looking in the same direction he was pointing as he continued to say, *"I want it."* It didn't seem to matter to him what *"it"* was; he just wanted it. Brandon just wanted to make sure everyone else knew how ridiculous they were for wanting any of it. Such a killjoy.

We made it to our seats, and our first seating lineup failed terribly. We learned Caisen couldn't sit by Faith, and Henry couldn't sit by Clay. Clay broke down in tears because he wanted to be next to Jordan. Faith panicked about sitting away from me. Brandon couldn't sit by anyone. It was embarrassing how big of a scene they caused over seating!

We swapped seats. This time, we learned Henry couldn't sit by Faith, and Caisen couldn't sit by Clay. Still, Brandon was ruining the show for everyone. The stares came from all directions as I tried my hardest to bring the game of musical chairs to a close.

After another swap, we established the family-seating lineup that would become routine. From end to end, it would go: Brandon, Me, Faith, Clay, Jordan, and Henry, with Caisen awarded Jordan's lap. He didn't necessarily love the idea, but each kid needed to be directly next to an adult. Success.

It took about thirty minutes before Brandon realized that the show was cool, the skating was impressive, and the Disney scenes were entertaining. We settled in, relaxed a little, and then the show ended.

"It's over already? That was short! That's not fair." Brandon exclaimed.

We took a nice family picture with the ice behind us, feeling like we had things under control.

As we walked out, Brandon remembered that we packed food.

"What? We have to go on a picnic? That's boring!" He shouted.

I asked if he had ever been on a picnic, and he said no. I told him that he would enjoy it and asked him to trust me. Fat chance! He fought us the whole way to Forsyth Park.

We knew this destination in Historic Downtown Savannah, full of huge mossy oak trees, would quickly become a family favorite. The centerpiece fountain was gorgeous. It had two kids play structures. It had huge fields for running and playing. It was a perfect location for us to go eat and play and enjoy the beautiful day.

Once we got to our spot, Brandon complained about the flavor of jelly on his PB&J. Yeah, he was a brat. Faith offered to trade. Brandon tried to rudely snatch the sandwich from her.

I grabbed the sandwich from him and said, *"You don't get what you want by pitching a fit, so you can thank her nicely, or you can eat the sandwich you were given. But, you won't be mean to her."*

He took a moment. After grunting and complaining the entire forty-five minutes since leaving the show, it took everything in him to force out the word *"thanks,"* and I handed him the sandwich. He then gave his first sandwich to Faith. I wasn't going to push it by talking about apology-etiquette just yet. Eye contact and tones would have to wait. Instead, I counted the victory.

The kids played for about an hour. Of course, Jordan and I had to take turns playing with them. I would have liked to just sit with my husband and enjoy the view, but the view was ugly when we were both sitting. They needed an adult fully engaged. But, at least we had learned a skill to bring out a positive outcome!

We made it through the rest of the day and through the nighttime routine. While Faith lay tossing and turning, I used the time to process. I was thinking about all they had been through, and what caused all of their difficult behaviors and attitudes. All of the paperwork, or lack of paperwork, indicated that the kids were happy, healthy, and age appropriate; however, we weren't finding this to be true.

The more I thought, the more questions I had. Only questions, though. No answers.

"Where do we start with Brandon? They said he has ADHD, but that doesn't cover all his behaviors? How do we figure out what else is going on?"

"Is Faith healthy? She has intense anxiety, talks like a baby, and likes things intended for kids between three and six years of age. There has to be something going on, but what?"

"Henry lies to make the others look terrible, so that he can bat his long eyelashes and smile. How do you teach someone to let go of manipulative habits? How will I help him to feel loved enough? And, how can I teach him to keep his hands to himself, when he's not even aware they're wandering?"

"Clay is so desperate for love and attention, and incredibly sensitive. Will that change, or will he always need extra emotional support?"

"And I can't forget Caisen, who rides the dog and sprints back and forth along the backside of the couches. Where do I even start with teaching self-control?"

I rolled into bed and found Jordan already asleep. Sure, I could have left him counting sheep, but my mind was racing. *"Jordan, wake up."*

I must have startled him because he bounced up asking, *"What is it? What's wrong?"*

"Nothing's wrong." Jordan lay back down, and I continued. *"I'm just really worried about how we're going to get through this. Will our house even survive?"*

He didn't miss a beat. Jordan rolled on his side to face me and said, *"Yeah, it's a lot, but if we don't do it, who will?"*

He was right. If we didn't take them, they probably wouldn't receive help, and I couldn't live with that. As I snuggled up in my cozy bed, an even bigger reality hit me. My husband offered me solid encouragement when I was feeling overwhelmed. It might have been the first time in our relationship that I really leaned heavily into him, and he responded beautifully. He caught me. I became overwhelmed with memories of Jordan stepping up to the plate with the kids: handing me Caisen as he snatched Brandon out of the air, tracking kids down in the corn maze, snuggling up with whomever needed a good squeeze, and developing great expressions with me, so that we could exchange whole conversations in milliseconds, without words, confirming that we were in it together. In the midst of the chaos, our relationship was growing stronger and deeper.

When morning came, we endured the usual chaos of the cats and dogs hiding while the kids tore through the house like a cluster of tornadoes. There was fighting, yelling, and running. We, as always, reminded them to walk and asked them to lower their voices. They, as always, said, *"Yes ma'am,"* as they carried on.

Out of curiosity, I asked Clay if he knew why he should walk, and he gave the right answer. *"So we don't run into each other or anything, and so that we don't scare the animals."*

That proved it. They knew what they should and shouldn't be doing, and why. And they seemed to think that they were doing what was expected. I couldn't help but wonder, *"Were the kids living in the same reality we were? Why didn't they have control of their bodies? Were their minds racing so fast that they couldn't actually track their actions?"* Again, more questions without answers.

As we were dropping the kids off at McDonald's, we went over the plans for the next weekend. They would be traveling on Halloween, but we didn't know if they were going to make it in time for trick-or-treating, since the trip was different. We were only five days away from Brandon and Henry moving in with us! And the other three had one weekend visit left before moving in. I was excited to move forward, but terrified at the same time.

We reminded them that in order to make the placement official for Henry and Brandon, there would be a move-in meeting declaring us as the new foster parents for the two kids. Both the kids' caseworker and our caseworker would be coming to sign papers with us. And, of course, the kids would be in attendance. Party at our house!

We exchanged hugs and kisses with the kids and said our goodbyes.

Between Halloween, the move-in meeting, and the excitement of the move-in becoming a reality, Jordan and I knew we were going to need every bit of Monday-Thursday to prepare for the whirlwind that was coming!

The drive home was about fifteen minutes, and Jordan and I talked the whole way. Not our typical exchange of summaries of the tough stuff we observed, the close calls we experienced, and then laughing at the situations we'd found ourselves in, but a deeper talk about the reality of our situation.

"The kids are not as healthy as the caseworkers presented. We need to get help lined up because we can only sustain them for so long the way they are now," Jordan said.

"You're right. And it's scary knowing that we'll be depending on progress to get through this. What if it doesn't come?"

Jordan was at ease as he said, *"It will come. God led us to these kids for a reason, and it wasn't so that we could all fail together. He'll get us through it, even if the struggles and complications are greater than we expected."*

As he spoke, I found myself admiring the subtle lines at the corners of his eyes. Age and experience looked sexy on my husband, a man I felt I was getting to know all over again.

"Again, you're right. But, He isn't going to wave a magic wand. He's expecting us to do a lot of heavy lifting, and we need to figure out our first few steps on this uphill journey we're starting. I think counseling is a must, right away. I think it's required anyway, but I don't want to wait. We need to get a team together."

"I agree," he said. *"So, ask the caseworker if they schedule it, or if we do, and who picks the therapist."*

"We also need to have the kids more thoroughly evaluated," I added, *"because a clearer picture will help us figure out what other resources will help. I don't want to guess-and-check."*

"Absolutely," he said. *"That's a given. You should make that request first thing in the morning."*

"I will," I agreed. And then it hit me: *"I guess I won't be going back to work any time soon. The kids are going to need my full attention, full-time, for a long while,"* to which Jordan nodded quietly.

It was a heavy realization because I enjoyed my last position. Before we knew which kids God picked for us, we naively assumed I'd be out of work a few months, to help with the transition. But, it was clear that these kids were going to demand more out of me than I could give if I split myself, and they deserved my best.

Despite the reminders from both family and friends that we could still change our minds, without judgment, we maintained faith that God had brought them to us for a reason. We knew that they were our kids, baggage and all. And we knew that if we didn't prioritize the kids, no one would. They needed us to be their advocates, and that outweighed our doubts, concerns or fears.

CHAPTER 13

COSTUMES, CANDY AND CHAOS, OH MY!

Throughout the week, we did some thorough brainstorming over whether or not we had everything we needed for the kids to move in, and about how we planned to address the kids' specific needs. It was the last week we would ever spend as a childless couple because on Friday, October 31st, all five of our kids were coming to visit and two of them would stay forever!

That's right! Halloween of 2015 was move-in day for Brandon and Henry! And, we were still trying to figure out the travel schedule. The initial plan was that the kids would drive across the state after school, arriving at our house late. However, I had posed two alternative options: Leave school early to arrive in time to do the foster-placement meeting before trick-or-treating, or, have the kids do Halloween at their foster homes, and come over the next morning.

At the last minute, it was decided they would miss some school and start the drive! So, we needed to make day-of purchases to be ready.

We had already bought Henry and Brandon their soldier outfits. And, through email, we were able to establish that costumes had already been arranged for Faith and Caisen. That left Clay, who was jealous of Henry and Brandon's costumes, so we went to purchase the same outfit for him. Caisen was the only one who already had a candy bucket, so we picked up four for the other kids. Pink for Brandon, purple for Faith, blue for both Henry and Clay. We were all set.

The caseworkers both arrived slightly ahead of the kids, at about two forty-five in the afternoon. They arranged themselves in our dining room. It was the calm before the storm.

The kids came rolling up about three o'clock in the afternoon, more crazy and hyper than usual. Caisen arrived in his Batman costume, with purple gum stuck ALL OVER HIM! I tried, but no one was able to tell me where the gum came from.

Henry and Brandon had paint spattered all over them from one of the paint sets they had brought. Faith only had a small backpack with her, so she put it on her back and helped bring in Brandon's suitcase. As a group, somehow, all of the kids, plus all of Brandon and Henry's belongings made it into the house. Well, all except for one of Brandon's flip-flops. I wasn't sure what happened to it, but it was gone.

When the kids got inside, they complained about being starved. They were taken out of school before lunchtime and didn't stop to eat along the way. So, it was three and they were hungry monsters. I mean, considering that they were monsters even with food, they were certainly cranky-monsters without it! Add in the crazed excitement of it being Halloween, and we knew we had no chance of a smooth foster-placement meeting!

We did the foster-placement paperwork with the caseworkers, while also trying to keep the kids contained in the living room with the TV, while preparing macaroni and cheese. Caisen stood on the couch back, sprinting from side to side. Jordan and I alternated who was stirring the pot, who was trying to catch the little madman, and who was listening to the explanation of the pages we were signing.

Brandon and Henry had pages to sign as well. Brandon signed first, with his current last name. Henry then signed, with our last name. Brandon got jealous and wanted to try again with our last name. He was upset that he couldn't have a new page, but settled for crossing out his first signatures to rewrite them with our last name. It was a circus, just to have them confirm that they knew their rights and our expectations. However, we knew that *"knowing"* the expectations didn't mean they knew how to achieve them.

I dished up the macaroni, telling the kids we typically don't eat in the living room, but the adults needed the big table. I handed each kid a bowl of cheesy noodles and a fork. I didn't stop to eat because I was still dedicated to getting through the endless stack of papers so that I could get back to the usual game of two-on-five. Otherwise, we were certainly going to fail the game of two-multi-tasking-adults-who-should-be-paying-more-attention-to-their-five-kids.

Silly me, I had thought it would settle down a little when the kids had their food. NOPE! They were spilling food, wanting seconds, not wanting to wait, and needing more.

Henry asked for either thirds or fourths, and I asked him to give me a second to finish my current signature, then I turned to find him eating the macaroni out of the pot that was still on the stove, with the serving spoon. I said, *"Get out of there; I said I'd get it for you!"*

He said, *"Yeah, but I didn't want to wait. I was hungry!"* He said it in such a *"duh, lady"* tone of voice, as though I should have known he wouldn't follow my silly request of him to wait two seconds.

There wasn't anything constructive I could say in response, yet, because he hadn't been through lessons on respect, listening, patience, or family roles. So, I got him some noodles, like I said I would, and sent him back to the living room, where the other kids were using the wooden coffee table as a springboard!

Brandon was the first I saw fly across the room. Then, Clay tried to copy him. However, Clay stood too close to the edge of the table, causing it to tip over when he tried to jump. So, instead of going up, he dropped straight down. At this point, Clay was crying as Caisen and Brandon were laughing at him. Henry didn't laugh because he was running to the table to be the next to jump, with his noodles in hand.

Faith was just staring at the TV screen, oblivious to the circus around her.

Eventually we got through all of the paperwork. Truthfully, I think the caseworkers were more overwhelmed and exhausted by being near our children than we were. They hadn't had much opportunity to acclimate to our regular level of crazy. They appeared to be thankful when the time came to exit our home, quickly passing right by one of our fire-evacuation plan drawings as they went out the front door.

We turned around to see Caisen jump from the table to the large couch. He popped up to join the other four kids in peeking over the back of the couch at us.

Jordan said it was time for the rest of the kids to get their costumes on, and they all took off in a hurry.

I promptly moved the coffee table from the living room to the garage. We were no longer going to be coffee table people!

When each of the kids was fully dressed, we handed out buckets. Caisen had a big, orange bucket with witches and ghosts on it. The other kids were handed their basic dollar buckets. I thought this was the final touch and that we'd be ready to go. But we weren't.

Caisen had a major meltdown about wanting one of the blue ones. However, we had already set it up so that each of the four kids felt special about the one that we picked for them, and I didn't want to take it back. Besides, Caisen didn't exactly approach it in the nicest of ways. Of course, he was only four, so his wheelhouse didn't include any nice approaches. Anyway, he threw his bucket across the room, which freaked out our still-hesitant dogs. He threw himself on the floor, screaming and yelling. However, it was his wording that struck me most.

"Clay shouldn't get a cool one! He's not cool, so he needs to give me the blue one. He should have this stupid orange one. He's stupid! He shouldn't get blue!" he screamed. Clay looked up at me, his face melted, and the tears began to pour.

After failing to soft talk this kid into calming, I finally barked, *"It's the orange bucket or no bucket at all. Your choice,"* and I took a seat on the couch next to the rest of the family to wait.

He eventually collected himself, somewhat. He was in his little Batman cape with snot pouring out of his nose, and gum everywhere. Whatever. It didn't matter. We were ready, and we were moving toward the door.

Then, Faith decided to hand Caisen her bucket, saying that he could use it if he wanted.

He snatched it, and said, *"I knew I'd get one,"* with a smirk on his face.

I was so upset that she rewarded his tantrum. We had finally calmed him down and demonstrated that he wasn't going to get what he wanted by being so mean. And Faith just decided that he should have what he wanted anyway. It was not cool!

I asked them both to hand me their buckets, and I switched them back. Caisen had another massive meltdown, but I wouldn't budge. I wanted to set the tone early that fits would not work.

Faith looked at me puzzled and hurt, and told me she thought she was helping. It was the same look of sadness she had when she tried to soothe Caisen after the pig-biting fiasco. She REALLY wanted to be the one to soothe Caisen and offer him care.

I pulled Faith into the hallway for a chat while Caisen screamed and rolled on the living room floor. I thought it was best not to give him attention, so I kept my back to him.

Her eyes were wide and her look was sullen as I spoke, *"I gave Caisen two options, and I don't appreciate you offering him a third option without talking to me first. Caisen needs to learn how to ask without pitching a fit, or he'll scream and yell every time he wants something."*

Faith nodded her head, but remained quiet. I closed with, *"I appreciate your attempt to help, but in this case, it wasn't really helpful. Next time, please check with me first."*

She didn't apologize for stepping in, but did say she would attempt to ask me first in the future.

Eventually, with the orange bucket in Caisen's hand, we were able to get out the front door. We had a 1950's girl dressed and ready in a beautiful poodle skirt, a little Batman, and three soldiers. It's a good thing we took the group picture early in the night, before it went further and further downhill.

"Stay out of their grass!" I said.

"We are," they replied, while they definitely weren't.

"Say thank you," Jordan said.

"We did," they shouted, as I could clearly hear that they were arguing about candy options.

"Leave the candy alone, until we get home and check it," we asked.

"We will," they said as they were snacking away, even little Caisen on Jordan's shoulders found a way to get into his candy without permission.

While all of this was going on, Faith and I were walking and talking. The conversation was odd.

"Why won't you let me like Frozen or other kid movies anymore?" she asked.

I was puzzled. *"I don't know what you mean. I like Frozen and many other kid movies. I probably won't encourage you to cover your room in posters, but I'm actually happy that you enjoy watching the movies and singing the songs. It's something we have in common."*

"Then why wouldn't you let me be Elsa for Halloween?" she asked.

My confusion escalated. *"Faith, I wasn't the one who bought your costume. I don't know why you couldn't be Elsa. Do you?"*

"Yeah. It's because we couldn't find one in my size."

I asked what that had to do with me, and she gave me a blank stare.

"I'm not sure why you thought I would try to steer you away from kids' movies, but I don't plan to. I will always do my best to support you and your interests, as long as it is appropriate and safe to do so." And just like that, the talk was over.

We came across a haunted house. Brandon, Henry and Faith seemed to enter without much hesitation. Brave young souls. I was a little worried about Caisen and Clay because of the intensity of the setup, but they were determined to go through the fog machines, up to the masked bowl-holders, and reach inside. They were a little more cautious. However, all five exited with great enthusiasm.

When we got home, we cycled the kids through their showers as we checked out the candy. Anything that was opened went in the trash, as we explained to them the safety issue. Once their buckets were cleared, they were told they could each eat three pieces. Brandon went through his entire pile meticulously. He arranged them, and rearranged them, and ended up with three different piles: his keepers, his three for the night, and the ones he was giving to us. Sweet, right?

Henry claimed it wasn't fair that Brandon was going to share because he shouldn't be the favorite. So, Henry picked a few to give us, followed by Faith and Clay. In fact, Faith outdid the rest of them by creating the fifty/fifty system, repeating *"one for me, one for them."* The only one who showed no interest in sharing was Caisen. He didn't care who was in the running to be the favorite. He wanted ALL of his candy!

When it was Caisen's turn to get bathed, I went in with the peanut butter and a washcloth. I was armed and ready to get the purple gum out of his hair and out of the creases on his neck. It mostly worked great, except the peanut butter left him feeling oily. That, and he had some redness due to the washcloth scrubbing. All things considered, though, I think he turned out clean enough. Which is more than I can say for the Batman costume!

Henry, Clay and Brandon got through their showers, and got their teeth brushed and their jammies on without much of an issue. Faith, on the other hand, had much of an issue.

She walked into the bathroom, and came right back out to say that she had forgotten her brush. That was no biggie; I had bought one for her.

Next, she realized she had no toothbrush. Good thing I had already bought toothbrushes during Henry and Brandon's Fall Break!

Then she said that she had forgotten her pajamas. That wasn't too big of an issue. I handed her a set of mine. They were pants and a button-up, long-sleeved top.

Lastly, she said she hadn't packed herself any spare underwear. I really didn't have an option to help her out with that one, and it was too late to run to the store.

I remembered seeing her carry in her backpack, so I asked what she had remembered to pack. Only a naked Barbie and a stuffed animal.

I told her to put the jammies on, underwear-less, so that we could wash hers for her to wear the next day.

"No underwear?" she exclaimed, with more gusto than I had ever heard from her.

"You'll have them back first thing in the morning," I said, recognizing that we were on the fast track with awkward conversations.

We tucked all the kids into bed, including Faith. I told her I'd be in there shortly, hoping that she might possibly fall asleep waiting for me while I got the laundry started and made myself a bite to eat, keeping in mind that I hadn't eaten yet.

I had just opened my string cheese when I looked up to see Faith standing in the doorway, eyeing me down. She about scared the living daylights out of me!

I asked why she was out of bed, and she said she was scared that I wasn't in there. I asked if she could please go back into her room and reminded her that I would be just a couple minutes behind her. I even explained that I hadn't eaten and I really wanted to demolish the string cheese.

She said no.

She said she was scared that the scary clown was going to come get her. I asked what she meant, and she said that she couldn't stop thinking about the scary clown from the street. I asked if she understood that it was just a person in a mask. She tilted her head to the side and said, *"Huh?"* so I explained that he was wearing a costume, just like she was. She said she thought she understood, but she still thought that he might be coming to get her, so she said she wasn't going to go to bed without me. So, the dogs got my string cheese, and I got the floor of her room. When I was able to sneak to freedom, three hours later, I ate a darn string cheese! I also moved the laundry over to the dryer and crawled into bed.

I wanted to talk to Jordan about the day, but the best I could do was give him a kiss goodnight. I didn't know what obstacles he encountered with the kids during the few hours we had awake with them, but I trusted he handled it all well. I knew he was a good man, and was well equipped to be an excellent dad, even though our kids were handfuls.

The next day, Faith wore an outfit that had been donated to her, along with her freshly laundered underpants. The other kiddos got dressed, as well. I would have taken Faith shopping if she was going to be with us longer than another day, but really didn't see the need to drag all five kids to Walmart (our closest clothing option), so we just committed to making it work.

After our over-the-top messy breakfast, where the kids were begging to have candy instead, we headed to the park. We were determined to burn the excess energy out of our Energizer Bunnies. We tried and tried. And tried some more. However, we found ourselves drained before we saw any signs of them slowing. When it got close enough to lunchtime, we headed over to the bowling alley on-post. None of the kids had bowled before, and we were still naïve.

We ordered everyone shoes, pizza, and orange pop. The kids didn't know it yet, but we were starting the transition away from caffeinated beverages, soon to be followed by limiting sugary beverages. The kids were having fun and being silly. They were eager to become great at bowling, and certain it would happen, but had no interest in actually learning how to do it.

About three frames in, everything changed. Caisen got mad and angry at every attempt he made, even when he knocked nine pins down. Clay became sad and cried. Faith didn't show much expression at all. Good or bad, she was absent-mindedly rolling along. Henry was doing well in comparison, which left him slightly chipper, which in turn triggered Brandon to fall apart.

Brandon screamed, *"It's not fair that Henry is doing better than me! Henry shouldn't be the one doing good!"*

Henry took it as a compliment and smiled, which made Brandon angrier, so Henry moved behind Jordan for safety.

While talking to Brandon, we used some usual phrases like, *"it's not about winning, it's about having fun,"* and *"Don't worry about what Henry is doing, just focus on doing your best."* However, it wasn't working.

Henry worried about how angry Brandon was getting with him and chose to play badly on purpose. After a couple intentional gutter balls, Brandon moved into the lead. It seemed as though maybe things would settle down, which would be good, even though I hated that Henry's good time was clearly spoiled.

Then, Henry accidentally had a good frame, passing Brandon for the lead, and there was no hope for recovery.

"I'm really sorry, Brandon," said Henry. *"I didn't mean to knock so many pins over."*

In the midst of it all, Caisen came up to me, and looked at me with his big blue eyes and said, *"Are we going to keep playing, Mommy?"*

It was the first time I had been called Mommy. Everything else faded away as I looked to Jordan to see if he had witnessed my perfect moment, but he hadn't. Someone else had though.

Brandon screamed back, *"She's not your mommy, your mommy is in prison. So is your dad. You have no parents."*

My jaw dropped. It was a significant blow for me to go from the highest of highs to the lowest of lows so quickly. And poor Caisen looked scared, like he thought he had been caught doing something wrong.

"Of course, Caisen, we can finish this game. There's two frames left," I said to the little guy, trying to hold on to the special moment. But it was gone.

"They aren't our parents. They aren't even anybody's parents. They didn't even teach me how to bowl. It's their fault. They only taught Henry!" Brandon shouted with his arms crossed over his face. He kicked his bowling shoes off, kicked at the ground, kicked at the ball-return machine, and kicked at the chairs, all with his arms over his face. *"Henry is a cheater! And bowling is stupid! I didn't even want to play."*

The families in the other lanes stopped playing to watch us. Embarrassed, I struggled to bring the fit to an end.

I felt bad for Brandon because all of his history left him so fragile, insecure, and angry. I felt bad for the other kids because Brandon's behavior impacted them in so many ways, in addition to their own behavioral difficulties. I felt bad for Jordan and myself because we were not given a set of keys or a blueprint to Brandon, or any of them. Of course, no parents receive instructional manuals, but some obstacles have more obvious solutions than others, and the solutions in our circumstances were not clear to us AT ALL!

I was stuck with the reality that my best wasn't good enough, yet. It was going to take my best effort over a long time before any progress would be made, and even then, there weren't any guarantees. It was an uncertain, uphill battle.

The most complicated aspect of our reality was while we couldn't stay cooped up in the house during this difficult phase, because the house couldn't handle it, we also felt out of place in public, because people seemed to make things worse with their glares and under-breath criticisms. Not to mention the fact that the fun of being out in public wasn't really fun for these kids yet.

The end result was we knew that things were going to be tough for a while, no matter where we were or what we were doing, and we weren't going to have any more days off to catch our breath. It was a tough reality to accept, but accepting it was our only option.

Anyway, when the first game was over, we got out of the bowling alley. No chance we were going to endure another round! Surprisingly, Caisen, Clay and Henry thanked *"mommy and daddy"* for taking them bowling. Our new titles had officially been assigned. I didn't even care that they were only sucking up to secure roles as *"good kids"* in contrast to Brandon's on-going fit. Didn't matter. I was counting it as a major win!

We kept moving throughout the day. Always moving. The kids did not come with a slow-down option. We decided to settle down and watch a movie before bedtime. Not because they had actually calmed down, but because we couldn't think of anything else to do. We selected Monsters, Inc. and let the kids each have three more pieces of their Halloween candy.

When the movie ended, everyone except Caisen got up. He was sound asleep, lying on his belly with his little head propped up on his little hands. Jordan reached down to pick him up and found that he had drooled gum and gum juice down his face, down his chin, down his neck, and down his arms. I'm not sure how he managed to get gum, because it wasn't in any of his three candy choices, but it happened. The gum came from nowhere and got everywhere! Sneaky little booger.

The four older kiddos got ready for bed while Caisen got another peanut butter bath. Brandon was the first one done and picked out a bedtime story for us to read to them.

As he handed me the book, I shared something with him. *"Have you noticed that certain jobs and roles have specific titles assigned to them, Mr. or Ms. for a teacher, and Dr. when you visit the hospital?"*

"Yes, ma'am," he replied.

"Do you think it would be rude to call those individuals by their first names?"

"Definitely," he said, *"and you could get in trouble."*

"Well, in this family I'll be performing the job of 'mom,' and no person should be attacked for addressing me as such. I don't expect you to call me mom, but please let the other kids make their own decisions about it."

"Ok, Mommy," he said. And that was that. I guess he just needed to hear it broken down.

We did our nightly reading before I moved to the next room over for another night on Faith's floor. It was beginning to feel normal. Too normal. She even made my floor-bed up with stuffed animals. I made a mental note to talk to her about a transition out of there after she moved in.

The next morning, we followed our usual routine. We drove Faith, Clay and Caisen to McDonald's, for what was intended to be our last drop-off.

I was actually excited to remind them that they would all be back in just a few short days with all of their belongings! Our transitional plan was almost complete.

While we waited for our last three kids to return to us, we got Brandon and Henry moving in the right direction. We went to Old Navy to get them school uniforms. They were both size eight, so I grabbed four khaki pants, four navy blue pants, and a handful of navy, white, and gold polos. I also grabbed two belts.

We enrolled them in school Monday morning, using our official foster-placement documents to certify we had the right to do so. Henry made sure that I wrote a note allowing for them to sign their papers with our last name, which was approved for in-class assignments, but not state testing.

I scheduled Brandon an appointment with the local psychiatrist, selected by the caseworker, to ensure his medication management would continue. And, we took the boys to complete trauma assessments with a local counseling clinic, which was also selected by the caseworker.

The trauma assessments were used to determine how much counseling would be appropriate for each child, not for diagnostic purposes. However, even without diagnoses, we knew that getting them into counseling would be beneficial. The assessor agreed. After a few minutes of watching the kids empty the bottom shelf of her display to crawl into the open space, and going through the items on her desk, there was no hiding we were dealing with some attention-span issues. This was in addition to the information gained by the trauma-screener.

With the assessor's support, I began pushing our caseworker for updated psychological evaluations to be completed. The assessor said the results would help the counselors tailor their therapy appropriately.

I was told the testing was several hours long over multiple appointments, but the enormity of the task was not going to deter me. We needed it.

On Wednesday night of that first week, Henry asked me to join him and Brandon for lunch at school the next day! Melted my heart.

I asked Henry what time his lunch was, and his response was, *"Huh?"*

I asked if he heard me, and he said, *"No, I was looking at the tree moving outside."* At least he was being honest, right?

Anyway, I got gussied up and enjoyed two marvelous lunch dates, back to back. I was seeing glimpses of my sweet boys tucked underneath the anger and manipulation. I was determined to keep digging them out!

CHAPTER 14

THINGS CHANGE
ALL THE TIME

So, we made it through our first official week of being foster parents to two young boys. We accomplished a lot in that first week! Particularly with the trauma assessments, which revealed a lot of emotional baggage to work through (Shocker, I know). We were told that the boys each needed two hours of counseling a week, plus two appointments with an aid who would help build necessary life skills in conjunction with the primary counselor.

We were committed to getting these kids all of the resources they could use, so I did not complain or argue when they told me that each kid would need four appointments a week, though it was a bit of a surprise. A super validating surprise though! The new information proved to me that I wasn't wrong or insane in my observations regarding the kids.

Also, the information proved that I wasn't wrong in my conversations with the caseworkers. I had been told repeatedly there was nothing documented that would indicate the kids needed additional resources. I continued to respond by pointing out that a lack of current evaluations wasn't proof they were healthy. I was frustrated that so many years had gone by without proper support in place, and I was motivated to fix it!

I didn't love that I couldn't pick my own counselors or set up the initial appointments. That was done by the caseworker, who just told me where to be and when. However, after the results of the evaluations were made available, I was permitted to schedule the future appointments. I didn't have much under my control, so I felt like this was a big win.

Another benefit to scheduling the appointments on my own was that I could tell the assigned counselor the last three kids would be joining us soon. Ideally, she could take that into consideration while we worked out our schedule. The even bigger plus was that the kids' state insurance, as well as this particular counseling agency, made in-home counseling an option. So, I decided that twice a week, for umpteen hours, sounded better than every day without end. So, the plan was for the kids to take turns rotating through appointments with the counselor and support staff, twice a week. It sounded miserable to me, but necessary. The plan was in place, rendering us ready for the three kiddos to return, but then we were hit with a new obstacle.

The day before the three kids were supposed to be delivered to us, I received a phone call from the kids' caseworker, letting us know there was a complication with Faith.

"Her foster mom brought her in to address some concerns about the placement," she said.

I stepped into the backyard so that I could pace while I listened.

She went on to say, *"She said she was sad that you wouldn't let her be Princess Elsa for Halloween."*

I stopped pacing and defended myself. *"We weren't the ones who went costume shopping with her. She came to us in her costume, so I don't know what the problem is there."* I'm sure I even used hand gestures as I spoke.

"That's odd," she replied. *"Faith also said that you wouldn't even buy her new underwear when she needed them. What's that about?"*

With more hand gestures, I responded, *"Faith didn't bring anything she needed with her. She didn't bring clothes for the weekend, her toothbrush, or anything. We made due, but it wasn't us who failed her."*

"She didn't bring anything?" she asked, with a tone that conveyed the same confusion I felt.

"A backpack with a naked Barbie, but we didn't find much use for that," I said lightly, though I knew it wasn't a light conversation we were having. I got back to walking, at a much faster pace.

"Wow," she said with a hint of disappointment. *"I don't even think I need to ask about this last one, but I will. Can you think of a reason why she'd be scared that you'd love the boys more than her?"*

After the hours I spent sleeping on her floor and talking to her one-on-one about whatever was on her mind, there was no way she developed that idea based on time with us. *"No! That's ridiculous. If anything, she gets more attention because she's the only girl."*

"Well," the caseworker said, *"I didn't think there was any problem, but I had to run it by you. I was pretty sure I knew what was going on after her foster mom said she wanted to keep Faith and said she'd be interested*

in adopting her later down the road. Seems like she's planting some upsetting seeds."

"Poor Faith," I said. "She's probably confused and frustrated in a tug-of-war that I didn't know was taking place. I'm sure that she'll be fine once she's here. She's been very happy with us. And besides, she'd be so upset if she got separated from her brothers."

"I agree. And I reminded the foster mom that it would take a judge's legal ruling to separate Faith from the boys, and I don't see anything to justify that," which was a relief to hear. *"Have you guys gotten counseling started? She's going to need help with the transition."*

"Yes, her trauma assessment is scheduled for Tuesday, since everything is closed on Monday for Veteran's Day. We need the placement paperwork to get her in school Tuesday, as well." I assured her.

"All right, then let's keep the plan as it is and see how it goes. Hopefully she'll see Clay and Caisen getting in the car, and choose to go with them."

I thanked her for her support, and shared my disappointment that another woman was causing further trauma to Faith, who had already experienced more than her fair share. But, there wasn't much I could do, other than wait to welcome Faith with open arms, and I was anxiously awaiting the opportunity!

When move-in day came, Clay and Caisen apparently loaded up quickly, beaming with excitement. Faith did not. She broke down crying, screaming that she did not want to leave her *"mama,"* whom she had previously been referring to in a much more formal way. She was saying she was scared that we wouldn't love her. She was saying that the only place for her was with her *"mama."*

The caseworker called and said, *"I wish I could have just put Faith in the car, but I was directed to leave Faith with the foster mom."* My heart stopped. *"This isn't over, though. We told her and her foster mom that we will develop a new transition plan, utilizing the support of a therapist."*

If nothing else, I at least felt good knowing there would finally be a therapist working with Faith. But that wasn't enough to offset my growing anger and disappointment.

I was angry that some woman was causing another obstacle in Faith's life, specifically a person who was assigned to protect her. It wasn't fair. She deserved better.

When Caisen and Clay arrived, they were happy to see us, but sad about Faith.

Caisen walked up to me and said, *"Faith isn't coming. Faith doesn't want to live with us. I don't think Faith loves us anymore."*

He continued talking about it through the entire placement meeting, when we were signing all of the paperwork for Clay and Caisen. I feel it goes without saying that it wasn't a smooth process.

We did, however, get a refresher course on our foster care rules. We asked for permission to get the boys haircuts, particularly Clay. We were told that since TPR had been granted, there were no longer any other parents to seek permission from. So, haircuts were up to us. This blanket permission did not extend, however, to medications or travel.

We needed prescriptions from doctors for any medications, including those that could be purchased over the counter. After submitting prescriptions to the agency to have them looked over, we would wait for approvals before administering medication.

For travel, we felt lucky they granted us a good chunk of the State of Georgia, since the kids' county and our county were so far apart. Most families needed permission to cross county lines. We did still need to get written permission to cross either of the state borders near us, which we planned to do frequently. We got the information we needed. We understood the boundaries in place as foster parents. We were ready to go.

We enjoyed the weekend with the four boys. We got haircuts, went to different parks, ate some of their favorite foods, and went to the beach. And, my personal favorite, we went to church as a family. It was the first time we were able to go to church with any of the kids because transportation-meet-up was always during church time. Brandon, being a fifth grader, went to the third through fifth grade group. Henry and Clay were together in the kindergarten through second grade group. Caisen was in the four-year-old class. Church went well, except for Brandon getting in trouble for being a bully on the Nintendo Wii.

We had lunch after church and then ran to Old Navy to get school uniforms for Clay. He was also size eight, which about brought me to tears. Between Clay being a big six-year-old, and Brandon being a small ten-year-old, they averaged out at Henry's appropriate size of eight, which meant I wouldn't be able to hand clothes down from kid to kid. I grabbed more size eight khaki pants, navy pants, and polos. My stock of size eight uniform attire ran deep.

Thankfully my four-year-old didn't need school uniforms, and even if he did, he wouldn't need the dreaded size eight.

Spontaneously, we took the kids to the movie theater. It was one of our favorite things to do as a couple, and it seemed like a good family activity, though we knew we were going to have to slow down on expensive outings like movies.

From left to right we sat Brandon, Jordan, Clay, me with Caisen on my lap, and Henry. It was much easier for two adults to separate four kids than five!

With about twenty minutes left in the movie, it hit me. It was a terrible, horrible, obvious smell. I must say, sitting in a room packed with people, smelling poop, and knowing with absolute certainty that it came out of one of my children, was one of the most unexpected, awkward, and undesirable moments of my life.

I investigated briefly. I leaned Caisen forward and sniffed him. It wasn't any stronger near his booty, so I fist pumped as I thanked God it wasn't the little guy sitting on my lap! However, this meant that one of my not-four-year-old kids just pooped their pants!

I sniffed to my right and left, and it was definitely stronger to my left. I looked down the line, and found that Jordan was sniffing, too. And he seemed to believe it was coming from his right. The only kid between us was Clay! And, he was watching the movie, laughing and gasping, as though everything was fine.

Jordan and I had a non-verbal conversation using shoulder shrugs and a wide variety of facial expressions, and we agreed to just stick it out. There was no use causing a scene.

When the movie ended, I strongly encouraged Clay to go use the rest room. He said he didn't need to go, probably because he knew he already had! Jordan pushed a little harder, and even offered to go in with him. He was hesitant, and his eyes got teary, but he went.

When he came back out, I asked if he was able to clean any of the poop out of his pants. He frantically exclaimed that he hadn't pooped and began crying. As Jordan gathered the other three boys up to walk out, Clay and I pulled up the rear together.

"Clay, it's ok," I said, as the tears in his eyes grew larger. *"I'm not mad. I need to know every time something like this happens, so I can help clean up."*

There was heavy reluctance in his voice, but he got the words out. *"It was me,"* with a whole river of tears pouring down his face.

I hugged him, and said, *"Thank you for your honesty, Clay. Were you able to dump most of it out in the toilet after the movie?"* Talk about an unexpected conversation.

"Yes, ma'am," he said.

On the drive home, we shared with all of the boys the importance of hygiene. Simply stated, I said that it was more important to make a bathroom trip than it was to avoid interrupting a movie, and that we would happily take any of them if they needed to go.

Now that the conversation about bathroom procedures and manners had been introduced, it seemed like the appropriate time to talk to the boys about the poop-chunks and streak marks we had been finding in each load of laundry. Each kid said they hadn't done it, but we had seen it in underwear belonging to each of them. No one seemed embarrassed, but mostly defensive and somewhat competitive as each one tried to brag that their bathroom skills were the most superior. So, we resigned ourselves to the realization that we were going to have to have this talk again, with each kid, with proof in hand.

When we got home, we got through the bedtime routine and went to bed. I got to sleep in my own bed, and it was glorious.

Monday morning came around, and there was no school. It was a long weekend for Veteran's Day, which also happened to be Jordan's birthday. When Jordan woke up, he asked if I had things handled inside enough for him to go outside and clean up dog poop. It was absolute affirmation that my life was crazy when my husband basically begged to go clean up dog poop as an opportunity to relax. But hey, who was I to hold him back! *"Poop-scoop away, honey!"*

The day continued. We were sad that Faith wasn't with us, but that didn't keep the rest of us from celebrating. We went to the park and then came home to watch some football. Clay, in true Clay-fashion, fell asleep lying up against Jordan. I wondered how long Jordan would have this effect on Clay! What made it even sweeter was seeing that Jordan also fell asleep!

The two of them snoozed all the way up until they heard the rest of us blowing up balloons. It was mostly fun, except the competition of who could blow the biggest balloon led the boys to pop everyone else's balloons while they were blowing up their own. Even though they were getting mad at each other, especially Brandon, who decided to attach balloons together so that his could be the biggest, they were all still happy about getting balloons ready for Jordan. In fact, I'd go so far as to say that the kids loved the balloons, almost as much as the dogs hated them. But what else was new, the dogs hated a lot these days.

We packed the balloons all around the dining room table, as Jordan pretended he had no idea what was happening. Truthfully, I think he was just happy to be given the direction to stay on the couch and watch more football.

Eventually, the kids were ready to call Jordan in for dinner. They raced through dinner as quickly as they could, still asking for seconds and thirds, though, before begging to dig into cake. I noticed the subtle smile on Jordan's face when I pulled the cake out; it was a camo-covered Army cake with the words *"Happy Birthday Dad"* written on it. Each kid claimed credit for being the special child who picked it out.

It may have been Jordan's most exhausting birthday, but he offered no complaints! It was a new era in our lives, and I think he actually enjoyed a few moments of it.

When bedtime rolled around, we got the little monsters tucked in. They had a big school day ahead of them. In the final moments before Jordan and I fell asleep we shared the sadness of Faith missing his birthday. *"There will be many more, honey. The kids even said so in your birthday song."*

When I pulled up to the school the next morning, Brandon and Henry went to their classes, while Caisen, Clay and I headed into the front office. I had been through the enrollment process the week prior, so I was ready. We quickly got Clay signed up and went to go meet his teacher. I was expecting it to go smoothly, as it did with the two older boys, but I was wrong.

His teacher came out of the classroom to introduce herself, and Clay cried. Not just a little. He was sobbing as he said, *"I want to stay with you, mommy."*

He wanted me. It was so sweet. My snotty, slobbery child had my heart in his hands!

"I promise, Clay, I'll be here to pick you up at the end of the day."

His teacher asked another student to come out and talk to him, but he hid behind me. A teacher aide walked us to the staff room so that she and I could talk to him, while Caisen rolled around on the floor. I wasn't having any success convincing Clay that he was going to have a great day, or that he would see me soon enough. Eventually, the teacher aide said that we should go, and that she'd make sure Henry could sit with Clay at lunch, to check in on him.

It wasn't easy for me, but I gave him a huge hug, told him that I loved him, and again promised to pick the three of them up, right after school. I picked Caisen up, and we left. I could still hear him crying for me as I exited the building, but the aid was confident that he'd be fine. If not, they had my phone number.

Then, it was just the little Energizer-nugget and me.

I wasn't planning on putting him in pre-K. I figured that he was getting enough socialization between being reunited with his siblings and spending so much time at different parks. Instead, I took him shopping to get activities and learning games for us to do together, looking forward to using our time alone to bond.

When we got home, I established a baseline with Caisen, in an effort to see what numbers, letters and sounds he knew. Apparently, he didn't know much. In fact, his table placemat had the alphabet on it, and each letter had a word and a picture with it. When I pointed to a letter out of order, he couldn't identify any of them. Not even the letters in his name. And, when I named different letters, he couldn't tell me any of the sounds. We certainly had our work cut out for us, but we had supplies.

We had a magnetic alphabet set for the side of the refrigerator with all of the letters, and when placed into the console, it would name the letter and its sound. We had little scissors, glue, crayons, and everything else needed for little kid projects. We had kits and activity books. What we didn't have was a calm, focused child. But, we made due.

When it came time to pick up the three boys, I felt more tired than when I had dropped them off. So much for calling their school time my down time!

When the boys came out, Clay had a huge smile on his face. Not because he was finally reunited with me, but because he had a fantastic day. He made friends and loved his teacher. Things were going well for him. He even blushed when I asked him about his meltdown earlier in the day.

After school, I took the four of them with me to the same office where Henry and Brandon had their evaluations, so that we could get Clay and Caisen's completed. All four boys were in the room with the assessor and me. There were some toys, giant papers, and markers. Caisen built one really long marker-stick by attaching all of the markers end-to-end. When it broke in half he completely lost control. He was screaming and yelling and throwing all of the markers. He was kicking things and even tore Clay's paper. Clay cried, a lot. He really liked his paper. The trauma assessment turned out to be traumatizing.

I wasn't surprised when the therapist came back with the same results as the first two boys had. *"These two kids have a lot of baggage, and would do best with two counseling sessions a week, plus two weekly sessions with a skills-builder,"* the assessor explained. I was actually excited that they required the same interactions as the other two because I already had it set up! We were well on our way!

After the appointment, we went back home. It was just my boys and I, for what seemed like forever. I was beginning to wonder if Jordan ever planned to come home, but then I checked the clock and found that it just wasn't moving as quickly as I'd thought. I was suffering through some slow-moving minutes.

And those slow minutes continued all week, with the exception of the minutes I spent on the phone with the caseworker discussing Faith's situation. Talking to another adult was certainly a treat - if only it had been under different circumstances.

These were the updates I received. The foster mom was given the direction to get Faith into counseling to help with the transition. That appointment was never scheduled. The foster mom was also directed to encourage Faith in the process. That also wasn't happening. However, whether the supports were in place or not, Faith was going to be loaded up on Friday to come for another visitation weekend.

Faith was scheduled for an extra two weekends of visitation with the expectation that she'd receive the support of counseling, to help with her anxieties. Without the support, her anxieties were growing.

Nevertheless, she came. She got to the house, walked in and said, *"I'm only here for a visit."*

The smile shifted on Jordan's face. I knew why because I was feeling the same hurt. She wasn't as happy to see us as she had been on past visits.

She walked to her room, and I followed her. She opened her empty backpack, and as she started packing some of the items we had bought for her inside, she said, *"I didn't want to bring very much, to save room to take all my things home with me. I didn't even bring my bunny because I didn't want to forget him here."*

As I was searching for the right response, Clay came around the corner and saw her packing, and asked, *"Why doesn't Faith love us anymore?"*

Though I felt sadness in that moment, I chose to stay positive and supportive, recognizing that she already had one too many adults trying to manipulate her. Therefore, I simply responded, *"Of course she loves you. Who wouldn't? Now, leave your sister alone and mind your own business."*

He rolled his eyes at me and walked away.

I still hadn't found the words to respond to Faith, so I just handed her the last of the stuffed animals in the pile she was packing, and asked if she had any requests for dinner.

By the end of the night, she was back to being her happy, lovey self. However, her language still made her plan to go back home to her *"mama"* very clear. By the end of the weekend, I was far sadder for her than I was for any of the rest of us. Her contradictory words and actions suggested she was struggling with being torn on the inside.

A text came in Saturday night to let us know that Faith's pick-up time was going to be a little later than usual, so we happily planned to take the whole family to church. On the way, the boys went on and on about how great our church was and how excited they were for Faith to go with them.

"Our class is so awesome, Faith. They play loud music," said Clay.

"And the groups are fun," Henry added.

"Faith, it's the best church ever," said Caisen, who seemed to enjoy chiming in wherever possible.

"They even have video games before it starts. I'll show you where our class is," said Brandon.

I enjoyed hearing their excitement, especially from Brandon. I was hopeful she'd enjoy the program as much as the boys did and that her heart was open to it.

At the end of the service, we first collected Caisen from the pre-school room, then made our way to the school-aged kids area. Thankfully, as we rounded up our remaining children, we counted five smiles in total. Brandon was the hardest to collect, as he didn't want to give up his remote control.

"I just have to finish this level," he said.

"The next kid in line can finish, and you'll be back next week," said Jordan.

"Can I play until I die?" he asked.

"Sure," said Jordan, as Brandon promptly died. *"All right, let's go."*

Brandon didn't hand the remote over.

"Just one more life?" he asked.

"You had one more, let's go," Jordan said, as Brandon hung his head and turned with us. A few steps away, though, he talked over the top of the younger kids to ask what we were having for lunch.

We made our way to the checkout line, foolishly thinking it could be that simple.

A volunteer intercepted me as my crew continued towards the exit and asked if Brandon was my son.

I didn't think it was the right time to share our family story, so I just said, *"Yes."*

"Well," she started in, *"he caused a fight today over the video games. We have set rules for how to take turns, and he refused to follow them. He even fought with me when I directed him to hand the controller over. Please talk to him about sharing, or he won't be able to play the games in the future."*

"Yes ma'am," I said. *"I'll talk with him. Thank you for letting me know."*

I refused to let Brandon's setback define my day, so I held my head high as I rejoined my family, and waited until we got to the car to bring it up, as softly as possible.

I started by asking each of the kids to tell us their favorite parts about their services.

"The music," said Clay.

"Coloring," said Caisen, as he handed me a stack of pictures he'd worked slightly hard on.

"I liked it all," said Faith.

"I liked talking to my group leader," said Henry, who clearly enjoyed hogging every bit of adult attention he could possibly get.

"I liked Mario Bros," said Brandon. Shocker.

"Speaking of Mario Bros, Brandon, it's important to share. Make sure you're following the rules," I said.

"Yes, ma'am. I did," he replied.

"Well, the volunteer in the room said that you could use some improvement on it, so let's work on it, ok?" I asked.

"Yes, ma'am," he responded, with gusto.

"Thank you, Brandon," I said, not because I believed he'd make quick changes, but because I appreciated that he didn't argue.

Our plan was to drop Faith off after church, but the caseworker texted, saying there was a problem. She told us that the pick-up was delayed, though the transport was ready to collect Miss Faith, and that we needed to act casually about it while she handled some things on her end.

We coordinated with the transport, who decided to stealthily follow us around like a hired private-eye, anxiously awaiting our updated directive.

We caravanned to a grocery store, after creating a list of items we *"needed."* Next, we stopped at Walmart, stating that Clay needed new shoes. All the while, I was texting the transport, so that he could easily stick with us. We didn't want the kids to hear me discussing our predicament.

A text from the caseworker confirmed we'd have time to grab lunch, so we texted the transport, letting him know we were headed to the Pirate's House downtown. The drive alone ate up a good chunk of time. Along the way, Faith talked about being excited to eat at the Pirate's House, but also reminded us that she'd be headed home to *"Mama"* afterwards. Jordan and I nodded along, while silently wondering what was happening behind the scenes with the caseworker.

When we arrived at the restaurant, Jordan sat down with the kids while I stepped outside to take the expected call from the caseworker.

She said, *"I'm sorry about the mess, but Faith's foster mom still hasn't set up the required counseling, and has now made a statement that she refuses to support Faith through the transition, and will do everything she can to prevent the placement."*

I felt a shift inside. I didn't witness any of the foster mom's actions firsthand, but I had no reason to doubt the caseworker, so I accepted the entire obstacle as true. I felt confirmation that Faith had been manipulated in her feelings towards us, which helped me to better understand why there had been a change in her. Understanding didn't change our circumstances, but it at least gave me a better sense of what we were up against.

She continued to say, *"There is no way Faith can return to that foster home because the foster mom isn't following our directions regarding Faith, so we're working on a new plan."*

Though relieved to know that Faith would no longer be stuck in this tug-of-war, I was also worried over how she would receive the news.

She went on. *"We're processing an emergency removal and discussing the options for moving forward. We can either place her in a new foster home for the two weeks that are remaining on her new transition plan, or leave her with you. How quickly did you say you could set up counseling to help her?"*

"Based on how fast the boys got in for their trauma assessments, I'm guessing Monday, Tuesday at the latest. And, as long as her assessment is complete, she'd begin her sessions at our house on Tuesday. The assigned therapist is already expecting her. And though I know you have the final say, I think that Faith would probably handle this shock better here, than she would at a stranger's house, though it will still be hard for her to process."

And in that moment, the decision was made. *"I agree,"* she said. *"I'll cancel the transport and she'll stay with you. I'll send a caseworker to you tomorrow to make it official. Does she have everything she needs? Because I don't think her foster mom is going to work with us on this.*"

"Well, she didn't bring anything with her, but we'll figure that out. The only thing I know she'll be really upset over is a stuffed bunny. Any chance of getting it back?" I asked.

She didn't have the answer I wanted, but it was the honest answer we needed: *"Not right away, but maybe we can ask about it later.*"

Once the plan was in place, there was only one thing left to decide. Who was going to tell Faith?

By the end of the call, I accepted that it wasn't up to me to decide by whom or how the news should be shared. Instead, I was given directions to take Faith home with us, and to call the caseworker back when we were in a place where we could talk. She asked me to tell Faith only that the caseworker was working on details and that she'd call soon to update us, which was true.

Jordan made an obvious nod at me, discreetly urging me to look back when he noticed the transporter breaking away from us. The emergency dissolution of Faith's foster home was already initiated.

At the house, Jordan got comfy in front of the TV with the boys, though it sounded like they were mostly jumping and rolling around.

Faith and I were in her bedroom as I called the caseworker, who asked me to use speaker phone. The caseworker bluntly said, *"There's an issue with your foster placement, and you won't be returning to that foster home.*"

Faith began wailing and slid down to the floor.

She continued, *"I promise, there was a plan for you to return, but that plan just changed. It wasn't supposed to be this way. I'm just thankful that you were with Jordan and Jessie when this happened, so that you didn't have to move to another house in the meantime. This is for the best, Faith. You'll see.*"

Just like that. Band-Aid off. The caseworker kept talking, but Faith wasn't hearing her.

I ended the call and sat down with Faith on the floor, a space I had grown to know very well, and held her. I acknowledged her pain.

"Faith," I said, *"I'm so sorry these really big things keep happening to you. I hate that you keep going through this kind of pain. I promise you, I will do my best to protect you from ever changing families again.*"

As she curled into my lap, I felt the snot and tears seeping through my jeans. It was a new experience for me, but one that I accepted. I knew, deep in my heart, that this was the first of many times I would show up to embrace this young girl as she snotted all over me.

Jordan came in the room and scooped Faith up. *"It's not fair that you should be going through all of this,"* he said to her.

My eyes met Jordan's, and in that moment, we felt deep affirmation that we were doing the right thing for these kids. The foster system shouldn't be their family. They needed something more, and they were worth every bit of struggle we would endure.

A text message came through, letting me know that a crew of caseworkers would be at our house the next evening to sign all of the placement paperwork. This meant Faith couldn't start school that Monday because we needed the placement paperwork first. I shared the news with Faith, who just stared blankly at me.

When bedtime came around, I was totally content with staying on her floor until she was sound asleep. I still looked forward to being in my own bed, but I didn't rush. She needed to know I was there.

I made my way into my own room, where Jordan and I spoke about the events of the day. We had been through a lot together, but holding Faith as her heart broke was new and difficult.

I recalled several moments from that day where our eyes met, and we got on the same page, non-verbally. Though our circumstances were harder than they'd ever been, he and I were growing stronger and more unified than ever. We were in the trenches together, fighting alongside each other in sync.

"I never imagined how profoundly this process would impact our relationship," I said. *"If anything, I expected it would be a strain on us. But I'm blown away at how naturally you are stepping in and embracing the struggle. You are an incredible man."*

"We are an incredible team," he responded, before kissing me goodnight.

The next morning, I took three boys to school, and then I took Faith and Caisen shopping to stock Faith's closet and drawers and to buy her school uniforms. We got everything we needed before the school day was over, then prepared the kids for round three of foster-placement paperwork, which would also serve as our November house-visit. Our caseworker arrived, followed by a substitute caseworker who came on the kids' behalf, who was able to make the trip on short notice. When the work was done, I can say with 100% certainty that he was happy to leave our house and was probably ready for a stiff drink. The kids had the ability to drive anyone crazy in a short amount of time!

After everyone left, we celebrated that Faith was officially placed with us, making it day one of our six-month requirement before applying for finalization. The next day, Tuesday November 18th, Faith began school, and all five kids participated in in-home counseling. It was a circus, but it was my circus.

CHAPTER 15

CHALLENGES MAKE LIFE INTERESTING

O ur fifth kiddo joined us November 14th and was legally placed with us on November 17th, just a week before Thanksgiving Break. We did the same things for her that we'd done for the others: enrolling her in school, starting her in counseling, and getting her an updated medical exam. As we were going through the steps, thankful that the drama over Faith's move-in had ended, we learned that we had again been naïve.

Instead of the drama ending, we found that it actually accelerated. On one of our social media sites, this post was drawn to our attention: *"Here's an update. This family is holding a child against her will. The 11-year-old they want to adopt did not want to live with them, so they "said" they* would continue weekend visits for another 4 weeks with her. She was supposed to come back to her foster home today, but instead they lied to her and now she is stuck in Savannah with people who treat her horribly. How could they lie to this child? These people that you consider perfect are not. There's your update and the truth."

I thought it safe to assume that this was a friend or acquaintance of Faith's last foster mom. However, my priorities were set appropriately, so instead of wasting a single second of my time defending our situation, I just deleted the entire profile. Faith's caseworker made all of the decisions regarding Faith's placement, and we did everything that was asked of us. That's all I needed to remember so that I could confidently turn my other cheek after that slap in the face. Besides, I knew I'd get my fair share of drama through parenting the kids!

Speaking of drama, our lives had changed. It felt like we were living in a sitcom. And to make things more complicated, it was almost Thanksgiving, and our Georgia tradition had been hosting Thanksgiving dinner for our closest friends, including Reagan and David. This year was meant to be extra special because the kids were going to meet their honorary Auntie Reagan, Uncle David, and Cousin Baby Jack.

I tried my best to find a way to make their planned visit work and to guarantee everyone's safety, but I failed.

I needed my best friend, but the kids were so chaotic and unpredictable that I had serious doubts about Baby Jack surviving the trip. To clarify, I didn't think any of the kids would do anything intentionally. However, things were breaking regularly, and we were having far too many out-of-control fits. I couldn't justify the risk, so I told Reagan we were going to have to postpone the meeting. It was one of the hardest phone calls I had ever made. It felt like I was letting go of a lifeline.

When Thanksgiving rolled around, we were on our own and we had a lot to do. Of course, we didn't need to insert the table leaf because it was already in place. However, we needed to roast a turkey, mash potatoes, butter rolls, make stuffing, open a can of cranberries, make a pink Jell-O fruit salad, make gravy, heat up some green beans, and pour the sparkling cider. This task was MUCH easier the few years prior when we had multiple families to split the work with, and fewer kids to distract and interfere!

There were some complaints throughout the meal, but mostly excitement. We went around the table sharing something we each were thankful for. Mostly the kids listed food items, but Clay said he was most thankful for his new family. Of course, everyone else quickly amended their statements to include bigger things to be thankful for. Brandon decided he was thankful for a mommy and daddy. Faith said she was thankful we were so nice. Henry said he was thankful that we liked football. Caisen said he was thankful that we could make such good food. They kept building on each other, all determined to have the best *"thankful"* of all. Competition aside, it was entertaining to hear what they were able to come up with!

After lunch, I put away the leftovers, while the kids played with some toys and watched a little TV. When the time was right, we loaded the kids in the car and drove to the movie theater. It was a Thanksgiving tradition in my home growing up, and I was excited to enjoy the activity with the kids. The movie was Annie, which seemed incredibly fitting.

We made it through the movie. It was sweet. The kids enjoyed it, but didn't seem to see the parallels to their own life. They were too high-speed and chaos-driven for introspection. It made me sad. It was so obvious they had so much rage, anger, frustration, guilt, worry, and anxiety, but they were never able to sit down and determine why. They had never been given the cues to process their experiences, or the tools to be able to find new ways for handling life's obstacles.

On a day like this, where it was so obvious that they were living such superficial, surface-level lives, my heart just ached for them. I was determined to get the approval for psychological testing to be performed, to go with the counseling we started. The kids needed the support. And I didn't care how big of a commitment it was to get the testing completed.

As we got in the car to drive home, I was thinking about how disconnected the kids were. It left me feeling stressed. I thought ice cream would be helpful, so I made a comment to Jordan about driving through Dairy Queen for dinner. Not only would we bypass the hassle of reheating leftovers, but we'd also get ice cream.

The kids heard the comment. Four were excited. One was upset.

I broke it down a little further for Brandon, but he was still clearly against the idea. However, things changed when we pulled up and saw that Dairy Queen was closed for Thanksgiving. I excitedly told them *"Well, I guess I don't get to be lazy. I'll pull everything back out, including more of the pink salad. And, we'll eat all the pies."*

I sold the new plan, by making it sound better than ice cream. And everyone accepted it. Everyone, except Brandon.

Brandon pitched a fit over wanting Dairy Queen ice cream. The kid who didn't want Dairy Queen was the kid who was now pitching a fit for it. I quickly became upset with myself for even considering it to begin with.

We reassured him, letting him know that we all felt the disappointment. We ALL were looking forward to ice cream. That didn't help.

We reminded him that we tried, but it was closed. That didn't help.

That's when it hit me. His fits weren't specifically seeking a change or adjustment. They were more a loss of control due to a surprise or disappointment. He wasn't asking us to go back to Dairy Queen. He wasn't misunderstanding the fact that they were closed. He was just so disappointed and was having a difficult time accepting it.

We continued engaging with him. The other kids chimed in about the pie still at home. He didn't even respond, trapped in his own bubble of rage.

By the time we got home, he was smashing the windows with his seatbelt buckle, kicking Henry's seat in front of him, and still screaming loudly. Sadly, Henry's seat was right in front of Brandon, and it was the seat that folded down so that the back-row kids could get out. However, with Brandon sitting there freaking out, the way out for Faith was blocked.

We weren't having much luck encouraging Brandon to come out of the car, or to let Faith get out. It didn't take long to realize that the back hatch was Faith's best bet. When we opened it, Faith began crawling out, but Brandon freaked further. He thought we would think he was *"bad"* if Faith had to crawl out the back, so he didn't want her to. So, his solution was to try to block her in the car while trying to crawl out the back himself. Because that would help?

We told him to stop and to go out the door so that Faith could follow him. He didn't want to. He was asked to calm down and think about it. Again, he didn't want to. When he covered his face and resumed kicking, Jordan motioned for Faith to crawl out. Brandon blew his top when he noticed, but there was at least enough time for Jordan to help pull Faith out and close the hatch.

I climbed back in the front seat so that he wasn't alone in the car.

Now, all of the doors were shut, child safety locks were on, and it was just Brandon and I. While Brandon fretted, Jordan called me on the phone so we could work out our plan. We certainly had to repeat ourselves a few times to hear each other over Brandon, but we got through it. It was decided that Jordan would take the other kiddos into the house and start reheating the leftovers. The plan was to eat dinner, eat pie, and watch the original Annie movie, as a family.

I wasn't sure if Brandon had heard the details, so I tried to strike up a conversation. I was hoping to distract him into calming down. It didn't work. And, at this point, I was feeling upset that I was missing out on leftovers and pie.

I went back to lines like, *"You won't get what you want by pitching a fit,"* and *"A fit will never get you what you want."* I even made the point of saying, *"Brandon, even if Dairy Queen was open now, we couldn't get you the ice cream because of the attitude you are taking. Let's calm down so you don't miss out on anything else."* I reminded him that we weren't going in until he got a hold of himself. He wasn't even responding. He just kept yelling. As I sat outside my house, I was wondering how I was ever going to help this kid. But I kept trying to remind myself that getting the evaluations completed would help us with some understanding, and then we could get the right resources in place. Surely things would get better then!

Eventually, Brandon calmed down enough to go into the house. I was still naïve enough at that point to believe the fit had ended, but I quickly learned that a child who is so stuck on something doesn't just move on. He may have seemed to calm down, but it was just an intermission.

When we got inside, he saw that the other kids were eating, and he flew off the handle again. He was screaming about them eating and also more about wanting ice cream. He was stomping and kicking close to the other kids.

We tried our best to help him join the rest of the group, but he wasn't listening. After enough-was-enough, I told him to go to his room. Of course, the screaming and yelling escalated. But, the point needed to be made that he couldn't ruin everyone else's good time.

I told him to go to his room and said that I'd bring dinner in to him. It took him a while, but I could see he was moving in the right direction. That felt big. I knew he didn't want to go to his room, but he eventually made it there.

He was inside the boys' room, slamming the door open and closed. It sounded like gunshots, as each sharp bang echoed loudly down the hallway. I wondered, *"What must the neighbors think?"*

As promised, I got his plate ready. When I took it in to him, I was surprised to see how quickly he was able to rip the blankets off his bed, throw his stuffies, tip over the laundry bin, and empty the closet. If only clean up could go as quickly!

I told him that if he didn't clean it up within the next thirty minutes, he would lose the option for pie. I set his plate of Thanksgiving food on the dresser and left the room.

I intended to be gone for ten minutes, but I heard the bunk beds bouncing around. I opened the door to see the Brandon/Caisen bunk bed rocking back and forth. It was slamming into both the wall, which was now decorated with a nice hole from the bedpost, and also into the other set of bunk beds. I came into the room and sat down inside the door. I figured he clearly wasn't calming down on his own, so I probably needed to stay.

I told him that the timer was still running and that he had a choice to make.

He said he didn't care. I was surprised, and actually thanked him for responding to me. I'm sure it shocked him, but it was the first time he had actually responded to me during a fit.

I continued to give him a countdown for cleaning up. When the timer went off, I said that his option for pie was gone. He was clearly upset, but he didn't have a whole lot of steam left to escalate.

He wasn't eating his food yet, so I told him that I was setting a timer on it, and I was going to remove the plate when the timer went off. He again said that he didn't care. However, I was able to talk him into eating the biscuit and some mashed potatoes. There was still another two minutes on the timer when he said that he was done. I took the plate away. I saw that the movie was almost over. Probably another twenty minutes. I set that as my own timer for getting him calmed down, cleaned up, and ready for bed.

I put his plate away and went back into the room. He was on his bed. Of course, his hands were crossed over his face. He hadn't cleaned anything, but it looked like he was done with the destruction portion of the evening. So, I climbed up onto Henry's bed and struck up a conversation.

"I'm sad that you and I didn't get to watch the movie that I had been looking forward to, and that we didn't get any pie," I said.

He grunted a little, still with his hands over his face.

"When you got stuck on the ice cream, it cost you Thanksgiving dinner with the family, pie for dessert, and a family movie," I said, as I noticed his breathing slowing. *"And not just you. I also missed out on those things with the family. I'm not trying to make you feel bad, but I hope you can see that I chose to stay with you and to be there for you, and that in a family, your choices impact you and everyone else."*

I noticed one of his eyes peeking at me from under his elbow. He hid it well, with his head tucked between his knees and his arms wrapped around, but there was no denying it was an eye I saw peering out.

"You weren't the only one disappointed about ice cream, but you handled it very differently. I pray that there will be a day where you come to me with your disappointments, so we can experience them and process them together."

I saw his body start to relax. He didn't look up, and he didn't say a word, but I felt his tensions were lessening.

"I promise I will try my best to teach you the skills and abilities to handle these difficult situations, so that things like this don't keep happening to you. I don't blame you, and I want to help."

We sat quietly for a few minutes, as I considered that Brandon didn't have control of many things in his life. Typically, things just happened to him. He didn't have many choices. So, when bad things happened, big or small, he developed the habit of falling apart. Brandon was completely out of control of his own life. It was an extremely sad thing to see.

When I felt it was suitable to ask, I suggested he clean up the room. He wasn't happy about it, but he got it done. I stayed in there with him as he finished up.

When he was done, the other kids came in to get snuggled up. We did a little reading before bed. Afterward, Jordan and I gave everyone hugs and kisses.

At last, I took my place on Faith's floor, where I was thinking about how glad I was that Reagan and her family didn't come. It would not have been a good time for them!

Utterly exhausted, I rolled into bed. I felt disappointed to have missed so much time with the family, even though I knew that staying with Brandon was the right thing to do. It still hurt to miss the fun stuff. Then it hit me: *"What if Jordan was upset with me for picking Brandon, or with Brandon for causing the fractured night?"*

I'm not one to let things fester, so I turned to him and asked, *"Do you have any regrets?"*

I expected a long pause, or a complicated answer. I was wrong.

He quickly responded with, *"No, I don't regret any of this. I actually feel like we're Brandon's only chance at getting a good life, and I feel good about giving him that chance."*

Tired or not, I grabbed his face and planted a big kiss on the man. Again, no hesitation on his part, and as we made out, I felt so lucky to get to know this other side of Jordan. Compassion and understanding looked so sexy on him. Being a dad suited him very well. And I propped myself up onto my elbow to tell him.

He pulled me down to lay with him, my head resting on his chest. He told me that he enjoyed watching me with the kids, and he was proud of how I was handling Brandon's challenges. I responded likewise, sharing how my heart fluttered seeing him snuggled with the other four on the couch, watching the movie and eating pie.

Before dozing off, we looked at some pictures on our phones. As we reminisced, we saw that the kids had physically changed over the short time we'd had them. Clay looked like a whole new kid, taller and thinner than he was when he walked in to that McDonald's only six weeks earlier. They were growing comfortable with us, and it showed.

I woke up the next morning, still aware of how much longer this holiday break from school would last and exhausted from the day before, but also refreshed that it was a new day.

First thing the next morning, Jordan ran to the store to grab two more gallons of milk. We were going through it quickly. As he left, I was called into the bathroom by Henry, who had found a large, slimy streak of blood across the toilet lid. I thanked him for telling me and went into Faith's room, not certain how to approach the conversation.

I knew I needed to say something along the lines of *"Hi Faith, I'm your new mom, it's nice to meet you. By the way, welcome to womanhood,"* but not in those exact words.

When she looked up at me, I asked, *"Faith, has anyone talked to you about having a period?"*

She stared blankly.

Second attempt: *"Have you ever noticed blood in your panties or anything before?"*

She got embarrassed and put her head down, like she was in trouble.

Third try: *"I saw some blood in the bathroom, and I wanted to make sure you are ok, and to come up with a plan about how to handle it."*

She looked back up, which I took as acknowledgement that I was on the right track. So, I discreetly sent Jordan to the store to grab a package of pads.

I continued, *"Is this the first time, or has it happened before?"*

"It's never happened before," she whispered.

Maybe her first period was a sign that she was also experiencing physical changes after letting go of heavy stresses?

I explained that menstrual cycles were normal, and they were something that all girls experience. I told her that it would typically happen once a month, for a few days, but that her periods might be different. I asked her to tell me every time that she started one so that I could make a note of it on my calendar, because doctors will always ask us for the date of the last one.

I tried to keep it simple, but it still seemed like her eyes were glazing over with the information.

Jordan came home with a variety of options. Regular pads, heavy flow pads, nighttime pads, and every other form of pad he could find.

I was candid with Faith. *"There are different ways to go about handling a period. At your age, pads are the only option I'll approve."* I explained how to get it in her panties right, and asked her to let me know throughout the day if she had too much blood pooling in the pad, or very little blood indicating a thinner pad would be ok. *"Oh, and don't be surprised if you feel cramping or icky tummy feelings."*

As much as I wasn't expecting to have this conversation only a week after welcoming my daughter home, I thought I handled it all right. And I thought I was in the clear. That's when she asked me, *"Why do girls have periods?"*

Again, I was candid. *"Girls' bodies were made to be able to have babies. When a girl's body grows enough, it starts dropping eggs once a month. If the egg isn't turned into a baby, then the girl's body cleans itself out with a period. I expect that you will have periods every month for a very, very, very, long time, because you aren't allowed to have babies until you're forty."*

She said, *"Ok."* And that was that.

I thought it went well, considering I hadn't spent any time preparing for this conversation.

CHAPTER 16

IN A RUT, SEARCHING FOR A GROOVE

As if Thanksgiving Break wasn't challenging enough, the calendar was telling me I didn't have much time to recover before Christmas Break kicked the kids out of school for another eighteen days! I tried to recoup while the four older kids were in school, but it wasn't going smoothly.

I thought that my one-on-one time with Caisen was going to be filled with bonding and play. I knew it would be exhausting, but I thought we'd get into a routine, and that I'd grow to enjoy it. That's not how it was playing out. Though I spent time doing crafts and activities with him, helping him to identify letters and sounds, and to tie his shoes, he seemed much more interested in spending his time throwing things at me, biting me, and chasing the dogs. He seemed to enjoy the chaos.

He was nonstop madness. At one point, our caseworker popped in to do a surprise visit, and while she and I were talking, Caisen screamed, yelled, kicked, spun, ran across the couches, body slammed the poor dogs, threw pillows, and complained of starving WHILE decorating my house with the Fruit Loops I'd already given him. I'm sure the caseworker had seen worse, though she didn't relieve my tension by admitting to it.

I used the face-to-face visit to again request psychological testing. Not because the kids were hyper, or because I thought there was something wrong with them, but because they were so scattered and deserved appropriate support. I didn't know when we'd get approved, but I knew to keep asking because a professional analysis and suggested resource plan could only help.

As if my day with Caisen wasn't struggle enough, I also had to survive the whole group of kids from two twenty every afternoon until bedtime. Of course, it was better on the nights when Jordan made it home around dinnertime, but that wasn't our norm. Jordan began a three-month cycle of staying at work overnight a couple nights a week as the Fort Stewart Military Police Duty Officer. Without him around to back my play and share the load, I worried I would burn out before Christmas Break, or during it.

Whether Jordan made it home or not, our afternoons were broken down into two categories. Not-counseling days and counseling days. On not-counseling days, I started by feeding them afternoon snacks, but they constantly pitched fits about the options, even though I stayed stocked on the things they liked. It was frustrating, but I could do it.

I was helping them complete their homework, even though they all got jealous of me helping anyone else. They were making up problems, just to keep me from helping the others. When I'd complete their imaginary problems, I'd move on to the next desperate child, causing the rest to get mad and call me back again. It was exhausting, but I could do it.

I was also able to make dinner. Of course, I was doing it while tending to one meltdown after another. Ironically, every time I touched food, a couple of the kids would pitch a fit about being hungry. Not before I touched food. Only after.

If I said, *"Great because I'm making dinner for you, right now, this very minute!"* then they'd respond with, *"But I'm hungry!"* and throw themselves on the floor in tears. I knew this was a common behavior in younger kids, but it was confusing to me at their ages. By the time dinner was ready, I was too exhausted to eat. However, I couldn't wait to eat until after I got them in bed because I was still on Faith's floor at night. It was tough, but I could do it.

And then there were our counseling days -- Mondays and Wednesdays at three in the afternoon, until around eight at night. I had hopes that these days would be smoother than the other days because there were two other adults in my house. I thought the extra attention would make for happier kids. I WAS WRONG!

On counseling days, I always prepped the kids for the ordeal on the car ride home from school. I got so good at the speech that the kids would say it along with me.

"When we get home, everyone gets a quick snack. Then, we read while we wait for the counselors to arrive and direct us. The lead counselor will tell us which kid she's going to work with first. The skills-builder will grab her first child. Then, I'll decide who takes a shower, while the other two kids do their homework, including thirty minutes of reading. We'll rotate

until everyone's done. If you're done early, it's quiet independent play while the other kids finish. Got it?"

As I pulled into the driveway, I already knew someone would pitch a fit about the snack options. Everybody would pitch fits about reading, even though it was a school assignment and not just my request. The kid who was picked first would pitch a fit about being first. The kids who weren't picked to go first, would pitch fits about having to wait. The kid who was asked to take a shower would pitch a fit about the shower. And the quiet, independent play thing was basically a joke on me because these kids didn't know how to be quiet or independent. But the expectation was made clear in the beginning, and we continually worked towards it.

When we walked inside, I put the dogs in my room so that they wouldn't be in anyone's way, and gave the kids a choice between fruit snacks, apples or peanut butter crackers. I thought it was a decent variety.

Within thirty seconds, Clay dropped to his knees, bent himself backwards, puffed his chest to the sky and screamed, *"I WANT GOGURT! RAWR!"* He growled, huffed, puffed, and cursed a little. It seemed as though he was shooting a beam of power out of his chest into the sky. Or, like his body had been possessed and the demon hiding inside was angry.

Anyway, when he was done screaming, he grabbed a kitchen chair and threw it at the garage door. This was new for Clay, and I couldn't tell if he was learning this from Brandon, or if he was now in a new stage of grief. Either way, he shoved the table, kicked the fallen chair out of his way, and walked out the door. He was in his socks, and it was December. I wasn't sure where he was going. I was torn, because I couldn't let the six-year-old go walking down the street by himself, but I also couldn't leave the other four behind.

The other four, by the way, who were supposed to be doing their reading while waiting for the counselors, were now asking me question after question about homework, why they have to read, and what was for dinner.

I stood in the doorway, not knowing what to do, when Clay thankfully stopped and turned back after getting just one house away. He stomped his way home, still angry about the snack options.

I again asked him if he'd like fruit snacks, an apple, or peanut butter crackers. He dropped back into his powerful kneeling position. I told him to let me know when his decision was made and walked back to the front door to see if the counselors were there. They weren't.

With my back turned, he yelled out, *"I HATE YOU JESSIE GA-GA-GARLAND!"*

I asked, *"Who's that?"*

He shouted, *"I HATE YOU JESSIE, JESSIE GAL-GAL-GAL..."*

Brandon, who was sitting on the couch with a book that he wasn't reading, chimed in with *"Galileo?"*

"Also, incorrect," I said.

"Well, whatever your name is," Clay growled, *"I HATE YOU."*

Just then, the first counselor pulled up. She chose to work with Brandon first, and he promptly lost his mind.

Then, the skills-builder arrived and called on Henry. He stomped towards her with his head thrown back dramatically.

That left me with Caisen, Faith, and Clay.

I asked Clay to take his shower first, thinking it might help calm him down, but he fell apart again. He was back on his knees, with his chest pumped upward, with some more hateful screaming.

I chose to ignore Clay for a bit, believing he'd eventually calm down and get his shower done, so he could stay in the insanely competitive race to be the first one to complete all of the stations on counseling days.

I turned to see that Brandon was still upset about being selected to do his counseling first, and hadn't yet taken any of the necessary steps to comply, starting with getting up. He was still on the couch, rolling back and forth, holding the book that he hadn't started reading. He had one arm across his eyes and was screaming that he shouldn't have to go first.

"Remember Brandon, it isn't our job to pick the order, just to follow the directions we are given," I said. He continued flopping.

I didn't want to step on the counselor's toes, so I backed off to let her do her thing. She, much like myself, wanted to set the tone that rewards were not given to those who behaved that way, and that she wouldn't wait all day, so after ten minutes were wasted, she told Brandon she was setting a timer for ten more minutes. She said if he didn't start his session within those ten minutes, she would close his session and move on to the next child.

"Yes," he chanted, *"Move on to the next kid and come back to me later."*

She repeatedly clarified, *"Brandon, this IS your session, and if you choose to miss it, then it's over for today."*

He really didn't want to miss his appointment, but he couldn't pull himself together.

When the timer went off, our counselor told him his session was over and called on Faith to begin hers. Faith got up and took her seat in the kitchen, oblivious to what was going on.

Brandon escalated. He screamed that he was ready for his session. The counselor stuck to her guns, alternating between ignoring him, and reminding him he had already made his choice, but he could make a better decision next time.

Of course, Brandon couldn't move on. Instead, he unloaded the kitchen cupboards while Faith sat and peacefully colored a mandala.

Throwing spices and bowls didn't get the response he wanted, so he moved to the refrigerator.

After the storm of chilled goods, Brandon took the refrigerator for a walk. Considering his scrawny body, knobby knees, sunken armpits, and a spine so visible it reminded me of a stegosaurus, I was actually impressed by the strength of this skinnier than skinny kid, though I had to act unimpressed. I didn't want to encourage him.

He took it several feet forward. Then he changed directions and took it several feet to the side. He pushed up against Faith, practically pinning her into her chair. Faith didn't even seem to notice. Our counselor's jaw dropped, but when Brandon looked at her, she wiped the shock off her face and looked like she didn't notice what was happening.

He moved on to the dining room, where he took the black and white clock off the wall and threw it onto the ground. It shattered. Brandon knew it was from my aunt, and to add salt to my wound, it was the one piece in my home that actually received compliments. I wanted to cry, but couldn't. I couldn't show him my pain in that moment because he would have struck harder.

Therefore, I held it together. Instead of responding with anger or frustration, I decided to shock him back. I asked to see his hands and arms, telling him I needed to know if he was ok. I was making a big deal about how worried I was that he might have gotten hurt when the clock shattered. He paused for a moment, looking confused. When I walked nearer to him, he covered his face back up and turned into a corner.

I didn't let it go. I told him I NEEDED to know he was ok. Eventually, he handed his arms out, still grunting. I said, *"Thank goodness you're ok,"* and turned back around. I wanted to disarm him without pushing my luck.

Somehow, I managed to keep the other kids away from the mess and rolling through their stations. Of course, Caisen cried about starting his bath and also when it was over. Clay cried about reading, claiming that his thirty minutes should be over only four minutes in. Henry hadn't even opened his book when he asked if he was done. Faith was staring at the wall, lost. And Brandon was still grunting into the corner. At least he wasn't destroying anything else.

Jordan got home as we were closing up with the counselors. He gave me a look of shock and awe at where the refrigerator was, and I nodded at him to go help redirect Brandon.

Our non-verbal communication was on point.

He went up to our Little Hulk, who peeked out at him, then immediately crossed both arms back over his forehead. Jordan grabbed him into a hug. Brandon didn't reciprocate. Jordan grabbed Brandon's arms and helped them into the proper hug position, saying, *"In this family, we hug with BOTH arms."* It took a few minutes of my telling Jordan what had happened, from the perspective that I wanted Brandon to hear, before Brandon calmed down. I worked hard to sell the *"I was so worried"* angle.

I then turned to say goodbye to the counselors, as Jordan grabbed a broom. When our eyes met, he said, *"It's not often someone moves our refrigerator out of the way for us. I might as well sweep under it while I can."*

Then, we had to get through dinner and bedtime.

After so many days of that same butt-kicking routine, it was time to start looking at options. I mean, I felt proud that I was surviving back-to-back days of total chaos and stress, but I realized that just because I *could* do it, didn't mean I *should*. I had nothing to prove and it was all taking a toll. Our journey with the kids was meant to be a long-term marathon, not a quick sprint. I needed some sort of built-in break.

Jordan and I talked about it, and the decision was made. Caisen needed a pre-K program, so that I could spend a few hours a day staring at a blank wall and drooling. I did a little research and found a pre-K center near our house. It wasn't my first choice, but my first choice had a waiting list, and I really needed more adults in my village.

I was so looking forward to getting his enrollment completed, only to find that Caisen's first day was a total train wreck. Not only did his teacher teach Caisen to spell his name *"Kayson,"* but my pick-up schedule had a major flaw. The big kids had a pick-up range of two twenty until two forty. Caisen had a pick-up time of two thirty.

The schools weren't close enough for me to pick Caisen up at two thirty and still make it to the other kids by two forty. Trust me, I tried. But at two forty, the kids were moved into the front office for late parents to walk in and collect them from the staff who clearly didn't enjoy babysitting after hours. Then we raced home for a typical round of counseling madness.

Picking the big kids up at two twenty to make it to Caisen by two thirty failed the following day. And, considering the fact that pre-K was getting Caisen into a much-needed nap routine, canceling pre-K was NOT an option! So, I had to think.

I didn't want to upset any staff members, and I didn't want the kids to have to worry about whether I was coming or not. And, for clarification purposes, we were still a foster family, which meant I couldn't ask someone to split transportation with me, carpool style. The kids could only be in our care, the care of approved organizations and institutions like church, school, daycare, etc., or other foster-approved families. I needed to find a way to solve the problem on my own.

That's when it hit me. I could solve two problems at once. I could sign the big kids up for the after-school daycare program. That way, they had someplace to go on counseling days, for the few minutes they needed to wait on me to pick them up, AND they had somewhere to go for a couple of hours on not-counseling days. This would reduce the number of hours I had all five kids with me, by myself. The idea resonated as a miracle, because my constantly chaotic time spent with the kids was hard on our individual relationships. I wanted more quality time with them, which was difficult considering the quantity.

Truthfully, I felt a little guilty about signing them up. I knew that we would all benefit from having a little less one-on-five time, but I still felt bad. I wasn't working a conventional job that required after-school care, and I wasn't physically unable to provide care. It also didn't help that the parents I ran into while picking up my kids started conversations by asking what I did for a living. I felt lazy telling them that I was a stay-at-home mom with my kids in childcare. I felt irresponsible spending the money on it, too.

Did I feel bad enough to take them out of care, though? NO. I felt deeply that we all would do better if they were in after-school care for a while. I tried to feel thankful that I at least had one week to test the new arrangement out before beginning Christmas Break; but, honestly, I felt sad at only having one week before the very long break started.

CHAPTER 17

STRONG PEOPLE ASK FOR HELP

I t was the last weekend before Christmas Break. A weekend didn't seem all that intimidating because my eyes were already looking ahead to Christmas Break. And really, what could go wrong in a weekend, when my precious children were so excited about our fun, planned activities, and also hoping to find time to make extra decorations and gifts? It was sweet, but also scary, because they didn't have much respect for scissors, glue, or lamps. I subtly worked on craft etiquette, like *"Be careful to leave the scissors where you can see them, so you don't accidentally grab them wrong"* while swooning over their projects.

I felt relief when our planned events came along. The first was a foster care Christmas party, put on by our local adoption agency. All of the foster and pre-adoptive families were invited to attend.

We got all dolled up, as best we could. For most of us, getting dressed up was fun. However, poor Clay was flopping around on the ground complaining about how weird his new clothes felt.

He did this each time he wore a new item. Typically, after rolling around and complaining about the weirdness for about ten minutes, the clothes ended up feeling normal. I hated hearing the complaining and whining, but it was also entertaining to watch him trying to stretch pants out with exaggerated squats and lunges, and kicking his legs around to test out new socks. This kid had major quirks! The strangest part of his dressing ritual was how tightly he would buckle his belt. I requested that he loosen it, saying his head might pop off if he squeezed his belly any tighter!

For the special event, Faith was given permission to dry her freshly washed hair. While she was drying her lengthy locks, I was gelling the boys' hair up in the bathroom, and that's when I smelled that something was burning.

I stepped out of the bathroom to investigate. I called to Jordan, who was in the living room on my right. He didn't smell anything, so I went left. It got stronger as I walked. I opened Faith's door and found the source. She had set the hair dryer down on the carpet, still turned on, while she looked for earrings. We promptly had a chat about fire safety.

When all of our crisis conversations were at good stopping points, we snapped our first selfie-of-seven. Of course, we couldn't share our picture with anyone because of the foster care rules, but I still wanted to capture our special moments.

At the event, our family took an entire round table to ourselves. One of the agency staff members came walking by, and Clay walked right up to him and asked where his present was, claiming that he was ready to open it. I'm not sure what shade of red I turned as I asked him to leave the gentleman alone, but I'm sure it was a deep one.

I pulled Clay aside to have a quick conversation about etiquette. *"It's not polite for kids to demand things of other adults. This applies to waiters, teachers, doctors, and other adults too. Instead, share your needs with your parents who can direct you or make a request for you. As far as the presents go, I'm sure they'll tell us when they're ready to give us directions. Until then, let's just hang out. Ok?"*

"Ok," he said, as he plopped into his chair and looked at Jordan. *"I'm hungry."*

We walked to the back of the building to join the rest of the party. There were some inflatable bounce houses set up and many kids laughing and playing. Our kids went to town, as many kids did. They all went down the inflatable slide every which way except for feet first, while shoving each other and anyone one else in their way. My kids got kicked off, one-by-one, but only after they had enough time to sweat off their hair gel.

When it was time to eat, the kids made it clear to the kitchen staff which dishes they liked and which ones they didn't. I looked at the man behind the counter and said, *"Thank you, it all looks lovely,"* but the damage had already been done.

While eating, we had another short conversation about etiquette: *"We should work on sharing compliments more willingly than complaints, especially since the agency had no obligation to feed us. Next time, you should wait until we get to our table to share your thoughts about the sides you didn't pick, instead of loudly proclaiming it to the entire kitchen staff. Does that make sense?"*

They all nodded.

Once we were done eating, an agency staff member announced that Santa had arrived. Santa called each of the children up to sit on his lap and claim their prize. Faith received a package with body wash, nail polish and lotion. Brandon, Henry and Clay each received a remote-control car. Caisen got a big plastic dump truck with a package of building blocks in the back.

Brandon threw his package as he began crying, claiming he didn't get anything special. He said it wasn't fair that he should get the same thing his brothers got. Caisen cried that he didn't get a remote-control car like the other boys. Henry and Clay were excited, until they realized that the batteries needed to be charged. Faith rubbed the body wash over herself, as though it was hand sanitizer.

Honestly, I didn't think the talk about quietly sharing complaints with us would last, but I didn't expect to have it go so wrong, so quickly. Jordan and I thanked the staff for a wonderful event, as we walked our hot-mess kids toward the door, and on to our next activity.

We had tickets to go to an event at our church called *"The Journey,"* which turned out to be a larger production than we had expected.

We were in the main auditorium enjoying a Christmas carol concert, waiting for our turn to experience the wonder of walking through history, to experience the living Bible. When our numbers were called, we made our way out the back door and were corralled into a large, old-style tent. Once inside, we were each given a piece of paper with a name and story on it. We were told to memorize our identities because our lives would depend on it.

While we were being briefed, some Roman guards came barging in, yelling at us, and shoving us towards the exit. The kids were clearly startled, evidenced by their screams and flinches!

Guards on horses waited for us outside, who shoved us towards a small ferry. The kids were both terrified and excited, and squeezed in closely. As we crossed the lake, they loosened up a bit and began to laugh at how dramatically they each had jumped when the first guard busted in.

When we got to the far side of the lake, we climbed off the ferry to begin the walking portion of the tour, where we would be going from cabin to cabin, watching the Bible come to life. We watched an angel appear to Mary, the same angel appear to Joseph, the relationship develop between Mary and Elizabeth, Caesar demand that all baby boys be killed, and so on.

Eventually, we passed through a large marketplace, where people were giving us samples of honey and bread. We saw goats, chickens, and sheep, which fascinated the kids. We also saw people dying wool, weaving blankets, and carpenters building things. To tell you the truth, it felt like being plopped into a scene in Aladdin, except with more of a biblical feel.

As we left the market and headed toward the manger scene, we passed some camels and even some white Siberian tigers. The Roman guards threatened to throw any who had lost their credentials in with the tigers. Again, the kids clung tightly. It felt great to be their source of comfort, whether they noticed or not.

Finally, we came to the manger and saw baby Jesus. The event was spectacular, and prompted a great discussion on the way home, particularly about the mean man who ordered that babies would be killed. We discussed how there will always be people working hard to make the world a better place, and also people who care about their own lives ahead of everyone else's. I strongly encouraged the kids to build reputations they could be proud of, and to encourage others to do the same.

The next morning, we went to church. It seemed like it was going to be one of our better church attempts, because our number didn't get displayed on the big screen, which would have indicated that the church volunteers had a problem with one of our kids. We went to collect the kids with a feeling of success, but ended up finding Henry had a new bracelet around his wrist. I wouldn't have thought anything about the bracelet, except Clay said to Henry, *"Hey, we were supposed to write special notes with those and send them to kids in need! You weren't supposed to take it for yourself!"*

Henry looked me in the eye as he tried to talk his way out of it. *"There was one left over and the teacher said I could have it."*

It was possible, but not likely. *"Henry,"* I said, *"there is still another service after ours, so the teacher couldn't know if there were any left over yet."*

His next quick response clashed with his first, making the lie obvious, so I asked him to return it. That was our window to pry Brandon from the remote control he was still gripping. It wasn't easy, or quiet, but we got him out.

We were all in the car, and I heard the seatbelts clicking. I turned around in my seat to engage Henry about what had happened, and I saw that he was holding a silver dollar. One that he did not have earlier that day.

I asked where he got the silver dollar. Clay responded for him saying, *"I found it! We asked the teacher what to do with it, and he told us to take it to the front desk. Henry told me he would take it to the desk for me."*

Henry didn't respond. He just looked down, angrily.

My words fell out of my mouth. *"Henry, you stole a bracelet AND a dollar from church?"*

He didn't answer.

I asked Jordan to drop Henry and me off at the front door. We walked back to children's ministries, where I asked Henry to give the lady at the desk the silver dollar. He told her he found it, and I chose to leave out the explanation of his intentions.

As we turned, he said, *"Sorry,"* with a bad attitude. As much as I wanted to correct his tone on the spot, I figured that the action of returning something he had claimed for himself was probably challenging enough for one day. We quietly walked back to the car and continued on our way.

Our next stop was the local Christmas tree farm. The kids were given directions to stay with us, and off of the smaller trees. That didn't work so well. I thought about putting each of the kids on leashes, which brought a smile to my face.

Once we picked the tree, we took a family selfie in front of it, making family selfies a new regular part of life. I then took three of the kids home with me, while Jordan kept two with him as he cut down our winner.

At the house, I pulled all of our Christmas decoration bins out of the attic. Faith was in awe. I set the box of outside lights aside so Jordan could hang them, and I brought the indoor décor and tree lights inside. Faith and I unpacked the tree skirt, stand, and lights, while Caisen and Clay looked through the ornaments.

When Jordan got home with Henry and Brandon, he invited the three middle boys to go outside with him. Caisen kept playing with the ornaments while Faith and I attempted to get the tree set up. I thought this was going to be a happy afternoon, until Faith stumbled a little bit and grabbed on to the tree as she tripped towards the wall.

I frantically shouted, *"Let go of the tree!"*

She cried. A lot.

I asked what was wrong, and she cried harder. I tried to understand by talking through the event, while she sobbed. *"Faith, you tripped a little and grabbed on to the tree. I said to let it go so that it wouldn't smash you, and you started crying. I'm not sure what went wrong. Did I upset you?"*

It took a while, but she finally responded, *"You care about the tree more than me!"*

In this moment, I was thankful that Faith was just about as skinny as Brandon, because it made it easy to scoop my eleven-year-old up like a baby, and pull her into my lap as I explained, *"I wasn't worried about the tree at all. The tree was already cut down, rendering it dead. You couldn't make that worse if you tried. I was only worried about what the tree would do to you if you pulled it on top of yourself."*

She cried more, but differently. I felt so sad that this girl had lived such a life where she assumed all raised tones meant someone was in trouble. But that wasn't true. My tone was raised because I cared, which seemed to be a new concept for her. She stayed in my lap, sobbing, for several minutes. I'm not sure if she'd ever been held as she cried before meeting us, but it was starting to become a regular thing. And truthfully, it seemed to be the first real lesson I had worked through with Faith.

Just as Faith began collecting herself, Clay came racing through the house screaming, *"I have to pee!"* We watched him fly by and noticed how quickly he came back out.

Apparently, he had pulled his belt too tight again, making it impossible to open it for nature's next call. So, he made the right choice of asking for help.

Just kidding. That's not what he did.

He didn't know he had a choice, so he peed his pants. Not only did he soak his pants and underwear with urine, but also his socks and shoes. And when he came out, he pretended it wasn't there.

I asked him if there was a problem. His response was, *"What? I couldn't get my belt off,"* with a tone that said, *"No, no problem here, lady."*

"Well, you should go change your clothes, and bring me that outfit so I can wash it, please."

He ran through the house a moment later, with no clothes in his hands. *"Clay, you forgot the dirty clothes,"* I said, and made my way to the laundry closet. He ran back down the hall and when he came back to hand me the mess, I said, *"Remember, your belt needs to stay a little looser, so you can unbuckle it when you need to."*

He muttered something at me as he took off for the front door. He didn't seem concerned that he had just peed his pants. That scared me more than the accident did.

As if this wasn't enough fun for one day, the boys then asked to play with their remote-control cars while Jordan finished stringing up the lights.

Caisen cried right away, but that was no reason to tell the other kids they couldn't play.

It started fine, but fell apart quickly. The cars were all on the same frequency, so their remotes were overlapping and hijacking each other's cars. They got mad and frustrated, and they each broke down in their own way.

It felt like the longest weekend of all time, and I could hardly wait to send them all back to school the next day, for their last week before the long, eighteen-day break.

When Monday morning finally came, I remembered that my school days weren't all that easy, either. Caisen really enjoyed pitching morning fits. Brandon hated rolling out of bed. Faith was extra lost and confused each morning. It felt like getting out of the house on time should be rewarded, but no one ever congratulated me.

We had the typical counseling shenanigans. We had the typical teacher notes indicating that my kids wouldn't stay in their seats, talked out of turn, wouldn't follow directions, and were constantly loud. And, since the kids had started the after-school program, we also got feedback from the facilitators who said the boys were too physical and wouldn't listen to directions.

I would have preferred praise for the kids at the end of the day, but I felt content just knowing I was sharing our chaotic blessing with other adults. It would have been selfish to keep all the joys to myself!

If nothing else, the feedback fueled my efforts to fight for psychological examinations. I mean, they were in trouble everywhere they went! I knew there had to be help out there, but I needed permission to seek it. I checked back in with our caseworker and was told that they were still working on it, and I just needed to be patient. My patience was wearing thin.

I considered signing the kids up for all of the available days of day camp offered during Christmas Break. They only offered camp on Monday and Tuesday of the first, second, and third weeks. It was expensive, and only for six days, but still worth considering.

I ran the idea by Reagan, thinking that having a place to stash the kids would allow her family to come for a softened visit! Reagan hadn't made a final decision yet, but I had a feeling I knew which way it was going to go and started getting my hopes up.

On Wednesday, I picked the kids up after school for counseling. I was greeted by Brandon, who wanted to know if he could eat the snack the program had offered him. I said we would take the snacks home and eat them when we got there, like normal. We were in a hurry to beat the counselors to the house, and since Caisen wasn't given a snack, I didn't want him to get jealous and pitch a fit. However, Brandon saw it differently.

"I don't want to wait! You drive too slow!" he yelled at me. I let a giggle out, as I told him that I would drive as efficiently as I could so that he could have his snack in the timeliest of ways.

As we drove home, Brandon got really worked up. However, I was still relatively entertained by the comment on my driving. Instead of engaging him, I just thought to myself how thankful I was that the counselors were meeting us at the house.

If they chose Brandon first, they could work through this one. If not, then they would at least grab a couple of the other kids, freeing me up for a conversation about why he felt it was so terrible to wait a whole ten minutes before eating his cracker-sticks and cheese. It ended up that they started with other kids, and I was on Brandon duty.

As we rolled through the routine, Faith had completed everything she could on her own and was waiting for her final sessions. She asked if she could work on her Christmas present crafts in her room.

I said, *"Yes,"* and reminded her of some craft manners. When I went to check on her, she had shut herself in her closet with her lamp on the carpet next to her. Another fire hazard, and another craft-manner that I hadn't thought to address ahead of time. I told her the lamp couldn't lie on the carpet, but didn't have the time to follow up with the reason why, because Caisen started screaming in the living room. She really needed to know the reason though because fire safety kept coming up. I made a mental note to check back in with her, but it must have slipped my mind.

Later that night, Faith crawled in bed while I was tucking in the boys. When I made it to her room, she was snuggled up with the same lamp. She had it pulled under the covers, squeezing it like a teddy bear.

She was confused when I quickly and abruptly took it from her.

She explained that she was cold.

I talked to her, in depth, about fire hazards. Then, I told her that the appropriate way to handle the chills is to grab an extra blanket, put on warmer jammies, or ask me for help. She accepted my solution, though I wasn't sure she'd actually hold on to the lesson.

By the end of the day, I was worn out. The next morning, I walked into the day care program headquarters and registered the four kids for six days of camp. I'd use the time to finish Christmas shopping, and breathe. It was the most excitement I'd felt in a while.

The next day was the kids' last day of school before the break, and Jordan was able to get off work by lunchtime. We enjoyed a meal together before braving such establishments as Toys R Us and Walmart. We knew that this Christmas was going to be bigger than any Christmas past or future because we were playing catch up. Most kids already had some toys, activities, games, and puzzles. These kids had accumulated very little. We'd been buying all of the needed items -the coats, shoes, uniforms, toiletries, car seats and everything else- while putting the wanted items on a list. A very long list.

We had come off of three months of list making in preparation for this spree. They needed bikes, which would come from Santa. Thankfully, the foster agency gave us three of them, so we only needed to buy two more. We also needed helmets. The agency got some stuffed animals, so we just needed to fill in the gaps. We also picked up board games, basketballs, a Barbie dollhouse, some Army toys, a Minion Fart Gun, Legos, and much, much more. Lastly, we got each of the kids an iPod touch, the one item they each wanted more than anything else. We did it because we hoped that maybe independent electronics would be a safer, smoother place to start, since sharing video games only resulted in tears, as each of the kids got beat up with remotes.

As I sorted gifts to be wrapped, I had a nice chat with Reagan where she shared some very good news with me. Not only was she coming to visit us, but her trip overlapped with some of the kids' day camp days, which would make it less overwhelming for everyone. They opted for a hotel. I agreed that would be the safest decision. The plan was for them to come down Sunday night, which was only two nights away. I was nervous, but also excited to see my best friend and for my kids to have their first visitors.

When we got off the phone, I briefly wondered if Jack would remember me? I felt a clear line drawn between my old life and my new life, separated by the day I met my kids. Instead of being sad over the months I'd spent away from my friend and her family, I was ecstatic that it was finally time to merge my two worlds. Chaotic or not, I was ready.

On cue, to ruin my happy moment, my alarm-reminder sounded, telling me to pick the kids up from school and to start the long school break. I said a quick prayer before responding to my bossy alarm.

CHAPTER 18

WHEN TWO WORLDS COLLIDE

C hristmas Break was starting, whether we were ready or not. Jordan and I went to pick up Caisen. Nothing too eventful. Just another yellow mark, which I had assumed would be his usual report. At least it wasn't a red mark leading us into our eighteen-day break! The plan was to continue urging him to go-for-green, believing it was possible.

Next, we went to the elementary school to pick up the other four. Jordan stayed in the car with Caisen while I walked into the gym to sign the four kids out.

Clay ran up to me with a new hole in his school pants, ketchup on his shirt, and dirt on his face. I asked what he had for lunch, and he didn't list anything that would have been eaten with ketchup. They had indoor recess that day, so I didn't understand the dirt. That kid was talented.

Faith, my sweet eleven-year-old, was in the corner coloring with a group of kids who I assumed to be either Kindergartners or first-graders.

The care provider explained to me that Henry and Brandon had gotten into a fight. That wasn't anything new. Of course, Brandon's hands were over his face as he was grunting, while Henry was directly arguing with the lady. The arguing, lying, and grunting was much more frustrating than the fighting. I longed for some honesty, even if it was the brutal kind.

I thanked the provider and wished her a wonderful Christmas Break.

On the drive home, we went over the usual, non-counseling-day reminders. Caisen would get in the bath, and the other four would start homework, followed by thirty minutes of reading. This routine was still hard to enforce, but I knew it was worth fighting through, particularly because I needed them to be busy with some sort of task while I started dinner. Therefore, I wasn't going to cave in, no matter how much whining and complaining was coming my way.

As we sat around the dinner table, we laid the groundwork for a successful visit with their new Auntie Reagan and her family. We talked about the fun stuff first and then moved into the behavioral requests. I told them that we needed to keep our voices low and movements slow so that we didn't scare Baby Jack or little Winnie, their wiener dog that didn't like kids. In fact, Winnie barely tolerated the child in her own family, only because Jack regularly let her lick the leftover food off his face.

After each request, they responded in unison with a cheery, *"Yes ma'am,"* using the same tone as when they were told to walk through the corn maze, just before they took off sprinting. I believed in their intentions, but their awareness and ability to follow through were still in question.

We transitioned into talk of our other Christmas Break activities, which didn't ease my nerves at all. When Clay showed excitement over riding bikes, Brandon was irritated by it. When Brandon made requests to swim, Henry said he hated swimming. The ups and downs of each topic were making my head spin.

When dinner was over, the four older kids took turns rolling through the shower, youngest to oldest. We were committed to predictability and routines.

Speaking of predictability, Clay pitched a fit about his shower. He was on the floor next to his bed, reaching into his drawers and throwing his rolled socks at me.

Henry saw an opportunity for a gold star and took his turn like a champ. He even did a little singing while in the shower. When he got out, I asked him what he was singing because I didn't recognize it.

"I don't know," he said. *"I just like making things up."*

Brandon didn't want to miss anything, even though we weren't doing anything in particular, so he was in and out of the bathroom in about fourteen seconds, including taking a shower and brushing his teeth. I pointed out how much dirt was still on him and asked him to try again. After doing a few alligator rolls on the floor, he complied. His second attempt took about three minutes, and he came out still dripping wet with water, shirt stuck to the top of his back. I assumed he'd learn eventually that drying off before dressing is easier, but learning wasn't his strong suit, and the stuck-shirt was becoming a regular occurrence.

I told Faith it was her turn, and she moved toward the bathroom. She forgot what she was doing and walked right past it into her bedroom. I reminded her to take her shower, so she turned back toward the bathroom but ended up at the front door getting into her backpack. I again reminded her she was headed to the bathroom to shower. I'm telling you, this girl was completely untethered.

I felt like I was getting in a groove. At least their theatrics and demands showed some consistency.

We survived Saturday. We had our usual fights over remote control cars, tantrums over Super Mario Bros, fits about showers, complaints of boredom, and claims of starvation. But, we made it. And, I was so excited for visitors to come that none of the kids' antics could kill my mood! I was desperate to see a familiar face and to share my new normal with someone.

Sunday rolled around, and we headed to church. When we checked the kids into children's ministries, they handed us stickers to put on each of the kid's shirts, with numbers that corresponded to the ticket they gave us. Much like a coat check. As usual, I sat with sweaty palms, staring at the number display, praying the kids' teachers wouldn't summon us. I'm not sure of God's reason for it, but our prayer went unanswered. We didn't even make it through the worship music before our number went up on the big screen. The guessing game began.

Caisen's classroom was closest to the auditorium. We stopped by, and his leaders said they didn't alert us. One down.

On the way to the school-aged kids' services, I wondered which of the kids was busted. Really, it could have been any of them. As we neared the front desk, we learned that it was most of them. It was not a proud moment when we saw three of our boys waiting for us with their heads hung low.

The volunteer explained, *"Henry and Clay were arguing, and we probably could have handled that, but Brandon inserted himself and the fight got out of hand."*

I looked at the boys. Clay and Henry slouched lower into their chairs, clearly feeling some sort of remorse or embarrassment over what had happened.

The volunteer continued, *"Henry and Clay are welcome to stay, but we aren't having any luck calming Brandon down."*

Brandon cut in, *"Because I didn't do anything. They just don't know how to do their jobs. I didn't even do anything."*

Brandon, sitting with his forearms over his face, continued to mumble to himself as I checked in with Henry and Clay. The two boys were then sent back into their class, as Brandon was asked to join us in the big service.

Removing him from the children's area frustrated Brandon more, but it needed to be done. He was still rambling that it wasn't his fault, with his arms across his face.

"I don't believe you started it," I said, *"and I didn't believe that you did any worse than the other two. If you were calm, you would have gone back into your service, but you still seem upset."*

"I'm not upset," he blurted. *"It wasn't even my fault. They should be in trouble, not me."*

"The fight wasn't the problem," I calmly stated, *"but after you chose to engage in their fight, you struggled to calm back down. You aren't with us as punishment, but as an opportunity to calm yourself."*

Being with Brandon was like being trapped on a Merry-Go-Round, that went 'round and 'round without the possibility of stopping. I wasn't sure we'd calm him down before leaving church, but I hoped we could redirect him before our guests arrived that afternoon because a frustrated Brandon was a guaranteed nightmare for all witnesses.

We made our way into the large auditorium, filled with more people than I would have liked. I tried to keep my arm around my little Hulk as we sat, and Jordan put his hand on Brandon's resting hand. Brandon seemed uncomfortable and confused, so I reassured him we had already moved on, and he could, too.

I wondered if he'd believe us, or if he'd continue to defend himself and would do so in an embarrassing, distracting manner. He looked like he was waiting for the other shoe to drop, as quiet as I'd ever seen him.

I tried to maintain a posture that would show Brandon I was focused on the Pastor, but I was actually reeling over what I knew about Brandon. Certainly, he was operating under some misguided assumptions, and we needed to pound him with some new messaging. We needed him to learn that our goal was not to punish him, or the other kids. Rather, we were using appropriate consequences and rewards to help guide better choices. The biggest lesson this boy needed to learn was that even if we were angry, disappointed or frustrated, we were still choosing to love him. If only I had a magic wand to aid in the process.

He wasn't going to internalize these lessons quickly, so we stayed focused on baby steps. The victory in this instance was that Brandon was able to calm down just as the service was ending. In fact, he had changed the story in his mind by the time we got the other kids and was bragging about being specially selected to go with us to our service. I giggled to myself, and noticed that Henry giggled as well. I was starting to see that Henry and I had similar senses of humor.

After lunch, we went to the park to play. I wanted to get some energy out of them before our visitors arrived, even if I had to stay *"it"* in freeze tag.

When we got home, the kids quickly found reasons to fight. I put the TV on and started the kids through the shower routine, beginning with Caisen. As Jordan rotated them, I got to work on dinner, overly excited to see my friend, and for her to meet the newest members of my family!

When they finally arrived, it was total chaos. Winnie was excited when they pulled up, as usual. She ran to the front door, clearly expecting to have a weekend filled with fun dog-play. When she was greeted by kids, she promptly found a hiding place behind the couch. Our dogs couldn't fit behind the couch, so Winnie ran back and forth along the back of the couch to see my dogs, who were running around the front of the couch to see her. Caisen and Henry were trying to push through our big dogs to squeeze their way into Winnie's space, which wasn't working well. They got trampled and Winnie avoided them desperately, but they stayed determined.

Meanwhile, Jack tried to walk in the house and couldn't get far. Clay, Brandon and Faith were in his face, overwhelming him. He tried to turn back to his parents, but couldn't find them from inside the crowd. I scooped him up; he greeted me with a smile. He remembered me.

When Reagan and David got inside, we did introductions. They acknowledged that Faith and Caisen were going to be the easiest to remember, but the other three were going to be tough. That made sense, considering they were all the same size - size eight. To be fair, they weren't the exact same size, because Brandon, the oldest boy, was actually an eight-slim, so he was slightly smaller than his two younger brothers. Thank goodness for belts!

It made my heart happy to see Reagan and David engaging with the kids, as the kids were hitting them with questions in rapid-fire style. It was Auntie Reagan this and Uncle David that. Faith grabbed Jack by the hand and led him to her room. They were going to play with her stuffies. She shut the door, so I went back and opened it.

Reagan made a comment about how cute they were back there playing. I urged her to keep her ears tuned, because if Jack began crying, Faith would probably try to resolve it herself, instead of getting help. My additional fear was that she might prevent him from leaving the room if he desired.

While Reagan and I were setting the table, all the kids played and chatted, loudly. It sounded like Faith, Jack, and now Caisen were doing well in her room. Jordan and David chatted with a clear view of the rest of the boys in the living room. And, Reagan and I were listening to all of it. Things seemed to be chaotic, yet smooth enough to still count as a success.

Just as I was beginning to feel comfortable, I heard Henry yelling, *"Stop it, Brandon! She picked me, not you!"* while Winnie screeched loudly.

I ran from the kitchen to see that Winnie gave Henry a chance and was sitting between Henry and the arm of the couch.

Brandon screamed, *"It's my turn, you already saw her!"* as Brandon grabbed at the dog who was trying to retreat into Henry's side.

I stepped in between them and Brandon's arms went across his face as he said, *"You always take Henry's side."*

I found that fascinating, but it didn't change the fact that Brandon was trying to force himself on a dog that wasn't interested.

I asked him to look at my face. He didn't. I asked him again. He reluctantly lined his arms up so that he could peek out from in between them. I asked him to put his arms down. It took a minute, but he did it. That's when I approached the lesson.

"Are dogs toys or living creatures?" I asked.

"The second one," he grunted at me.

"I agree." I responded, *"So it isn't really fair for us to make her choices for her. If she made the choice to sit by Henry, we should let her. And maybe if we respect her choices, she'll give you a chance, too."*

"No. That's stupid. He had his turn."

I asked, *"Who should choose where Winnie sits? Winnie, Henry, or you?"*

No answer.

"Do you remember when I told you that Winnie was scared of kids?" I asked.

He nodded.

"That makes it special that she chose to sit with any of you kids. If we are calm and respectful, maybe she'll choose to do it more." I paused briefly, as he seemed to be considering my words. *"But, if you grab at her while yelling, it will probably make her more scared."*

The guilt made his arms go right back up.

"I'm not upset with you, Brandon," I said, *"but I would like you to be more respectful of the dog. We don't grab at our animals, and we shouldn't grab at anyone else's, either."*

I hated that every incident, no matter the size, required such detailed conversations. The kids didn't have the trust to blindly follow my lead or directions. Also, their history didn't help them to develop common sense. It was taking a lot of work to rewire them.

When Brandon settled back down, I returned to the kitchen to find that Reagan had dinner set and ready. I was surprised to see that food-prep continued WHILE I was dealing with a crisis. She was sitting at the table and gave me a pathetic look as she giggled.

"You told me how easily the kids trigger and how quickly things escalate, but it's still hard to believe how such a small thing could turn into such a big issue," she said. *"How do you keep from laughing in those silly talks?"*

That, to me, was validation. *"You call that a big issue? You haven't seen anything, yet,"* I said, before joining her in giggling about the silliness of fighting over a dog.

Anyway, dinnertime came, and we had many plates out! Jordan and David sat at the dining room table with my kids, while Reagan and I sat with Jack in the kitchen.

After dinner, we confirmed our plans for the next day. It took us a little while, with all of the interruptions and redirections. But, when we figured it out, Reagan's family left for their hotel.

We finished the bedtime routine of brushing teeth and getting jammies on, and closed the night out with a little bit of reading. It wasn't easy to settle them down after all the excitement of having guests, but we got through it.

We had to go back into the boys' room several times to ask them to quiet down. Caisen earned himself a timeout, but that wasn't anything new. After the boys settled, I moved over to Faith's floor, which was really getting old.

The next morning went mostly as planned. There were many loud voices all going at once. There were many fast feet pattering through the halls. There was some complaining and arguing. All of these things had become the general atmosphere in our house, which is why we stayed on top of our reminders and redirections. I was certain I would one day succeed in taking my house back! In the meantime, I accepted the zoo we lived in.

By nine o'clock in the morning, we were out the door. First, Jordan and I dropped the four kids off at their day camp. It took a little while because we were getting an unsolicited explanation of the itinerary and a tour of the place. Truthfully, I didn't care when lunch was, or where the bathrooms were, because I was eager to experience my moment of freedom. As we walked out the door, I looked at Jordan and said, *"Four down!"*

Next, we drove to Reagan and David's hotel where I traded Jordan for Reagan and Jack. Jordan and David were off to enjoy a guys' day, and I was going to enjoy the day with Reagan, after arranging the car seats and booster seats for Jack to fit in the middle row. I was thrilled to spend a day with my bestie, each of us with only one son.

First, we met up for breakfast with another of our friends and her young daughter. Just three moms with their little kids! I planned to blend in with the other moms, but I struggled while looking at the menu, which drew attention.

Caisen pointed to the pancakes on his menu, and I read to him that there was an option for either two slices of bacon or two sausage links. I asked him which he'd prefer, and he looked at me like I was talking in a different language.

"But I want the pancake," he said.

"Of course," I reassured him, *"We'll order the pancake. But you also get to pick which side you want."* I used my hands to gesture as I described the items, *"Bacon is flat and long, and the links are shorter and round. Sound familiar?"*

He just stared at me and blinked a couple times, like I was hurting his brain.

I asked the waitress if I could do one of each, and she said no, *"either two slices of bacon, or two links."* I didn't understand why it was a problem, but it wasn't the time or place to push it. I just wanted a nice breakfast with mom-friends. So, I ordered him the bacon, figuring he could try my sausage, and we'd know better for next time. In the end, he liked both. Not that he said as much, but he ate it all. I was thankful he wasn't a picky eater!

After breakfast, we all headed to Toys R Us. I had returns to make and some planned purchases. Reagan and our other friend had lists of their own too.

I slyly told Caisen we were shopping for other people, so that he wouldn't mess things up by blabbing before Christmas. It was going mostly well. Except, Caisen wanted everything and was getting worked up. Thankfully, he wasn't the only kid behaving this way, so I wasn't bothered by it. But, the louder he got, the harder it was to ignore.

Soon he escalated to be the worst in the store, and as embarrassment crept in, something spectacular happened. Jack took an item out of the little plastic toy cart that our friend's daughter was pushing, and then she picked up the entire cart like a champ and whacked him across the back with it. He tumbled. They were both screaming and crying. I couldn't help but laugh. The two moms apologized to each other, and I felt relief that it wasn't my kid.

When we got home, we put the boys down for naps. While they slept, it was just Reagan, me, and the dogs. We sat on the couch and talked about everything and nothing at the same time. It felt oddly normal, yet long overdue.

It was also short lived because the little ones woke up with full tanks of energy. Caisen was so entertained by Jack, who was trying to climb up the bunk bed ladders and was bouncing on the bed. He also thought it was funny the way Jack was playing with his toys. Caisen kept face palming himself when Jack *"didn't use it right."*

When the time came, we loaded Caisen and Jack up in the car and headed to go get the rest of the kids. Jack got more and more overwhelmed as they piled in, and it showed on his face. I felt his pain. It was always a full car.

The three back row kids were competing for Jack's attention with dramatic faces and flailing fingers. Clay was looking sad because he wanted to sit closer to Baby Jack. Caisen was chatting away about how our day went.

At one point, Jack dropped his sippy cup, and all the kids went crazy yelling to Auntie Reagan that he dropped it.

Reagan said it was ok and that she'd get it when we got to our destination. However, Jack enjoyed my kids' response, so he proceeded to throw his shoes, socks, and a stuffy overboard. He thought it was hilarious when they responded so loudly and with face palms.

We drove straight to Reagan's hotel. She hopped out to go ride with David, and Jordan hopped in with us. Jack typically couldn't handle Reagan's absence, but he was so distracted and entertained by my crazy children that he hardly noticed she had left.

We drove to B & D Burgers. Once inside, the greeter asked if Clay and Henry were twins. It wasn't the first time this had happened. Clay loved the question and always said yes. Henry hated the question and abruptly exclaimed that they weren't. Thankfully, we were quickly seated.

First, my kids began fighting over who would sit by Baby Jack. Brandon did not win, so his arms went across his face and he began chanting about how unfair it was. Then, there was fighting over who would sit by Auntie Reagan, Uncle David, Jordan and me.

Eventually they were all seated, and the waiter came to take our drink order. It was an exciting night, so we ordered the kids Sprites, with the explanation that once the first cup was empty, they were switching to water.

I tried asking each kid what they wanted to eat, but they were more interested in fighting over who had which colored crayons. They all wanted the colors that the other kids were holding even if they didn't have a purpose for that color at that time, just in case they needed it later.

While trying to bring our volume down a notch, I again gave them their food options. It was a nightmare. Every time a kid gave me his order, the other kids began changing theirs. We went around a few times before each kid was ready with their final answer. But, at that point, the waiter was nowhere to be seen.

While we waited for the waiter to return, we attempted to chat, but every other sentence was *"Sit back down!"* My kids were determined to stand and kneel in their seats because it was making Jack laugh. They were also climbing around each other in the booth. It was obnoxious, and David's face showed shock. I reminded him that the kids were emotionally younger than they were physically.

In one perfect moment, Caisen was messing around with a little more energy than he could control, and despite his best efforts, he couldn't recover. In slow motion, his torso tipped over, and while trying to compensate, his feet rotated directly over him. As he continued to rotate, he hit the back of his head on the table with a good thump, and he continued to roll. Next, he slid backwards and head first off of the bench, onto the floor. The last thing we saw going down was his feet.

The crashing sound caused most of us to gasp, as we were clearly worried. Then, he bounced back up and screamed, *"I'm OK!"* with his arms raised over his head like a champion! I couldn't do anything but laugh. This was my life. This was my circus. Reagan was going to be taking some great stories home with her.

The best part of Caisen's crash was that it distracted Brandon back into a good mood. Even though he wasn't sitting next to Jack, he resumed making funny faces at him and trying hard to get him to say his name. However, despite Brandon's efforts, the only name Jack chose to say was, *"Clay."* And just like that, Brandon was upset again.

After dinner, Reagan and David said their final goodbyes to the kids, because they were going to be heading home the next day while the kids were at day camp. They may not have learned how to tell Clay and Henry apart yet, but the relationships had started and the hugs goodbye were precious. I was so happy that my worlds were colliding! I'm not going to lie; I cried when I saw that my kids had just been officially welcomed into the family!

The next day, I dropped the four older kids off as planned and went to drop off Caisen. He and I walked into the building -- and right back out.

Unbeknownst to me, they had a rule about dropping kids off by nine o'clock in the morning, so our nine thirty attempt was a no-go. Mom-fail.

The roughest, toughest consequence of this misunderstanding was the realization that Jordan and I had to entertain Caisen while organizing and wrapping all of the kids' Christmas presents!

We weren't able to get everything completed before it was time to collect the other four kids, but what was left would wait until after Faith was asleep. It was December 23rd and there was no camp on the 24th, so we had no time to spare. I felt the pressure.

That night, the kids were excited to have met Auntie Reagan and the family. They were excited Christmas was so close. Clay was excited that he was done with day camp for the week because they made all kids six and under wear life vests in the pool, which uncomfortably rubbed his armpits. All in all, there was a lot of excitement. It was great to see, but made bedtime more difficult. Eventually, we got through the necessary steps and only had to walk back in about eleven-teen times to ask them to stop talking, arguing, yelling, and bouncing around. Oh, the joys of having four boys in one room.

Then, I sat on Faith's floor. I lay there for about an hour, and she was still tossing, turning, and trying to strike random conversations about where I thought unicorns lived and which of the Care Bear stuffies was my favorite. I tried my best to wait patiently, but I didn't have the time. When she rolled over and tried to hand me another stuffed animal, I had a special response for her.

"This isn't a slumber party," I said, *"and I actually have my own bed waiting for me."*

She stared blankly, which I accepted as her go-to look.

"I still have things to do before bed," I told her, *"and I can't wait any more hours for you to sleep. I'm going to my room, across the hall. I'll listen for you, but I can't sit here anymore."*

She didn't handle it well. Her eyes were no longer blank. They were glossy. I worried she was scared, so I explained a little further.

"I have Christmas stuff to do, and if I don't get my tasks done, there won't be presents."

All of a sudden, she was fine. *"I'll be fine, as long as you check on me,"* she said.

"I will, Faith. Don't worry."

I walked out the door, feeling free, and I heard her say, *"Good luck."* I looked back and saw she was smiling at me, with a big, cheesy, present-hungry grin. I smiled and sped up, before she had a chance to change her mind.

Jordan and I intentionally talked loudly while wrapping, so she could hear us. We also took turns checking on her, always finding her smiling and waving. I didn't think she needed the checks, but she thought so, and I wanted to be sure I held up my end of the promise. I couldn't risk moving backward in our pursuit of trust.

We didn't finish wrapping, but I was struggling to keep my eyes open. Jordan checked one last time and found that she was asleep, so we closed up shop and went to bed, together. Neither of us had the energy for chatting, so we shared a quick kiss and went to sleep. I can't be certain, but I think I had dreams of ribbons and glitter paper coming to get me. It was my first Christmas as a mom, and it was exhausting.

CHAPTER 19

AH, POOP

Having Reagan visit and having Jack remember me, were all the Christmas presents I needed. I asked the kids if the visit was enough for them, and they said no. So, we continued with our scheduled plans for Christmas Eve and Christmas.

Christmas Eve obviously came first. We tried to keep the kids entertained because their fits were no fun. We brought out coloring books and crayons, which lasted about fifteen minutes. When they whined and complained, we reminded them that Santa wasn't going to like their bad attitudes. It helped, to an extent. We put on the TV, which worked for about twenty minutes. When they whined and complained, we reminded them that Santa wasn't going to like their bad attitudes. It barely helped.

We went outside to play with remote control cars, but that was over before it even began. When they whined and complained, we reminded them that Santa wasn't going to like their bad attitudes. It almost helped.

We went to a park, which lasted about an hour. When they whined and complained, we reminded them that Santa wasn't going to like their bad attitudes. It helped, but only slightly.

We took the dogs for a walk, and we barely made it down the street before the kids whined and complained. We reminded them that Santa wasn't going to like their bad attitudes. It may have helped, but not enough for me to take notice.

We tried to keep rolling all day. I didn't want to have any major meltdowns on Christmas Eve because I knew I didn't want to burn out over the next fourteen school-less days. I was in prevention mode like my life depended on it.

As we finished our dinner, I patted myself on the back because we only had a handful of fifteen to thirty-minute-long tantrums throughout the day. However, when shower time arrived, not even a Santa reminder could help.

Caisen lost his mind, which wasn't new, but also wasn't on my list of things I wanted to deal with.

I did my best to calm him, but it wasn't working, and we didn't have all night. He screamed and kicked, and flipped the light switches up and down, which I'm sure he learned from Brandon, until Jordan scooped Caisen up and plopped him in the tub. Caisen tried to act like he was mad, but his fake anger faded when some bath toys plopped in beside him.

About ten minutes into his bath, Jordan popped in to check on him and shouted, *"Hey Jess, you need to come look at this,"* so I moved toward the bathroom. I wished I could un-see what I saw.

Apparently, Caisen had gotten out of the tub to poop and then climbed back into the tub. Without wiping. We know he didn't wipe because he scooted himself over the edge of the tub to get back into the water, which left a large amount of poop smeared along the tub wall.

Caisen looked up and said, *"Huh?"*

I must have given a confused look in return.

Jordan asked, *"Did you notice the poop right next to your face?"*

Without breaking eye contact, Caisen said, *"It wasn't me."*

Jordan processed out loud. He pointed out that the poop-smear wasn't there when he put Caisen in the bathroom, no one else had come in or out, and that Caisen was the only one in our family short enough to cause such markings.

I chimed in to say that we weren't upset, but that we needed him to let us know about problems like that because it wasn't ok for him to just be hanging out with his poop. I also said he needs to do a better job with his wiping.

"I already do a good job wiping." The poop streak didn't sway his confidence.

Without first admitting a problem, the step of fixing it surely wasn't around the corner. I made a mental note that I needed to address hygiene-denial with him, and that I might as well talk it through with everyone else again, too.

Next shower should have been Clay's, but he lost control. I considered sending him to bed without a shower, as he rolled on his bedroom floor throwing socks at me, but I didn't want him to think that future fits could get him out of showers.

With a strong mom tone, I made it clear he wasn't going to be watching TV or hanging out with the family until he was ready to follow directions. I mean it was just a shower, for Heaven's sake!

I let everyone else go ahead of Clay while he continued to buck around in his room. And when I say, *"buck,"* I mean it literally. He was aggressively flopping around much like a bull does while trying to rid himself of riders. It probably goes without saying that he was screaming, *"I hate you,"* at me, with an occasional *"You're mean,"* or *"You're stupid."* What a darling.

During Clay's episode, Henry, Brandon, and Faith showered and brushed their teeth. Brandon had to shower twice because he was only in the bathroom for about thirty-seconds, and I knew that this early-pubescent boy needed at least a few minutes to rid himself of the B.O. he had developed throughout the day and properly clean his pearly whites.

When everyone else was finished, I went back to Clay and said, *"You're going to miss story time if you don't get yourself in the shower in the next three minutes."* I let him see that I was setting the timer on my phone.

He screamed so loud and deep that his face turned bright red and looked like it might explode! He dropped to the ground like his soul had just been crushed. He laid motionless, for two of his three minutes. I softly let him know that he had one minute left to start his shower.

He rolled over, grabbed his jammies, and stepped toward the bathroom. I noticed that he hadn't grabbed clean underwear. I could have told him, but I didn't think he could handle the news. He was under too much stress already. Instead, I said, *"Thank you for making the right choice. Once you're ready, we'll start the bedtime story, together."*

When I heard the water turn off, I grabbed him some Minion underpants and stood outside the door. When he cracked it to yell for me, I cut him off by shoving his britches through the small opening. He giggled and thanked me. His giggle made up for the fit he had thrown, mostly.

After reading The Soldier's Night Before Christmas, we passed out hugs and kisses to the boys. We wished them each sweet, Christmas Eve dreams and made our escape.

We followed Faith to her room and after tucking her in, I assumed I could go to my room again. She cried, loudly.

"Faith," I said, *"you were fine last night. And I know you'll be fine tonight, too. I'll be nearby. I love you."* I smiled softly as I turned and walked out the door.

She ran after me.

"Faith," I said a little more sternly than I meant to, *"you were fine last night. What makes tonight any different?"*

She stared blankly.

"Does that mean you were only fine because I told you I was getting your presents ready?"

"No," she said. *"It wasn't because of the presents. I really need you to stay with me."*

I sighed deeply.

She had her usual blanket and pillow setup on the floor waiting for me, but I refused to lie there. I didn't even sit there. I sat up against the wall, next to the door. *"We aren't having slumber parties in here. I'm only sitting here to meet your need. I have my own room, bed and husband waiting for me. I need for you to be able to sleep on your own, so I'm going to slowly transition out."*

Surely it wasn't what she wanted to hear on Christmas Eve, but it needed to be said. It was time to help her develop age-appropriate skills and abilities.

When she fell asleep, Jordan and I went into the garage and assembled a basketball system, complete with a backboard, rim, net, and both water and sandbags to anchor it. After completing that task, we moved all of the gifts to the living room and set up for Christmas. We made sure the stockings were filled and hung nicely. We stacked presents tall and wide. We had basketballs and helmets inside, hinting at the hoop and bikes waiting outside. When everything looked just right, we happily tucked ourselves into bed. It was another late night in a long string of late nights, but I felt encouraged. We were about to celebrate our first Christmas as a large family, and I was finally going to start working my way back to my own bedroom, which was my Christmas gift to myself.

The next morning was Christmas. We walked into the living room, and the first thing I heard was Brandon's screechy voice saying, *"Our other Christmases in foster care were way better than this. At Granny B's house, we had presents all the way down the hall."*

There were so many presents in our living room and all he could do was complain? I was hurt by his initial reaction on our first Christmas together, but deep down, I wasn't surprised.

As we began digging into gifts, it seemed as though many things were near misses. I mean, it was obvious they loved all of their gifts, based on their posturing and gestures. However, their words indicated they would prefer different colors, or wanted what someone else got, and they definitely wanted more.

Jordan and I tried to maintain our smiles as the kids critiqued everything they opened. It hurt that our work wasn't appreciated, but no one in our home deserved blame. It was another moment where Jordan and I had to suck it up and lean on each other. So, each time our eyes met, we silently offered each other affirmations, with subtle smiles and eye gestures.

When the kids were done opening gifts, the real madness began. They were tearing through packaging, tossing things in every direction, and loudly screaming over the top of each other that Jordan and I needed to install batteries and open tough boxes. We recognized this was probably happening in every home that celebrated Christmas, but that didn't make it any less overwhelming.

There were only two of us, and five of them. So, we asked each of them to grab just three things they wanted us to finish opening for them immediately, saying we'd get them started with those items, and would finish the others while they began playing. This did not work well.

They were so upset and sad that they couldn't have ALL of their own things freed from their boxes at once, even tags off of clothes, before anyone else had help opening any of their things. They were so desperate and pathetic. I'd never seen so many tears on Christmas morning!

As soon as we possibly could, we sent the kids outside. We figured the bikes would eat up a good chunk of time. And truthfully, if I was going to give up seventy-five percent of my garage to seven bikes and one pulling cart, then I wanted to see them used. And when the need arose, we also had the basketballs and new hoop that would occupy time and energy, right?

Hardly.

First, Clay and Caisen both cried that their bikes had training wheels, and Henry cried that his didn't. We asked Clay and Caisen to do a few passes with them on, to be sure they were ready, and they took off on the bikes. While the others were working out the kinks of riding, Jordan put the training wheels back on for Henry. It didn't take long to assemble them, but to Henry it was an eternity.

It wasn't long before all five of them were riding around. Brandon had the tension so loose on his bike that his feet were circling way too fast, but he wasn't actually going all that fast. He kind of looked like the horrible neighbor from the Wizard of Oz, the one who took little Toto and put him in the basket, then rode off with him on her bike. I think it was the intense posture. All I could hear in my head was the music played during the tornado. I smiled at the visual, recognizing that Brandon often played the role of the wicked witch in my life.

After only four passes, it was obvious that Clay and Henry both needed to lose the training wheels. The wheels weren't helping them and were mostly just in their way. Caisen, on the other hand, needed the extra wheels. He was a little madman, who also seemed to be magnetically drawn to the other kids' bikes.

Clay was excited to get the extra wheels off.

Henry panicked. He asked if we could get him knee pads, elbow pads, and wrist guards first.

Clay hopped right on his two-wheeler and took off. He crashed into everything, but that wasn't stopping him, or even slowing him! He had the wind in his face and nothing else mattered. So, after his third crash into the same garbage can, I moved it. It may not have been bothering him, but I still felt it was the good parent thing to do.

Henry, on the other hand, was overly terrified. Jordan was helping him balance and giving him all the right cues. He didn't pick it up as quickly as Clay, but he was doing way better than he gave himself credit for. He was certain he was going to crash and die, but he wasn't even wobbling. His skills grew much faster than his confidence. After about five passes, he was riding on his own. He was anxious, but he was doing it.

While we were bonding with the younger three by helping them learn to ride, Brandon was teasing them and criticizing them. When they ignored him, he complained he was bored. He decided riding bikes was stupid and tried to get the other boys to quit riding too. It didn't work. That made him mad, which triggered the first fit of Christmas Day.

Brandon grew louder and angrier, chucked a basketball down the street, and attempted to tip the basketball hoop. So, I led him back into the house, where he fully unleashed his anger on the back of the couch. I heard the wood in the back of the couch buckling with each kick.

I'd love to say this was the only fit of Christmas. But, no. I'd love to say they were all resolved quickly at least. But, that would be a lie. I'd love to say that the day was great, all things considered. But that would be a stretch.

A neighbor brought us a package of large stick pretzels, dipped in chocolate and covered in sprinkles. She was my Christmas Day miracle! I gave one to each of the kids and saved the rest to be a special treat for Jordan and me, after getting the kids to bed. It was something to look forward to.

As if the fits weren't enough to keep us busy, we had ANOTHER hygiene parenting-emergency. I will never forget that on our first Christmas together, Caisen came out of the bathroom with poop on his fingers. Jordan found it and told him to go wash his hands. He threw himself on the ground. Who pitches a fit about washing poop off their hands? Caisen, that's who!

Jordan picked him up and took him into the bathroom, which smelled terrible, as usual. Upon inspection, Jordan found that Caisen had been throwing his toilet paper in the garbage can instead of the toilet. However, there was only one square in there. After some discussion, it was determined that Caisen only rarely wiped and only with one square. Sometimes that square would rip, and his fingers would get *"dirty,"* and he would throw the square away.

No wonder his undies were so disgusting!

As Jordan tried to explain proper wiping etiquette to him, AGAIN, Caisen maintained his stubborn attitude of *"I am doing it right."*

As I stood there watching the conversation unfold, I wondered if the kids would ever seek improvements and growth. Or, would they live with poop in their pants and on their fingers forever?

At least now I knew why that bathroom always smelled extra bad. I mean, people told me that their kids' bathrooms smelled, but I felt ours was extreme. Poop left out told me I wasn't just being sensitive.

And to be clear, the poop and pee tissues in the trash bucket was in addition to the still prevalent problem of the boys peeing all over the bathroom. Pee around the toilet seemed to be a normal thing, but pee on the wall across from the toilet was disturbing to me! I tried to accept that boys were just gross, but then I remembered Faith's period smear and our ongoing conversations about proper pad disposal. Therefore, I decided that all kids were gross, not just boys.

I did my best to hold on to the notion that flaws are potential. If that truly was the case, then the sky was the limit for these kids! Their potential translated to hope for me, that one day, I wouldn't have to talk about bodily excretions of any kind while also prepping a holiday feast.

As we took our seats for an early ham dinner on Christmas Day, Clay asked, *"Who is your favorite?"*

I wasn't going to name any one child because that would cause a problem. Also, I was still in shock over the disgusting bathroom behaviors we had just readdressed. I had no favorite, and I didn't see the benefit in announcing which of them I saw as the least challenging.

Jordan responded with a standard, *"You're all my favorite."*

I said, *"Butter is my favorite,"* in a silly tone. Three of the kids laughed, reminding me that she was a dog.

Clay seemed confused. He must have thought I misinterpreted his question. So, he tried again, speaking louder and slower this time. *"No, I meant which one of us is your favorite?"*

"I understand your question," I said, *"and I still pick Butter."*

He teared up in frustration and asked me again, so I told him I was being silly. It was sad to me that he couldn't pick up on my tone or facial gestures enough to recognize silliness.

Henry was listening to the whole thing with great anticipation. When I refused to answer, he broke out in tears, exclaiming, *"I'm nobody's favorite!"*

More tears for Christmas. Awesome!

Clearly, he needed reassurance. *"Henry, you five were our favorites out of ALL the kids waiting to be adopted. We CHOSE you, because you are ALL a favorite!"* His expression changed, though a few more tears escaped.

Sadly, encouraging Henry triggered Brandon. I certainly didn't say anything to imply I liked any one of them over the others, but Brandon quickly got irritated. Maybe it was the effort I put into easing Henry's pain. Or, maybe it was disappointment for not being named the only favorite. Or, maybe it was just discomfort with having such a loving moment. Either way, he fussed. And, considering how much fussing he had already been doing, I knew a big fit was on its way.

Before leaving the table, Brandon asked if we could watch *"How the Grinch Stole Christmas,"* one last time before packing up our Christmas movies and decorations. His tone told me he expected us to say, *"No,"* but we said, *"Yes,"* and asked everyone to get through their bedtime routine quickly, so that we could get the movie started.

I did the dishes while Jordan got the kids ready and into their movie-watching positions. Not only had we established assigned seats for movie watching, but also for sitting at the table, riding in our vehicle, and for restaurant table formations. We certainly were doing our best to establish routines.

I came around the corner to join them as the previews were ending, and they looked so calm. I was on the verge of having a *"look at my beautiful family"* moment, but it fell apart before it really came together.

Just as Jordan hit play, Brandon decided that the movie was going to be boring, even though he picked it out. His hands went over his face and he mumbled, as per the usual. I tried to throw him off with, *"Anyone want another chocolate covered pretzel dipped in sprinkles?"* But it was too late. There was no turning back.

Of course, the other kids went crazy with excitement over treats, which were only offered to distract Brandon. I couldn't tend to Brandon and serve the others, so Jordan got pretzel duty, and I got Brandon. I could have shed a tear over losing my treats, but my attention turned to Brandon as he executed a perfect alligator roll. I caught myself admiring that he never hurt himself while aggressively rolling across the floor, knowing that I couldn't lose control like that and come out unscathed.

I knew his rolls meant serious business, but I couldn't help but find the humor in a ten-year-old rolling around on the floor, back and forth, yelling about how unfair it was that he should be allowed to stay up late to watch the movie he had requested. Though he worded it differently, there was no way to make his circumstances sound bad.

I looked at my phone and saw it was getting late. If we waited much longer to start the movie, we'd have to cancel. I asked Brandon to leave the room until he was calm. Silly me. Bad idea.

He threw his shoes at me and kicked the couch some more. I'm sure it hurt without shoes, but he didn't want to hear me ask about his feet.

I walked to his room, knowing he would follow me. I didn't like being his target, but at least it gave Jordan room to start the movie with the other kiddos, without me, because I was in the boys' bedroom with a lunatic.

I offered Brandon encouragements. I asked him to take deep breaths. I asked him to slow down and try to figure out what he was upset about. No matter my tone or angle, he seemed to be getting worse. I thought maybe he just needed to get it out of his system, so I stopped talking.

As I sat there quietly reflecting on my own sadness over missing another holiday movie, I watched him unload the clothes out of the closet. Not just his, but his brothers' too. As he aimlessly ruined my closet setup, I began to picture that he was my very own Grinch, and that maybe when he was done with the clothes, his heart would grow, and he'd revive my night.

No such luck. Instead, he headed to the dresser. After unloading each of the drawers, he then tipped the dresser over. My little Grinch was escalating, so I tried intervening again.

"Brandon, is this really better than watching the movie?" I asked. "Really, think about it. Is this how you want Christmas to end?"

He looked right at me as he picked up and dumped the boys' shoe bucket. Such a punk. Since he looked right at me as he dumped the shoes, I thought maybe he was doing it for attention. If that was true, then I must have been wrong all along for thinking it was lack of control. Right or wrong, it was worth exploring the possibility.

I tucked my head down in a way where I could still see what he was doing from my peripheral vision, but I had to look like I wasn't paying attention. I sat on the floor with my arms around my knees as he destroyed their beds. He threw everyone's pillows, tossed their stuffies, and pulled off blankets. The room was a disaster, and he was showing no signs of stopping. All the while, the rest of my family was in the other room, laughing at the movie and eating my treats.

He began rocking the bunk beds back and forth, and I closed my eyes, which were still tucked downward, in order to hide my disappointment. As I sighed to myself, he put some extra umph into the bed and pushed it over, directly at me. Thankfully, I looked up in time to see it coming and was able to catch the rungs of the ladder in order to keep from being totally smooshed. But that didn't detract from the realization that he tried to smash me under the bunk beds.

I couldn't push the beds back up while still seated on the floor, so I called for Jordan, who came racing in. He grabbed the beds and helped me to push them back up, freeing me.

In a split second, I processed so many emotions. I felt betrayed, but then ruled it out, because Brandon didn't owe me loyalty. I felt endangered, but it didn't make sense to react as though the danger was still present. I felt relief because I wasn't hurt. Then I noticed I felt relief that Brandon wasn't hurt either, which prompted me to consider his feelings.

His arms were over his face, so I couldn't read much off of him. I did see that his eyeball was peering through the crevice of his elbow bend, so he must have been attentive, waiting to see how I was going to handle the situation.

Jordan started to yell at Brandon. *"What were you thinking? You could have killed her!"*

I saw Brandon tensing back up, so I asked Jordan to leave.

Jordan looked at me in severe protest. He clearly did not want to leave me in an unsafe, vulnerable position, which was sweet. But Brandon wasn't going to stand down if Jordan didn't leave.

I strongly urged Jordan with some exaggerated eye movements, and he did end up leaving, but not before he said to Brandon, *"She deserves your respect and an apology."* Then, he walked out the door, but sternly said, *"This door is staying open."*

I had no argument.

If someone had asked me earlier how I would respond if one of the kids tried to really hurt me, I don't think I would have guessed correctly. I felt so many conflicting emotions and was still recognizing some of them. I felt sadness over the boy who was so badly hurt that he couldn't just enjoy a happy day, a happy night, or a happy anything. I felt sorry for this kid who was too scared to trust, and would rather sabotage potential relationships than experience the pain of things inevitably going wrong. I felt frustration that I couldn't prove myself to him on a more convenient timeline. The more deeply I felt, the more I knew I needed to express my compassion more than my frustration, fear or anger.

Without a doubt, that was God's prompt in my heart. There is no other way to explain how or why I saw the situation in such a sympathetic way. I should have been scared or defensive, but I felt the urge to be more nurturing.

I proceeded with caution, taking the time to consider my wording. I was deliberate with my words when I began speaking, *"I'm not mad at you, but I am confused. I don't quite understand what we did to make you so angry, and I don't think it is necessary for you to express anger the way you did. You could have seriously injured me, or even killed me."*

Brandon grunted, but he didn't argue.

"And that's not all of it," I added. *"If you continue to lose control like that, there's a possibility that the person you hurt isn't able to protect themselves, like maybe one of the other kids. Even when you're upset, I don't think you'd feel good about truly hurting someone."*

He started mumbling, but I couldn't make out his words. I was losing him. I took a deep breath, and fought the frustration that was coming up. It wasn't the right time to be offended that he was dismissing my concern of how dangerous he was. Instead, I complimented him for keeping his hands to himself while I spoke. It was much better than his typical approach of breaking and throwing things.

"We have made the commitment to stick with you," I said, *"through all of the challenges that arise, but we'd prefer a different way of working through those challenges. Do you think maybe you could work on talking to us, instead of pitching fits?"*

"Uuhn," he grunted.

"Maybe we could practice," I suggested, *"so that it gets easier over time. How about you tell me why you were so upset about watching a Christmas movie before bedtime?"*

He crossed his arms back over his face and screamed, *"That movie is stupid! You never let me pick the movie. You always make me watch whatever you want to watch. You don't care. You're mean."*

"I'm sorry you feel that way, Brandon," I said. *"I thought you wanted to watch the movie because you asked if we could. If you didn't want to, you could have told me. I would have listened."*

173

There was no direct response. Just more hands-over-face posturing with a lot of grunting and mumbling. It took another hour before he settled down, which was about the time the other kids finished the movie. I held it together long enough to get everyone in bed, including my transitional position of sitting in Faith's doorway, until I was able to tuck myself in.

As I lay in bed, my mind reeled about the possibilities of Brandon's rage leading him to grab knives, or throw heavier objects at me, or something else terrible. I hated thinking the worst of Brandon, but I was concerned. I knew our love and support was going to make a difference for him and the other kids, but only if we could get the right additional resources lined up.

After such a scary ending to a complicated Christmas Day, I felt desperate to get the psychological evaluations completed, which was the step needed to initiate diagnosis-specific treatments. Brandon needed help. The other kids needed help. As a family, we needed help. We needed a clearer picture of what we were dealing with, the extent of the dangers we might be facing, and how to best help each of them.

In the meantime, we just accepted that Brandon had a fit waiting just below the surface, always. And we just kept working through them, hoping for a breakthrough, someday.

I received a phone call on Sunday saying that the two days of day camp for the second week of break were cancelled because they didn't have enough people signed up. And Jordan had to work. These extra days with the kids gave me plenty of time to witness more meltdowns, note more triggers, and rule out all possible solutions.

During the rare moments where no one was falling apart, we played games, we girls painted our nails, and we did anything else I could think of to keep everyone moving and stimulated. My favorite activity was our family bike rides through the neighborhood. I rode Jordan's bike so I could pull Caisen's bike-cart attachment, while the rest of the kids rode around me. If it weren't for these rides, I probably would have lost my mind.

The best part was that I couldn't hear all the kids complaining at once. I could only hear whichever kid was closest to me, and I could handle one kid complaining at a time. Besides, I knew we were all getting fresh air and exercise, and I had a great playlist of Disney songs playing. With the breeze in my face, I could almost believe we were a happy and healthy family.

It was a long week, but we made it. We brought the New Year in together. About that time, we got a letter from the kids' caseworker saying she was taking a different position and would no longer be working with us. We were assigned a new contact and worked out a plan to get her up to speed.

She was a new employee, so I felt bad that she landed our crazy group of five, but I was sure that all of our little complications would quickly help her learn the ins and outs of being a caseworker.

When the following Sunday came around, I got another call letting me know that the day camps for the following Monday and Tuesday in-service days were also cancelled. So much for help during the 18-day break. And, Jordan worked almost that entire stretch. Even though I counted down the minutes for each day to end, I was proud to say I made it. I got through it. It was a difficult two and a half weeks, but we all survived.

When the kids went back to school on Wednesday I didn't know what to do with myself. I thought about cleaning, or meal prepping, or laundry, but I deserved better. After I dropped the kids off at school, I went home, greeted my dogs and cats, and crawled into my bed. I slept deeper and more peacefully than I had in months. I would have stayed in bed all day, but it was Wednesday, and I couldn't use after-school care because Wednesdays were counseling days. But I got every minute of restful sleep that I could manage before getting in my mom-mobile.

Picking the kids back up for counseling felt like being asked to run a sprint at the end of a marathon. My tank still felt empty, and I didn't feel ready. I'm not even sure if I was able to form words while Clay cried over the snack options, or as Caisen dropped to the floor in anger over his bath. I was glossy-eyed and worn out, even after my glorious nap.

But, I was there, doing my best.

When Jordan got home that night, he helped with dinner and set the table. He tried to help the kids with homework, but they weren't receptive to him. They wanted me and my attention. He kept trying though. He's sweet like that. Little did I know that it was all an effort to butter me up before he dropped a mental bomb on me.

As soon as we got the kids in bed, he told me that he just learned he was going into the field for twenty-one days at the end of January, through mid-February. Just what I wanted to hear before going to sit on the floor in the hall, outside Faith's room. The wood floor was uncomfortable, but I could see my bedroom. I was getting closer and closer. And after just two hours of twiddling my thumbs, thinking about the days ahead of me and occasionally sighing loud enough for her to hear I was still there, I was in my bed, next to my husband. Just where I needed to be.

CHAPTER 20

PATIENCE AND PROGRESS

I t was a new year, but things weren't feeling new or different. After knowing the kids for three and a half months, we were still stuck in a phase of overwhelming challenge. And without psychological evaluations, we still couldn't seek any additional support, which left us on our own to change the circumstances we were living with. We stepped back, hoping to find a fresh approach based on what parenting styles we knew weren't working and what approaches still had potential.

We contemplated the specific rules and regulations foster families are required to follow, as well as the general suggestions. The foster care guidelines indicated that timeouts should start with the same number of minutes as the child's age, an idea we only briefly entertained. However, considering how reminders and warnings were already triggers for the kids, we decided they needed a buffer.

Instead of using their ages, we decided the kids would earn a solid two-minute time out for breaking a family rule, with the understanding that the minutes would steadily increase if we were met with a fit, disobedience, arguing, etc. We knew we couldn't change too many things at once, so we picked three offenses to work on, with hopes of adding more rules as they developed control.

We sat the kids down to get them up to speed on our new system: *"Every time you run in the house, you'll earn a two-minute time out. It is ok to be excited or to rush, but we expect walking-feet."*

"What if you don't see us running? Will we still be in trouble?" Clay asked.

"That's an interesting question. Our goal is to have you make good choices, so every chance I get, I'll draw your attention to a bad choice, to

help you learn to make a better one next time. If I'm not there to remind you, then I hope you'll start reminding yourself to do a good job anyway."

He nodded.

I continued, *"Every time you bully, intimidate or mistreat an animal, you'll earn a two-minute time out. It is ok to pet the animals and to love them, but only when they are ok with it. If they want to leave, you must let them. That's how respect works."*

Brandon chimed in, *"But they never let me pet them. I only get to pet them if I make them."*

"Well, Brandon," I said, *"if you work hard on calming down, I know they'll be more comfortable around you. It all starts with you and how you choose to behave."*

"OK, then I'll just never pet an animal," he said, as though he was just clarifying.

"Our third rule is about keeping our hands and feet to ourselves. Being upset is ok, but hitting or kicking furniture or others is not. You can talk about your feelings, you can even shout about your feelings if you need to, but it isn't ok to hurt people or break things."

As I spoke, I noticed four of them looking at me like the rule didn't apply to them, and the fifth child moved his arms across his face as he let a grunt out. To make things worse, Henry even seemed pleased to see Brandon being picked on individually. I drew attention to it.

"Brandon, thank you so much for the proper demonstration. Hey guys, Brandon felt embarrassed or irritated about the rule, so he covered his face and grunted. He didn't hit or kick anything, just grunted. Brandon, there is nothing wrong with that right now. Maybe later we'll work on more tools, but for now, that was the perfect way to handle the situation. All of you can take note of this, because every one of you has let a bad attitude turn a small problem into a big one."

Henry no longer seemed pleased.

"I need you all to understand that we will still talk to you about other problems as we see them, like separating too far from us in parking lots, or troubles at school. But, we're going to focus on these three rules, first. There will be reminders, we will encourage you, and we will warn you when you're getting close to a consequence. However, if you don't choose to follow the rules, a two-minute time out will be assigned, and it will keep growing until you make the good choice to serve it." I couldn't tell if they were actually internalizing the information, or just staring at me waiting for it to end, so I tested it.

"Lastly, we'll have a weekly ice cream outing for those of you who show you're working hard to do a good job," I said, and they noticed.

"I'll never get ice cream," Caisen said, as the other four lowered their heads.

"Caisen, if you give your best, you'll earn ice cream. I know you can do it," I said. *"And that applies to all of you. We aren't expecting you to be perfect, we only want to see you try, and we'll reward you for giving your best."*

The approach felt soft, but we knew we needed to motivate them if we were going to re-train their instincts. We thought that punishing them for being scattered and unaware would only slow the process down, even though some people around us, both family and friends, joked about how a few good beatings would straighten the kids right up. Building trust was a priority, so discipline had to take that into account.

Welcoming the New Year was a great time to revamp our discipline routine, but also a time to figure out what our birthday celebration routine would be, particularly because Clay was about to be our first celebrated child. Jordan and I picked some days where I'd take two kids at a time to go pick Clay a present, telling Clay that I was running errands, letting the other kids in on the secret, while Jordan took everyone else to the park. It was a team effort.

Also, I had been making the transition out of Faith's room and was ready to make the big move from inside the doorway, to outside it. Faith wasn't excited about the transition, but it was necessary. It was also necessary to have our last *"stop peeing on everything"* talk with the boys, and finalize their proper wiping techniques. It was time they cleaned up after themselves with some basic personal responsibilities, and we knew just the way to encourage it.

It went something like, *"If I do a single load of laundry without finding any poop chunks, then we'll celebrate with an ice cream night!"*

We were desperate for them to settle into our routines, count on our follow through, and gain comfort in our predictability. We stayed consistent with our school, counseling, and church routines, and used a giant dry-erase calendar on the wall to help everyone stay with it. We worked on building trust and expected consistency would help cultivate it. And, to balance it all out, we aimed to play as hard as we worked and pray even harder. Certainly, with such an arrangement, big changes were coming.

Clay's birthday came and he requested that I make him spaghetti and a chocolate cake. After dessert, he opened the gifts that the other kids had picked out for him. They were all excited to watch him open the presents they picked out. It seemed like his birthday had a possibility of succeeding.

Halfway through the gift opening, Brandon fell apart about how unfair it was that only Clay was getting gifts. I was frustrated to have Brandon ruin our good time, but emotional meltdowns weren't punishable because it isn't a crime to have feelings, as long as the feeling doesn't become destructive to people or property. They were exhausting though.

His little complaints grew into a full-fledged fit. He said things like, *"I should get a minion toy and teddy bear, too!"*

I asked him if he actually wanted either of those items.

He said, *"No, but it isn't fair that he gets them!"*

I tried to explain that Clay got things we thought Clay would like for his birthday. And, if he thought we did a good job for Clay, then the odds were in his favor that we would get him the things that he wanted for his birthday. I tried to play up the idea in his mind that he'd have a special day too, but on his own birthday.

"I shouldn't have to wait for my own birthday. Or, he should have to wait. It's not fair that he gets a birthday, and I don't!" he screamed at us, over and over.

"Everyone will get a birthday. I promise. Each of us gets one each year," I explained, feeling silly for even having a conversation about it.

"Fine," he said, *"then Clay shouldn't get the teddy bear. I picked it out, and I don't want him to have it because it isn't fair,"* as he took his arms off of his face to grab the small, tan teddy.

He was right. It wasn't fair. Not the bear, but the fact that Clay's big brother was trying to steal his birthday presents. Even more, it wasn't fair that these kids had been without love for so long that they couldn't share it. These poor kids, they were all desperate for love and affection.

Eventually we were able to settle Brandon down and take a family selfie to remember Clay's birthday. It may not have been a perfect celebration, but it was another experience under our belts as parents, and I prayed that our family would grow and improve as the days went on, with the consistency of love and structure in our lives.

After a couple of days of constant first-strike reminders, second-strike warnings and third-strike timeouts, we learned something. The kids had no yellow lights built into their minds, only impulsive, reactive green lights. They couldn't avoid the strikes and continued to grow in anger and disappointment. However, the new disappointment in their actions told me that they were trying.

Trying or not, it was miserable. I wondered if I was the meanest, worst parent in the world because my kids were ALWAYS in trouble for relatively small things. And big things. I wondered if I could survive twenty-one days without Jordan if things stayed the way they were.

Instead of focusing on the stress and worry about what my life would look like, I chose to give it all up to God. In that moment, I felt reminded that I wouldn't feel good about myself as a parent if I didn't do the hard work they needed me to do. They deserved someone willing to work on their impulsivity while they were still young, because the real world would not be as soft or compassionate in teaching them the lessons later. Bottom line, they needed me to work for them. It was a hard challenge to accept, but I knew that God had a plan for us.

That night, after getting the kids in bed, I sat against the wall across from Faith's room. Technically, this was outside her room. Progress. And my timeline for getting to my own room decreased to just one hour.

The next afternoon, I got a text from the kids' old caseworker. She was on our side of the state for a conference and asked if she could see the kids after her meetings ended. I thought it was sweet that she thought of us, so we agreed to meet up for dessert.

A little later, she texted that she wasn't alone at the conference. She would be accompanied by a co-worker we didn't know and also one of the kids' prior foster parents. I had no worries about the co-worker, but my heart started racing when I thought of the past foster parent.

She was the first foster parent the kids lived with. The kids didn't have many great memories of life before this foster parent, so her home represented the first safe and happy place for them. Though I was excited to meet this significant player in their lives, I was also concerned about the timing. We were in the middle of transitioning in consequences, and we were going to see a person who the kids had raised up on a pedestal. I was nervous they would see her and wish to be with her instead.

Not to mention, I knew that she was a friend of the foster mom who tried to prevent Faith from moving in with us. What if the night didn't go well? Could any unwanted drama arise because of it?

I called Jordan at work, and we decided that we'd like the opportunity to meet one of the key players in our kids' lives, and we thought that it might be exciting for the kids, which outweighed any anxieties.

The former caseworker asked if they could surprise the kids. I initially thought that sounded ok, but then decided I wanted the kids to know in advance, to prevent anyone from getting the wrong idea about walking into a restaurant to see a former foster parent with a former caseworker. I'd feel horrible if anyone had the initial response of thinking they were being given back.

When we told the kids, two of them were excited, two were interested, and one kid seemed indifferent. Not exactly what I was expecting, but it was what it was.

When we pulled up to Dairy Queen, I was nervous. I prayed it would be smooth and comforting, for everyone involved. When we walked in, their former foster mom gave me a big hug as the tears streamed from her eyes. She also hugged Jordan and each of the kids, as did the caseworker. She didn't look the way I pictured her. She had such a loving, caring look in her eyes. Before we even started talking, I felt thankful that the kids had spent time with her.

The kids took turns sharing our adventures and asking Jordan or me to tell specific stories. They thought of memories I hadn't thought of recently, and it made me feel like we'd been together forever. The night was fun and light, and then it was over. God answered my prayer for a comforting night.

We took the kiddos home and through the bedtime routine with some hiccups, but nothing major. And I was in my own doorway that night, just a couple feet down the hall from Faith's doorway, with my big toe still visible to her. To me it felt unnecessary. But, it was important for Faith, who could no longer see my face.

The next morning, one by one, all of the kids crawled into our bed, for the first time. It was extra warm with the seven of us and two dogs. No cats, though. They took off when Caisen came in.

It was a touching moment for me. It was the first time that I felt a real family bond. They were finally becoming MY kids! I thanked God for the moment.

Just then, when I was starting to feel that they were mine, a reminder came by way of a phone call, that they weren't. The state maintained their rights, the control, and the power.

I answered the unknown number and was greeted by another new caseworker. He called me to schedule his monthly visit, which would also be his opportunity to meet the kids. On that same call, I tried to explain that we scheduled our visits during counseling times so that the kids didn't lose any more minutes of normalcy than they needed to. They could just roll through their stations, including their caseworker chat, at one time.

However, he wasn't really listening and cut me off abruptly. It wasn't a good sign.

First, he came in and told us the order in which he wanted to talk to the kids, except a couple of them were already in counseling sessions. I told him which kids were available, and the timeline for the kids who were busy, reminding him that counseling was our first priority.

Instead of talking to the kids who were free, he just headed into the kitchen and asked the primary counselor questions, which wasn't even a typical aspect of home visits. He could have reached out to her at a different time.

The counselor who he chose to distract was working with Henry and Clay at the same time, which was a sensitive task. They were playing a game together, working on sportsmanship and respect, while also being slowly encouraged to see each other as friends.

Sadly, the kids weren't even on their way to seeing a friendship yet. So, when the caseworker called away the attention of the counselor who was monitoring the situation, things fell apart quickly. Henry moved some pieces around, cheating. Clay was trying to call him out for cheating, so Henry called Clay a liar. Clay knocked some pieces over as he yelled at Henry.

The counselor's rule during team-up sessions was that if someone starts to pitch a fit or fall apart, then they'd have to leave the table until they regain control, or they miss out on the rest of the game. In this case, she said that Clay needed to go catch his breath.

This made it worse because Henry hadn't gotten in trouble for his actions yet. And Clay didn't have the trust to believe that Henry would also be addressed. So, he fell further apart.

The counselor recognized what was happening, so she wrote her contact info down and asked the caseworker to contact her later, while she wasn't in session with kids.

Brandon, who was still waiting to talk to the caseworker, wasn't doing well with all of the attention going elsewhere. I recognized his groaning as a sign that a fit was coming and approached to redirect him.

The caseworker came between me and Brandon to address the rude noises on his own. The grunting picked up. Brandon's face was covered. The alligator rolls started. Brandon was mad and so was I. I had a chance to redirect Brandon when I first noticed his mood, and the caseworker came in like a wrecking ball.

Of course, when the three boys were all freaking out, Caisen decided to join in, for the fun of it.

Faith just stared blankly, probably scared about what was happening. It was complete chaos.

It took everything in me to not kick the man out. Trying to redirect a stranger who didn't seem to care to know the details of our family seemed impossible, but I had to try. After all, HE was the one with whom I'd be coordinating permissions and reports. I wasn't feeling good about it.

Finally, after he set off each of the kids, knocked the counselors off task, and looked over our necessary logs and ongoing paperwork, he left. And I got to work putting my family back together again.

I didn't know things could get worse, until they did.

The next day, I received a phone call from the counselor. She said that she got a follow-up email from the caseworker, asking her to comment on the problems he recognized with our placement. He apparently wrote that things were too chaotic, considering that the paperwork said the kids were fine and dandy, and his assumption was that we just weren't a good fit.

I was furious. This guy, who had no history with my kids or our journey, dared to indicate it was our fault that the kids were crazy? His reason being that there was no paperwork to match what he was seeing, even though I'd been begging to update their paperwork with fresh psychological examinations. Plus, HE was the one who triggered the afternoon to fall apart, even after I tried to prepare him for how to best navigate the visit. Oh, I was fuming,

And I wasn't the only one! It was insulting to our entire team. Thankfully, the counselor was not shy in her defense of our placement, home and the kids' progress. She was proud of the elements of progress we had been seeing, and told me she let the man know that he needed to back off. She also requested that the kids receive psychological evaluations, so they could see a psychiatrist to help with medications. With that piece not yet in play, she told him that all of the improvements we'd seen were due to our structure, routine, discipline, and support through counseling.

To achieve any progress with such emotionally reactive children was a point of pride for our whole team, and it wasn't ok that he dismissed it. After taking a few deep breaths, I called the caseworker. *"I understand you're concerned that the kids' behaviors don't quite match the packet of papers you inherited on our family. I can assure you that the disconnect took place before the kids came to us, and we have been requesting psychological evaluations for months, intending to have their conditions updated and accurate. And those requests have been well documented in my weekly reports."*

Thankfully, I felt he was listening.

I continued. *"We were told that we could wait for the evaluations to be completed before accepting their placement, or make them a priority while still moving forward with the placement plan. We chose to accept the kids without updated documentation, knowing that God brought us to them for a reason, but it's time to have the evals done."*

"Yes ma'am," he said. *"I agree; we need to get everything updated. I'll look into it."*

"Thank you," I said. *"We've been doing our best to help the kids, despite their obvious struggles, and without the proper resources. Getting everything moving forward is crucial for us."* I had made my point, and expected him to respond. When he didn't, I took it as permission to make another: *"And while I have you on the phone, I'd like to remind you that the dynamic between our five special needs kids is fragile, documented or not, and I need you to go with the flow better on visits."*

By the end of the call, he apologized for the chaos of the visit and also for jumping to conclusions. I accepted his apology and moved on, recognizing that the man was going to be on our team. There was no room for grudges, hard feelings, or drama.

Even though the incident resolved, I still felt uneasy knowing I wasn't legally the mom I had emotionally grown to be, and that at any time, a new stranger could be assigned to us who might dissolve the placement. The risk was unsettling, to say the least. It was taking everything in me to stay afloat, doing all of the mom-like things, while being treated like a glorified babysitter. In order to stay focused, I had to give all the hard feelings up to God. He didn't hide the truth from me, but He helped me keep it in perspective.

CHAPTER 21

A JUMBO ROLL
OF RED TAPE

While sitting on the wood floor outside my room, I could hear Faith tossing and turning. I had heard that melatonin was something that might help her, but I couldn't give it to her, as I did not have the right to make such decisions on her behalf. Protocol demanded that I get a prescription from a doctor, who didn't have the right to administer meds, and submit the request to our caseworker, who would pass it to the necessary people for review. As I sat on the floor, I stewed over how ridiculous it was that I couldn't even authorize basic supplements.

To make matters worse, we had not been assigned to a primary care provider, which was needed in order to schedule appointments with a family doctor, so if I wanted the prescription, my only option was to take her to the Emergency Room. I felt silly even imagining myself in the waiting room of the Emergency Department, waiting for a doctor to come talk to us about an over-the-counter sleep aid.

Luckily, a solution presented itself, disguised as another no-choice situation. Faith was riding her bike down the middle of our street. We were on a slow cul-de-sac, so this was normal. The other kids were also riding, and I was watching from a cozy lawn chair in the driveway.

I saw when she swerved. It was big and deliberate. She swayed back and forth, with more and more commitment. Eventually, she swayed with a little more force than she could control, turned the handlebars too far, and ended up ramming herself in the stomach with the right handle, causing her to topple over the front.

I was mostly surprised, though also impressed. I had never seen anyone crash into themselves on a clear, flat, and open path before.

I quickly got to her, and she looked stunned, too.

"Are you ok? What were you doing?" I asked.

She said, *"I was pretending that I was pulling Caisen in the cart like Dad does, and I wanted it to be a fun ride for him. I thought he'd like it if I was swerving and being silly, so I was doing my best."*

Shock. I felt shock. The kid fell because she was trying to make the cart-ride fun for the four-year-old. But, there was no cart and no four-year-old. This was my kid. This was my daughter.

With foster rules, I needed to be in direct supervision of each kid, so I had to make everyone come inside with Faith and me. I couldn't give her any pain medication, anti-inflammatories, or any tummy-soothers for her increasingly upset tummy.

The next rule I had to adhere to was the mandatory phone report each time a child got hurt. I made the call and was told to report back if there was any change in her condition.

A couple hours later, Faith's upset tummy took a nasty turn. She puked. This was my first opportunity to see that these kids had never been groomed to seek a toilet, sink, tub, pot, outside, etc. Instead, she puked all over the couch. I mean, ALL over the couch including the cushions, pillows, and throw blankets.

Again, I knew her tummy was legitimately upset because it had just been aggressively shaken up with a blow from a handlebar. My instincts were to work through it with rest, but it wasn't my decision to make. I called the foster agency with the update.

They mandated that I take her to the Emergency Room. I had no choice or say in the matter. However, I'd need to wait for Jordan to get home because he didn't have available space in his truck to come pick the other kids up from me, and I really didn't feel like taking them all anyway.

It was about six thirty in the evening, and Jordan wasn't home from work yet. I called him and used a stern-mom tone to convey how crucial it was for him to head home, because I did not want to take all of the kids to the Emergency Department with me, and I did not want to stay there all night. He granted my desperate request, and I fed the kids and got them started with their bedtime routine while I waited for Jordan to make the twenty-five-minute commute home.

After grilled cheese sandwiches and tomato soup, Caisen went into the bathroom and got undressed for his bath, when he noticed he had forgotten to grab his jammies and clean underwear. Naked-man ran from the bathroom, past Faith's room, into the boys' room. He grabbed the needed items and turned to head back to the bathroom, but didn't make it.

He was cut off by Faith sticking her head out her bedroom door to puke again.

She projectile puked up and down the hall and up and down the walls, leaving Caisen trapped in his room, with the water still running in the bathroom. Faith curled into the fetal position and cried.

I listened hard, hoping to hear Jordan's truck pulling into the driveway so I could hand over the barf-torch, but no such luck. To make matters worse, my naked four-year-old was starting to look green.

I gave Caisen directions to stay in his room, turned off the bathtub faucet, tried to reassure Faith, and attempted to keep the nosy other boys from getting into the mess. It was a circus. It was my circus. And on top of it, I was cleaning up her spew, while trying to suppress my own urge to upchuck.

As soon as I had cleaned enough to be able to step over the remaining mess, I grabbed Caisen and carried him to the bathroom. At least I had a good place to stash one of my disgusted children.

Then I got back to work with plastic Walmart bags, paper towels and Lysol wipes. Scooping and dumping the chunky mess was an incredible test of my self-control. I'm not going to lie. My gag reflex was fully engaged, the smell was horrendous, and I would have rather cleaned poopy underwear than the spray of spew that lined my hallway.

Just as I swiped the last Clorox wipe, Jordan came through the door. I handed him the bags filled with a full roll of vomit-covered paper towels for him to throw away, feeling he got off easy, while Faith and I left for the Emergency Room with her foster-placement paperwork in hand. I still didn't have an insurance card for her, but our newest caseworker texted the numbers I needed.

We were in the waiting room a long time before Faith made a bed out of three chairs and got some sleep. I sat there, patiently watching as my phone battery got smaller and smaller with each passing hour. After two and a half hours, it was finally our turn.

When Faith shared her story of what happened, the doctor asked if she was kidding. I vouched that she was not, and he held back a laugh as he confirmed that the puking was normal and fine.

Faith looked at me with a smile and told me that I was right. I smiled back, believing I had just won another battle in the ongoing attempt to prove she could trust me.

As I thanked him for his time, it dawned on me. I was in an emergency room, with a doctor, who could approve of melatonin.

He looked at me curiously when I asked and said, *"You don't need a prescription for that. You can just go pick some up at any Walgreens or CVS."*

I shared the foster care policy, and he wrote us the note.

I texted the update to the caseworker that we'd completed the required emergency room visit before heading out the automatic sliding glass doors.

It was about one-thirty in the morning when we got home. I rolled Faith into bed, without melatonin. I quickly scanned and emailed the paperwork over to the caseworkers, who would then move it around to get the required signatures, before letting me know when it was approved to begin giving the supplement to her.

By the time I was done, Faith was already asleep, without me near her. Even as tired as I was, I still felt giddy over it. However, my second wind kicked in and my mind raced. I had two new problems.

First, what would I have done if Faith's incident happened during Jordan's twenty-one-day field exercise? I would have had no other choice but to take all five kids with me to the Emergency Room, which was not appealing in the slightest. It scared me how real the possibility was that there might be some complications with Jordan gone, and my resources were very limited.

I decided to ask for help and made an urgent mental note to call Reagan and my mom in the morning. It wasn't the kind of call I could put off. To be clear, foster care rules wouldn't let my mom or Reagan watch the kids for me if there was an emergency or anything, but at least I would have another adult with me to help lessen the load, with or without an emergency.

The second problem was that Jordan could only fit one kid in the back-seat of his truck at a time, and foster care rules wouldn't let us put anyone up front. Plus, Caisen's car seat didn't fit in the back, which ruled him out from riding with Jordan all together. Essentially, if Jordan was the only adult I could count on, I really couldn't count on him for much. It became clear that he needed a vehicle upgrade.

The next day, I recruited Reagan, Jack and Winnie to come down for a couple days during the first week of Jordan's absence and for my mom to fly out for the entire middle week. I was to be on my own the rest, but I was thrilled at how many days I was going to have support.

In response to our second problem, we traded in and got Jordan a new truck. A four-door, black Chevy, which was a dream come true for Jordan. He had his ideal specifications saved in the notes app on his phone, waiting for the day that I'd give the green light. I was sad to spend the money and sad to see the old truck go, but I knew it was for the best.

It felt amazing to arrange solutions for our problems. And, the streak continued!

I got a phone call from a psychologist's office, confirming an initial intake appointment for a psychological evaluation for the following day. Good thing they called to confirm the appointment because the caseworker never shared with me that such appointments were scheduled, and I would have hated to find out after-the-fact that I'd missed an opportunity.

Disappointment with the last-minute notification wouldn't have been helpful in my conversation with the receptionist, so I kept it to myself as I asked the questions I needed answered: *"What is the name of the child you're calling about?"*

"I have Clarence (Clay) and Henry starting together. Are they your sons?" she asked.

"They are in my custody, along with three others. I just wanted to make sure I show up with the correct kids. Could you please repeat who it is you work with, so I can look up an address?" I wondered if she thought it odd that I didn't already know, since many people set up their own appointments.

She gave me the necessary info, so I asked my next question, *"What time?"*

Again, she answered, leaving me to ask my final question, *"Can you please tell me if any of my other three kids have appointments scheduled with you?"*

She told me that all of them had appointments scheduled. I followed up to get the dates and times of the remaining obligations and headed to my master-calendar on the wall to plug the new information in. As I tinkered with my color-coded dry erase board, I realized it didn't matter to me that the caseworker forgot to tell me because I got what I needed. It also didn't matter that Clay and Henry were scheduled to go ahead of Brandon. I would have prioritized them differently, but at least they were all scheduled. And it didn't matter that I only had one day's notice to work out a plan to take two kids to a lengthy appointment over an hour away. I knew I could make it work. I had to.

I looked at my organizational masterpiece on the wall and was happy I had slightly more notice for the rest of the initial appointments that would be completed by the end of the week. I also wrote their follow-up appointments, which would take place while Jordan was gone. I even got the heads up about the day I'd receive everyone's results, which would be soon after Jordan returned. There was a plan. I may have been left out of the loop, but at least there was a loop, and I was in it now.

I was gleeful over the idea of progress and felt everyone deserved a celebratory spaghetti dinner. While we ate high-carb delight, I told the kids about the appointments coming up, *"From what I understand, these appointments are going to help us get as much information as possible so we can help you grow up to be the strongest, happiest versions of yourselves that you can be. With this new information, I can better fight to make sure you have everything you need, and I promise I will always fight for that."*

The kids nodded, but mostly continued slurping noodles. They may not have been as progress-driven as I was, and I wasn't even done yet.

I looked at Faith and said, *"Speaking of growing in yourselves, I really think it's time you start sleeping on your own."*

She looked up at me, like a deer in headlights. I saw the panic starting.

"I haven't been inside your room for a while and you've been doing great. You know where my room is if you need me. I think you're ready. So, tonight, when you go to your bed, I'm going to mine."

She stared at me blankly, stunned.

I repeated the *"you're ready"* part, while reassuringly nodding my head at her.

She flashed me a coy smile and got back to eating.

That night, just as I had said, I went to my room after getting everyone tucked in. Jordan and I talked aloud for a bit, trying to make the distance sound small to Faith. After an hour passed without a peep out of her, I said to Jordan, *"I'm getting my first full night of sleep tonight. Things are looking up."* We exchanged a victory kiss and went to sleep.

I'm sure I was dreaming something lovely when I was suddenly awakened by Faith standing over my face. I popped up, startled, and asked what was wrong

"My tummy hurts," she said," and I threw up."

I glanced at the clock and found it was just after midnight. So much for my peaceful slumber.

I woke Jordan and we all walked to her room. She had puked spaghetti all over her floor, the walls, the doorway, and her stuff. Everywhere. Jordan got to work cleaning it up like a champ, and I grabbed some extra towels, sheets and the puke-pot.

I knew that it was the anxiety that drove her to be sick, but I wasn't about to tell her that. What if she became too scared to try the separation again? Instead, I said, *"You must have had too much spaghetti."*

When she agreed, I giggled to myself. She was so gullible.

We got her in her bed and went back to ours. However, she came back in about an hour later, to tell us that she puked again. I looked. She completely missed the pot. I mean it wasn't even close. This kid. Anyhow, after getting her cleaned up and in bed, again, she stayed there.

It may have been a rough first night apart, but we made it. And to my surprise, the next couple of nights went smoother. So much so that I thought we were out of the woods, but it ended up being like every other time we thought we had succeeded.

It was a night like most others, and we had gotten everyone in bed. Jordan and I were in our room, folding and putting away our laundry when I heard a creak at the door, but then it was quiet again, so I figured it was nothing. When I heard a second creak at the door, I asked Jordan, *"Is there a child at the door?"*

He checked. Faith stood there.

He asked her what she needed, and I heard no response. I imagined she was staring at him blankly, as usual. He asked if she was feeling ok and still no response.

I walked over. I asked what she needed, and I got a stare. I told her that I couldn't help if I didn't know what the problem was, and she still stared.

I gave up. I was tired. She clearly wasn't ready to talk, though she must have had something to say. Either way, I said that she needed to crawl back in bed and that if she ever decided to share her thoughts, she knew where to find us.

Maybe thirty minutes later, Jordan and I were lying in bed, and we were hinting to each other that we felt like we were catching our stride. I was in my own bed, obstacles weren't surprising us, and we weren't emotionally responding to every little thing that came up. We were adapting.

Without notice, Faith came barreling into the room. She was moving faster than I'd ever seen her move as she made a loud and desperate exclamation, *"I know why I was standing at your door. I looked at a scary app at school that I wasn't supposed to and now I can't sleep because I'll have nightmares! And I'm sorry I lied by not answering when you asked."*

It was the most direct and precise she had ever been with us. I don't think she even took a breath as she spit it all out. I was so proud. I sat up to have a chat with her about what she saw and why it was scary, while she stood there, panting.

It was an app rated appropriate for ages eight and older, and the premise is that you are working through some levels when some random things blast up on the screen to startle you. It seemed minor, but it posed a major problem for her. She knew that it was just on her screen, which wasn't even in our house. But, she couldn't help but feel panicked by it.

As I listened, I pondered over what options we had within the foster care regulations. She couldn't sleep with us, like many parents would do for their younger children having nightmares. Of course, Faith was physically older than that, but not emotionally. I also wasn't going to go lay in her room with her either, because I didn't want her to grow dependent on my being on her floor again. We were stuck.

I scooted to the middle of my bed, so that she could lie on my side as we figured it out together. While Jordan and I were talking it through, she fell asleep. Jordan picked her up and carried her back to her room. Problem solved.

I was thankful that fear drove her to open up with us, though sad she had to experience it. And it helped me to realize that even though the rules may have told us we weren't her legal parents yet, the bond that was developing was telling me something different. It was great affirmation as Jordan hit the road for three weeks.

CHAPTER 22

CALLING FOR BACKUP

After months of work establishing and reinforcing both clear expectations and routines, it was the dreaded time to put myself to the test. Jordan was going to be out of reach for twenty-one days, with the exception of one night to restock and refuel, which happened to be the night my mom was flying into town. Other than the one night, I was prepared to be the only authorized transport or supervisor for my five crazy kiddos for a long three weeks.

The first couple of days were full of typical chaos, typical meltdowns, and typical rule-breaks. The only problem was that I didn't have anyone to entertain the kids who weren't involved in meltdowns, so typical problems were slightly more complicated than they otherwise would have been. I can honestly say it wasn't my favorite weekend.

I took the kids on bike rides, to give myself a break from hearing their whining. I put on the TV, to give myself a break from hearing their fighting. I made their favorite meals, to give myself a break from any backlash. I did everything I could, within the standards of the routine, to help it go smoothly.

The kids went back to school on Monday. Oh, how I loved Mondays. Tuesday was great too, because Reagan came down with Jack and Winnie. My dogs were obviously excited to see Winnie, and Winnie seemed happy that the kids were in school when they arrived.

We got them unloaded and set up in the house. Jack's pack-n-play was set up in my closet, and Reagan's phone charger went on Jordan's side of the bed. We also shifted the booster and car seat in my car to make room for Jack. Once we were set, we relaxed for a bit before I warned Reagan to brace herself for pick-up time.

Caisen was the first pick-up destination, and he was visibly excited to see Jack, causing him to squeak and squeal so much that I had to wait a couple of minutes before asking him what color he had earned at school. It was yellow, of course, so we went through our classroom behavior pep talk.

We headed to the elementary school, and I could see on the kids' faces as I walked into the child care room that bad news was coming. The supervisor let me know that Clay and Brandon got into a big fight, to include spitting, hitting, and choking. The kids immediately got defensive, trying to blame each other for the problem. Typical. I apologized to the supervisor as we left.

As we walked out the door, Brandon grew increasingly uncomfortable because I hadn't spoken to him yet, other than to tell them both that I didn't want to hear the arguing. Brandon's arms went over his face, and the grunting began as we all climbed into the car. Some of the kids happily said *"hello"* to Reagan and Jack. Brandon did not.

I heard what I needed to from the other kids, who were all too happy to rat out their brothers, which was that Clay stuck his tongue out and spat towards Brandon. Brandon spat a loogie at Clay. Clay said he was going to tell. Brandon hit at Clay, who shoved Brandon away. Brandon grabbed Clay by his sweatshirt as he tried to run. By holding onto Clay's sweatshirt, he was choking Clay. That's when the teachers finally got them to separate.

We were driving toward McDonald's because they offered one dollar and ninety-nine cents kids meals on Tuesdays, which meant I only had a few minutes to get the conversation wrapped up before getting to our destination. I addressed Clay. *"Stop annoying your brothers so much. Stop spitting at them. Stop taunting them. Stop instigating them. It doesn't matter that Brandon did worse. You started it, which makes you in trouble."*

Clay asked, *"What's taunting mean?"*

"Trying to get somebody to react badly," I answered.

"What's incubating?" he asked.

I took a deep breath, annoyed that this kid was missing the point. *"That's when you use lamps to help eggs grow. But I wasn't talking about incubating. You must have misheard when I said 'instigating,' which is trying to do something small to cause someone else to do something bigger,"* I answered, *"like when you spat at Brandon knowing that it would annoy him and he would react. You might think you're out of trouble because he responded badly, but you still started it."*

Through all of this, Clay seemed so content. He enjoyed being annoying. He enjoyed getting his brothers into trouble. It was his way of exerting some control. He and Brandon were not a good fit for each other.

Brandon, by the way, was hearing the entire conversation and was growing increasingly agitated. He was going on and on, mumbling, *"It was Clay's fault because Clay started it,"* even though I clearly recognized that fact already.

I could see some confusion on Reagan's face. It's like she couldn't tell if the issue with Brandon was real, or if she should be laughing at the ridiculousness of the whole thing. A struggle I knew well.

I shifted my attention over to Brandon and after agreeing with him about five hundred times that Clay started it, I explained that Clay didn't choose how Brandon responded. I said, *"Clay is responsible for his actions and reactions, just as much as you are responsible for your actions and reactions."* Brandon didn't like that.

We pulled up to McDonald's, and Brandon was still escalating.

Thankfully, the McDonald's playplace had some great big windows, so I sent the other kids in with Reagan, knowing that I still had direct eyesight of them, while Brandon and I continued our conversation in the parking lot, outside the car.

I would have preferred to have the chat in the car because I could more easily contain Brandon if he fully lost it. But, he got out when the other kids did, and it wasn't easy getting him back in.

I told Brandon, *"I'm not as upset as you seem to be. Really, I'm proud that you stopped engaging with Clay when the adults told you to,"* reminding him that recently it had been difficult to get him to hear others while he was angered. I felt it was progress.

I knew that a ten-year-old choking a seven-year-old was a big deal, but I needed to recognize all of the baby steps taken toward improving the circumstances. That's why I went on to explain that I believed he was trying to do better, I appreciated his efforts, and I asked him to continue to work at it. I also explained the consequence to him, which was a time out at home, so that he could begin to process it. He wasn't happy, but he wasn't angry either. It really was progress.

It took us about fifteen minutes before we were able to join Reagan and the rest of the kids, where I found that Clay had lost a tooth. I was awarded the prestigious position of tooth-bearer and saw that the tooth was much more metal than tooth. About that same time, Brandon apologized to Clay for how badly he responded to Clay for being so annoying. I giggled, but agreed. Clay was annoying at times.

Clay said, *"Thank you?"* like a question, and *"Sorry I'm annoying."*

We went on with our evening. Brandon remained on edge, but he still engaged and played. In fact, Brandon helped Jack move through the large play structure in order to experience his first slide.

No matter how frustrating my kids could be, there were also many precious moments to remind me that they were just kids, and they didn't deserve the trauma they'd experienced. They were kind of like roses. Of course, they had many thorns, but they were still roses. I could see in the way they interacted with Jack that they really were sweet-natured kids. They had good hearts, good intentions, and the potential to be kinder, gentler people. I sat back, ignored the yelling and arguing, and just enjoyed them playing with their little cousin.

After dinner, we went home. Reagan got to work on Jack's bedtime routine, as my three younger kids cycled through showers and reading, and my two older kids explained to me what was needed on their newest school project. Of course, I also gave Clay his tooth to place under his pillow.

I enjoyed having Faith and Brandon in the same grade because I could usually count on at least one of them to bring home their homework, permission slips, or flyers from their teachers, and our copy machine made it possible for the other to still get their work done on time. After making a copy for Faith, they both got to work.

It didn't seem like a terribly difficult project. They were just designing a poster board to highlight at least seven scenes from the book they had been reading as a class. I told them both to get a blank piece of paper first to either list the scenes they wanted to include or to lightly sketch out a very rough draft, while I went digging through the garage to find where I had stashed poster board. However, from the garage I could hear that Brandon wasn't moving forward with the planning phase of his project.

"It's going to take too long," he yelled, which prompted me to quickly get my booty back in the house. I didn't want anything to break in my absence. I found him flopped to the floor crying, and it didn't even look like he'd read the grading rubrics yet.

"Brandon, you are such a great artist, you'll be able to complete this assignment easily, and you can even choose to enjoy it. You're getting to color while you wait for your shower. Sounds great to me," I said.

He kept rolling, but he wasn't hurting anyone or anything, so I shifted my attention to Faith.

Faith wasn't crying, but she wasn't making progress either. She just sat there, holding a pencil, staring at the wall.

I said, *"Faith, what's the book about?"*

Stare.

"Do you remember any of the characters? Or what was happening?"

Head tilt.

"You know, in the book?"

Excited head nod.

"Well, make a list of some of the things you remember. Then, start scribbling some drawing ideas down to plan how you want it to look."

Her eyes went glossy and rolled backwards. Well, not totally backwards. But, her left eye did roll out of focus.

That was typical for her. Especially later at night. We tried to request approvals to get her eye looked at, but we weren't gaining any traction. I took her response as a signal she was too overwhelmed to move forward at the current time, and I shifted my attention to Brandon.

Brandon was doing alligator rolls while complaining that he wasn't going to get any playtime.

I asked, *"If you had play time right now, what would you choose to do with it?"*

"DRAW!" he yelled at me.

"Great because that's what your project is! All you have to do is draw some scenes from the book! You'll love it!"

He sat up, but clearly wasn't happy.

I told him that the sooner he got to work on it, the sooner it would be done. I grabbed crayons for them, and they both got to work, kind of. Faith was slower than a herd of turtles moving through peanut butter, but she was working. I just had to keep reminding her *"what"* she was working on.

Brandon got his list of ideas ready and then wanted his poster board. Instead, I asked him to do a draft because I had no extra poster board for redo's: *"You can practice scribbling your pictures, to make sure you know how you want to draw them, and you can see where things will fit."*

He grunted at me a couple of times. I launched a final attempt to catch him with some logic: *"There's no need to rush it. Two-week long assignments are not meant to be finished in ten minutes. They are supposed to be done over time, to the best of your ability. It won't take much time, but it will make your final product much nicer, and I'm looking forward to seeing what you come up with."*

Letting him know that I was excited to see the end product seemed to help, slightly.

After getting Jack to sleep, Reagan came out and sat in the living room with Caisen and Clay. Henry was taking his turn in the shower. I walked over to join her on the couch and came across Brandon's shoes on the floor in front of the TV.

We have a rule about putting our shoes away when we take them off, because we have dogs that steal them and cats that puke in them. I knew Brandon liked having shoes, so I asked Brandon to come put his shoes away.

The dude lost it. He must have been fragile over the whole *"Do your homework well"* scene, and this little request was enough to put him over the edge. He fell out of his chair, back onto the floor. He flailed around like a fish out of water. He was crying. He was screeching. All over putting shoes away.

Reagan's face again revealed confusion. She said, *"You told me his big fits are over ridiculous things, but this is totally not what I pictured! I imagined it being defiance or something. This is just so sad!"*

Yes. Yes, it was sad. And frustrating. And for a kid who was concerned about his project taking too long, I was concerned about him recognizing these wasted minutes.

Just as soon as I'd finished my thought, he voiced it loud and clear and took it further than I had time to predict. *"It's not fair that Faith gets to keep working while I have to stop and put away shoes! She should have to stop, too!"*

"Putting away your shoes will be over so fast, and you can get right back to work," I said, hoping for the best. It took a while, as it always did, and when he finally picked the shoes up and took his first steps towards his room, Henry came out of the bathroom.

"Brandon, it's your turn," he said.

As Brandon dropped to the floor, boneless, his arms flicked the shoes up into the air. One made a loud thud as it hit the ground. We didn't hear the second shoe land because Brandon's back absorbed the noise. He arched backwards and screamed like he was being attacked.

Reagan couldn't help it. She giggled. He cried. Good times. It took every bit of patience in me to finish out the night, which made closing the door behind myself after kissing the boys goodnight ever more satisfying!

While chatting with Reagan, a few exchanges stood out to me. First, she told me that on the first trip, she really only recognized the abundance of energy harnessed in my kids. It was nice to have someone validate the level of chaos they maintained. Next, she described how after retrieving the kids from school, she was able to see that Brandon didn't like earning consequences, or taking responsibility for his mistakes. However, those things paled in comparison to what she observed that night. She saw that he couldn't even handle the small obstacles in a day, where no trouble was associated with them. *"He's extremely reactive, and I don't even know where you start to change that."*

All I could say was, *"It will take us a long time to develop trust with him. Maybe when he begins to count on us to uphold our commitments, he'll start to feel a little more stable. At least, I hope we can teach him that the world doesn't have to be as bad as he's seen it to be."*

After a few more minutes of chatting, I felt ready for bed. Thankfully, Reagan was there and she reminded me that I still had a tooth to collect. I had completely forgotten.

I snuck into the room with four boys sleeping, recognizing that waking even one would be disastrous. I reached under Clay's pillow and pulled out a handful of trail mix. No tooth.

After searching and scrambling, I admitted defeat and asked Reagan to give it a try.

She came back out with a tooth, but it was more tooth than metal. NOT the tooth I had been carrying. She also showed me the two batteries and fruit snacks she collected.

The next morning, Clay came to us, showing that he did receive a quarter for one tooth, which he had lost shortly after getting into bed, explaining why I didn't know about it. However, he still had the mostly metal tooth.

I tried to be clever, *"Oh, the tooth fairy probably only had room for one tooth at a time, or she didn't have enough money for a second tooth on such short notice. I totally understand why she took the healthier tooth on her first trip, and I'm sure she'll be back for the other one tonight."*

After getting the kids to school, Reagan and I paused our plans to fill my freezer with ready-to-go meals, in order to satisfy our curiosity. We checked under the rest of the kids' pillows and found thumbtacks, magnets, candy wrappers, crumbs, clothes, and a few other random items.

We also checked inside the pillows. We found a box of Band-Aids that I didn't even realize I was missing, bags of chips, packages of fruit snacks, a box of candy I didn't recognize, a stale slice of bread, warm Gogurt, peanuts, and two Capri Suns.

Once we started searching, we couldn't stop. Not until the surprises were all found. We checked dresser drawers and found freezer meals, no longer frozen. We found a box of macaroni and cheese. We found a banana and two apples. We also found many more candy wrappers.

I don't remember the prompt, but we also ended up checking the heater vents in the bedrooms and found far more treasure than I could have imagined. In total, we found three boxes of granola bars, some playing cards, many fig bar wrappers, some random trinkets, some Capri Sun wrappers, and a pack of gum. Quite the find.

When we accepted that our scavenger hunt was over, I set everything aside to talk to the kids later. I was super excited to jump into meal prep because stocking up on freezer meals for crazy nights felt like a lifeline in the making. As an added bonus, I did more sitting as Reagan did more meal prepping. It was the best pampering I'd had in so long, and I enjoyed it all the way up until it was counseling time.

In the car, in addition to working through the usual counseling day reminders, I also let the kids know about what Reagan and I found. Fear showed up, and I couldn't tell if it was fear of trouble, or worry over what they'd do without their stashes. Either way, I addressed both.

"It makes me sad that you feel the need to take food and hide it. I hope I'm not doing anything to add to your feelings of neediness about food. But, now that I see how much of an issue it is, I want you to know that you aren't in trouble, and I want you to hear something important: I promise, I will always provide you with the food that you need."

That's all we had time for before jumping into a regularly insane counseling session, where I prompted each kid to share with the counselor about the food issue that had come to light. It was a madhouse, as usual, but we made it. And the experience felt special to me because Reagan saw some tougher sides of the rest of the kids, further deepening her understanding of what our struggles looked like. In fact, I was certain that Baby Jack would be traumatized over the intensity of it, but it turned out that he was actually entertained by the loud noises and fast movements. Winnie, on the other hand, was not entertained at all! Poor pup!

Reagan packed up Thursday morning, and I thought she seemed extra chipper. Or maybe I just imagined myself packing and knew I would feel chipper, which made me feel guilty. I hadn't even known the kids a whole five months yet, and I was already fantasizing about packing a suitcase. Before the kids, when Jordan and I talked about adopting, we knew it would be difficult. We weren't caught by surprise in that respect. But, five kids was a lot, especially when one of those kids was Brandon. I was suffocating and wondering if I was ever going to be enough for them.

As Reagan left, she gave me a hug and told me that I was doing a good job. I cried. I cried because she was leaving, because she validated me, because I wanted to go with her, and because I still felt God urging me to stay. My home no longer felt like a safe and happy home, but God needed me there anyway, and He was doing big things, I just knew it.

In the midst of a stressful time, her willingness to come participate in my crazy world was an emotional boost for me. Not only was life better by having someone around to share it with, but also the extra love and support went a long way. A thought to live by.

CHAPTER 23

THE SECRET TO HAPPINESS IS LOW EXPECTATIONS

When Reagan left, I had one night to get prepped for the next phase of my adventure. The next morning, my mom called as she boarded her flight. I wished her safe travels and once again asked her to let go of her expectations. She was hoping to shower each child with attention, have special projects to connect with each one, and possibly even give me room for a ten-minute bubble bath.

I told her that was crazy talk. She didn't seem to understand why, assuming that my *"difficult kids"* were probably similar to her most difficult child, my brother, Chris. I didn't see the need to argue with her, since I knew the kids would quickly make my point for me, so I just reminded her to keep her expectations low.

Jordan got home for his one-night refuel just in time to pick the kids up from school with me and head to the airport. I couldn't wait for my mom to meet the kids, and vice versa. I wasn't certain about how the time would go, but I knew that my mom was about to get a crash course on the new life we'd been living, and I was anxious to hear her thoughts.

I know it was hard on her becoming a foster grandma from a distance. I don't say foster grandma to lessen her role. Rather, there were a lot of complications caused by choosing this route for becoming parents, and my mom would have enjoyed being more deeply involved. This was her chance.

I took Faith and Brandon into the airport with me. The others were circling with Jordan in the car. We met Grandma Roxie at the baggage claim, and she instantly cried. The tears streamed down her cheeks as I wondered if she was going to suffocate my kids with her tight hugs. It was a beautiful thing.

She climbed into the backseat with the kids as I loaded her bag into the back. She, like I, wore minimal make-up. She didn't need it because her smile could light up any room on its own. It also didn't matter what mom wore or how she did her hair, because her energy made her the spotlight of any crowd. However, her dark hair was half up and she wore a mint green sweater. Bright colors were usual for her, whereas I prefer blacks, whites and greys.

We stopped at Steak-n-Shake for dinner. It was busy and loud, but mom kept a happy face. She was trying to smooth out bumps with the kids, specifically Brandon complaining about his crayon colors and drink options, by being enthusiastic and animated. I enjoyed watching her, taking it in while it lasted, knowing her batteries wouldn't stay charged for a full ten days of such high output.

We got home, and the kids went berserk. There were fits over showers. There were complaints about hunger, even though we had just eaten. There was dog riding. They didn't hold anything back.

About thirty minutes in, my mom looked at me and said, *"Hey Jess, how about you go take that bubble bath?"* with an incredibly sarcastic tone that showed me she was catching up fast.

Instead of saying, *"I told you so,"* I pretended that I didn't sense the sarcasm and said, *"Great, see you in ten,"* and then I giggled at the notion.

She rolled her eyes, and I added, *"Are you still thinking that my challenging kids are similar to yours? Or are you now seeing that something is different about their struggles?"*

Abruptly, she exclaimed, *"They're nothing like Chris. This is a circus."*

Instead of being embarrassed over the kids' behavior, I found pleasure in sharing my daily life. When Caisen got out of his bath, my mom asked if she could read to him and anyone else who wanted to listen, some books she brought. No arms had to be twisted. Caisen ran to his bed.

I called out, *"Walking feet, please."*

My only request was that the kids still take their showers when it was their turn, which prompted Clay to race down the hall.

I yelled out, *"Walking feet, Clay."*

Jordan and I joined the rest of the kids in the boys' room for some stories. I loved watching how my mom brought the books to life, and Jordan's smile told me he was enjoying the show, too. I loved even more seeing the kids squished up next to her. Caisen was wedged so tightly against my mom's thigh that I couldn't really tell where he stopped and she began. It was one of the most meaningful and beautiful things I had ever seen because it was obvious that my mom wanted each of these kids to feel loved. They were not foster-anything to her. There was no waiting period before they were hers. I don't think I could have really identified the feeling earlier, but I recognized that I was having to work really hard at trying to love the kids, but seeing my mom seemingly all-in was truly a life-changer for me.

The next morning, Jordan returned to the field, my least favorite way to launch a weekend. The kids didn't seem too upset by it, as they had a grandma to more thoroughly break in. She worked so hard to keep them entertained, but their attention spans were small and individual needs were great.

First, there was chalk drawing outside. Then, three minutes later, there was basketball. Then, catch with baseballs. Then, jump-roping. Then, Simon Says. Then, bikes. Then, more basketball. Then, she was tracing the kids with the chalk so they could color themselves in. Then, she was making up games and grasping for ideas.

Yes, I was playing, too. But, I was mostly just building the kids back up as they took turns falling apart. One was mad that he wasn't outlined first. Another was mad because he missed a shot. Another was mad because catching a baseball was hard and therefore for losers. Another was mad because he crashed into a light post on his bike. These were all small things, but not to my kids.

By lunch time, mom and I were both tired. So, macaroni and cheese was the choice. After lunch, the kids pulled out toys, games and stuffies. It was messy, but messes can be cleaned. And if it could keep at least three kids happy at a time, then I was all for it.

My mom agreed to play a board game with the kids, and she learned that games with them are more exhausting than they are worth. She's a total game-person, but it was hard having to coddle each kid and smooth everyone's feelings, particularly after someone throws a game board over.

By about two o'clock, my mom got up and headed into the kitchen. She pulled out a couple dishes, and I got curious about what she was up to.

"What are you doing, mom?" I asked.

She responded with, *"I'm getting dinner started."*

I took pleasure in delivering the bad news: *"But it's only two o'clock, mom."*

She desperately exclaimed, *"Time doesn't move in this house!"*

My thoughts exactly.

She reluctantly resumed her place at the board game, just in time for Henry to send it flying again. He was frustrated, which then caused the rest of the group to deteriorate.

Mom looked at me with concern, and I said, *"Just another day in the life."* Then I moved on to address Henry, as she put the game back together with the other kids.

The day slowly rolled along, and mom was happy when it was finally an appropriate time to disappear into the kitchen. Which is funny, because she never used to rush into the kitchen. But, in this case, it was a break from the kids.

After dinner, showers, and reading, we had a good ten minutes left before bed.

Mom roped them all into playing the alphabet game and explained that we'd go around in a circle, giving responses to particular categories in order of the alphabet.

We did a round of animals and a round of favorite names before Caisen cried over not being able to find a good response for the letter J in the category of places.

Then she switched to *"would you rather"* questions.

Then she tore papers in some odd cadence. I don't think she even knew what she was doing.

I called out *"two more minutes"* and she abruptly responded, *"Oh, come on!"*

At *"one minute"* she dropped her head down on the table, then picked it up for the final stretch.

At *"bedtime"* she did a pathetic happy dance, which looked a lot like a seizure.

And it was only Saturday. Which was only day two out of ten. Poor Grandma Roxie.

Mom came with us to church on Sunday, and I think she appreciated the break from the kids even more than she enjoyed the sermon. I felt the same. The rest of the day was a lot like Saturday. Tough, but with many sparkling moments.

Then, my favorite day of the week came. MONDAY!

I'd love to say that we had great mother-daughter time while the kids were at school, but those precious minutes were reserved for mom's recouping, which basically meant zoning out. And as the week went on, recover-time got more and more serious. Especially after she was introduced to counseling days!

As I shuffled to put the dogs away while the kids snacked, problems started to arise. I knew our chaos would be eye opening for my mom, who agreed to hang out in the boy's bedroom with the kids who weren't in showers or sessions.

After the first round of tantrums over snacks and tasks came to an end, the second round built on it. Clay was asked to take his shower and Brandon was asked to do a session. Clay had already finished his reading and one of his sessions, so he jumped up to get his shower done, realizing it was putting him in the lead with completed tasks.

Brandon wasn't as compliant because he wanted to shower instead. He wanted to shower before Clay so that Clay wouldn't be finished with the entire array of tasks before him, even though Brandon still needed to get his big session completed and was wasting time.

Clay tried to get into the bathroom as Brandon was pushing him. Clay got the door shut, and Brandon began pounding on the door.

"Brandon, your session won't get done without you, so you should probably go knock it out," I said, and he eventually worked his way into the kitchen, where he gave lame effort. He was rolling around, upside down in his chair, groaning and complaining of boredom. But, it wasn't boredom. He just thought his time would be better spent in the shower.

Clay got out of the bathroom. Brandon was still in his session, and Henry was reading in the room with Grandma Roxie. It made sense, so I sent Henry to the shower next.

Brandon flipped out again. He was focused on winning an imaginary race through the shower. The counselor wasn't getting anywhere with him, so when his session ended, she reminded him that he has a choice of sitting there miserable or sitting there engaged and happy, but either way he has an appointment with her to sit there. He chose miserable that day, but the hope was that he'd learn how to make better choices in the future.

Brandon was directed to go into his skills-building session. He didn't seem interested.

Meanwhile, Clay went into his big session. And he was excited to play Go-Feelings, a version of Go-Fish that prompted discussions of the feelings indicated on the cards.

Brandon got more upset when he saw that Clay was happy with his session, saying that he would have been happy if he had been able to shower first, *"It's your fault my session was bad because you didn't let me shower."*

Brandon paced through the house, arms across his face, chanting about the injustice.

The skills-builder pursued him, with her long maxi skirt swaying back and forth as she race-walked to keep up with him, with the dogs whimpering in the background, clearly wanting to walk laps around the house with them, if it wasn't for the baby gate separating them.

Brandon kept peeking to see if she was still following him and continued to pick up the pace in an effort to ditch her. He was doing lap after lap through the living room, to the dining room, through the kitchen, and back to the living room. I was getting dizzy watching them.

I had to intervene a few times to try and talk him down, while the skills-builder caught her breath. He gave me the time of day by peeking through his arms at me, allowing me to see one eyeball, and quieting down to listen. I enjoyed this new connection, but I chose not to compliment him for it, because I didn't want to remind him of a worse behavior.

I didn't want to press my luck with the new connection, so I made my interactions brief and stayed focused on my task of preparing dinner. To be honest, it was only frozen pizzas, but I knew it would be a victory if there were any food to eat.

I could hear some issues between my mom, the kids, and the dogs developing in the back of the house, so I popped the second pizza in the oven and went to check on my mom. She looked overwhelmed by the kids who had finished their reading and moved on to playing quietly and independently, except for the quiet part. Just because we asked them to be respectful of the kids still in sessions didn't mean they'd actually do it.

It didn't help that the dogs, who were shut in my room, were agitated by Brandon's pacing and were speaking up about it.

My mom asked, *"Is there a secret for getting the collar and leash on Cinder?"*

"Why?" I asked, wondering if she was planning to ditch me and take them for a walk instead.

"Because I can't figure it out," she said. The desperation in her voice was clear as she continued. *"The whining is driving me nuts. I want to bring them in here with us so they might settle down, but I can't make Cinder sit still enough to get her collar on her. And I can't just open the door because I know I won't be able to get them back in the room once they are free."*

I nodded my head along with her as she continued, *"I tried straddling Cinder to force the collar on, but she bobs and weaves faster than I can move. She's making me feel old."*

A giggle fell out of my mouth and before she had a chance to call me on it, I grabbed the collar from her. I showed my mom up by lassoing the dog with ease. I handed her the attached leash with a proud smile, but when I turned, I let out a sigh of relief because it didn't always go so smoothly for me. I didn't tell her that, though.

I got about two steps down the hall before my mom asked if she could trade me places.

"If you want, but you'll regret offering," I told her.

She gave me an inquisitive look.

"I'll happily stay in the back room so you can take over dinner and be on Brandon duty," I said. *"Go take a look and let me know if that's how you want to play this..."*

She was only gone about twenty-five seconds before coming back to say, *"Nope, I'm good."*

I resumed my place encouraging Brandon to see that he was being unreasonable, up until the buzzer went off on the pizza. I excused myself to pull it out.

He followed me. After I set the pizza on the stovetop, I knelt down in front of him, with my hands slightly holding on to his still-raised elbows, as I talked to him with full eye contact. I was reminding him that the counselors were here to help him gain control and insights, but he couldn't gain either without giving them a fair chance.

I believed in the information I was sharing with him; however, I was bursting with glee in my mind over the eye contact.

Brandon continued complaining about the shower order while I sliced pizza. Eventually, enough was enough, *"Dude, the entire family is waiting on you to do a good job so that our entire team can finish out the session and begin dinner."*

It wasn't the easiest concept for him to absorb, but he did sit down to finish his last session as I plated the pizza and poured milk.

In the end, my mom had seen enough to understand that things escalated quicker for our kids than most, their triggers were smaller than most, and their skills for working through complications were far less developed than most.

As she did the post-dinner dishes, she told me that seeing the kids, especially Brandon, helped her to understand that progress for our family was going to be slow, complicated, and a little outside of standard. I felt validated and excited because I knew the comparisons to my brother were going to stop abruptly now that she had this new image in her head.

We continued through the week, acknowledging more of the same challenges, plus a few more. There were a handful of quirks that stood out for different reasons. It isn't possible to remember all of the details of everything we experienced that week, so these few stories were the ones she would have held onto for everyone back home.

The most entertaining quirk for mom took place during our wacky-spaghetti night, where the kids helped us stick dry spaghetti noodles through slices of hotdogs before we boiled them. Most everything was already on the table, except I was holding a jar of applesauce and a bag of salad as I asked each kid which side they preferred.

I started with Faith, but she just stared blankly.

"There's no wrong choice, Faith," I said, but she continued to stare.

I moved on to Clay, mom, Brandon, Henry and Caisen. I gave them each the side they selected before moving back to Faith. She was still staring.

"Well, which one of them do you like more?" I asked, and she cried.

I noticed my mom's jaw dropped.

I cheerfully said, *"Applesauce it is,"* and poured some on Faith's plate. She wiped her tears and smiled.

After I got the kids initiated with their showers and TV routine, I joined my mom in the kitchen. She was finishing up the dishes, which seemed to be her favorite task of the day. It also seemed to be the only time she had to pause and reflect, which meant that validation was on its way.

She looked up at me and said, *"I just can't figure out how something so small can cause tears for Faith. Truly, I'm at a loss."*

I looked at her and with my most serious tone I said, *"Something small? Applesauce vs. salad is no small thing, Mom,"* and we both laughed. It became our inside joke.

The most heart-wrenching quirk of her trip occurred later that night, when we were tucking everyone into bed. When I told Faith goodnight, she didn't lie down or say anything back.

I asked if something was wrong, and she stared at me. The staring was getting on my nerves.

I sat on her bed and reminded her that I couldn't know her thoughts unless she shared them.

After twenty minutes of my guessing, she came out with it. *"I looked at that scary kids' app again, and I can't stop seeing it in my head."* The tears streamed down her cheeks.

I tried to work through it with her, but she was resistant to my approaches. An hour and a half later, she was still refusing to lie down. I finally gave her the direction to get set for bed, and she delivered a statement that I immediately knew would stay with me forever.

She barked, *"My mom was never there for me!"*

My heart was broken for her, long before this moment, but this was such a great reminder as to *"why"* we were going through all of the chaos with them.

I said, *"I know she wasn't. And that isn't fair or right. But, have I EVER let you down?"*

"No," she replied.

"Have you ever needed me, but weren't able to find me?" I asked.

Again, *"No."*

"So, when I promise you that I will be here if you need me, do you have any reason to question whether or not I will follow through?"

A final, *"No."*

"Faith," I said, *"I love you, and I promise that I will always do my best to make sure you never feel abandoned or neglected again."*

With that, she lay down. I gave her a kiss on the forehead and she went right to sleep.

When I walked out of the room, I could see that my mom had overheard the exchange. She was sitting on the couch with her own tears flowing. When I sat next to her, she grabbed my hand, and we both just cried. In that moment, I knew my mom was beginning to understand why we were giving our best to kids who drove us nuts. No matter how difficult it was, they deserved to be loved.

As if my mom wasn't observing enough, she couldn't leave without experiencing some of our more disgusting quirks. She found, just like Jordan and I did, that there is never a good time for the adults to shower in my house. In fact, she only got one shower in her entire ten days and regretted that one.

Truthfully, you couldn't take showers after the kids were in bed because there was no hot water left and a morning shower certainly wasn't worth the risk of waking any children up. During the day, there was too much coming-and-going, plus exhaustion was a shower-defeater. The struggle was real. By the end of her trip, she grew to understand that the only hygienic necessities were to get deodorant on, teeth brushed, and the previous night's tears washed off. If those three things happened, it was a successful day.

The most exciting development of the trip emerged on the backside of a tragic discovery. We were in the car listening to the Disney station, and my mom and I were singing away. I mean, we were really belting out. The kids thought it was hysterical, and their giggling fueled our increased enthusiasm.

The song *"Bare Necessities"* from the Jungle Book came on, and we totally nailed it, even the fast parts. However, as the song came to an end, my mom noticed that the kids hadn't been singing.

"Why aren't you guys singing with us?" she asked.

I nodded along in sadness as the kids answered her, blurting out over the top of each other, *"We've never seen the movie."*

Her mind was blown. She looked at me like I'd failed them and asked, *"Why have you not been watching Disney movies with them?"*

"I have been," I assured her. *"I have a decent collection of movies that we've been working through, but I don't have all the "classics,"* and they're expensive. Let's be honest, there are so many other things to spend the money on."

She accepted my answer, but not the circumstances. She was adamant that all children should see the Classics. To fix it, she started a list and went through our favorite Disney movies. I could tell she was fighting tears over the number of special movies the kids had not seen.

During her visit, we didn't have a lot of down time. However, the next free chunk of time we had was spent in the movie section at Walmart. She grabbed several titles and made time to watch a couple before she left for home, starting with the Little Mermaid. Not only did the kids enjoy it, but also it was a special moment for mom and me to share with them.

After working to remedy their movie history, mom realized there might be other unacceptable missed life experiences. She moved on to compile a list including necessities like camping and s'mores. At first, she was getting information I already had, but she continued to push deeper. When she got into things like putt-putt golf and riding horses, I began to take notes, too.

After putting the kids to bed on mom's last night, I asked how her week went compared to what she expected.

She said that she was only slightly surprised by the magnitude of each kid's baggage, letting me know that she truly had been listening to me. However, she went on to say that she wasn't prepared for how their baggage affected each other and our abilities to interact with each one.

She said that she came with an idea as to what would be good or fun for each kid, but didn't calculate how to do it without isolating the other kids. The fact that the comforts for one often were triggers for others left us in a complicated position.

Having someone else identify the fragile nature of our family was so fulfilling for me. I hadn't quite found a way to describe it to others, so I typically didn't even try. We often found ourselves in uncomfortable circumstances, like at the Zaxby's when Brandon dismantled the booth or at Jordan's work gathering where Brandon kicked the other boy, and all I could think to do was smile and apologize.

Even when there wasn't a problem, or before a problem developed, I hadn't yet found my response to people saying, *"What a blessing,"* when they heard about our circumstances. Though it was a very nice thing for them to say, it didn't ring true for me. It didn't feel like a blessing, even though I knew it was a God-thing. It was hard. However, it was also worth it. It was complicated, and I didn't feel like I could correctly convey that in short exchanges. Thank goodness for the few people who came and took the time to find out for themselves because it was lonely feeling like no one understood.

Over our ten days together, we had high moments, we had low moments, and we completed tasks like psychological evaluations and counseling appointments. We were busy and productive, and just when I felt she was falling into the groove of things, it was time to close-up shop. Probably for the best though, because I could see she was tired. The last thing I needed was guilt over aging my poor mother.

So, I accepted that it was time for mom to say goodbye to the kids. First, the bigger four as they got out of the car for school. She teared up a bit.

Then, we dropped Caisen off. At the door to his modular classroom, she said, *"Caisen, can I have another hug goodbye?"* To which my Caisen and the other Kayson in his class turned around and grabbed her tightly. She laughed at the extra-kid hug.

The floodgates opened when she got back in the car.

I took my mom to the airport to say our difficult goodbye. On the one hand, she wanted to stay. She didn't want to leave me to handle the work on my own. She didn't want to miss out on all that we were doing with the kids, knowing that it would be some time before she would be with us again.

On the other hand, we had wiped her out. She was in serious need of a recharge.

We parted ways just before the security checkpoint, but I quickly had a *"whoops"* feeling and turned back. Thankfully, she also realized that we hadn't taken a picture together through the entire trip, so she turned back, too. If we hadn't caught our error in time to get a quick selfie, there would have been no proof of our time together. She left, with a promise that we'd remember to pull our cameras out the next time.

As I walked out of the airport and got into my quiet car, I sighed in sadness. I was to be on my own for a few days, and the notion was heavy. I prayed that February thirteenth would come quickly.

Though I prayed for it, it didn't actually feel like it went quickly at all. Thankfully, it wasn't long after I'd gotten the kids in bed on that last night when I heard Jordan's truck pull into the driveway. I cried in relief. I made it. I got through it. I was a survivor. I probably looked ridiculous to him, as I approached him with snot and tears all over my face, which ended up on his uniform. I didn't feel bad though. That's what the washing machine is for.

As I held on to him, I expected we'd have time to focus on each other. I was wrong. One of the kids also noticed his truck pulling up, which resulted in all of the boys coming out to see him, which caught Faith's attention, too. They were all up. After I'd worked to get them all down.

I didn't want them to see my tears, but it turned out that they don't notice things like that. They were all grabbing at Jordan and pushed me out of the way in the process. I was chopped liver to them, and I was ok with that. I watched for a few seconds, happy that Jordan was being welcomed home so sweetly, but also wanting them back in bed.

Jordan must have read my mind, because I don't remember sending him any specific call signs or signals, and he told me to go lay down while he handled tucking the kids back in. He was my hero.

As much as I would have loved to pass out, I didn't. I waited for my husband to come to our room, and I verbally unloaded on him while he unpacked his field gear, which took close to an hour. He laughed at the funny and shocking stories I shared and groaned at the tough stuff. He also shared some of his tough moments from the field, and I couldn't help but think that I'd rather have been sleep deprived, dirty, and frustrated at work over being stuck at home with the kids.

Knowing what I'd just been through, I couldn't understand why Jordan would feel happy to be home, so I asked him, *"How can you possibly feel happy to be back here?"*

"Because I missed you," he said. *"I kind of missed seeing the kids, but not really. I just missed being with you."*

I cried, again, and he reached for me. He pulled me into him and just held me for a minute. Considering the man had been missing his wife for three weeks, I'm surprised I got a full minute of consoling before he put the moves on me. I was so happy to have him home that I responded in kind.

We woke up on Saturday, February fourteenth knowing that the kids were expecting to do something fun for Valentine's Day. We also had a few errands to run with Jordan, which was typical after he got home from the field. As a family, we grabbed some lunch on the way to the park. Brandon was upset about the lunch choice, so he pitched a big-ol' fit as the other kids began to play.

After a good thirty minutes, it was time to continue with our day. However, Brandon still hadn't *"gotten"* to play. Instead of getting in the car, he began throwing rocks at the car and at me. It didn't feel like Brandon was settling down, so Jordan took the other four kids to get his errands done and left me with Brandon. I hoped Brandon would get a clue soon, so that people would stop glaring in our direction, and I could rejoin my husband.

He did not. He ran alongside our exiting car, kicking at the tires, while I avoided eye contact with the other parents at the park. He threw more rocks at the car, until it was out of range. Then he went back to aiming at me. I gave reminders and warnings and incrementally increased his timeout length.

The time didn't add up as quickly when he switched to throwing pinecones at me. Then, he reduced his efforts further by only throwing them near me, since I was taking the fun out of it by sitting in a grassy area, enjoying the sun with my back to him.

Two hours passed before Jordan had finished our errands, and I gave the word we were ready to be picked up. Brandon earned the honor of serving a one-hour time out. He didn't like the consequence, but he was exhausted enough to roll with it.

I can honestly say that my 2015 Valentine's Day was the least lovey-dovey in so many ways. I mean, I had never had things thrown at me for an entire two hours before. However, it was also the most lovey-dovey, because it was the first Valentine's Day where I got five goodnight hugs and kisses. Well, six, if you count Jordan's. I was so happy to have him home!

CHAPTER 24

STRIVE FOR PROGRESS, NOT PERFECTION

W e had been working so hard to balance our seemingly endless counseling appointments with elements of normalcy, and it worked for a
bit. However, we needed a shift. Since there was nothing we could remove,
we talked to the kids about adding something into our already demanding routine.

Our talk revealed that they all wanted to play sports. Jordan and I grew
up in sports. We learned a lot of life-lessons that way and enjoyed our experiences, so we loved the idea of giving the kids the same opportunity. We
knew it would be more difficult for the older kids to start up because of the
years of participation that they had missed. But better late than never.

We discovered which sports were offered for the upcoming season and
let the kids pick. Faith chose volleyball, and I became hopeful we could
bond through it. The boys all chose soccer. I didn't know anything about
soccer, but I was ready to learn.

This new time commitment changed my world. In addition to helping
the kids with their homework and school requirements, the visits from their
caseworkers, their counseling days, which were changed to Wednesday and
Friday, I also had five kids on five different sports teams, with five different
schedules.

And let me tell you, their schedules were not consistent. The only
schedule rules were that each kid would have three appearances a week
between practices and games, and the practices and games would all be
between five and eight, Monday-Thursday and anytime on Saturday. Other
than that, the schedules changed from week to week. So, I had to be flexible.

It was worth it to me, though, because sports introduced concepts like punctuality, hustling, dependability, consistency, etc.

We made it clear to the kids that if they signed up, then it was a season-long commitment. We told them they could choose not to play additional seasons, but the practices were mandatory to stay on the teams because of the way a team counts on having all of its members present.

There were many tests of this rule. Brandon would be in a full meltdown, and we'd need to be leaving for practice, whether it was his or someone else's, and I'd have to find a way to get him out the door, even when everything in me wanted to leave him behind.

"I just don't feel like playing today."

"Then you're off the team."

"But I want to play in the game."

"Then go to practice, today."

"But I don't feel like playing today."

"Then you're off the team."

"But I want to be on the team."

"Then go to practice, today."

The rounds would go on and on and on.

I felt tempted to quit everyone's teams, but thought that was a little extreme. I didn't really want him, or any of them, to be off their teams, and I also didn't think it would be fair for their teammates to wonder if or when they were coming.

Somehow, I got each of the kids to every one of their games and practices, with the latest we showed up being about ten minutes. I chose to view those days as victories anyway and as reminders of why I had to start prepping the kids to leave long before most other families would have.

The other fun aspect of sports was the dinners-on-the-go. Other than some kids discount nights at local restaurants, I packed dinners. I enjoyed throwing their food to them as we all sat around, watching whoever was currently playing.

As we were working out the kinks of our new routine, we had some wonderful highs and lows.

For me, every night that Jordan could join us was a high. Whether it was to help with the end-of-night shuffling, or to take the kids who had completed their sports obligation home while I finished up, or to just come hang out and watch some of the excitement, bottom-line, I just really enjoyed having him around.

I also enjoyed the view of my kids, as they were reading and doing homework on the sidelines when they weren't in a practice or game. In the beginning, I felt silly carrying a large tote filled with books and pencils for their homework, but the more they utilized them, the prouder I felt over their progress, especially considering the distractions all around them.

I also enjoyed the rare opportunity to step in and coach Faith's volleyball team. Her head coach had to miss a practice from time-to-time, and I was happy to stand in, if Jordan was available to cover the other kids. I played hard, the girls worked hard, they learned stuff, they laughed, and they certainly dripped some sweat. Throughout the season, Faith and I also spent a good amount of time passing the ball back and forth, counting how many exchanges we could get. Our number increased over the six-week season, and I was proud of her for it.

Another high was watching my kids navigate the world of having other adults guide them, direct them, and criticize them. It felt nice to share the burden of sculpting my young kids. Anything they heard or learned from their coaches was a little something less I had to take on.

Though the highs felt very high, there were also lows, including every time my kids displayed poor sportsmanship. For example, there was the day we watched from the sideline as Brandon called his teammates jerks for not passing him the ball exactly when he wanted them to.

Or, the time Caisen ran away from me in a parking lot, while onlookers commented on how cute he was.

Or, trying to put the kids to bed after they had crossed the line of too tired. The later sports nights were brutal.

Or, having to handle all of the chaperoning on my own. Oh, how I longed for carpool privileges.

Or, receiving all of the negative statements and stares from other parents when my children did something clearly uncalled for or rude. The comments made, both under breath and full breath, indicated that others assumed the kids were learning their behaviors from us, or that we weren't parenting well enough to correct our unruly kids. The most common phrase I heard on the sideline was, *"Discipline your kid,"* always after my kid did something embarrassing, which was almost always followed by a, *"Hi mommy,"* with an obvious wave in my direction.

No matter the blowback, I tried to keep the foster-secret to myself, because I wanted sports to be the one place where the kids could just be kids and take a break from our foster-reality. I didn't want any foster stigma to isolate them from the other kids, though they seemed to stand out anyway.

Though I tried to keep our status to myself, it got awkward when mom-friend relationships seemed to be developing, and I didn't divulge when the opportunity presented. So, instead of lying or pretending, sometimes I let the conversation roll.

It never went well. I usually got questions like these in response:

"Where are the real parents?"

"So, you're not actually their mom?"

Or worse, *"So you're not actually a mom?"*

"Do you regret it?"

"How much do you get paid for that?"

"I'm surprised your husband agreed to that?"

Occasionally I'd get, *"Are you sure you want to go through with this? Because, you can't really fix broken kids. You know it's going to break your marriage, right?"*

One of the toughest comments was, *"It isn't official yet, so you can still back out, right? Too many people think they have to stick with it because of guilt, but that's no reason to do this. You need to do what's best for your marriage and back out before it's too late."*

As much as I knew that I had no chance of making mom-friends if I didn't open up, I also recognized that sharing opened the door to unwanted criticism, lectures, or inappropriate interrogations. As an advocate, I tried my best to handle the complications gracefully. As a human being, each exchange was hurtful, and I felt myself withdrawing further and further.

I eventually accepted that it wasn't the right time for making friends, and I just needed to focus on the demands of my mom job. I spent my spare moments planning and executing fun things to do as a family, like frequent beach days. We stayed busy, we stayed alert, and we celebrated the many small victories along the way.

One night, while we were sitting around our large dining room table eating dinner, Henry teared up and asked, *"Can we please change my name?"*

We told him that the plan was to only change their last names, which the kids thought had already been done. In fact, a couple of the kids fought back with intensity when anyone called them by their legal last names. We had ongoing conversations about how to politely respond when someone didn't know their preferred last name.

Anyway, he got more worked up, saying that he wanted a whole new name.

Clay chimed in, saying that he'd prefer to be called Ken.

Henry said that he wanted to be Jordan Junior. But, he said he'd settle for a new middle name.

Caisen piped in to say that he wanted to be Jordan Junior, too.

Clay said if he couldn't be Ken, then he'd like to be another Jordan Junior.

Brandon said he wanted a middle name starting with L, so that his new initials could be BLT.

Faith said she really wanted my middle name. I told her my middle name was Marie, the same as hers, except mine didn't have a spelling error. So, she decided that she just wanted us to correct the spelling of her middle name because Maie just wasn't doing it for her.

We brought it to a close by agreeing to consider middle names. As everyone transitioned from the table, I recognized that no one had begged for thirds. They were obviously feeling some trust in that moment and left feeling content. I didn't draw attention to it, but my heart took notice.

That night, Jordan and I talked it through and decided that there was no harm in changing their middle names, since it's what they all wanted. We brainstormed middle names for each of them, feeling so sentimental about picking names for our kids.

The next night, we told the kids that we picked a few options for each kid, names that were meaningful and significant to us, that we wanted to pass down. But, we were keeping their first names, despite their pleading. Learning new names would be too complicated, considering what was already going on.

We started with Faith. Easy, correct the spelling to Marie.

Brandon. We offered him two L-names with meaning to both Jordan and me - Lynn and Lee. He chose to be Brandon Lee, which met his desire of being BLT.

Henry was disappointed he couldn't be called Jordan. But, he was pleased with the name Henry Bennett. Bennett was Jordan's middle name and had been carried down a few generations. He beamed as he said, *"Dad was the middle kid, and I'm the middle kid. And Dad's middle name is Bennett, and my middle name is Bennett. I'm the most like Dad!"*

I was so happy to see him happy.

Then it was Clay's turn. Technically, his name was Clarence. The other kids had also been given nicknames, but they all ditched them as quickly as possible. By the time they made it to us, they only made fun of their old nicknames, even their own.

Except Clay. His seemed to stick. When we addressed Clay, he said I could start calling him Clarence sometimes, which I took as a request, so I began to use them interchangeably.

Anyhow, my grandfather was Clarence Raymond. My uncle shared the same middle name. I had lost both my uncle and grandpa far before I was ready and had always planned on passing their middle name down. Considering my child already had my grandpa's first name, I was hopeful that he would like the middle name I leaned toward for him.

When I told Clay about my history with the middle name *"Raymond,"* he smiled so big. However, Clarence had a hard time making *"r"* sounds, so it sounded like he was bragging about being Clawence Wemand. For the next few days, he asked me to help him learn to say it correctly. If nothing else, Clarence had a strong work ethic.

Lastly, it was time for the little man. He was on the same boat as Henry, badly wanting to be called Jordan Junior, or JJ. When we asked what he thought of the middle name James, he loved it. Except, for the next few weeks, he kept saying that his name was Caisen Junior.

"Caisen what?"

"Caisen Junior."

"Are you sure?"

"Whoops, I forgot again. I'm Caisen James."

He was silly, and cute.

Then, the conversation transitioned to the rest of our family. The kids wanted to hear more about the people they'd share names with, then more about our parents and our siblings. As they showed interest in our family, I took it as a sign they truly believed we were their forever family.

I knew that we had missed a lot with our children, and I knew there was no way to go back to experience or recreate their earlier years. Renaming them was a monumental opportunity. We were real parents, doing real parenting, with our real children, counting on every small victory to keep us moving forward through the struggles. Between improved eye contact and sporting events to look forward to, I found it easier to balance out my perspective.

Speaking of moving forward, we found proof we were making progress while the kids and I were eating our kids-night dinners at McDonald's on a typical Tuesday night. We were all smooshed together in a booth. Clarence was sitting on the inside and shared with the group that he needed to go to the bathroom. His only obstacle was Brandon, who was sitting on the outside.

"Brandon, could you please lean forward so Clay can step behind you?" I asked.

Clay went to step behind Brandon, but Brandon leaned backwards instead of forwards, causing Clay to trip on Brandon. He didn't use his arms to brace himself, which I thought odd, as he fell flat onto the floor.

At the same exact time, a McDonald's employee was walking by and accidentally stepped on his outstretched fingers. She couldn't have planned the timing if she tried.

In the past, Clarence would have curled into his own little ball and faced the problem on his own. But, this time, he turned for me with his giant blue eyes and wide-open arms. I scooped my big, heavy baby up and was holding him as the server brought over some ice for his skinned hip and red fingers.

Brandon grunted, *"It's his fault, I didn't even do anything,"* which I interpreted as his feeling guilty over the mix-up. He hadn't learned the skill of apologizing, he didn't want to be in trouble, and he didn't want to be blamed for the problem, so he just loudly defended himself.

I needed to focus on Clarence' physical pain in that moment, so I abruptly said, *"Brandon, no one is blaming you. It was an accident. If you feel bad, you can apologize for the accident, but pitching a fit won't help anyone."*

He seemed confused, which was fantastic, because it meant he had heard me. However, he put his arms over his face as he tried to work it all out.

He was quietly mumbling to himself, but I still heard bits and pieces. He said something to the effect of, *"I shouldn't be in trouble, but Clay shouldn't either, so who gets the consequence? I shouldn't. But he shouldn't. But he got hurt, so someone needs to be in trouble."*

I actually giggled about the turn of events with Brandon as I was holding Clay, who was not giggling. Clay held the ice on his fingers and then on his hip, then back on his fingers. When he felt recovered, he headed to the bathroom and back to the playroom.

This enabled me to address Brandon, who couldn't understand how no one was getting a consequence. He couldn't identify the difference between accidents and intentional problems. Further, he couldn't see the difference between an accident resulting from a miscommunication and an accident resulting from a broken rule.

I gave him examples of broken rules that lead to accidents, like running through the house and plowing into someone coming around a corner. You don't punish the plow; you punish the running that caused the plow. But, in the case of Clay's McDonald's wipeout, the cause of the fall was just a miscommunication about which way to lean. There was nothing punishable about that, even though the result was not good.

Brandon nodded at the example, but I could see through the gap in his arms that he was still puzzled. *"If I didn't do anything for a consequence, why would I have to apologize?"* he asked.

I explained that apologies aren't just used as an acceptance of fault, but also as a way of sharing that you feel sorry about an outcome, situation, action, or event, and you just want the other person to know that you care.

It was one of our better talks, and his arms came down as we finished.

Next, without being directed, he walked up to Clay and apologized for accidentally tripping him.

I was astounded. Did I actually connect with Brandon? Did he really offer up an apology on his own? What led Clarence to reach for me when he fell? Was I dreaming? Would Jordan believe me when I told him what happened?

That night, it was a challenge to find the words to describe for Jordan how I felt. And even if I could find the words, there was no way for me to get them out through the tears. I was moved. I had been pouring into the kids for five months, and I was finally seeing a tangible shift in them.

A couple days later, we received the results of the psychological evaluations. Just about all of my suspicions were confirmed, plus a few other quirks were noted. All five kids had Attention Deficit Hyperactivity Disorder (ADHD). No surprise there! In fact, to determine whether or not ADHD is clinically present, the difference between two calculations must be greater than fifteen. The difference in my kids' numbers was large, with the most severe being forty-six! They were not mild cases!

In addition, Brandon was diagnosed with Reactive Attachment Disorder (RAD), and Caisen was given a provision for it. RAD is the most severe form of attachment disorder. The basic explanation is that about eighty percent of a person's brain cells develop before the age of two. If a person doesn't have access to certain things, like relationships, nurturing, social exchanges, and positive modeling, then some areas of the brain basically don't develop properly, and the life lessons they learn are deeply skewed by their inappropriate circumstances. Therefore, the person is left with any combination of traits like being selfish, controlling, manipulative, falsely charismatic, highly addictive, drawn to fires, and indifferent.

Caisen's provision meant that he was too young to be formally diagnosed, but there were enough consistent symptoms to request that he be tested for the disorder at an older age.

Caisen and Brandon were also observed to have Disruptive Behavior Disorder (DBD) with features of Objective Defiance Disorder (ODD), which means that they sought chaos and disorder through disruption and were more comfortable in confrontations than in harmony.

We also received various diagnoses of mood disorders for each child and an interpretation disorder for Faith, with indicators that the others might have difficulties with their processing too.

Additionally, their IQ's were tested. From oldest to youngest, the IQ's started off better than I had guessed, at average, and improved as we worked through our lineup, with the younger three deemed to be geniuses, rating in the superior range of intelligence. Since we weren't seeing that play out in their daily interactions, I accepted the challenge of revealing their aptitude, through lessening their baggage.

I was hopeful after learning that each of the kids had the intellectual ability to logically understand what some of their problems were and to understand the implications, that they could possibly develop an interest in learning compensation skills.

Lastly, each child was assigned a number to represent the likelihood of them making full recoveries. The psychologist told me that when he calculated the results based solely on the many hours of testing, those numbers were not good. However, when he factored in the progress we had already observed, the resources we were committed to utilizing, and the parenting approach we described, the numbers improved.

Even better than explaining the dynamic to me, he also wrote it up in the packet of documentation that I'd be giving to the caseworker. Let's just say, I was more than thrilled to know the caseworker would be seeing such a glowing review of our parenting, especially after the earlier conflict when he assumed we'd been the problem regarding the kids' behavior. And with the updated psychological evaluations in the kids' file, their health on paper would finally be an accurate representation of how they were presenting in life. They deserved that, after nearly four years.

Though their difficulties outweighed their strengths in that moment, I left that meeting with a hopeful heart. I was aware that the cause of their being so far from living out their potential was due to preventable, unfair living circumstances, but I couldn't change any of that. All I could do was facilitate the steps forward, and I was refueled in my mission to do just that.

And, now that I had documentation of their difficulties, I was going to get better support through more specialized resources. The counselors could adjust their approaches to account for the specific diagnoses, and we were assigned a psychiatrist.

Just like that, my life went from crazy, to crazier.

Getting the kids through psychiatry appointments was the opposite of entertaining. They did not do well in office settings. I took the kids in one at a time, and their behavior was equally disastrous. Faith kept trying to call my attention away from the psychiatrist to have a chat of our own. Caisen was throwing the doctor's stuffed animals up in the air. Brandon rolled on the ground in boredom. Clarence was getting into the desk drawers. Henry started crying as the doctor asked questions. If nothing else, they made it easy for the psychiatrist to see what we were working with.

An unintended consequence of taking the kids in individually meant that I had many follow-up trips to the pharmacy. Since the medicines were controlled substances, they could not be called in. I had to actually show up with the paper prescriptions and then wait for them to be filled. Because they all started their medications on different days, their refill dates didn't line up, either. My new norm became visiting the pharmacy between two-to-three times per week. And my wait was always long.

Thankfully, there were some great changes in some of the kids.

Henry went from being in trouble daily, to being perceived as helpful and respectful. He hadn't learned integrity, so his newfound hint of self-control was only exercised when he thought an adult was watching. However, the praise he gained for making good choices, I was certain, would become a goal for him, which might help him to let go of some of his other, less charming instincts.

Clay also had a big response. However, giving him some self-control actually revealed that he enjoyed being an instigator, and he used his new tool to annoy people with much more precision. Truthfully, the small adjustment in him reminded me even more of my younger brother. His gains also opened the door enough for us to have chats about what he wanted in life and what character traits would get him there. Each time our talks went deeper, I felt more connected and motherly.

Caisen gained a better ability to earn green at school. Of course, it didn't happen every day. He was a playful and silly young boy. However, he gained the ability to choose, at times, to avoid some undesirable consequences. If only I could motivate him to choose success at home...

Medications helped him to gain better control of his thoughts; apparently, what he thought was that he should have all of my attention. And he thought that it would be easiest to gain it by being mean to me. That made sense, considering the diagnosis we had explained to us. But, at least he was seeking my attention. It showed me that I mattered to him.

Sadly, Faith's gains were small if any. We were hoping to see the light bulb come on. However, the medications only gave her flickers, at best. At least she had good intentions. She wasn't getting into trouble. She was just floating through, missing out on her own life.

Lastly, there was Brandon. His impacts were not good. We were told that it would take six-to-eight weeks to see if the medications were a good match and that he might be extra irritable while his body adjusted to the chemical changes. I laughed at the idea, not believing it was possible for Brandon to become more irritable.

As it turned out, it wasn't a laughing matter. We found this out while playing at the park.

Jordan had met us there after work one evening and attempted to play catch with Clay. When Jordan threw the Nerf football to Clay, it bounced off of Clay's chest, and Clay ran to grab the ball. As he picked it up, he got blind-sided by Brandon. After Brandon knocked Clay to the ground, he sat on him. Then he kicked him in the face, with his heels.

We intervened as best we could. While I used my mom tone to say, *"Brandon, get off of him, NOW,"* Jordan ran the short distance to the boys. He couldn't physically grab Brandon, so he grabbed for Clarence instead, pulling him up to his feet from underneath Brandon.

However, here's the ridiculous part. When Brandon was told that he had earned his measly little two-minute timeout, he freaked out. *"Clay started it,"* he screamed, *"because he tried to get the ball that I wanted. If you can't see that Clay should be in timeout, not me, then you're stupid."*

If we'd learned anything about Brandon, we learned that he couldn't recover quickly. Therefore, there was no use in pretending we'd get back to the fun. Instead, Jordan loaded Faith, Henry, Clay, and Caisen into his truck and took them to Wendy's, understanding that I'd join him whenever Brandon was ready to calm down.

After my crew left, I sat in my car with the windows down so I could hear Brandon's ranting and watch him intently. When the sun went down, the air got cold, and I turned my heat on. As the show went on, I enjoyed some alone time with the music on.

After thirty minutes of screaming about my stupidity, Brandon ran out of steam. He noticed it was cold and climbed in the car for heat. I called Jordan, who had stopped at the house to change out of his uniform, and coordinated our timeline, while Brandon sat silently with his arms folded.

I hung up with Jordan and shared with Brandon that our food would probably just be coming out when we got there, and we'd be able to eat with everyone else. He seemed indifferent.

I tried to talk to Brandon about what happened, and he struggled to see things from my point of view. His mind was made. All I could do was stand my ground in hopes that he'd later figure it out.

I felt like we'd taken a step backward with Brandon, but I also felt like we were never actually ahead. Every time I thought I was making progress, I learned I wasn't, or that it wasn't very much, or that there was more challenge hiding underneath. I had no confidence in the relationship, or where it was going.

Between the highs and the lows, I really didn't know how to feel. I thought maybe we had the right setup for gains to come through constant prayers, the strictness of our routines and disciplinary responses, their new medications, our ongoing therapy and our developing sports experiences. I knew there was no magical cure, and it wasn't up to us how the kids handled the opportunities in front of them, but we had at least arranged a platform where improvements were possible. Those possibilities had to be my focus.

CHAPTER 25

A PICTURE IS WORTH ONE THOUSAND WORDS

D ay-to-day life was challenging. I was spread thin. Logistically, I was over-booked between psychiatry appointments, caseworker visits, counseling appointments, homework/reading obligations for school, and sports. I was emotionally exhausted due to the overwhelming abundance of bad attitudes, melt-downs, intentional defiance, testing limits, challenges for control, fear of vulnerability, lack of trust, inability to see value in compromise, and an overwhelming sense of *"life isn't fair"* and *"I hate this"* from my kids. Each aspect was understandable, but so heavy to live with.

Not to mention the changes that came through starting medications. Of course, it took the edge off of the kids' impulsivity issues, but giving clarity to children who are both defensive and offensive brought its own variety of concerns.

Not only was Brandon still in daily meltdowns, but his arguments were more hurtful. He would scream that I was a terrible parent and that his other parents would have been much nicer. He even screamed that he wanted to take back everything that he had drawn for us, send it to any one of his former parents. He aimed to be hurtful when he was upset.

No matter how hard he fought, we stuck with the phrase, *"A fit will never get you what you want."* The kids also used the phrase, *"You get what you get and don't pitch a fit."*

I was determined to teach all of them that fits would guarantee they don't get their way, every time, without fail. I was tempted to give in often, but knew that negotiating with them would give them hope that their tantrums would work, which was as dangerous as striking deals with terrorists.

Brandon wasn't learning, so he continued to push the limits. It was hard to understand his motivations. His responses of screaming, yelling, arguing, shutting down, rapid firing door slams, furniture tipping, furniture kicking, furniture moving, alligator rolling, insult sharing, light flicking, shoe throwing, and down the road walking did not help him, in any way. In fact, it cost him. So, why even do it, unless he was just stuck in a bad rut?

Clay, however, wasn't stuck. He was deliberate. I think he was aiming to get attention, and he knew just how to do it. I had to work extra hard to settle my emotions as he was aiming to push my buttons. I had to step over him as he flailed on the ground over things like wanting to change the TV channel, wanting a book that someone else was reading, or wanting a different snack option.

Though I was tempted to give in, I held firm and continued to address his instigating, prank-playing, lying, fake-tears, then real tears, non-poop wiping, squirming, rage-screaming, chair throwing, food scarfing, dramatic and dirty approach to life. I was conflicted between wanting to enjoy the time with him at this age and wanting him to fast track on some growing up.

Henry wasn't stuck like Brandon or attention seeking like Clarence. He wanted to stay under the radar. I thought of Henry like a person who just met their new boss, after years of enjoying a laid-back supervisor at work, who, metaphorically, allowed him to show up late, take extended breaks, and take off early. And, he seemed to feel an injustice by now having to exist under a new, by-the-book boss. He did not like being held accountable for his behaviors, especially ones he'd grown accustomed to getting away with.

Instead of adapting to our expectations, he decided to try a new manipulation tactic: trigger someone else so he looks better in comparison. I noticed Henry going into the living room one day, where he took a seat near Brandon. I listened closely and heard Henry quietly say to Brandon, *"Ice cream sounds really good, don't you think? We haven't had ice cream in a while."* I could see on Henry's face that he was up to something, and it didn't seem to be about ice cream.

He was planting a seed in Brandon's mind, and it worked. Within a few minutes, we saw the alligator rolls. Once Brandon was well into his fit and I was attempting to calm him down, Henry seized the opportunity to approach me for a hug while batting his eyes, saying that he loved me.

The little punk. Each time I called him out for triggering Brandon on purpose, he was appalled. He would say, *"But Brandon, blah-blah-blah,"* which would push Brandon further over the edge. I believe his attempt was to distract me, so that he could make his escape. But, I always came back for him.

I always told Henry that I only chose to follow up with him because I cared about him enough to notice his habits, but he maintained that I was just being mean to him. I continually reminded him that his habits were not from his heart, and I wanted to help him replace the survival habits he'd learned with happier, healthier ones. He called it unfair. I called it love. Meanwhile, we kept working on accountability and integrity by addressing the lying, cheating, manipulating, instigating, and sucking-up.

Then there was Faith. She was still just floating along. She was always smiling, always talking like a baby, and very hot and cold with Jordan. When he gave her directions, she wouldn't even look at him or acknowledge him, but she'd accept every hug from him she could get. When he gave the other kids directions, she would cut in to explain how I did it differently so they didn't need to listen to him. When Jordan called her out for being disobedient, she ignored him, then I'd get pulled in, and I'd make the point clear to her that Jordan also deserved her respect.

After she processed, she would come apologize to me for not listening to Jordan, but she wouldn't apologize to him. Even if I told her that the apology was meant for Jordan because he was the one she hurt. Instead of addressing him, she'd just glaze over and stare.

Then, before bedtime, she'd go collect her bear hug from him like nothing happened.

Aside from her daddy-issues, she was mostly sweet and easygoing. I was thankful to have at least one child who didn't scream and yell at me. However, since she was so quiet, I had to push myself into approaching her. She wasn't going to bring her problems to us, so I needed to remember to go to her. In the meantime, we kept working through her blank staring, eyes glazing, baby-talking, confused thinking, passive approaching, dad-disrespecting way of life.

Lastly, there was Caisen. He certainly wasn't as big or strong as Brandon, even though Brandon wasn't big or strong. However, Caisen's fits were growing to resemble Brandon's with the door slamming, light flicking and furniture kicking! He wasn't stuck or illogical, like Brandon. He was stubborn and controlling. He was growing to be my biggest adversary.

He held nothing back when he fought. It was clear that we'd be experiencing his biting, kicking, throwing, head-butting, bed-destroying, couch-kicking, pinching, eye-gouging, copy-cat light-flicking, screaming, yelling, toe-to-toe way of life for a while.

I just kept telling myself that God had a plan, and He'd get us through, one day at a time.

Before we knew it, it was Faith's twelfth birthday, which was also April Fools' Day and my dad's fifty-eighth birthday. I enjoyed knowing Faith and my dad shared a birthday.

Going into gift opening, I accepted that Brandon was going to behave similarly as on Clay's birthday. And he did. Sadly, this time Caisen joined him.

I chose to focus on the good stuff, like Faith enjoying the super young, girly things we bought for her. We stuck with her interests, but bumped her up from the four-six age ratings to the eight-ten range. The dolls were intended for a slightly older child, and the crafts required a little more focus and attention. I didn't expect her to jump all the way up to a twelve-year-old girl just yet, but we laid the foundation for her to steadily grow.

Not long after Faith's birthday, I found some unexpected relief. It was Easter morning, and we were all dressed in our best. The four boys had matching little suits. They fought against matching, but they each wanted the same color. Since none of them was willing to try a different color or pattern, matching was the only option. Jordan coordinated with the boys. Faith and I wore dresses and make-up, with our dried hair down.

Foster care rules demanded we not post or share pictures of the kids for privacy reasons, but I asked our neighbor to take a family picture for us anyway, even if only for ourselves. It was a rare moment of our family looking and feeling so great, while also celebrating something so important. While holding my smile for the eternity it took to get the rest of the family smiling, I had an idea.

I didn't say anything when I took off running, in my high-heels, into the house. I'm sure my sudden departure left my crew feeling confused, but I was on a mission. I knew how to take a picture we could share and post!

I grabbed our favorite snuggie, which is a sleeved-blanket, to use as a backdrop. It was our favorite because it was covered in the colors and logo of our favorite football team. Jordan and I stood in front of the blanket, holding it up like a curtain for the children to stand behind. Each of the kids stuck their hands over the blanket or through the armholes of the blanket to better reach us. The younger kids struggled, so Jordan and I squatted lower, and lower, until they could all properly place bunny ears, since it was Easter, on Jordan and me. Though their faces could not be viewed, their unidentifiable fingers served as proof that the kids did exist.

I posted the picture. It was the first visual I had shared publicly. Before this, the only pictures I shared were of the five backpacks or five jerseys or five baseball mitts. This was the first time I had shared with the masses any picture that contained child-flesh.

The responses were funny. Mostly people said things like, *"So, maybe you really do have five kids."* It felt amazing to share a glimpse of what my life had become. In a world where people share so much, I could share so little, making this one picture meaningful. It was proof, of sorts, that I really was a mom.

I continued to seek those happy moments in order to help offset the weight of the struggles. We diligently sought activities that would pique our interest, as well as distract the kids into feeling loved, all while combining brainpower to find new ways of creatively capturing our family on camera.

It was hard to balance the adventures and the routines, but we didn't want the time after our last games on Saturdays or the afternoons after church on Sundays to go to waste, and fighting in the house always felt like a waste. We just needed to remember to submit travel requests to the caseworkers for activities outside our approved travel boundaries.

We were thankful that our radius was greater than most because we had to travel with the kids back and forth between the county where the kids went into foster care and our county. However, we still needed travel passes to cross the Florida-Georgia Line or over into South Carolina to visit Hilton-Head and enjoy the tourist attractions. If we didn't get our request for permission in early enough, then we couldn't go.

We had frustration over the travel passes, not because we couldn't entertain ourselves in Georgia, and not because approvals were hard to get, but because I hated living under the restrictions. The inability to be spontaneous was another reminder that we weren't in charge of our own family. Like every other rule, I had the option of wallowing in my own self-pity, or keeping a backup destination in mind. For us, Jekyll Island in Georgia was the place to be when we couldn't go to our favorite beach, which was just a few miles further down the interstate in Florida.

Our frequent beach trips, whether they were in Georgia, Florida or South Carolina, helped to tire our kids out on the weekends, which helped bedtimes go more smoothly. The sun and waves at any beach could zap them. Like most kids, they got cranky when they were tired, but the window of crankiness between the beach and bed was small enough that we chose to do it again and again.

We used our backup destination a few times a month, got approvals for other beaches when we could, and stayed on the lookout for additional adventures, like the magic show at the Children's Museum. It was local, so we didn't need a permission slip.

It was a Saturday, so Jordan and I split our eyes between the many volleyball and soccer games taking place. When the first three kids were done playing, Jordan took them home to get started on showers, leaving me with Faith and Caisen.

We got home a little later than the first crew and walked in to find Brandon in a meltdown. It didn't look like he would be coming out of it any time soon, and we needed to hit the road for the magic show, so Jordan and I had to make a choice. Either one of us needed to stay behind with Brandon, or everyone would have to stay behind.

This was the first time we couldn't calm Brandon down in time for an event we knew he'd be sorry to miss. As disappointing as his loss was, we decided it wasn't a good reason for the other kids to miss out, so I took the four and left Jordan with the one.

I had a flicker of hope that Brandon would collect himself and catch up when he noticed what had happened. But he couldn't. He was stuck, and there was no shortcut for freeing him, which meant no chance for Jordan to join us. I felt sorry for Jordan to miss the fun with the other four, but I also felt relief it wasn't me. I'd already missed movies and dessert and family bike rides.

At the show, my kids fought over some of the goodies that were tossed out into the crowd. Then they called out to the magician, demanding that he throw additional items out to them. Then they yelled at him for throwing the wrong things.

A proud-mom moment, and I'm sure that the glares from the other parents were out of jealousy.

The coolest aspect about this magician was how he utilized many animals in his show. He had a scene with a tortoise and a hare and also some birds and reptiles. The kids loved it, until he pulled out a large snake. Three of my kids were noticeably concerned, but not as severely as Henry, who broke out in full tears when he saw the snake.

The magician invited all of the kids to come up to touch the snake and take pictures with it. Three of my kids reluctantly went up. Henry was terrified and sobbing. I told him he didn't need to go up there, but then he got mad at me for suggesting he was scared.

It was a reminder that I couldn't advise my kids to hold back. The idea needed to come from them. I could only support forward progress, even though other parents looked at me like I was trying to unfairly force my kids into things. One lady even mumbled to the mom next to her, *"Poor kid, his mom is traumatizing him."*

They didn't know our circumstances, and I couldn't abandon Henry to go inform them, so I shook it off, as always. I tried to maintain a smile as I continued talking to him.

Anyway, when we got up to the snake, the magician teasingly said, *"Not to worry, he likes everyone... Except for the kids wearing orange shirts."*

Henry was wearing an orange shirt. The tears flowed again. The magician was clearly oblivious to the distress he was encouraging. What a mess.

"Henry, he was teasing. The snake is very nice," I said.

Henry did not find the magician's joke to be funny, but Clay did. He laughed and told Henry, *"He's so funny, and his snake is soooo cool!"*

Eventually we got a group picture. Clay, Faith, the magician, and myself all had our hands on the snake's body, holding him up. Caisen stood at the snake's face, laughing at the tongue that kept popping in and out. Henry was at the tail, with his hands clasped together. He touched the snake briefly and celebrated his bravery with a big teary-smile for the picture.

As soon as the show concluded, we made a break for the car, where I called to check in with Brandon and Jordan. *"Brandon is exhausted, so he's fighting less, but he's still upset. I'll try to get him in the truck to meet you guys for dinner, but take your time getting there because Brandon won't be easy to get moving."*

When we got to the restaurant, I called Jordan for a progress report: *"We're pulled over on the side of the interstate because Brandon freaked out when I told him that we couldn't make the magician start the show over for him. I can't drive while he's shaking my seat and throwing things at me. I'm sorry, but it's going to be a while longer."*

He wasn't lying; it did take a while. And when they finally arrived, Brandon didn't know if he should start an entirely new fit over being jealous, or a fit over feeling guilty for causing our group to split, or if he should just be excited to hear the stories. His face struggled to pick an emotion and just kept rotating through them. It was sad, but also entertaining. Thankfully, he felt special because we ordered a stuffed jalapeño appetizer that he'd always wanted to try, so he mostly held it together.

While at dinner, Reagan called to talk about meeting up the next weekend for a day trip in Myrtle Beach, SC to visit with her family, including her mom who was flying in to see them. Myrtle Beach was close to being in the middle between our two homes. We knew it was a big, touristy city, so there would be plenty of things to do to fill up a day of visiting.

I happily committed to submitting a travel request.

The kids overheard enough to get excited over the possibility of seeing everyone, and I had to remind them that it wasn't fully decided yet. We needed permission first. I hated telling the kids that we needed permission because I felt like it was a stab at my authority. However, we had gotten the hang of the travel system, so I was fairly certain it would be approved.

Within a few days, I had a printed copy of our travel approval. We were all so excited because it had been a couple of months since we last saw Reagan and Jack and even longer for David. Plus, I was looking forward to introducing my kids to another important woman in my life, Reagan's mom.

We changed up our routine and went to church Saturday night, to free up all of Sunday for our day trip visit. The circumstances felt good. Very good. Which had me worried.

CHAPTER 26

BELIEVE IT OR NOT

I t was adventure day! We couldn't wait to get to Myrtle Beach for a fun, touristy day with some of our favorite people! We started the three-hour drive so early that the kids were more than halfway asleep. With hubby at the wheel, I was feeling relaxed and enthusiastic about the day to come.

About twenty minutes in, Jordan began nodding off. We traded places, and I continued feeling enthusiastic, but from the driver's seat, singing as I drove. I was peppy and determined that nothing was going to ruin my day!

We arrived much earlier than the rest of our company, intentionally. We started with Ripley's Believe it or Not museum, and the kids were mesmerized. They may have touched things they weren't allowed to, or crossed lines they weren't permitted to, or ran when the signs said not to, and possibly even screamed at each other a few times, but they also laughed and excitedly shared the things they learned with us. Considering the good and the bad, I was much more moved by their apparent happiness than anything, so it was a win.

We finished our first attraction just in time for our highly anticipated meet-up. The kids were beyond ecstatic at seeing Baby Jack, who was equally thrilled. Truthfully, seeing the proof that the relationships were developing was more than a little satisfying.

The kids gave rounds of hugs to Reagan and David as well, and also to the plus one adult, Reagan's mom. It was wonderful to have yet another person investing in conversations with our kids and making them feel special, as we walked together toward a mirror-maze. The kids were giddy on the way in, which may have contributed to the chaos, causing us to lose a kid or two or three, but only briefly. Or, somewhat briefly.

In between losing them around the corners of the confusing maze, I enjoyed watching their confidence lead them straight into mirrors, moving faster than they were supposed to. It was a great, natural reminder to walk inside the maze, though my kids didn't respond well to natural consequences, so they kept bumping heads and knocking knees.

I may have also collided with a tilted mirror a time or two, but in the scheme of things, the crashing made for some great laughing all the way to the end. There was a brief panic when I only counted four kids at the finish line, but relief when I realized I was only missing Brandon, not because I wanted to lose him, but because I already knew he'd stray. The relief was nothing compared to my surprise at still having the rest of the kids! Incredible improvement over the corn maze experience six months earlier.

We visited the Ripley's Aquarium, and they were all fascinated. They got bored before we wanted to leave, crawled on things they weren't supposed to, and gave me heart attacks by trying to hide at the most inconvenient of times, but they still enjoyed seeing the giant megalodon jawbones and different species of sea-life. Though it felt like I was herding cats, I also felt less anxious about it. The chaos was feeling normal, and so were the glares we received from employees urging me to control my children.

We took all the kids to the park to burn some energy. We set them free on the play structure with little guidance, which turned out to be an error. If I'd given a little more direction over how to supervise a young one, maybe the child who was chaperoning Jack would have intervened before the toddler walked through the structure right off a ledge.

The child, cough-Clay-cough, said, *"I told Jack not to jump, but he wouldn't listen."*

I made my confusion apparent as he blamed the baby, by tilting my head and displaying a puzzled look. Apparently, it wasn't common knowledge that the chaperone sometimes intervenes. Jack survived, and Clay learned the lesson that you sometimes have to grab the toddler to keep him from falling off, because toddlers don't always listen.

The kids resumed playing with an enthusiastic game of tag, while we adults enjoyed some much-needed social interaction. We talked about life in Georgia, Reagan's life in North Carolina, and what had been happening with our friends in Oregon since we'd moved away. We giggled at some of the kids' silly quirks, and when the game of tag got too physical, we rounded up the kids to capture some new headless pictures to share on Facebook. Literally, it was a photo of the seven of us sitting on a brick retaining wall, focusing on our feet, our hands in our laps, and cutting off just below the shortest chin.

Our creative family pictures became my special way of sharing our story, while also following the rules. The perfect balance of doing what was right and connecting with our network.

Other than Jack walking the plank, the park went as well as it usually did. I was proud that we didn't unearth any new triggers or earn any bruise-related phone calls. After eating a quick meal together, our company headed for home. We did not, because we had one last activity in store, a short and exciting 4D ride that brought us right up to bedtime, just as planned. We had the kids change into their jammies and brush their teeth before hitting the road for our three-hour drive home. I felt like a superstar mom.

Jordan pulled over to fill up with gas at the middle mark of our drive. I went into the station to grab drinks and snacks for Jordan and myself, to help keep us awake for the rest of the trip. As I was walking down the aisle, I saw Faith come sprinting through the parking lot and into the station.

I called out, *"Faith, no running inside."*

She desperately screamed back, *"But I'm peeing my pants!"*

At first, I thought this just meant that she had to go badly. I mean, she hadn't told us about needing to go or anything, but she was clearly in a hurry.

I joined her in the two-stall bathroom and saw her shorts/skirt combo and underwear were on the floor of the nasty, germ infested gas station bathroom, just underneath the right stall door. And they were wet.

I asked, *"Faith, do you need help?"* and she didn't respond.

I locked the door to the bathroom and asked her to come out of the stall. I directed her through rinsing her items out in the sink, wringing them out as best as she could, and attempting to start the drying process with the hand dryer, which wasn't really working out.

While she was drying, I noticed I hadn't grabbed my phone from the car. I said to Faith, *"I've got to go update Dad. Lock the door behind me and do not open it for anyone but me. Do you understand?"*

Very quietly she responded with, *"Yes, ma'am."*

I let Jordan know what was going on, and wasn't surprised to see his jaw drop and eyes bug. I felt the same shock when I first noticed that our twelve -year-old daughter had just peed herself. And especially shocked that she'd never given us a courtesy warning.

I went back into the bathroom and found her clothes were as good as they were going to be. She got dressed, and we headed to the car, where Jordan gave her his sweatshirt to sit on, thinking it would absorb the moisture and keep her from feeling too horribly uncomfortable.

We attempted a follow-up conversation, but when we asked why she didn't say anything, she said, *"Why would I? We weren't near a bathroom so it wouldn't have helped."*

I was a little taken aback as I slowly said, *"But we could have pulled over to use one if we knew that you needed to go."*

"Ohhhhhhhhhh," she said, with a giant smile. She seemed so impressed by my idea.

"Faith, we'd much rather pull over to let you use a bathroom, than clean your pee out of your clothes and the car."

"You'd pull over just so I could use a bathroom?" she asked.

"Yes, we would. So, please let us know the next time you need to use a bathroom, even if you don't see one. That way, we'll have time to find one. Ok?"

"Ok!" she said, without embarrassment, shame or remorse. Like it wasn't a big deal at all.

In hindsight, I knew to ask if anyone had to use the bathroom before the drive. But, I didn't know to keep asking throughout the drive. I assumed they'd let us know when they needed a potty-break outside of gas stops. Lesson learned.

We got home and transitioned the kids into bed. It wasn't as smooth as I had hoped, but the bumps weren't outside the realm of understandable. At least I didn't need anyone to change into jammies or brush their teeth. Point for mom.

Once everyone was tucked in and asleep, Jordan and I tucked ourselves in. It had been a mostly good day, but I was still thinking about the weirdness of learning that our twelve -year-old daughter would pee her pants if she didn't see a bathroom with her own two eyes.

I couldn't imagine the specific circumstances leading her to just sit there with a full bladder, holding it in, not knowing that we would have helped her if she'd asked. The poor girl had been left to solve problems on her own, and it was going to take time to change the habit. And it was going to take time for me to learn exactly what questions to ask and when, to better set up successes. Just when I thought I was getting a handle on some things, I learned that I probably had many more obstacles in front of me.

As I drifted to sleep, I recognized sadness that our Myrtle Beach trip was over, because I didn't have anything else on the calendar to specifically look forward to. Instead, we rolled right into the Monday morning school routine, like my special daytrip hadn't even happened. Life just resumed as normal, which for me meant I'd get a tantrum from Caisen within ten minutes of waking up. The little booger was escalating his morning crankiness.

I no longer saw him giggling as he noticed he put his shirt on backwards or as he got his foot stuck in the leg of his tangled pants. Gone were the mornings of watching him chuckling as he failed to get socks on, which I didn't know people could fail at. His new routine started with grunting and groaning, and not even trying to get his tasks completed. I would sit next to him, reminding and helping, and he just didn't want to.

On top of that, he was also distracting his easily distracted brothers. This was just one of the difficulties in having four boys in one room, finally requiring me to make some changes. I couldn't allow one kid to cause problems for the others anymore because they each had enough problems of their own to worry about.

So, I continued to use the cadence *"bathroom, teeth, bed, and clothes"* as I woke the kids in the morning, but I altered the meaning for Caisen. I'd grab his school clothes while he was taking his turn in the bathroom, so that they were ready for him in my bedroom when he got out. That gave the other boys the space to get their tasks done and to get out of the room. When the room was empty, Caisen could go finish up with his bed.

And let's be real. He didn't sleep under the sheets or comforter. Only under the blankie that was on top. So, making his bed was as easy as somewhat straightening his blankie so that it was ready for him to snuggle back up with at night, and putting his stuffies back on his bed. Simple task.

However, to Caisen, it was an opportunity to fight. He sure seemed to love a good fight.

Therefore, his response to my new routine included throwing his stuffies and blankies around his room before making his way to the bathroom, throwing his shoes at me in my room, messing up his brothers' beds in their room, and often taking off the shoes he'd gotten on his feet to throw them at me again.

I tried my hardest to keep focused on the long road ahead of us, repeating to myself that, *"If it was a blessing that Brandon felt comfortable enough to show us his baggage that first weekend, then it must be a blessing that Caisen was now showing his baggage, personality, and difficulties. It has to be a blessing, because it gives us a chance to start working on his real struggles. So, be thankful. It's a blessing."*

Even if it was five forty-five in the morning. Still a blessing.

Then, his new approach infected our afterschool normal, the sports prep normal, and the bedtime normal. The kid was showing me he had many tricks up his sleeve to unleash on me.

Truthfully, I tried to believe in the blessings of Caisen's developing presentation, but I wasn't having success. I was crumbling under the constant confrontation, and the revolving meltdowns were keeping me from seeing Caisen as a sweet little four-year-old and instead was painting a picture as my burden. I asked God, *"Why are you doing this to me?"* many times a day. Some days, I asked many times per hour. In the worst hours, I'd go hide in my closet for fifteen seconds to confess I thought He'd made a mistake with me. *"God,"* I asked, *"How could you possibly see me as capable of helping and loving a second child with this much anger and rage?"* I asked, feeling that Brandon was already too much.

God answered, but not the way I wanted.

It was mid-day when I received a phone call from the pre-K center, asking me to bring Caisen a spare outfit. I indicated that there was a spare outfit in his backpack, to which they said that they only found socks and two shirts.

Why had the little punk taken the spare pants out of his backpack?

I grabbed extra clothes and made my way to the school. When I got there, I was told that he was sitting on a garbage bag in the back of the classroom. I collected Caisen and caught a noticeable stench as we walked to the bathroom, letting me know I was in the beginning of a bad memory.

Caisen's school uniform consisted of a tucked in polo shirt and khakis that happened to have a fleece lining. And it was a hot, muggy, humid, Georgia day. The fleece lining combined with the heat was the perfect combination for melting poop, causing it to run down to his shoes and socks, which were the first things we removed. And, his tucked in shirt allowed for the poop to run up his back.

I updated my prediction. This was no longer the beginning of a bad memory, but an undeniable realization that I was having a nightmare.

After peeling his shirt off, we tried to work his pants and undies off, but found that they were stuck to his body. There was so much poop. It was mushy, runny, clumpy, and basically smooshed in everywhere. I was fighting my gag reflex and had no chance of hiding it from him. A healthier kid might have cried in embarrassment, but not this kid. He saw me gagging, and he was smelling death too, but he just stood there.

I mentally checked back in with my original plan to bring him a change of clothes, clean him up a bit, and let him finish the school day. But, that was no longer an option. I needed a hose.

My new mission was a lofty task for my already run-down self, but I did in fact pry the sopping clothes off of his sticky body and stuff them into the plastic bag. I didn't want to unnecessarily dirty additional clothes, so I skipped new undies and just put the replacement pants on him, viewing them as my car-barrier. I survived the raunchiest smelling ten-minute drive of my life and then carried him at full arm's length to the bathroom, where I sprayed him down with the dog hose-attachment.

Although I hated to be wasteful, the bag of poopy clothes went straight into the outdoor trash bin. There was no possibility of any other route. Problem solved.

Well, one problem solved. I still needed to figure out what had happened and how to prevent it from happening again.

Throughout the cleanup process, I'd asked several times why he hadn't just gone into the bathroom. I mean, this behavior was not typical for him. Maybe for Faith or Clay, but this was a first with Caisen. Granted, he had sub-par wiping skills, but this was more than just a wiping failure.

He shrugged his shoulders and mumbled, *"I don't know."*

I deserved an answer, so I stuck with it. Eventually, he told me that he was playing outside and the teacher was talking to someone else, so he just went on with his duty-business.

Not fair! I mean, he had no problem with interrupting me! But, he didn't want to interrupt her? What the heck!

While addressing the mistake, he let a little more information slip, and I pieced together that he was lying about choosing not to interrupt. He only told me that because he thought I'd be proud of his choice to prioritize manners. In actuality, he didn't want to miss out on outside time, he tried to save his duty until they were doing something else. However, he couldn't wait. So, he just made the choice to poop-it-out, and continued to play in the sandbox.

Sadly, even after pooping himself, he still didn't approach the teacher. He continued to play until someone noticed the smell and narrowed it down to him.

Gross.

I saw this horrible situation as God's reminder that Caisen was only a small, misguided child, not a burden. He wasn't a punishment or a practical joke. He was a kid with some real needs.

God did not give us ready-made, beautiful, loving, kind, hard-working, selfless, grateful children.

However, God wasn't cursing or punishing us, either. He had a deep and personal love for each of these five kids, and He was gifting Jordan and me to them, counting on us to help them become the beautiful, loving, kind, hard-working, selfless, grateful children He knew they were meant to be. He made a promise to provide for us just as much as He had made a promise to the kids. And, He was holding up both ends of the deal, even when it seemed we were surrounded by difficulty.

And surrounded we were.

Faith's pee and Caisen's poop weren't my only run-ins with bodily refuse that week.

It was Friday, and I was doing the kids' laundry. That wasn't anything new, considering I was doing loads daily. I kept praying for the loads to improve, but today was not the day the kids earned ice cream.

First, I came across one of Clay's shirts, with blood on it. That kid was always getting nose bleeds, or scrapes, or scratches. His clothes regularly had holes, blood, and food on them.

Next, I came across some skid-marked underwear.

Then, some chunk-filled underwear.

Then, I came across a shirt with puke on it. I thought that was weird because I didn't know any of the kids had puked. It was Brandon's shirt, so I made a mental note to talk to him about it later.

Finally, I reached in and pulled out one of the most offensive clothing items I had ever grabbed. I quickly connected the dots and realized that while Brandon was puking, he was also unloading diarrhea into his boxers and shorts. And he didn't tell me. He just put them in the laundry bin and left them there for me.

I scrubbed my hands, many times. And then I scrubbed them some more.

When I came back in to finish the laundry, I was wearing re-purposed kitchen sink gloves. I made a decision in that moment that I would never touch the kids' laundry again without a hazmat suit. Or at least some tall, rubber, kitchen gloves. How were we still struggling to get on top of the foul-substance-laundry situation? Why couldn't we get beyond hygiene?

After finishing the load and thinking it through, I felt sad I didn't know to ask Brandon how he was feeling until AFTER I touched diarrhea. I didn't like that he was in the bathroom alone, with no one to get him water, a towel, or a change of pajamas. Don't get me wrong; it was disgusting, but not as much as it was sad.

I needed to talk to the kids about letting me know when things happen, for their own benefit as well as mine. They needed to know that finding their unsanitary treasures was the equivalent of a rude, cruel, prank. But, more importantly, they deserved to have someone love them through their tough, uncomfortable moments. The kids deserved parents to help them with the difficult times, even more than hubby and I deserved a break, a vacation, or another day trip on our calendar.

CHAPTER 27

SPEED DIAL

We had successfully navigated our first sports season and only had one end-of-season pizza party left, which happened to be Brandon's. Unfortunately, it was the hardest for me.

Jordan couldn't join and Caisen was having an extra difficult day.

While the other kids were eating pizza and juice, Caisen was head-butting me and screaming. I never was able to find a reason. He was just going to town. He threw his shoes, and he swiped items off of the table. He screamed a lot. He pinched me and whacked me several times. Not only was his aggression hurting me, but it was also embarrassing. I mean, he wasn't two or three. He was four years ten months old. That's fifty-eight months, calculated that way because it's what you do with babies. Seriously though, he was close to five years old, drawing more negative attention than the terrible toddlers who seemed to be much better behaved than he was.

I tried to ignore him. Then, I thought about retreating to my house forever. But, being trapped with them there didn't seem any better. Besides, I had just paid the registration for all five kids to begin t-ball/baseball/softball, which also required me to purchase five cleats, gloves, balls and bats. We needed to stick with our routines and commitments and maybe they'd learn more discipline and control in the process.

But, that couldn't help me in the immediate situation. I wanted out of there as soon as possible, so I planned to make my escape after the trophies were presented. Not only did we have to get a couple kids to their baseball meetings, but I also really needed to move on with my terrible day.

As the trophies were handed out, Caisen threw himself on the floor. I scooped him up and carried him out as he was wiggling and squirming so badly that he ended up over my shoulder. He was too big for me to carry him any other way while he was in a tantrum. However, it gave him the perfect position for pounding and punching me in the back. Which he did, all the way to the car.

To make matters worse, in an effort to get him in his car seat, I hyperextended my elbow.

I was trying to remain focused on the sad fact that he missed the opportunity to experience these stages earlier in life, when it would have been appropriate. I was just the lucky recipient of his catching up on life. Good for him. Not so good for me.

I was fighting the urge to consider God's calling in my life a curse. It was a tough fight, and it took everything in me to remember that God had a plan, there was an explanation for the phase of nightmare I was in, and that He would see me through.

With my elbow throbbing and my too-old toddler still challenging me for control, the added bonus was the disciplinary restrictions in foster care. Since smarty-pants Caisen knew we were restricted, he pushed harder. It felt like he was asking, *"What are you going to do about it?"* each time he let me have his wrath.

He would dart through parking lots if he didn't feel like getting in the car to go home. A growing timeout wouldn't even catch his attention.

He would cause scenes in public, without any holding back. Being told we would leave, and following through, didn't bother him.

He would destroy things at home and seemed to enjoy it. Loss of privilege and stuffed animals didn't faze him.

I kept trucking along, day after day, from early morning meltdowns to late night meltdowns, surprised we got to and through any appointments and practices, which was the criteria I set for gauging if I was a total failure or not. My focus was getting the kids out of bed, eventually getting them back in, and connecting some dots in between. That was enough, until it wasn't. At his age, Jordan and I were supposed to be his heroes. It wasn't fair that I was missing out on happiness.

Not only was a shift needed in order to salvage some sanity, but also for his safety and security. He needed to know that he had loving parents who were in control. He deserved that. I needed to find a way to force him into accepting appropriate family roles.

So, I increased his consequence scale.

He seemed to enjoy his stuffed animals. But taking them away for a night wasn't making enough of an impact. Instead of losing a stuffed animal for the night, he would receive a warning that he would lose it for good. If he didn't back off, the stuffy would become a hostage. If that wasn't enough, the stuffie would be sacrificed into the garage garbage can. It had to be the can in the garage, because he was tall enough to reach in the kitchen bin and pull the stuffies back out. I couldn't have that.

I felt that the permanency of the consequence would eventually give him a reason to comply.

It certainly didn't work the first night. He just got more and more invested in doing the wrong thing, thinking that I should give in before him. He kept escalating, in what seemed to be an effort to force me to cave in.

Like that was going to happen.

He lost fourteen stuffed animals that night. He punched me and kicked me down the hall each time, thinking if he were bad enough, I'd give in and return the stuffies to him. He was wrong. He was going to learn the lesson that you can't go backward and erase consequences.

He would have lost more if it were up to him, so I adjusted the process on sacrificial stuffies eleven, twelve, and thirteen. Jordan got home during negotiations for number fourteen, which gave me further opportunity to tweak my wording. We were, after all, the adults, so it was our job to set up success.

"Hey Jordan, maybe you could talk to Caisen about what he wants for this Mickey Mouse stuffy. He's already lost thirteen other stuffed animals and is still making the same choices to hit me and throw things at me. I need Caisen to learn that it's his choice what happens to Mickey, and he can let me know what he chooses with his actions."

It took some real convincing, but he was able to save that last Mickey Mouse and began to learn through the process that he had control over the situation. He could choose how bad a consequence gets by ceasing or pushing. We knew the lesson wasn't going to fully stick right away. He was stubborn. But it was a start.

For the next few nights, he lost between one and three stuffies at a time. Good thing we had a lot of stuffies donated to us, which got us through two weeks of lesson learning. I was determined that it would fully click with him before getting to his most favorite stuffies. I'd do what I needed to, but I hoped it wouldn't go that far.

A week and a half into our standoff, I felt it might be the storm before the calm. I know, it usually goes the other way, but I felt like it was his last surge before falling into his place in the family.

It was a counseling day, and he flared up. I set him up to succeed, but he didn't want to. He wanted to fight. But he also wanted to keep his stuffies. When the choice was made that one of his precious little babies was going in the trash, he followed me down the hall, into the garage, and up to the trash can, punching me and kicking me the entire way, while calling me a meanie in between unintelligible screams.

My heart broke for the little guy, who was so desperate to get his stuffy back. If only he had chosen to save the critter before my countdown hit zero, instead of throwing another shoe at me. My heart also felt a hefty dose of guilt and embarrassment as I traumatized my young boy in front of the counselors. Thankfully, after that session, the still relatively new skills-builder said that she was proud of me for sticking to my ground, there would be a day when he would finally submit, and that day would be worth all the struggle.

I felt relief. I prayed she was right. Jordan was gone a lot, I was holding up a very heavy plate, and I desperately needed to believe progress was coming.

I hoped he'd begin to feel he was a son with loving parents, and I was scared for his life otherwise. I did my best for him by standing my ground, talking through his choices and options, suffering through counseling nights, getting the kids to their sports obligations to burn energy and get adult reinforcements, and giving each kid a hug and kiss at night. Even when I was exhausted, burnt out, beat down, and uncertain.

The only problem was that the progress felt so slow, and the foster rules were burdensome. Mostly, the no-carpool rules, the restricted discipline options, the inability to offer over the counter medications, the lack of rights to travel, the lack of rights to share pictures, and the requirement to call in every bruise I found.

And that bruise thing grew to be a big deal with so many rambunctious kids. Over Spring Break, I thought I was going to flood the incident phone lines.

First, Clay crashed into Henry on a family bike ride. Clay got a red, puffy eye. I called it in.

Then, Henry crashed into a mailbox while riding his bike on our street and ended up with a red scratch on his upper cheek, close to his eye. I called it in.

Then, Caisen came home from his day camp with a bruise on each of his cheeks. He and another boy were acting like monkeys playing cymbals and smashing each other in the face with blocks. Oh, and he continued the monkey-slap at t-ball practice with another boy. I called all those marks in.

Then, Faith went to catch her first pop fly from the outfield. She had her glove up, she was lined up, and then she moved the glove so that she could better watch the ball, all the way to her forehead.

The timing was terrible, because I had to leave her to go pick up Henry and Clay shortly after she was knocked in the noggin, since their practice was ending. I hated leaving her, but she didn't want to leave her practice, which had thirty minutes remaining, and I couldn't leave the boys waiting with their coach that long. My best option was to hustle to the boys and back.

Before leaving, a couple of parents graciously offered to bring her over to the boys' field for me when they finished, but I had to decline. Foster rules said I couldn't accept carpool. Since I hadn't disclosed to the other parents that we were a foster family, the mom continued to offer, demanding that it wouldn't be a problem.

I would have felt support through accepting the convenient offer of having Faith transported to me, but the fact of the matter was she could only wait on the field with her coach in the event I wasn't back in time. Accepting that, my two remaining options were to share our foster status with the other parents, or offend them by essentially saying their help was not appreciated.

I shared.

The other moms seemed to understand my dilemma, while also changing their posturing. They shifted their weight away from me and ended the conversation abruptly.

I left to get the boys and got back in time for Faith, recognizing I could have protected our secret a little longer. No going back though. As I collected my young lady, I saw that her eye had begun swelling and changing colors. I called it in.

When pain and worry crept into Faith's expressions, I handed her a bag of frozen peas and stuck with statements like, *"I'm so proud of how you handled your first sports wound."* When Jordan got home, he shared his sports injury stories and talked up how cool it was to have a sports story to share.

The bruise grew over night and encompassed her whole eye socket by morning. She maintained a positive attitude about it up until we pulled into the parking lot for Spring Break day camp. Out of nowhere, she became frantic and worried she'd be made fun of.

I honestly told her that anyone who made fun of her was not someone she'd want to be friends with. Kind people don't make fun of other people's wounds, and there will be some kind people in there. She nodded in acceptance, and we made our walk to the front doors, where she froze.

Her brothers went inside, which was for the best. They weren't helping by reminding her that the bruise was still growing and darkening. While saying goodbye to my insensitive, blunt young men, I noticed a familiar young girl sitting at one of the craft tables. It was our little next-door neighbor, who was also in Clay's class at school. *"Psssst, Grace, come here,"* I said.

I asked, *"Do you think Faith should skip camp because of her eye?"*

Grace looked at me like she thought I was kidding, then looked at Faith's eye and said, *"No, she should stay,"* clearly hoping she would stay and play.

Faith said, *"I don't want to get made fun of."*

"I won't make fun of you, and I won't play with anyone who does," she replied, and just like that, they walked in.

During that same week, we also had a Brandon-bruise. He was drinking a Gatorade at the end of a baseball game and was trying to suck as much air out of the bottle as possible, so that the bottle would hang from his lip. And he succeeded. Repeatedly. So much so, that he gave himself an upper lip bruise. Technically, it was a hickey, which looked like a mustache.

When I called in his five o'clock shadow, I laughed so hard that I actually cried. I'm sure the lady on the other end was confused as to why I was so entertained with his *"injury,"* but I couldn't help it. It was one thing after another, and each thing was sillier than the one before. If I didn't keep a sense of humor about their incidents, I wouldn't have been able to bear the babysitter-like feeling of being told to check in with the authorities every time something happened, big or small.

Anyway, just when I thought that each of the five kids had completed their turn for the week, the kids went back through the lineup. Clay got another face mark, Caisen got a big scratch and bruise on his forehead, just a couple days before school pictures, and Henry got another bruise. The incident reporting line earned a special place on the *"favorites"* list on my phone, though it wasn't actually a favorite of mine. To balance out the foster care obligations, we continued to seek true *"favorite"* experiences.

It was a sunny Saturday in early May, and the seven of us were playing at our favorite park in downtown Savannah. We spontaneously decided to take the kids to see a late Jukebox Musical, requiring us to eat downtown while we waited for show time. It was a semi-pro Broadway production theater that Jordan and I loved to go to, and a rare opportunity for the kids to stay up past bedtime.

We sat in our typical order, with Brandon on the aisle.

The kids tried to sing along to the classics, even though they didn't know the words. Clarence sang the wrong words the loudest. One of the ladies from the show grabbed Brandon to dance with her in the aisle, and he showed everyone his terrible dancing skills. We all laughed, even Brandon.

As the show progressed, the kids got quieter and their eyelids moved slower. When the curtains came down, Caisen reached up to me to carry him out to the car. It was happening! He was learning to reach for me. He was beginning to depend on me. My prayers for this child were being answered!

We parked a long distance from the theater, which made it difficult for me to hold him up! However, I was so happy that he reached for me that even though Jordan offered to take him from me, I sucked it up and carried him the entire way.

Most of the kids fell asleep on the way home and transitioned into bed easily. It was a great day. I was still anticipating a meltdown, but it didn't happen.

Knowing that they were capable of getting through a day without major meltdowns made me cautiously optimistic for Mother's Day, which was just a few days later. I was seeing enough progress to feel hope.

My very first Mother's Day came, and one of the highlight moments was when the kids woke me up and presented me with the necklace they picked for me, that said, *"Mom"* inside a heart. They also made me some great cards and pictures. Then, we went to the beach, and when they were in the water, I was on the sand far enough away that I couldn't hear them arguing and fighting. I also loved the key-lime pie that came after dinner.

On the other hand, the kids fought over who should give me the necklace and over who should get credit for picking it out. They fought so hard that Brandon slammed Clay's head into one of the corner-walls. It left a mark, so I called it in.

Brandon couldn't process whatever emotion he was feeling over having hurt Clay and earning an incident report, so he defaulted with rage. Jordan took the other kids into our room to watch cartoons on our bed while I worked to calm Brandon down. I thought I might be getting better at it, even though I didn't enjoy it. And no matter how hard I worked at it, the process reminded me we were still far from having a healthy mother and son relationship.

Next, the kids complained the entire way to the beach. Then, they fought the entire time we were at the beach. And, they all fell apart when it was time to leave for dinner. Lastly, Brandon and Henry pitched an additional fit after dinner because they learned that we were not going back to the beach, since it was time to head home for showers and bedtime. A couple chairs were tipped over, which drew some unpleasant looks, which did not make me feel like, *"Mom of the year."*

When we got home, the kids all talked about how great the day was. They didn't see what I saw. I was happy for them, but also thankful that Jordan had the next day off, so he could take me to the beach with the dogs for a redo, while the kids were in school. We just walked up and down the coastline with the pups and then got ourselves some frozen yogurt. It was a better attempt at my first Mother's Day, and a couple's break from our home life reality.

We couldn't use babysitters or anything, so we hadn't had much time without kids. That block of five hours together was so needed. The conversations were stimulating, the interruptions were minimal, and there was a lot of laughing. Mostly, laughing at how ridiculous our kids were and how crazy we were for doing what we were doing, but laughing nonetheless.

While enjoying our wet and cold beach day, we committed to introducing the kids to another *"first"* experience.

Well, a modified version.

Backyard Camping. We picked up a ten-person tent on the way home, to make sure the kids had enough space that they didn't have to touch each other. When the following weekend rolled around, we set it up, brought out their pillows and comforters, and let each kid pick out a stuffy. We used a battery-operated pump to inflate a mattress for Jordan and me, after determining we were too old to sleep on the ground when we knew we had a blow-up option.

We grilled hotdogs for dinner and when everyone was ready, we tucked ourselves into our massive tent.

It wasn't easy to settle the kids down, but we weren't expecting it to be. They wiggled and rolled, bumped into each other, argued, then wiggled some more. The dogs rotated who they were laying on top of, which actually made each kid happy, until the dog moved on. Eventually, everything became quiet and still.

When morning rolled around, the earliest to wake proceeded to wake everyone else. We took a couple group photos to capture our newest family memory, including setting a timer to get a picture of Jordan and me at the tent door with all the kids giving thumbs up in the windows. We packed up and headed to IHop for breakfast. Another family-first.

Though the weekend wasn't perfect, it was easily the best weekend we'd experienced together. More than seeing progress, I was finally feeling it.

The progress with Caisen felt like a huge weight was lifted. Like some dark clouds were finally moving on. My stern mom-look and convincing mom-voice finally meant something to him because I'd used them so often, and then I consistently did the work of helping him process what it meant. Additionally, Faith, Clarence and Henry were moving along, which left the darkest clouds surrounding Brandon.

My despair over Brandon was compounded when the counselors told us that Brandon wasn't making enough progress to indicate we were on the right track. Logically looking at our situation, I understood the concern. I knew Brandon had made small gains, but they weren't nearly as obvious as the other kids'.

They explained that Brandon didn't want help, so traditional therapies wouldn't work. Since his fits were dangerous and frequent, we were given some other options to look into, particularly residential treatments, which were programs where we'd send him away for many months at a time.

When Jordan got home later that night, I shared the news with him, and asked, *"If we have to send him away after adopting him, does that mean we failed?"* I truly couldn't wrap my head around it. It scared me to consider such drastic alternatives, and I felt helpless.

"Slow down," Jordan said. *"We won't even have the rights to change his treatment plan until we finalize the adoption. Keep doing your best because it is enough, since the other kids are improving."*

He was right. There was no need to get ahead of ourselves. And, I felt proud that we were seeing notable progress in four of the kids. But I couldn't help but wonder. Would we ever be enough for Brandon? Would we ever experience the kind of breakthroughs with him where we felt deeper bonds and saw better potential in his future?

CHAPTER 28

FULL CIRCLE

W e had been playing by all of the rules and going above and beyond with fighting for and with our kids for what seemed like an eternity. It had been over nine months since hearing about the kids at that crazy used-kids sales conference, nearly eight months since we met our kids, and just over seven months since the court ruled to terminate the birth parents' rights. We were still waiting for the paperwork to come back from the courts allowing us to transition from foster care status, back over to foster-to-adopt.

I braced myself when my phone rang with a familiar number, just after dropping the kids off at school. Typically, the caseworkers only called with new demands, or new reasons for our timeline to be extended. I took my deep breath and accepted the call.

The caseworker from the kids' original county started with the good news. *"The court documents were finally released,"* she said, which was the domino we'd been waiting on. By itself, it didn't mean anything, but it opened the opportunity for us to transition from a foster placement to a pre-adoptive placement.

"And," I asked, *"what's the bad news?"*

"There isn't any!" she said. *"We'd like to meet at your house, tomorrow at two o'clock, to sign all the papers."*

"I'll call Jordan." I said. *"What papers will we be signing?"*

"We'll go over it all tomorrow," she said. *"Basically, it's the paperwork needed to switch your placement and make your intentions to adopt the kids official."*

I immediately called Jordan, who got the ok from his leadership for the afternoon off. It was really happening!

The next day, while the kids were in school, we adults sat around our dining room table signing the three-inch stack of papers, three separate times, so that each party could retain an original copy. We indicated the kids' to-be names, so that the next round of documents would reflect them accurately. We signed the contracts that initiated the court process and went over the new rules. It took a couple of hours, but the resulting milestone was worth every minute.

The new rules were basically the same as the old rules. We still needed to entertain monthly caseworker visits by each of the agencies. We still needed permission to cross state lines or to give medication. We still needed to call in bruises and marks. We still needed our evacuation plans displayed and our emergency kits assembled. We still needed to send in our weekly and monthly reports. We still couldn't post pictures. We still couldn't use carpools, and we still couldn't hire babysitters.

Though most everything stayed the same, there were some subtle changes. For example, we could refer to ourselves as a pre-adoptive family instead of foster, and we could list the kids as foster child dependents in the military database. Also, we felt further along in the process and feelings matter.

While enrolling the kids as military dependents felt like a step forward, it also came with difficulties. The kids had to sign their new ID's with their still-legal, old last name. The kids were disappointed that they couldn't sign our last name, then frustrated when the military representative forced them to sign in cursive, which they had not learned. The kids and I questioned why the woman cared how they signed the name they were anxious to drop, but nonetheless, she spent about thirty minutes coaching the kids' penmanship.

We hired a lawyer to arrange the legal aspects of the adoption, got to work planning a finalization celebration trip for the kids to meet all of our family in Oregon, and coordinated to give others a chance to travel in as well.

Though we were looking forward to our big court day, life essentially continued as usual, until mid-May when we walked out our door for Caisen's pre-K graduation ceremony, indicating school had ended and summer had shown up to take over. The feeling of doom was compounded when Brandon caused a scene over wanting to be in the center of the family picture underneath the pre-K graduation banner.

He shouted, *"It isn't even a real accomplishment. I could have graduated pre-K better than he did!"* A rotten way to start the summer.

We also had some happy moments mixed into the chaos. For example, I felt giddy as I asked a friend to take family pictures for us. She was the same friend whose little girl whacked Jack with the little plastic shopping cart when he tried to grab a toy from inside it.

Even though it hadn't been made official yet, we decided we were close enough to start thinking about how we wanted to share our very first public family photo, which meant we needed a great one. I used Pinterest to find some picture and prop ideas to send to my photo-friend, so that we were on the same page when picture day arrived.

In preparation, she gave me the advice that planning a family picture would not be a challenge of picking out seven coordinating outfits. Rather, it was a task of building one large outfit. It took three shopping trips before I had just the right combination of blues, denims, whites and teals. I also planned for a military family photo, where Jordan would wear his uniform, with the three boys in their Halloween soldier costumes and a red/white/blue outfit for Faith, Caisen, and me.

On picture day, my friend had the backdrops and locations picked out, and I had a chalkboard to write our message on and seven wooden letters, painted blue, to form the word *"FOREVER."* We had a plan, we were in sync, and then it was time to smile.

Everyone got the memo, except Brandon. First, he pitched a fit that he was asked to hold the letter *"R."* He also didn't want *"E." "Those letters aren't special,"* he said, *"because there's more than one. I want to be F, O or V."*

It wasn't an easy fix, though, because we were standing in the best-looking lineup, and I didn't want to misspell the word just to please Brandon. *"Dude, every letter in this word is special and important. Without you, we'd be a FOEVER-family, which doesn't sound cool at all. Please be the very important "R" in our FOREVER-family."*

He reluctantly agreed, and even smiled, until our friend asked him to put his arm around Clarence. *"I'm not touching him,"* he said, with a disgusted tone of voice and look on his face. Brandon's problems weren't big that day, but they were there.

If nothing else, I learned something. Not a lesson like all the others, where I immediately found myself wrong, but a sad, lasting truth. There was always a problem with Brandon. Or, at least, a problem with Brandon was always coming. No matter what I did, no matter how I worked with him, it wasn't ever going to be enough. And though I felt competent to handle the obstacles, I was realizing how much I hated it. I desperately wanted to enjoy a situation, any situation, with my family, which didn't seem possible with Brandon around. Then, I felt guilty for thinking so negatively.

While enjoying a self-pity-party one morning, I checked my email. My pity-party ended when I noticed one from our lawyer because I knew she was sharing our court date. Except, I was wrong. It actually contained a list of things still needed in order to file the petition. Some things I could provide, and some required me to be the middleman between the caseworkers. Self-pity party resumed.

While waiting on the real news that court was scheduled, I spent the weeks splitting my time between Brandon's meltdowns and coordinating everyone's counseling, summer camps, and activities, while also planning a trip to celebrate with the rest of our families in Oregon. To be safe, I requested travel permissions for our family trip and also for a week-long church camp for Faith and Brandon. I knew the process for travel approvals for them to go out of our supervision was more intensive than the ones for family travel, so we started early. I got nervous when the caseworkers said we'd be finalized in time and therefore didn't need approval letters. I prayed they were right.

Knowing the legal system wouldn't bend to accommodate my travel itinerary, I pushed our big trip to the very end of the summer, so that we'd have the most time possible to get to court. I prayed it would be enough because the flights weren't refundable. I didn't have the ability to adjust the dates for the camp, though.

Jordan and I talked daily about Brandon's troubles, usually prompted by me, feeling alarmed by some new angle of Brandon's wrath. No matter my concern, though, Jordan's faith never wavered. At least, not that he let show. *"I know God led us to the entire sibling group for a reason and to back out on Brandon would cause irreparable damage."*

I believed that to be true, though I also felt that Brandon already had irreparable damage. *"If Brandon can be helped, I want to see it through. I'm just not certain it'll make much difference."*

As we spoke, we stumbled onto a different perspective, in the form of questions: What would the other kids think about our love if we changed our minds on Brandon? Would they worry they could also lose us if they had bigger challenges arise? Would I feel guilty forever for assuming Brandon was a lost cause? What if he could be helped, and the breakthroughs were just around the corner?

With so many unanswered questions, neither of us was willing to say the words that would let the other off the hook. And the words from others weren't enough, not even a text from Jordan's dad, reminding us that there was no shame to be had in backing out.

We didn't know God's plan for us, and we decided to give Him more time to reveal it.

We continued on our journey, trying not to let Brandon's destruction be our focus. I purposefully held onto the fact that Brandon didn't ask for his baggage or for the habits he'd learned. He was a victim, even when he was our offender. Also, summer break was an opportunity, not a punishment. Not easy perspectives to hold onto, but necessary to try. And, when all else failed, I could look at the calendar and count down the days for Faith and Brandon's week-long summer away camp, even though we still weren't finalized and still didn't have their travel approvals.

Though I was eager for their trip, I noticed Faith was slightly panicked about sleeping away from us. I reminded her that she didn't have to go, but she really wanted to. I tried reassuring her, by sharing stories of the camps I'd attended when I was younger, but it didn't seem to soothe her any. I changed up my approach and played Devil's Advocate.

"You're probably right." I said. *"It's unsafe. You shouldn't go. You should stay at home, with me, forever."*

She looked at me like I was crazy, and I dug in deeper.

I used my best, most animated storytelling voice. *"In fact, I heard they put dirt in their food and slip snakes and spiders into the children's rooms, just to test their faith that God will protect them and provide for them."*

"No, they don't," she demanded, *"because then no one would ever go back."*

"Fine." I said. *"Believe what you want."*

"I will," she said.

Honestly, I was thrilled that I'd just found a way to quickly impact my child. She didn't have the trust to internalize my words without proof, but she did have the ability to find the answers on her own, if I prompted her correctly. Reverse psychology worked!

Just in case, Jordan and I developed a back-up plan. We made her a build-a-bear, with a recording of our voices, telling her goodnight and that we loved her. She'd have it if she needed it and so would the other four kids because we couldn't just make one for her. That'd be rude. I seized the opportunity to post a picture of the five bears and felt creative about it.

Everything was ready for their travel, except the most important thing. Everyone seemed certain we'd be finalized in time. But we weren't. Two days before camp, we were given an overwhelming list of what was needed for the travel approvals, which seemed impossible considering the time constriction. The caseworker dug into it with us, but it wasn't up to either of us how quickly the camp personnel could respond with background checks on the volunteers and other necessary pieces of information. We worked as fast as we could and waited anxiously to see if the camp directors could satisfy the requirements for us in time.

As the kids went to bed that night, we hadn't received an answer. We had only one day left, and I felt both powerless and hopeless.

I hated that I didn't have control, or even a say-so. In my old, pre-kids life, I felt confident that if I set realistic goals, and if I gave my best to achieve them, that I'd find success. But that was no longer true. The new understanding was that I needed to give my best, and then some more, and then wait and see if other people would allow for success. It was belittling and discouraging.

I checked my email obsessively the following day, uncertain if I should be helping Faith and Brandon pack, or not. By the grace of God, the approval came together, just in time. I don't know what I would have done if it went the other way, and I was thankful I didn't need to find out.

I was peppy on the drive to the church, even though it was only six in the morning. And, after saying goodbye to Faith and Brandon, I felt relief. I felt no sadness in saying goodbye to Brandon. Instead, I felt energized and free, like my chains had been broken.

I experienced so much joy with the younger three kids in those few days, and I thought it was the perfect way to refresh my mindset. Of course, we had obstacles too, but far fewer of them. We went to the zoo and fed the giraffes. We watched movies at home with popcorn. We played at the park. We had some bumps, but mostly, we had fun. I focused on Caisen's giggles, Clay's ridiculous questions and comments, and Henry's sincerity. I felt myself relax, and I heard God's affirmations that things were going to be ok.

And things were ok, until I felt the pressure in my chest as we drove to pick up my older two after a week that went far too quickly. I had to force statements like *"I missed you guys,"* and *"It's so good to see you. Give me a hug."* I tried to focus on the notable growth in Faith, as she talked about the friends she made and the lessons she'd learned. But it was overshadowed by Brandon, interrupting her to brag about being labeled, *"the annoying boy."* Didn't he know that was a bad thing?

It took almost no time before Brandon's presence was impacting the whole family, again, which felt significantly heavier after experiencing a small stretch of peace.

I tried to remember that Brandon was also a victim, but wasn't having much success. I tried to remember that God was in control, but that had me questioning why He would do something as horrible as give me Brandon. Again, I shared my feelings of despair with Jordan, and he simply said, *"You're wrong, Jess. God didn't give Brandon to you. He gave you to Brandon, because Brandon needs you."*

It wasn't going to do me any good to argue with God, or with Jordan, so I set my eyes on the week ahead. Faith and Brandon were registered for one church's day camp, while Henry and Clay had a different church's day camp, which left me alone with Caisen for a few hours a day. Also, Brandon, Henry, and Clay had a night football camp, near post, hopefully allowing for Jordan to watch some. It was a lot to coordinate, but I knew it would be worth having other adults pour into my kids.

Monday through Wednesday went as planned. Caisen and I enjoyed some chaotic one-on-one time. Faith said that Brandon seemed fine at their camp, though he complained a lot. Henry and Clarence raved about their camp. The days were successful.

Football camp was interesting. Brandon was quickly labeled the *"I can't kid."* He didn't like the name, but he certainly used the phrase enough to warrant it. Negative attitude or not, at least he was another adult's problem for the time being. Henry and Clay, though, were giving solid effort. Clay had butterfingers and Henry was scared of contact, but they both tried their best.

By Wednesday night, I thought we'd found a decent groove. Maybe I'd found the secret to surviving life with Brandon: keep him busy and tire him out! Or, maybe not...

Thursday started the same as the days prior. Caisen and I swam and did crafts, and then picked up Faith and Brandon from camp. We brought them back to the house to eat lunch before picking up the other kids.

Pause with me for just a moment. In case this situation lead-in is sounding familiar, it's because you've read it before. We've finally caught up to the scene I promised you we'd revisit, way back in the beginning of the book. Ok. Resume.

After lunch, Brandon asked to play with his iPod, which I knew was danger-ous. He was either going to pitch a fit for not getting to play it, pitch a fit while playing it, or pitch a fit when play time ended. I gave permission, hoping to get a few minutes of peace, maybe more.

While at the house, I got a call from Henry and Clay's camp director because Henry fell off a cargo net apparatus and bit into his lip. I was told it wasn't bad enough to require immediate attention, but depending on how the afternoon went, it wouldn't hurt to have it looked at. I figured his lip would either close up and survive football camp, or it wouldn't, and in that case, Jordan could take everyone else home while Henry and I went to the Emergency Room.

It would have felt good to have a plan, but it wasn't up to me.

I called the agency to get the incident documented, and the caseworker who received the call, not surprisingly, told me I needed to get Henry in to a doctor to clear the injury. It wasn't time sensitive, but it needed to be done, so that there would be documentation that we made care available to him.

I let her know that we still hadn't been assigned a primary care physician, to which she responded, *"An emergency room doctor will suffice."*

I shared that Henry, and two of his brothers, had football camp later in the evening, and she said it would be ok to visit the ER afterward.

"Oh, goody," I thought.

When the timing was right, I gave Brandon a ten-minute warning for turning over his iPod, letting him know that we needed to pick up the other two kids. He said, *"Ok Mommy. I won't pitch a fit."*

I gave Brandon a five-minute warning before leaving. He said, *"Ok Mommy. I won't pitch a fit."*

I gave Brandon a two-minute warning before leaving. He said, *"Ok Mommy. I won't pitch a fit."*

"It's time to go, everyone. Load up," I said.

Brandon flopped off the couch screaming, *"You didn't even give me a warning. You're a terrible parent."* He alligator-rolled several times before throwing his iPod at me, still yelling.

I asked him to put his shoes on, and he refused. *"I'll only get ready to go if I get five more minutes, since you didn't tell me it was almost time."*

"I did tell you," I said. *"And we don't have five minutes. Put your shoes on."* I shifted my eyes to my other two kids. *"Faith and Caisen, please get in the car,"* I said, as I discreetly grabbed the shoes that Brandon had no interest in putting on. My eyes went back to Brandon to say, *"Brandon, I'm not going to have an injured Henry waiting on a late mom. Let's go."*

I got in our SUV, with his shoes behind my back. I acted like I was going to leave him, wishing I really could, hoping he'd take the bait.

As predicted, he followed us out the front door. He kicked the garage door a few times until I was in the driver's seat, then he banged on my window. I ignored him, knowing that my participation would only make things worse.

He pounded on the hood of our truck as he made his way around to the passenger side. He opened the back door and climbed in, but didn't close the door behind him because he wasn't preparing to leave with us. He just wanted to scream his insults directly into my ear.

Once he was fully inside the car, I hit the gas enough to then hit the brakes and have the door shut itself. Child safety locks did the rest, allowing me to calmly say, *"Buckle up."*

Brandon put his seatbelt on, out of habit, which I took as a sign I could start making my way through the neighborhood. Without missing a beat, he shouted, *"You wouldn't even let me get my shoes, you're terrible."*

Let him? I flat out told him to get his shoes, just like I gave a countdown. He was impossible.

I handed him his shoes, and he wasted no time in throwing them back at me. He didn't like solutions. He continued screaming, *"You're not even a good mom. You're the worst mom there is."*

We turned onto the main highway between our house and the church, which didn't have a shoulder or many side streets. When the timing couldn't be worse, Brandon unbuckled himself and tried climbing into the front seat where Faith was sitting, to get out the passenger door.

I didn't know he could still shock me, but in that moment, he did.

I wedged my right arm against the front passenger seat, attempting to be a barrier of protection for both Faith and Brandon. I hesitantly looked for a place to stop, scared that if I found one, he'd push through my arm-wall and out the door. I could picture him barreling his way down the highway, barefoot, with his hands over his face. He had no awareness of danger. Keeping the car moving was not safe, but it was safer than stopping while he was enraged.

We were two miles from our exit when he escalated and got through my arm enough to grab Faith's handle and crack the door open. My heart skipped a few beats as Faith gasped and yanked it closed. It took solid effort from Faith and me both to get Brandon's scrawny self back to the middle row.

I didn't know what to do. I thought maybe I could call 911 and ask to be escorted somewhere safe, but it would burn whatever small bridge I'd built between Brandon and me, if I'd built one at all. I knew this because that's what happened when his past foster parents called the police on him.

Or, maybe I could discreetly flag a passing patrol car, so Brandon wouldn't know it was me who alerted the authorities to our unstable situation. I was willing to accept the ticket for having an unbuckled minor, if it meant I'd have some help, but no marked police cars came into view.

I couldn't find a solution, because there wasn't one. Nothing was going to fix our problem because he wouldn't grow through the experience. He wasn't interested in growth. He was impossible.

Brandon pushed forward a second time, with more determination. Faith and I fought hard to limit his attempt to another door-cracking. The close calls were going to be the death of me, if it wasn't the death of one of them first.

Caisen didn't seem to notice what was happening, which was a blessing. However, I knew he'd notice a crash, or worse, he'd notice if Brandon pushed Faith or himself out the door. I couldn't let that happen, but felt powerless to prevent it.

After being defeated two times, Brandon slammed himself into a seat in the middle row, shifting his attention back to my failures as a parent. He grabbed his seatbelt and slammed the buckle against the window several times as he screamed at me, *"You can't even make me put on my seatbelt. You're useless. You can't do anything right."*

Part of me agreed. I mean, I knew I wasn't the cause for his rage, but I also wasn't able to find a way to help him. It was impossible.

He continued to yell at me the last few minutes before I pulled into the church parking lot, but I couldn't let him distract me. I had another problem to focus on.

I realized I couldn't safely leave Brandon unsupervised in the car, reinforced by our pre-adoption supervision-restrictions. But he also wasn't in the right mood where I could trust taking him inside with me, and I needed to sign Henry and Clay out.

I wracked my brain for a solution and sweat a few bullets before remembering that the camp director called me about Henry's incident, which meant his number was in my recent call log.

I dialed the number, shared a watered-down version of my predicament, and asked if he could email an incident report about Henry to our caseworker, in addition to bringing me a hard copy. Once the easy request was out of the way, I also asked if it was possible for him to facilitate an employee walking the boys out for curbside pickup. It wasn't the first time I had to ask for an exception because of Brandon, and it wasn't getting any less embarrassing.

Brandon heard my special request and lost his mind, because he didn't want me to think he was the reason I needed Henry and Clay escorted out to me, even though he was the one and only reason. This told me he cared what I thought, but not enough to be respectful or obedient in the first place.

He then buckled himself and said, *"See, I didn't do anything wrong. We can go in."*

The kid was impossible, but at least he was buckled in time for me to park the car. Regardless, my mind was made up; we weren't going in, no matter how frustrated it made him.

Clay's camp counselor brought both Henry and Clay out and indicated to me that Clay made a commitment to being a Soldier for Christ. I asked Clay to tell me what that meant, and he said that he was ready to put Jesus first in his life, and do his best to represent Jesus well. I was very proud.

I checked out Henry's lip and called it into the caseworker. I let her know that an email was being sent with the details, and she said I needed to get her a doctor's note indicating we had it addressed. It was a reminder that I didn't have the final say in my kids' treatment yet and confirmation that there would be an ER visit in my near future. But, it would have to wait until after football.

I updated Jordan as we drove to the football field, then turned on a Christian youth CD to rock out with for the rest of the drive. Well, all of us except for Brandon who was still upset. It didn't bother me that he wasn't singing because he sang like a dying seagull anyway.

I felt relief as Brandon walked away from me, toward the coaches.

As Faith and Caisen did cartwheels and somersaults in the grass, I took a seat to watch my football boys warming up. During the first drill, I saw a child grab on to the back of Clay's shirt, so he turned around and decked the guy.

A true follower of Christ.

I made a mental note to talk to Clay more about what it means to be a Soldier for Christ and about how his actions will have to adjust some in order to let God guide him.

Not long after, Brandon missed a pass that he thought he should have caught. Clay laughed, which made Brandon mad, so he tackled Clay and hit him a couple of times.

I got to be the parent that screams from the sidelines. *"Brandon and Clarence, knock it off!"*

A bit later, they were given a water break. Clay and Henry ran up a little hill with the rest of the participants to the water cooler, but Brandon walked over to Faith, Caisen, and me.

I said, *"Hey bud, you've got to learn to ignore Clay because tackling him and hitting him is going to get you in trouble."* That was it. My whole statement.

His hands went above his face as he went on and on about how it wasn't his fault, and it wasn't fair that I was getting him in trouble instead of Clay.

"I didn't get you in trouble because that doesn't even make sense" I said. *"I just respond to your choice."* I kept it simple, calm, and non-offensive, but he wasn't having it.

When all of the kids got back on the field, Brandon did not. I told him the drills were resuming, but he kept yelling, *"You should've gotten Clay in trouble, not me."*

As if the attitude wasn't bad enough, his grammar was tough for me to ignore.

I tried walking away from him, but he stayed on my heels, screaming, *"You're a terrible parent, definitely the worst mom I've had!"* As we crossed in front of the grandstands filled with parents and siblings, toward the parking lot, he threw sticks at me, yelling, *"My other moms didn't get me in trouble for anything, so you just don't like me. You like the other kids better, and that's why you get me in trouble. You don't even care."* He had a real knack for drawing attention.

As we got to the car, I interrupted to say, *"If I didn't care about you, then why would I be spending so much time and energy on you?"*

"You only care about yourself! You make us do the things that you like. You never let us do anything we want. You don't care. You don't even like me."

He sure was making it hard.

I climbed in the car and locked the doors, thinking he might get bored if he didn't have direct access to me. He hit and kicked the car while calling me a moron, so I let him in to muffle the sound for others.

He barged in screaming, *"I'm going to collect everything I ever made you, even the picture I drew for dad's birthday because I'm sending them to one of my other moms that was better than you."*

I calmly responded with, *"I'm sorry you feel that way,"* and *"I wish I could make it better for you,"* and other similar statements, hoping he'd simmer down.

It was hard being the punching bag for this kid, but he needed to take the punches. It wasn't fair to me, but it was clear he couldn't carry his burden on his own.

Brandon got it all out with fifteen minutes of camp remaining, and he headed back like nothing had happened.

Jordan pulled up slightly after the meltdown. I updated him about Brandon's fragile state and Clay's new commitment to the Lord, and then headed out to the Emergency Room with Henry and his hamburger lip.

When we finally saw the doctor, he said that Henry's cut would heal quicker if he put two stitches in, and arranged for the procedure.

The stitches were not easy for Henry, but he held my hand as the doc worked, with tears rolling down his cheeks. I felt bad, but I shook off the negativity and offered him encouragements.

When we got home, I initiated another Brandon-talk with Jordan. Just as I'd done many times before, I vented to Jordan about how horrible my day was, thanks to Brandon.

Jordan gave me the space to verbally vomit, before responding. He said, *"I'm impressed at how you survived the driving nightmare, and it scares me that you were in that situation. And you're right, things aren't working well the way they are, so let's talk about options."*

"Well," I said, *"we don't have permission to change his therapy until after finalization, even though his therapists say it isn't working. That leaves us two choices. Call 9-1-1 during one of his fits, where they'll likely have him hospitalized. Which would deem him unsuitable for adoption until he's stabilized. Which might not happen while we're still living here. So, it would probably sever him from our family permanently. Or, we can do nothing until finalization and just hope that we find something that works, later."*

As I explained the options, I felt a shift in my heart. I didn't like option two, but I couldn't live with myself over option one, knowing Brandon probably wouldn't land on his feet well after additional trauma like that. I hated to admit it, but I knew he was our son to walk with, even without a clear step forward. As it sunk in, I cried. It was one of those days.

We still didn't have an official countdown for finalization, which meant we didn't even have a timeline for when we could change Brandon's treatment plan, but we got to work researching possibilities. We knew it was a hard, uncertain road, but the kid couldn't walk it alone. He needed us.

To distract myself from the enormity of our situation, I buried myself in the details of our celebration trip. I talked to three people about it: Reagan and my sister-in-law, Trish, were asked to consider booking overlapping trips home with their families, and my mom was asked to look into vehicles and sleeping arrangements. I also tried to get travel permissions, just in case, but got denied. We booked flights under old names, just in case. And, we prayed a lot that the process would be completed in time, so that the kids could ride in cars with aunts and uncles, and go outside with cousins while we were inside.

The only detail left to decide was whether or not we'd announce our trip home to Oregon. On the one hand, it would help with planning. On the other, it would give people time to worry about Brandon breaking their things. We leaned toward keeping it a secret, so that anticipation couldn't get the best of anyone. In fact, I grew appreciative that we didn't receive full disclosure of the extent of Brandon's challenges before bringing him home, because the magnitude would have intimidated us!

CHAPTER 29

ADOPTION DAY

After signing mounds of necessary forms and hiring our lawyer, all we could do was wait for a court date. It was torture. We urgently needed to change up Brandon's treatment. He was losing control up to three times a day, for up to three hours at a time, and always over something too small to consider valid. It was a trauma-kid's version of the terrible two's.

The counselors reminded me regularly that Brandon might be a candidate for long-term residential treatment, which made me cry. To make me feel better, they gave us another option to look into, which had me cautiously optimistic.

After another round of research, we decided to try Eye Movement Desensitization and Reprocessing (EMDR) first, to see if there was any hope of treating him at home. I found an EMDR practitioner and saved the info for the day I'd receive the parental right to schedule his first appointment. I prayed we'd get court date news quickly and that God would guide the new treatment.

While we waited for a court date, Brandon's late-June birthday came and my early-July birthday came. They were both terrible, and a reminder we were getting dangerously close to our Adoption Celebration trip, which required a finalized adoption to celebrate.

I desperately waited, overwhelmed by the stakes of having already purchased our flights.

For a while, whenever the lawyer or caseworker called, I got giddy believing they had news of a date. After a few letdowns, I stopped getting excited over the calls, recognizing they were calling to discuss another obstacle.

This game went on from May twenty-second until July sixth, when I got THE call. There had never been a call more satisfying than the one that told us we were scheduled for court, the morning of July 8th, just two days away.

And, in the blink of an eye, it was Adoption Day!

We had the boys in the same matching suits they wore for church on Easter. Jordan was in his Army dress uniform. Faith and I wore blue dresses. By looking at us, you'd never guess the kids hadn't been ours all along. We looked like we belonged together, and we felt we were a family too. Hurdles and all, we were in it together.

We took our seats in the large courtroom, along with some of our closest Georgia friends.

Unlike our first court appearance, the routine of taking care of the quicker cases ahead of the complicated ones benefited us. And instead of presenting our personal details in front of the audience, they moved our group into a conference room.

Our lawyer presented our case to the judge, including our qualifications, some background information, and what she'd observed to be true about our family.

Next, the judge asked Jordan and me if we were sure of our decision.

Though Jordan and I both said, *"Yes, sir,"* I also said a silent prayer that went like this, *"God, I hope you know what you're doing. Please stay with us on this journey, today and every day, because we can't do it without you."*

The judge then asked the kids what they wanted their names to be, and they all shared, even Caisen who got the whole name right on his first try.

Then, he signed the papers. It took ten minutes, tops. That short and sweet encounter was all we needed to bring our foster experience to an end, well worth the eleven months wait from the day we learned of the kids' existence, and the twenty-three months wait from our first adoption meeting, way back when Jordan returned from Afghanistan.

As of that moment, we could give our kids medication or supplements if we wanted to! We could cross state lines, country lines, and any other lines we wanted to! We could choose who could watch or transport them! And, we could choose what treatment options to pursue and schedule our own appointments.

Which reminded me... I paused my happy-dance in order to make a quick call, to schedule Brandon's first appointment with the practitioner who utilized EMDR, to begin just after our Oregon trip. It was my first priority as an official, legal mother, and I felt empowered as I completed the call.

I couldn't think of a better way to share my overwhelming joy than to post our first official family picture, because I could, and I wanted to, so I did. In our chosen photo, we were wearing our one, large, blue, family outfit, holding a chalkboard sign. I used an app to add this text to the board: *"After 1,540 days in foster care, we stop the count because today is Adoption Day!!!"*

I briefly reflected that even though the judge made our family official, giving us the rights we had been seeking, he didn't give us our family. God did. God decided that these five beautiful, messy, crazy, silly kids would be ours. The judge just agreed.

Also, the judge's decision didn't mark the end of our journey. He just allowed us to move on to the next phase, which was using our adoption decree to request new birth certificates and social security cards, which were necessary before we could update the kids' names in legal databases, like the ones used for military dependents and insurance.

We knew that this phase was going to take months. Thankfully, the adoption decree, on its own, enabled us to update the kids' names at their schools and to remove the caseworkers as emergency contacts, which we did right away. It was our second act as legal, official parents. Victory!

Once the excitement settled, we realized we only had a few days to get ready for our trip to Oregon. Since Jordan and I came from the same general area, planning was fairly straightforward. However, we chose to keep the trip a secret, to relieve our worriers of any room to worry. We didn't want anyone to anticipate burden or chaos. We just wanted to show up with big smiles and win everyone over with big hugs!

Also, the kids weren't great with stepping out of routine, and we'd never done a big trip together. Jordan and I had no idea how the kids would react. I didn't want to hurt anyone's feelings by saying, *"We're coming, and we'll see you sometime, but we don't know when, because it depends."* I was sure that some would have understood and given us space for flexibility, but I didn't have the mental capacity to risk any unnecessary tension from anyone wanting a travel itinerary more concrete than I could provide.

Besides, who doesn't like a good surprise? The thrill of planning it was making me feel good, even while living with Brandon. That was no small feat. Since I recognized the secret was making my heart happy, there was no way I was going to give it up. Our lips were sealed, except for necessity.

Though the surprise aspect gave us some freedom to arrange our trip how we saw fit, it was also a bit of a challenge to set it up for success. Certainly, success would not be defined by rolling up to an event and having a bunch of snotty, poopy, angry, monsters barge in to meet their new families. No. That wouldn't be success at all.

275

It also wouldn't be kind to spend a week bouncing around with one side of the family, without even letting the other side know we were in town. Obviously, after the first, *"SURPRISE!"* the rest of our network would find out, so we needed to pick the right way to unleash it. There were many pieces to consider in my very large puzzle, with a goal of building happy relationships.

After mapping out some different scenarios, we developed a flexible, yet guided, master plan, including our first targets: the bulk of Jordan's large family, who would be lured to a small vacation home, where we'd all be trapped for a few days.

There's no need for notice before adding an additional seven people to a sleepover, right?

We knew how we wanted to start our trip, but knew we couldn't pull it off on our own. We asked my mom, who was already aware of our trip, to get us to her house from the airport, tucked into bed for the night, fed breakfast in the morning, and sent on our merry way in a vehicle of her arranging, with the necessary car seat and booster. She agreed. We also asked for life jackets because you can never be too prepared. And she accepted the challenge of tracking some down.

We also enlisted the help of my sister-in-law, Trish, who was married to Jordan's brother, Jacob. Thankfully, when I shared our travel ideas with Trish, she and Jacob agreed to be a part of it and booked their travel to Oregon to overlap with ours. They also accepted the challenge of getting Jordan's entire family to their family lake house. They needed to appropriately urge everyone to attend, without sharing the reason why. No small task, I'm sure!

Knowing the initial arrangements were in good hands, I continued working through our additional visits, including a couple of days out in Eastern Oregon to hang out with my dad and all the family out there, time at the beach with my mom and all the family that could join us, a birthday party at Jordan's sister's house for their mom, daily outings to take the kids to experience some of our favorite childhood spots, and a big potluck party so that our entire network of friends and family could come meet the kids and catch up with us.

Of course, we couldn't send out any invites for the party until after we'd arrived and launched our surprise at the lake house. We confirmed with Reagan, who arranged the party, that she would hold off on sending the invitations until after our big reveal.

We had our highest priority activities scheduled, and we also left some time blocks unplanned so that we could be somewhat flexible to what options arose and how the kids were doing. We prayed the surprise would work well, that our travel would go smoothly, and that hearts would be sufficiently softened for everyone to gain insights and understanding as to what we'd been going through, without being overwhelmed.

All that was left was getting ourselves packed for three weeks all the way across the country.

CHAPTER 30

MAY YOUR ADVENTURES BRING YOU CLOSER TOGETHER

W e started our trip very early on a Friday morning, braced for 3,000 miles of travel spread over the course of twenty-six hours with five kids. Nineteen days required some serious packing, so each kid had their own travel backpacks and little suitcases on wheels. Jordan and I also had carry-ons and suitcases. Plus, one additional suitcase dedicated to beach towels and Caisen's water-floatie. I was surprised, but not surprised, about how much space towels for seven took up!

The driving went mostly ok. The kids were still dazed from the early morning wake up. Brandon was the only one who protested going back to sleep and complained the entire four-hour drive about being bored. Just complaints, though. No fits.

When it came time to walk ourselves into the airport though, Brandon fell apart and apparently lost the ability to carry his stuff. So, only four of our kids wore their backpacks and rolled their suitcases.

Brandon walked with his hands over his face, complaining that we weren't in Oregon yet.

I got to wear Brandon's backpack. I shoved my purse into my carry-on, wore my carry-on with the strap slightly strangling me as it crossed my body, and pulled my suitcase while balancing the towel suitcase on top of it.

Jordan wore his Army print backpack, rolled his giant Army duffle, and carried Brandon's bag.

I was burnt out on Brandon's grunting and whining, so I called dibs on not sitting by Brandon.

I got Caisen instead.

Jordan and Brandon were just across the aisle from Caisen and me, while Henry, Faith, and Clarence sat together in front of me.

Lucky for Jordan, Brandon slept the entire way.

Not so luckily for me, Caisen squirmed, whined, and complained the whole way.

Our next obstacle took place while we were waiting in between flights. We had the kids sleeping on the floor, since it was way past their bedtimes. It was a relaxing moment for us, until a lady walked through, rolled her bag over the top of Clay, and then stepped on his finger. Then, as she pulled her suitcase over Caisen, she loudly complained about the kids sleeping on the floor.

My tired, defensive thoughts wanted to say mean things and let her know that she should use her eyes before using her feet. However, I tended to Clay and Caisen instead.

Clay handled it well. His fingers hurt, but he was too sleepy to pay it too much attention. It didn't take long before he was back asleep.

Caisen, on the other hand, took some soothing. I picked him up and held him as I walked around the perimeter of the moving sidewalk a few times, waiting for him to calm back down and fall back asleep.

At that point, I sat down and wondered for a while about how a person becomes so callous that they would actually blame the sleeping children they stepped on, instead of recognizing that they had been the ones to do the stepping. Besides, I was sure that most of the people around us preferred the kids were asleep, snuggled with their build-a-bears, instead of being loud and obnoxious.

Our second flight landed in the middle of the night, slightly more on the morning side. We were greeted near the security point by my parents and younger sister, who rallied together to bring both their own getaway vehicle and my older brother's van, stocked with a car seat and booster and also life jackets for our adventures.

Technically the van belonged to my older stepbrother because he was the son of my stepdad. And, technically I had a stepsister, from that same stepdad. However, I was so young when our families merged that I didn't remember life before that brother, sister or dad. So, as far as I knew, they weren't step-anything. And, to take it further, it was technically my half-sister who greeted us, but I only knew her as my little sister.

As luck would have it, my older brother's wife was out of town for our entire visit, which prompted them to offer us their van. We knew from our earlier experiences how expensive van rentals were, so their offer was a blessing!

We made our way to the parking lot where my mom and I loaded the kids, each with their backpack and bear, into the van. After Jordan and my dad situated our suitcases in the back, my mom gave the van keys to Jordan, who looked at me before handing them right back to her, as we both darted for her car. Jordan climbed in back with my sister, and I sat in front with my dad, and I locked the doors. Bye-Bye, Grandma Roxie, and good luck!

She didn't seem nearly as burdened, as I felt relieved. In fact, she seemed happy to take the kids. Which was good because I was happy to legally leave them in her care. It wouldn't have worked if the kids hadn't already met her, but she was familiar to them. I knew they'd be ok.

We drove to my mom's house and threw the kids straight into bed for a few hours of sleep. The four boys were in the living room on couches and cots, Faith was in one guest room, and Jordan and I got my old room, which sent my sister into the other guest room. She agreed though, because she didn't want to be next to the boys.

Breakfast time Saturday came quickly, and heads popped off their pillows when my younger brother barged into the house to introduce himself and swipe a ham, egg, and cheese croissant breakfast sandwich while it was still hot.

Chris, my little Bro who wasn't very little at all, tossed the kids around, goofed off, taught the kids the secret uncle/nephew handshake, and gave the kids nicknames. I particularly liked that he renamed Caisen, *"Meatball."* He made a playful first impression on the kids and then headed to work.

We took our cue to hit the road. I felt bad using my mom as a stepping stone, but she knew she'd see us again later in the trip. We said our good-byes and took advantage of the two-and-a-half-hour drive to quiz the kids on everyone's names before bombarding Jordan's family in Central Oregon.

As planned, Jacob and Trish had a lot of the family gathered at the lake house, which was Jordan's parents' vacation home, for the weekend. When we got close, Trish let us know that nine of the ten people we were hoping to surprise were down at the little day beach near the home, while Jordan's dad stayed back. We knew that meant he was relaxing in his recliner, either reading or watching TV.

We stopped by the vacation house first to say hi to his dad, Cliff. It wasn't always easy to get a smile out of Jordan's dad, who passed his stoic expression on to Jordan, but we got one that day. We introduced each of the kids to their Papa and briefly chatted with him about our travels, before heading down to the beach.

We drove my brother's van very near the group's gathering space and reverse-parked with the back of the van lining up with their chairs and coolers. As we backed up, the group glared toward us for crowding their space, and we giggled to ourselves.

Most everyone was there, except one of Jordan's brothers and his wife, who were out on their boat. Of course, Jacob and Trish had been expecting us, so they smiled when they recognized we were the ones crashing the party place. However, it took a moment for Jordan's mom and sister to put it together, because they had no context for recognizing the kids.

Jordan's mom, Margaret, stared at me a second before realizing it was me. Her shock was compounded when she saw Jordan come around the back of the van. She reached for us and cried before even noticing the kids, who were falling out of the van one by one. It took a few more seconds for her to fully grasp what had just happened. Her face showed so much excitement and happiness.

Jordan's sister, Jamie, cry-hugged us next. It had been far too long since we'd last seen Jamie and her two kids, Jennifer and Justin. We were all sad that her husband, Jeff, couldn't make it for the weekend, but we knew we'd get to see him later in the trip.

I made my way to Trish and her daughter, Sophie, as Jordan checked in with Jacob. It had been two years since I had seen my dear friend on my Germany trip, and I had been anxiously awaiting our reunion. We began introducing the kids to everyone when the last members of the group, Jackson and Chelsea, brought their boat in to see who the rude people were who invaded their beach space.

Factoring in that Jordan called Jeff on the way, the only two family members unaccounted for were Jordan's older brother, Jayce, and his lovely wife, Heidi, who were in Washington, DC. Considering the short notice, I thought the turnout was impressive.

As we visited on the beach and played in the water, I looked around and was pleased that we held to our surprise. It was a little excitement for me to focus on as we approached the trip, and it had the desired effect of being a carefree first meeting. Well, somewhat carefree. I guess I forgot to tell the kids that bodies of water in Oregon were colder than the Georgia beaches, and they cared very much about that small detail. They squawked and squealed as they slowly made their way into the lake.

Later, at the lake house, we pulled out some board games. I stayed attentive to Brandon, trying to prevent any of his small frustrations from growing. His frustrations included things like irritation over someone else having a lucky move in a game, while he had what he thought was an unlucky move, complaints of boredom, and complaints about the climate. Really, it was anything he could think of. Considering the lack of sleep and the exhaustion from playing in the sun and water, I knew a fit was a real possibility, and certainly the last thing we needed.

After each interaction with Brandon, I received some well-intentioned encouragements about how to better see him, like *"Boys will be boys,"* and *"A little competition never hurt anyone."* Also, *"He's fine,"* and *"Don't worry."* Another one that came up more than once was, *"Aren't you concerned you'll embarrass him or shame him?"* and, *"Maybe you should wait until you're behind closed doors to talk?"*

It was odd to me, until I remembered that they'd never seen one of his fits. They didn't know that waiting to re-direct wasn't an option. They were giving me advice on how to parent under healthy circumstances because they didn't see Brandon's special needs on his exterior. As I tried to field the concerns and share context for our parenting approach, I found that part of me would have been ok if he threw a fit, so they'd better understand. I knew he'd paint the picture much more clearly than I could explain it.

That wasn't realistic, though. I couldn't allow a fit for such a silly reason. Instead, I shared information about our journey and relied on the fact that everyone would see more of our complications over time. Thankfully, nobody got pushy or defensive.

When bedtime came around, all seventeen of us took our spaces, mostly in sleeping bags. As I lay, I reflected on how amazing it was that our kids finally met some of the important people in our lives, and those people met our kids. It was an exciting and emotional day.

In the morning, we all enjoyed a pancake breakfast before heading down to the lake beach. While the rest of our group went out on the boat, our party of seven waited, reviewed everyone's names again, and complained about the cold water and the sharp yet slimy rocks.

Though we'd practiced, it was still hard for the kids to keep so many names straight, especially because Uncle Jackson and Uncle Jacob looked so much alike. And a few times, they confused their uncles with Jordan too! The kids were lucky Uncle Jayce and Uncle Jeff weren't there, otherwise they'd have four Uncle J names to keep straight.

I reminded them that it was ok to make mistakes with names because everyone else was working on the kids' names too. Three of my boys were the same size and had some similar features, which made it hard for most new people to keep them straight. Heck, it was hard for people who weren't new, too. Especially if they weren't seeing the kids side-by-side.

After a while, it was time for some boat shifting. Everyone who was onboard climbed off, except Jackson and Chelsea, and the kids' cousin, Jennifer. Jordan and I helped our kids out to the boat, and we all went for a ride.

We took the inner tube with us, which is a large, inflatable, donut-shaped device that you haul behind a boat. None of the kids had ever been inner tubing before, or boating, for that matter.

Brandon asked to ride on the tube first. He was fearless to the end, and entertained us all when he was finally tossed from the tube and skipped across the water a few times before going under.

Next was Faith with her cousin Jennifer. They were silly and dramatic about the bumps and splashes, but relatively quiet otherwise. They were both twelve-year-old girly-girls, but they were also both shy and reserved. Though I thought they'd bond on their own, we found that they did best with the adults prompting and facilitating conversations.

Next was Clay, except he was too scared to go alone, so I went with him. I lay next to him, but straddled my arms around him, pinning him down with my outstretched arm and my armpit pocket.

He started all smiles and laughs, but gradually let more and more fear show with bugged eyes.

I asked him what was wrong, and he screamed, *"My arms are getting tired! I'm going to fall!"*

I told him I had him pinned and asked him to let go of the handles briefly, so I could show him. He did, and seemed to exhibit some relief in realizing I had him.

He was fine for a little bit longer, before letting the fear creep back in.

I again asked what was wrong, and he said, *"Your arms will get tired, then we'll fall!"*

"Clay," I said, *"I've got you covered. Uncle Jackson won't go any faster unless we ask him to, and I promise you, what we are doing right now isn't enough that I'd drop you. And even if I did, we'd be fine."*

I may have been bouncing around behind a boat, but I could still see that my child was too scared to enjoy the activity. And, I wasn't going to convince him to trust me while his instincts were telling him he was in danger. I needed to prove he could trust me.

"I have an idea," I said. "What if we choose to let go and fall off together, instead of being thrown off? That way, it's our choice, and we're in control."

He agreed.

We counted to three and let go.

He got water up his nose, but was otherwise physically fine.

Once we were out of his perceived danger, he let all of his emotions out. His chin was quivering as he ugly-cried and sobbed, while still bobbing in the water. We hung out in the water for a good five minutes, just the two of us, talking about trust.

"Clay, did you notice any fear on my face while we were riding?" I asked.

"No," he said.

"How about in my voice? Did you notice fear there?" I asked.

Again, he said, "No."

"Could you hear me talking you through the experience, encouraging you, and telling you that we were ok?" I asked.

He said, "Yes," but it sounded more like a question.

"Did it sound like I was lying to you?" I asked.

"No, I didn't think you lied," he said.

I was so excited about his answers, because it was the perfect setup for a much-needed lesson.

"Clarence," I said, "there may have been a time where you needed to decide for yourself when you were safe or when you were in danger. But that isn't the case anymore. You now have responsible adults with you who will make safe choices for you."

I could see his face relax, as we bobbed, so I continued. "You can always look at my face to see if I'm worried and if I'm not worried, then you shouldn't be. That's true for every situation and for all kids with responsible parents, like you, Clay."

His tears changed, and he seemed to be looking at me differently. Even though our eyes were fairly level, it felt like he was looking up to me.

I'm sure we could have talked more about his past disappointments and some other times where Jordan and I had proven we were trustworthy, but our boat crew told us we needed to load up. I agreed. I didn't think anyone would continue to enjoy boating if they witnessed Clay or me get run over by one.

Next, Caisen was ready and anxious, and he picked me to go with him.

I pinned him in with my armpit, just like Clay. When he got tired, he got nervous that he couldn't hold on, just like Clay. I told him that he was ok because I was holding on for both of us, which was hard for him to accept, just like Clay. They had such similarities in their need for control.

When the timing was right, I suggested we let go on our own, and he agreed.

Of course he did. It was the only option where he'd be in control.

Again, water up the nose, but otherwise fine. And, no emotional repercussions. He was a champ.

Next up should have been Henry, but he panicked before even getting up from his comfy seat. I sat with him and reassured him that I wouldn't let anything bad happen. In the meantime, Jackson took us around the lake, Jordan talked with the boys about their rides, and Chelsea chatted with Faith and Jennifer.

I recognized the opportunity to relax, but it was foiled by Henry's escalating drama. He wasn't ready to accept that I would be there for him and that he could trust me. I was tempted to say, *"Fine, then don't go!"* but that would have made it worse. It wasn't that he didn't want to go. He was scared, and his trust was stunted. If I had given up on him, then he would have given up on himself, too. In that case, we would have seen his disappointment and anger, which wasn't the right step forward.

Eventually, he was able to climb on the tube with me. We went slow and steady, and I talked him through the entire event, just like I did with Clay and Caisen. Those lengthy conversations helped the kids to step out of their comfort zones and into unfamiliar experiences, but they were taxing.

When the time came that Henry was ready to be done, he also chose to let go, which resulted in more water up the nose. It was worth it, though, because he was so happy he chose to ride with me, and I was happy that we had worked through another obstacle together.

As I climbed the ladder onto the boat, I was torn. Each victory reminded me that my efforts were worthwhile, though I knew they were baby steps. It wasn't easy having to prove myself over and over and over and over again, and so frequently each day. We were far from having true trust, but we were closer. I prayed God would use our baby steps to achieve something great.

As I wrapped up in a towel, Brandon asked to ride with Jordan. And they got crazy.

Jordan stood up on the tube over Brandon, who was rolling around and goofing off. Jackson lined up a good wave and tossed Jordan off.

Chelsea held up the orange flag, that tells other boaters we had someone in the water, as Jackson circled back for Jordan. Instead of holding on, Brandon decided to be cool and stand up, like his dad had.

He also got tossed. But, in a different area.

So, Jackson circled back to get Brandon, leaving Jordan out on the busy lake by himself.

Once Brandon was onboard, we again went over the rules of boater safety, explaining that an orange flag means there was someone in the water, and if people saw us going for him, then they wouldn't know to also look for Jordan. Therefore, next time his partner is tossed, he should try to stay on the rig until his partner is recovered. Totally not a big deal, but certainly a lesson worth learning.

Instead of registering the lesson, Brandon felt guilty and got upset. He covered his face with his arms and began grunting. Once we had Jordan in the boat, Brandon wouldn't look him in the eyes, because he thought Jordan would be mad at him.

While we were swapping people out, I had a talk with Brandon, focusing on the fact that making a mistake or misunderstanding a procedure wasn't a reason for anger. *"You just needed to receive the information and move on,"* I said.

If only he could move on.

Jordan then took a turn on the wakeboard, which is like a snowboard or skateboard made for the water. The kids were totally awe-struck. And, it impressed me that my sexy thirty-two-year-old-hubby still had it in him. He might not have caught as much air as he used to, and he certainly didn't last as long as he had in the past, but he still got out there and looked good doing it.

I called Brandon's attention to Jordan as he moved back and forth across the water, and he forgot he was upset.

Next, I took a turn on the kneeboard, which is what you'd think it is, a board to kneel on. I had fun spinning around, riding backward, jumping around, and basically just goofing off, though not to the level I used to. The kids seemed impressed, which I hoped would give me better credibility with them.

It didn't take long before I was totally wiped out, opening the door for Brandon to take another turn as we made our way back toward the beach spot. It was perfect, really. The rest of us were relaxing on the boat, and Brandon was a good twenty-five feet away.

Even with the couple of smaller meltdowns and the abundance of fear, I still had a great time! However, I was exhausted by three rounds on the inner tube, holding a child and myself onboard, while also over projecting calm and cool, and by three big-emotional-response conversations, plus my round of kneeboarding where I rode until I had nothing left.

When we anchored, Jordan jumped into the water for me to hand the kids down to him. As he shoved each one toward the shore, I realized how thankful I was to have him. In fact, I thanked God for Jordan in that moment, recognizing that my husband had to entertain and guide the other four kiddos each time I had to focus on one. I loved our partnership and loved being able to count on him.

When we got back to the house, the kids pulled the board games back out.

I tried to just lay back and relax, but I had to balance it with responding to more of Brandon's smaller issues. I was too exhausted to respond to a bigger fit, so I felt the pressure to resolve the bumps before they grew. I focused on my wording to help him see he was getting frustrated over small things.

I knew our non-standard parenting style stood out because I was again told to let Brandon be, while Jordan was asked why we didn't just wait and address his attitude later, in private. Based on the suggestions, I believed we came across as over-protective, strict, or just dramatic, but they didn't know Brandon like we did. And though they didn't know why, we couldn't do as they suggested, because Brandon would learn it's ok to be bad, as long as it's in front of others, so mom and dad will ignore it.

We had a system that sometimes helped, and we needed to stick with it. Brandon wasn't a typical kid; he was a trauma kid. In fact, each of our kids had some quirks that dictated how we could parent them, which wouldn't inherently make sense to anyone on the outside, looking in.

As before, everyone seemed receptive to our explanations, and it was nice to have that support.

That night, Trish and I went on a long walk. As much as I knew our trip was meant to connect our kids with the rest of their new family, I also knew that I was running low on steam after so many months of digging deep. Walking with Trish was therapeutic, as we talked about everything and nothing, as old girlfriends do, and I was in no hurry to get back to the house or my kids.

When we finally returned, the kids were getting tucked into their sleeping bags, which were spread across the floor. I learned that it wasn't as smooth for Jordan as it would have been with me there, but that didn't hurt my feelings at all. I'd been receiving the brunt of the tough stuff, so it was ok with both of us that he would pick up the extra slack from time to time.

Truth be told, I found Mr. Persistent to be extra sexy each time he proved to be both dependable and willing. Just like the day the refrigerator went for a walk, and the day the bunk beds were tipped on me, and the day I had rocks thrown at me for hours, he did his best to absorb what he could. I was the primary caregiver, and therefore the kids aimed most of their baggage at me, and Mr. Persistent often stepped in as their hero, and as mine!

I leaned down to kiss each kid goodnight before stepping into the hallway to give my husband a better kiss goodnight, out of view. I climbed into my sleeping bag on the couch and fell asleep fast.

Caisen woke early, as usual, and found his Papa Cliff was also up. I watched through the window above my couch-bed as Cliff and Caisen wandered down the road together. My heart fluttered when Caisen grabbed his Papa's hand, and Cliff smiled down. If only I had taken a picture!

Later in the day, we made the kids their very first s'mores. We weren't about to let some uncooperative weather stop us, so we made them at the stovetop, reminding the kids that when there's a will, there's always a way.

For the third day in a row, I watched as the kids played board games with whomever they could gather, and it went fairly successfully. It helped that their Nana, who was sitting at the table with five of her grandkids, was being direct and clear over the rules, so that no one could manipulate the game through cheating. She took the lead, and I was free to relax.

When the time came, we watched a movie to help the kids settle down for bed. They were disappointed it was their last night, and so was I, but we knew that we had many other relationships to tend to. When morning came around, we took family pictures and said our goodbyes, looking forward to meeting up with everyone again later in the trip.

Though the weekend went better than I'd hoped, I made a mental note to expect an abundance of parenting suggestions as we visited with the rest of our friends and family. I wished I'd anticipated it so that I could have prepared some shorthand answers, but I didn't. I was distracted by kid stuff and travel stuff. Instead, I just felt thankful that Jordan's family was willing to accept our super-involved, lengthy-chat parenting approach. I knew they didn't understand it, but they were open to learning about our journey. What a splendid first gathering!

CHAPTER 31

POKING THE BEAR

We were all sad to say goodbye at the end of our lake house trip, but we knew we had many more people to see and things to do. In fact, we didn't have a single hour to spare.

We used my mom's house for one night of transitioning, again. It was hard to believe it had been almost a full three years since my last visit to my childhood home! We spent the evening catching up and goofing off with my parents, my little sister, my not-so-little little brother and his wife Laura.

This was only the kids' second time seeing their uncle Chris, and they were all over him. Literally. They were climbing up his back, grabbing onto his legs, doing their best to be squished against him as much as they could. Meanwhile, Laura was taking selfie-pictures with each of the kiddos and teaching them some basic Spanish words. It was light and fun, and then Chris and Laura left for home.

Not long after, Jackson and Chelsea, who had just spent the weekend with us at the lake house, came over to join us as we walked to the nearby ice cream shop and then over to the park behind my mom's house to play. As we walked, I noticed my kids grab the hands of their aunt and uncle. The bonding was real and true, and my heart was happy!

As soon as I could swing it, we got the kids in bed and fast asleep.

Well, except for Faith. She came to our door and said, *"I'm too scared to sleep."*

I knew that it wasn't actually a fear thing because she said it with a begging tone, more than a scared tone. I walked her back to her room, to figure out what the real problem was.

After some prodding, she blurted, *"No one here cares about me. It's like I'm in foster care!"*

I felt sad for her.

I asked what she meant, and she said, *"At the lake house, everyone looked loved and happy, even the boys, but not me. Everyone was a stranger to me. I thought they'd love me like family."*

I felt bad that I'd failed to prep her properly about the process for developing relationships, but also recognized it wasn't a natural thing to anticipate. It was just another unexpected challenge to walk through.

We talked at length about her feelings. I reassured how much I loved her and cared about her, and that I wasn't the only one. I explained that it would take time to build meaningful relationships, so she shouldn't feel bad that the feeling wasn't there yet. Lastly, I told her, *"We still have plenty of time for the relationships to grow, but it will only happen if you reach out."*

She understood and seemed motivated to keep trying. She finally went to sleep, which was good because we needed some rest before launching our next mini-trip, three hours away, to meet my dad's side of the family in another part of Oregon.

Along the way, we stopped at Multnomah Falls, which was my favorite waterfall, with a good hike up to the top. I assumed that Caisen would be our most challenged hiker and planned to take turns carrying him.

I was wrong.

I thought Brandon would be our biggest complainer, and that we'd need to spend a good amount of energy encouraging him and enticing him.

I was wrong.

I thought Henry would be the first to quit, and that we'd have to motivate him to keep going a little further at a time.

I was wrong.

I thought Clay would be our workhorse, and that he'd blaze his way up the trail.

I was wrong.

I thought Faith would just roll along, following the group like a lost puppy.

I was wrong.

Faith and Clay were pathetic. I mean, yes, there were some fairly steep parts, but nothing that they couldn't handle. The five-year-old was leading the way, so I knew it was doable. Jordan stopped at each switchback with Caisen, Brandon, and Henry and waited for me to drag Clay and Faith up the trail.

I'm sure other people thought that we were mean parents forcing our crying daughter to hike, but that wasn't the case. She didn't want to go back down, she didn't want to stop, she didn't want to miss out on the top, she didn't want to disappoint us, and she was scared she might not make it. So, she just cried. A lot. And Clay joined her.

Truthfully, I was prepared to handle the blowback from the other three. I was surprised and irritated that the difficulty came from these two. It felt like I'd never have a successful happy family moment, because if it wasn't one kid, it was another, or two.

Eventually we made it to the top, and the view of the Columbia River, and Washington on the other side, helped to ease my frustration and disappointment. The view held a special place in my heart, and I enjoyed sharing it with our kids.

From the top of the primary waterfall, there were two options. We could go back down, or follow the path along the flowing waters further back into the gorge, toward my most favorite place in the world. We took the path going further.

The trail was mainly flat yet crooked, with some shorter rocky hills. When we got to our desired spot, we helped the kids climb down from the trail to an off-the-beaten-path landing. We helped them cross some low logs over parts of the creek, to a smaller waterfall that pooled in front of an open space of pebbles and logs.

This space, this special, beautiful space, was the exact location where Jordan had proposed to me, nearly seven years earlier. I felt at peace standing in the place where we made our first commitments and also amazed at how much our lives had changed since then.

The kids had Jordan and me stand in the traditional proposal position so that they could take a picture.

They took some silly pictures of us. I took some silly pictures of them. Then, we got everyone but me situated on our special big log. I set the timer on my camera, sprinted across the open space, climbed the giant log as fast as I could to join my family, and took a family picture. We repeated the process, to get full-group pictures of us climbing around and playing. Considering the challenge getting up the trail, the time we had to play around really made it all worthwhile.

To venture out of our personal oasis, we had to help kids across logs and water again, and up the fairly steep edge that led back up to the trail. The way down to our car was much smoother than the trip up, and I was thankful for it.

We drove a little further through the gorge, before stopping in Cascade Locks to enjoy a little picnic with another view of the river, and the hills and mountains of Washington on the other side, while we waited for Uncle Chris to catch up to us.

When Chris pulled up, Brandon and Clay jumped in the truck with their uncle, which felt to me like winning the lottery.

Our next stop was my Dad's house, where the kids met their Grandpa Ernie and Grandma Linda, and slowly met many more aunts, uncles, and cousins. As everyone was becoming acquainted, we loaded up plates for the kids, with fried chicken, chips, and watermelon. There were other sides, but my kids knew what they liked.

And yes, that included dessert when it came out.

There were twenty-one people inside and outside the house, all wandering and chatting.

The kids enjoyed the big gathering, but mostly invested their time in the three cousins who were old enough to wander around and play with them. It was quite the group, quite the excitement, and quite the time.

I enjoyed talking with each of my family members. It had been over three years since our last trip through town! Everyone had experienced a lot of life in those three years, and I loved being back in it, catching up on all that had been going on.

After dinner, we attempted an updated full family picture, and by some miracle, we actually got a few good ones to pick from!

Next, our entire group walked over to the local park, because everyone loves a good park.

I watched as my kids climbed all over their uncle Chris.

I watched as my kids climbed all over the playground with their cousins.

I watched as Jordan chatted with my dad and brothers.

I watched as my dad made the rounds, taking pictures of the family. His contagious laugh seemed to catch everyone!

I watched as Linda performed her Grandma-duties of playing with all of her grandkids, hugging and kissing on each of them, all while sporting a beautiful smile. There was no denying how much she enjoyed having so many grandkids around at once!

I sat back, relaxed, watched, and socialized. Of course, there were reminders for the kids to follow playground rules and manners, but nothing triggered into fits, which made the night feel easy. It also felt odd, though, because I'd prepared for a little more struggle with the kids and the parenting inquiries that would accompany it.

Go figure. I wasn't prepared at the lake house, when I needed to explain, and was expecting to explain here, when there was no need. I was getting use to assuming wrong.

I felt proud of the kids over how they'd been handling being out of routine, around many unfamiliar faces, and in unfamiliar places.

We all walked back to the house and most everyone departed. We scattered the kids' sleeping bags across the living room, all around the couch their uncle Chris had claimed. You'd think Chris was Superman the way the kids looked at him and reached to touch him.

Just when I'd finished patting myself on the back for getting the kids down, Faith came forward with an issue. She didn't want to be separated from everyone. Even though she wasn't. She was on the outside perimeter, but she was only an arm's distance from Brandon, in the same room as all the other kids and Uncle Chris.

It took me a moment of trying to wrap my head around the problem, before I decided there wasn't a problem. She just wanted reassurance. *"Faith,"* I said, *"you would be sleeping alone if we were at home. However, since we aren't at home, you get to sleep with everyone else. You are not separated or alone in any way. You can see where Uncle Chris is sleeping from where you're at, and your Dad and I are only a few steps away, in the guest room."*

I gave her a second goodnight hug and kiss and reminded her that she was loved. And, once she was ready, she and the rest of the kids went to sleep.

We woke up and had cereal for breakfast, before Caisen and Henry excused themselves outside to help their Grandma Linda water her pretty flowers.

While the rest of the kids played with farmhouse toys and plastic hardware tools, my dad suggested we spend the day at his hunting cabin in the mountains. He had everything needed for a campfire lunch, and we had swimsuits for playing in the lake. As I was counting towels and packing sunscreen, one of my sisters dropped her daughter off to spend the day with Grandma Linda and Grandpa Ernie, while she went to work.

I noticed a contrast between my niece's relationship with her extended family of aunts, uncles, and grandparents, and Faith's relationship with them. I said a prayer that bonding would happen for her. I wanted Faith to feel the love around her, enough to start healing.

We loaded everyone up. We pawned Brandon and Clay off on my dad, Linda, and my brother, which opened space for my niece to climb in with us. Our young guest was social and engaged for the whole drive, but I knew that Brandon was probably more social, yet disengaged from reality for the entire drive in the other rig. I felt like I won in the arrangement.

When we got to the cabin, several activities began.

My dad and brother pulled out some BB guns to teach the kids to shoot, using pop cans, or sody-pop cans, as my dad would say, as targets. I tried to provide some context for why they'd need to keep an extra eye on Brandon, and Clarence, and Caisen, and Henry, and Faith, but definitely Brandon, however they both respectfully dismissed me. They had it under control.

They were confident they could handle a course on gun safety. I was confident in them too, considering they had a wealth of experience to draw from, especially my dad, who was a retired State Trooper, and had spent his entire life hunting and fishing. He knew guns like the back of his hand, or better. Still, it felt odd that they didn't want my explanations, or need them. They accepted the kids had baggage, committed to keeping a close eye on the group, and that was that.

As I sat back and watched, I saw Brandon and Clarence swing the guns around carelessly, but their teachers were all over it. They corrected the behavior, repeatedly, and reminded the kids to point the guns to the ground when they weren't shooting. It felt nice to observe someone else show consistency in their expectations of the kids, and I felt reinforced through the experience.

Later in the morning, Jordan and I took turns taking the kids off-roading on the four-wheeler. When it wasn't their turn, the kids roamed around and played in the dirt, while my dad started a campfire.

Things were going mostly great. We had no injuries, meltdowns, or fights. However, we did have a moment where my youngest was certain he could reach into the goldfish pond to grab something he wanted. When Grandpa Ernie told him that he wasn't going to be able to reach it, Caisen thought he knew better, so he reached further. And he fell in.

It was shallow enough that he could stand back up and reach to his Grandpa who pulled him out. The shock of his unexpected cold swim certainly showed on his gasping, bug-eyed face.

Thankfully, the fire was going, making a perfect heater for Caisen to dry off and warm up.

Henry, Brandon and Clarence resumed with the guns. They were shooting at different targets and seemed to be improving. They all wanted pictures of themselves holding a gun with the cans they had shot. I happily snapped the photos, noticing how proud they each looked.

When it was time, the kids gathered around the fire pit to roast weenies. We loaded their plates with buns and condiments and the chips of their choice. They were sitting around the fire, as happy as could be, listening to my brother tell an enchanting story about a plane crash on the property from long, long ago, where a treasure was lost and never found. They were mesmerized, and I wasn't surprised. Chris had a storytelling gift.

After lunch, we pulled out the s'mores staples. The kids were so excited because they had just learned about the amazingness of a good s'more. This time, though, they got to roast the marshmallows over the fire, and they were giddy. I'm thankful my dad had plenty of long skewers for roasting, because asking them to take turns or wait wouldn't have ended well.

Next, we attempted to go swim at the lake. Four of my kids were in their swimsuits, with our suitcase full of towels in tow. Faith, Henry, and Caisen got in the van with my niece, and Clay climbed in his Grandpa's truck. We were missing one kid. Brandon.

When we told him that we wanted to go swim, he yelled that it wasn't fair that we wouldn't let him find the treasure.

He paced the perimeter of the cabin, and kicked pinecones and rocks, while he ranted, *"You just don't want me to find the diamonds. You don't care. You just don't want me to be the one to find the treasure. You only do what you want."* It was pathetic. It was frustrating. It was somewhat embarrassing.

"Brandon," I said, *"it was just a story that Uncle Chris made up, to entertain you."*

"No," he demanded, *"Uncle Chris would never lie to me. You're the liar."*

I didn't follow him around the cabin because I didn't want to add to his aggravation. While he was on the far side of the house, I asked Henry to switch vehicles, knowing that Brandon should be in the van with me, if I ever calmed him down.

I again tried to offer my dad, brother, and Linda an abbreviated course on how the trauma and drug abuse affected Brandon, but they all assured me it wasn't necessary. Although I felt relief that they didn't expect clarifications on Brandon's struggles, I was also perplexed. Why didn't they want to know *"why"* he was the way he was?

After finding myself wrong about so many lessons I thought I'd learned about the kids, especially Brandon, I had a real soft spot, rather a deep insecurity, over being wrong. Essentially, I had lost my confidence that I could read situations and people, and I was questioning my instincts. I knew it was silly, but I couldn't shake the feeling.

Brandon paced many laps around the cabin before he was ready to hear me. I spoke slow, soft, and steady. *"Uncle Chris didn't lie, he told an entertaining story, much like a book or movie. Instead of worrying about the details in his elaborate tale, we'd really like to go to the lake. Are you ready to join us?"*

He nodded his head, wiped his tears, and climbed in the van while letting us know he'd rather be in the other vehicle. Chris hung back at the cabin, while the rest of us left for the lake, much later than planned.

The kids barely got the tips of their toes in the water before deciding it was too cold for their Georgia-peach bodies. Over time, they got both feet in the water, but decided the lakebed was too slimy/squishy. They had been spoiled with Georgia/Florida beaches and had become water-snobs.

I was on the bank telling them that they would warm up if they just got out there and played. While I used the, *"do as I say,"* approach, my dad shocked us all with *"do as I do."*

He climbed into the lake fully dressed, which included his socks, shoes, and hat. As he swam around he called out to tell them they were missing out.

The kids clearly thought he was hysterical, as they grabbed their bellies and laughed. They slowly moved toward him, making their way out into the water, where he tossed them in the air, over and over again.

It was a side of my dad that I hadn't seen before, and I loved it. Especially when he laid back and floated with his sneakers sticking up out of the water. He was a big teddy bear. The kids were having fun poking at the bear, while Jordan and I sat on the bank taking pictures.

For a moment, everything was right. In fact, it was the best moment the world could offer, until Grandma Linda climbed out into the water, proving me wrong by making it better. She was out to her knees, splashing with the kids, laughing and smiling over each dripping-wet hug she received.

My Uncle joined us at the lake, letting us know that his daughter and two grandkids were up at their campsite. While Jordan chatted with him, I joined the group in the lake. My initial reaction was to agree with the kids, it was chilly compared to the Florida/Georgia beaches, but I didn't let it show. I put on a brave face, dunked myself completely, and committed to moving around.

Once warm, I asked Faith to swim across the lake and back with me. I had seen her swimming form and endurance and figured she'd do well. Especially if I were there to encourage her.

I was wrong.

We were about three quarters of the way across when she gave up. I thought she was joking, but she stopped swimming and started treading. I knew that we were closer to the far side than the edge we started on, so I encouraged her to finish, which she reluctantly did in a few short stints.

We took our time catching our breath, knowing the strength needed to get back to our group. I talked game plan: don't push yourself to go too fast, or you'll get tired early. Also, don't go too slow, because stretching it out too long will also hurt us.

We started when she said she was ready, and we made it less than half-way before she looked at me and said, *"I'm done."* Like it was no big deal.

I was confused. I looked at her and simply asked, *"What do you mean, you're done? We're in the middle of a lake. Getting to the shore would make us done."*

"I don't feel like swimming anymore," she said, and just stopped swimming.

It was so weird. She said it the same way that one would say they were done with a meal.

I reached out to support her and asked if she was cramping or out of breath.

"No," she said. *"I just don't want to swim anymore."*

She didn't seem to understand the problem with stopping in the middle of a lake. *"You know you can't stay here, right?"* I asked.

She gave me a puzzled look as she gave up on treading, like I was the confusing one. As she went limp, I grabbed on to her, tucked her under my arm and began side swimming. She didn't help at all.

She wasn't a small child and we still had half a lake to go. After switching from one side to the other a couple of times, I realized I wasn't going to make it as-is while hauling my twelve-year-old cargo. I rolled onto my back so I could use both arms, moved her between my legs, and she leaned back and rested her arms on my legs like she was reclining in a lawn chair.

The lake began feeling bigger and bigger. Every time I looked up, I wasn't as close as I thought I was. I was exhausted, and I was disappointed that my daughter couldn't dig deep or finish strong. Those things are learned, and she hadn't been taught. Instead, she'd learned to just check out, or turn off.

I thought things were already worse, until I looked up and saw the rest of family exiting the lake, making their way to my Uncle's campground. I had no back up. There was no rescue team in place. We were too far away for me to call for any of them, and Jordan thought my hand gesture was just a wave. He was wrong, and I was out of luck.

My arms were burning, I was out of breath, and I kept telling myself to keep a steady pace. I asked her a few times if she was ready to help herself across, and she wasn't. What was wrong with her?

Several times, I wondered if I should give up, too. It was working for her, wasn't it? Except, I was the parent, and if she were ever going to learn the value of working hard, I'd have to continue to model it for her.

To my surprise, we made it across; rather, I made it across for us. We walked the path toward the campsite and found that the boys had moved on to tossing a football around. I tried to tell Jordan how the lake swim went and how I wasn't so confident we'd make it, but got distracted because Clay was making some interesting faces each time he reached to catch a ball. By interesting, I mean that he looked like he was trying to violently bite off his own ear.

We visited with our extended family for a bit before heading back to the cabin. The kids dried off and wandered around a little bit, while Jordan helped my dad pack up. I made use of the time by writing a thank you note with my finger in the dirt we'd accumulated on the back of my older brother's van. There was a lot of dirt to work with, making it an ideal canvas.

I took a picture of my message so that I could share it with my brother at the appropriate time, as I wondered if they had any idea that we'd be taking their van out on such a big, dusty adventure.

Once ready to leave, we assigned seats. I again pawned Brandon off on my dad, brother, and Linda, along with Henry. Henry hadn't ridden with Chris yet, so he was ecstatic when given permission to climb in the truck. In return, we called dibs on our niece, again feeling like the victors.

I convinced the crew to stop off at a viewpoint to take another big family picture out in the mountains. Well, the only one who really needed convincing was my husband, who was over the pictures and not happy about slowing up the drive. He was a trooper though.

Everyone climbed over the road railing and walked about one-hundred feet, so that I could balance the camera on the edge of the van, line up a shot without the rail in it, set the timer, and sprint to the group in time to smile pretty and pretend that I wasn't out of breath. The view of a large drop off and a curtain of trees behind our family photo made the effort worthwhile. And it was pretty easy getting everyone back into their same seats to finish the drive back to my dad's house.

The ride in our rig was nice and smooth. There was potential for things to be different in the other vehicle, but no need to worry about something out of my control. However, upon departing the vehicles, the potential for difficulty became my reality.

Brandon was upset. Turns out, Brandon was complaining that Henry got to sit by Uncle Chris, instead of him. Brandon's wording was a little less logical, though. He said, *"I never get to sit by Uncle Chris,"* even though Brandon had sat by his uncle on the drive up to the cabin. He also said, *"Henry always gets to,"* even though it was Henry's first time in a vehicle with their uncle. Even after the information was shared with him, he continued to rant that, *"it wasn't fair."*

The kid was bonkers!

Again, my dad, brother, and Linda got to see the result of Brandon's nonsense frustrations. And again, I was thankful he didn't lose physical control, because I would have felt terrible if he'd tried breaking their windows with seatbelts or throwing his shoes at them. Instead, he just yelled, whined, and complained. Not a big deal on my scale.

I can't say I blame Chris for developing a migraine and quickly taking off once we got to my dad's. In fact, I wondered if I could claim a migraine and leave with him. I didn't, though, because I wanted pizza. I went with my dad to get the cheesy-goodness and left Jordan and Linda with the kids!

I'm glad I did, because my dad had a story to share with me.

My dad described that while he and Linda were driving Henry and Clay to the lake, it got quiet in the backseat. He told me he asked them why it was so quiet, and the two kids held up a roll of duct tape, asking if it was his.

He said yes, so they asked what he used it for.

He jokingly claimed to use it for everything because duct tape is a fix-all tool.

Again it got quiet, so Linda asked why they were asking about the duct tape.

That's when they shared a memory of having their mouths duct-taped shut for talking when they shouldn't have, or for being too loud.

It wasn't the first time I'd heard about the duct tape stories of their past. I'd also heard that Clarence had been strapped in a car seat and sprayed down with a hose. They certainly had some tough experiences in their past, and as much as I hated that they had memories like that, I liked that they felt comfortable sharing them with their grandparents. It meant they felt safe, and they were bonding. Also, it gave my parents a glimpse into the kinds of experiences that helped sculpt the kids' behaviors and beliefs, without my explaining anything.

Truthfully, I'd never done a pizza-pickup-run over that kind of conversation before, but our time was limited and both the talk and the food were necessary. We got the pizza back to the house, ate every bit of it, and let the kids know it was time for us to say goodbye. There were hugs, kisses, and some tears. Then my dad handed us a package of his smoked salmon to take with us, and we were all smiling again, with more places to go and people to see.

We got back to my mom's house fairly late and threw all of the kids in bed, where they fell fast asleep. Well, except for Faith. She again took an extra round of goodnight hugs and kisses.

Jordan and I talked briefly as we lay in bed that night. I told him, *"I feel like everyone is accepting of the kids, which is great, but I'm surprised that it feels like I'm on the outside. I can't really figure out why, but I don't feel the same being back here."*

I guess Faith's insecurities were rubbing off on me? I don't know. But I felt out of place.

CHAPTER 32

ALONE IN A CROWD

The next seven days were a whirlwind. Unlike the two mini-trips we had just completed, the middle phase of our trip was scattered. We used my mom's house as our home base, with many daily adventures taking us to-and-fro. Some of these were our own choices, and other choices were made for us.

We were sent to a water park with our lake house crew, which allowed Reagan to prepare for our Adoption Celebration party at the park behind my mom's house. We could have been helpful with the setup, but I wasn't going to argue with a direction to go swim with Jordan's family instead.

The indoor aquatic center, which I enjoyed frequently as a child, had a wave pool, three water slides, a diving board, a little kid's area, a hot tub, and lanes. We spent time playing together, but I enjoyed the span of time where we ventured out on our own, because Jordan and I enjoyed some alone time in the hot tub.

We could see the kids pop out of the waterslides and jump off the diving board. I felt good about Caisen's water skills, recognizing how he and I both benefited from our private swimming adventures.

As Jordan and I sat there, feeling toasty warm and kid-free, I felt different emotions arise. I realized I was moved by how graciously the kids had been welcomed into our family and by how well they'd been doing on the trip. However, I wasn't feeling as personally encouraged as I'd hoped. I thought there'd be more pats-on-the back for Jordan and me, but there weren't many at all. No one knew the depth of the burden I was carrying, other than the general fact that we had five kids, which wasn't the real weight of our stresses. The kids' special needs and emotional struggles were demanding, and I felt very alone with it, even while surrounded by a strong network.

I shared my feelings with Jordan, and he partly agreed. *"I get it,"* he said. *"But I'm more relieved that the kids are doing well, even if it means we don't get the understanding or support we need. It's better than having to deal with their meltdowns in front of everyone."*

"Is that really better?" I asked. *"I'm exhausted, and I need nurturing encouragements to refuel with, and I'm not getting them."*

Caisen plopped out of the steepest slide, and I didn't see him coming up to the surface. I watched cautiously and stood in the hot tub, but it was a false alarm. As he made his way to the edge, I took a deep breath, recognizing my ongoing stress. Stress from the travel, stress from feeling misunderstood, stress from being too exhausted to engage, and stress from having nothing to talk about except the kids, because I'd given up every other aspect of my life. Simply put, I was stressed. Not too stressed to appreciate my time alone with Jordan, but stressed enough that my eyes were on the slides more than on him.

Jordan put his arm around me, probably because he was getting hot and it was more comfortable to lift his arms out of the tub, and said, *"Jess, it really doesn't matter if anyone here sees or knows what we're doing because we're doing it 3,000 miles away. We're only here for our kids to meet the family, and then we're going home. This has been a long summer, and you're doing better than anyone could expect, even if they don't know it."*

Jordan wasn't usually sentimental, but he sure did pull it together when I needed him. I could tell by the look in his eyes, and the way he tightened his arm around me, that he was thinking he'd just earned some points with his wife. And he was right; he'd earned points.

When it came time, everyone headed into the locker rooms and got party-ready.

We parked at my mom's house and walked to the park. People had already gathered and were set up in lawn chairs. Potluck style dishes were placed on banquet tables, in front of a picture display Reagan set up, showcasing the favorites of the memories we hadn't yet been able to share.

The kids said hello to the few people they'd already met, but then darted over to the play structure with the other kids in attendance.

Jordan made the rounds, floating from group to group, while I had more of a speed-dating set up. I stood still, but the person in front of me rotated steadily. I had the same conversation on repeat:

Other person: *"What a blessing."*

Me: *"Well, there is blessing in it, but it's a challenge, too."*

Other person: *"But they must appreciate everything you're doing."*

Me: *"Maybe one day, but they're just kids. Right now, they struggle with all the changes, because they're used to a very different lifestyle."*

Other person: *"They will, though, just wait."*

Me: *"Maybe. We certainly pray for it. But even if they don't, it's still worthwhile."*

Other person: *"Why wouldn't they?"*

Me: *"They're hurt. One of the boys pitches three-hour fits, up to three times a day."*

Other person: *"Welcome to parenthood."*

Me: *"Yes, parenthood is messy, but trauma kids have burdens on top of typical kid problems. They hadn't learned trust, which makes appropriate behavior a little more complicated."*

Other person: *"Kids are kids. All kids have their challenges."*

Me: *"Yes, they do. And attachment disorders are at the center of our challenges, since they haven't had many lasting relationships. We're trying to help them learn healthier ways of interacting with people, but there's no guarantee that they'll fully overcome their baggage."*

Other person: *"They look normal to me, and they're playing with the other kids just fine. Maybe you're overthinking it. You just need to take a step back and let them be kids."*

Me: *"Yeah, they're acting fine, but... Oh, never mind, you're right. It's in my head and the kids are actually healthy and wonderful, and our home is full of laughter. And we have a pet unicorn."*

Well, maybe I didn't end conversations like that, but sharing the abbreviated details of our story wasn't accomplishing anything. It was as if people envisioned a ready-made family and didn't consider the unhealthy, unsafe circumstances that brought us together. Based on the warnings we received against getting involved with foster kids, people understood there would be hardship, but they apparently thought the hurt would magically disappear once they were adopted. And since my kids chose not to reveal any of it, I looked like a dramatic, attention-seeking liar. I felt so lonely.

I overheard Jordan talking to a friend about the upcoming college football season, so I decided to talk about other things and to be more tight-lipped about our situation. If they wanted to know the difficulties of adopting older kids and/or sibling groups, they'd ask. If they didn't ask, then they weren't prepared to hear that the blessings of adoption are complicated.

While safely chatting with a friend about her new job, I noticed the kids digging into the recycling bag. I wondered what they were up to, but didn't ask. Not long after, Jack was being pushed around in a racecar made out of a large trail mix box, with a helmet made out of a twenty-four-pack Pepsi box. Safety first. There was laughter over the kids' creativity, and I felt Jordan's words lead me to one of God's best lessons. Jordan had told me he felt relief that the kids were doing well, so I chose relief, too. And God said not to worry, so I gave it all up to Him. I knew He'd have a plan for how to fill my love-tank, since it wasn't happening the way I envisioned.

While choosing to have faith, it hit me. The problem with my interactions was due to a lack of context for others to filter our story through. Those who engaged were doing so based on whatever context they decided to apply. They weren't coming to us with questions about our journey, rather an assumption about what it would look like. In a matter of seconds, my theory came together:

Everyone has a cancer story. If someone hasn't personally had cancer, they know someone who has been impacted by a loved one's experience. Therefore, when we hear mention of cancer, it's safe to say, *"cancer sucks,"* or something similar, and everyone understands where you're coming from. However, not everyone has an older child or sibling group adoption story to draw from, or even a special-needs child story, and therefore they try to relate using the closest thing they have, which is parenthood generally.

My mom had at least given us the benefit of assuming our parenting story was more similar to her experience with my brother, who was difficult, versus believing it was a story of ease and obvious blessings. But even that model was inaccurate. Older-child adoption circumstances are different because of the impaired ability to trust and lack of common history to draw from. Our kids had been in a failed family, a failed placement, and multiple foster homes, which changed the way they saw family, and therefore changed their roles within ours.

Jordan and I knew the similarities and differences. We knew the kids were still kids, needing the same things other kids need, but we also knew we had a lot of life-lessons to go back and re-teach. But why would others know the details of the cause that moved us, when God led them down a different road? And I finally understood. They wouldn't.

I needed to brainstorm how to better advocate for kids like mine and families like mine, so no one else should have to feel so misunderstood. Maybe more quality time with each person would allow the conversations to go deeper. Or, maybe I could pick the right stories to remedy naive assumptions. Or, maybe I could write a book, which could be made into a movie, so that a context for families like ours could be available. But, none of those things would immediately reverse my struggle at our large picnic.

As I wrapped up my inner-revelation, I refocused on my friend, who was just finishing the details of her career move. I congratulated her, and she asked when I'd be going back to work.

"That's a good question," I started, *"We thought it'd be about six months or so before we'd stabilize enough for me to re-enter the workforce. But, that guess was made when we were planning on two kids. Realistically, I don't see the opportunity for work coming soon, but I miss it."*

"Why would you miss working?" she asked. *"You get to stay home all day."*

"Well, I loved my work," I said. *"And I impacted soldiers' lives. I know I'm impacting these kids, too, but they don't say, "thank you" like my soldiers did. This is a thankless venture and a tiring one, and a few hours a day of outside-the-family work sounds refreshing."*

"Remember," she said, *"you chose this."*

Whoops! I shared my thoughts and feelings and got burned AGAIN. I needed to tuck my own story away tightly, until I found a way to spread context. But then again, hiding my journey couldn't be good for me either. Maybe ripping my hair out would help?

"Yes," I said. *"You're right. And I don't regret our choice, even when it's challenging."*

With that, the line moved, and I got to visit with my older brother and two of his kids. I showed them the picture of the dirt-message on the back of their van, and promised we'd bathed the van since then and would do it again before returning it. His chuckle told me he didn't mind. I asked some questions to get caught up with my niece and nephew, and I was amazed by how much they'd grown since I last saw them. While everyone was missing out on our Georgia lives, we'd also been missing out on everyone's lives in Oregon. The distance was taking its toll.

As I looked around, I saw Clay and Caisen sitting on Chris's feet as ankle weights. Their weight didn't stop Chris in his tracks, like it would for me. He could move, while also growling down at them and exchanging silly faces. The kids were doing great and relationships were forming because of it. I was happy for everyone but me. But I was determined to find a way to make it better, for me and for others in similar circumstances.

Reagan brought me a plate of food to snack on, saying, *"I noticed you hadn't been over to the buffet line, but you need to eat."* I couldn't have asked for a better friend than Reagan, and even as I was feeling misunderstood, she proved she saw me clearly.

However, before taking my second bite, my mom took my plate, saying, *"The rain is coming. Quick, get in some pictures before people leave."* I wanted food, but my mom was right.

I had a line of people saying goodbye, and it was hard not to cry over each one. It didn't matter what I was struggling with on the inside. What mattered was that I loved every person in attendance, and I was so thankful that they each took the time to come see us. I knew they loved me and my family, and would be there for us if I had a specific request of any of them. Our network of supporters was strong, and I missed being near them all.

After the bulk of our guests left, a few people braved the rain to either continue interacting with the kids or to help with cleanup. Jordan tried to get out of cleanup by goofing off in the back of the small U-Haul that was used for transporting the banquet tables. Jordan thought it would be funny to close the door on the kids, forgetting that little Caisen wasn't old enough to find total darkness funny. The sobbing was loud, and Jordan stopped laughing to tend to his terrified child.

After the situation calmed, my Aunt Anne crawled in the back of the U-Haul. She told jokes, asked questions, and made silly faces. Within minutes, the kids were putty in her hands. Her love was obvious, because Aunt Anne wore her heart on her sleeve. Her willingness to engage with the kids brought me to subtle tears. She looked at them with sympathy, and I felt touched that the same woman, who offered me joy and support as a child, was now offering it to my kids.

My young brood might not have known that day, but I had no doubt they'd learn over the years how lucky they were to gain Aunt Anne, Uncle Paul, and Cousin Hope as family. I had nearly thirty years' worth of special memories shared with them, of kids concerts, family barbeques, and competitive cribbage tournaments, and I knew with certainty the kids had just started to collect memories of their own. In addition to all the other aunts, uncles, cousins, grandparents, and friends the kids had gained, the kids' love tanks were filling fast.

Lucky them. I mean, lucky us.

When we finished cleaning and loading, we were all exhausted, yet satisfied. After saying a few more goodbyes, four of the kids walked with Jordan to the greenway, which is an open, grassy space in the neighborhood with a path through it, that happened to connect the park and my mom's backyard. Caisen stayed with Reagan and me, as I said my final goodbye to yet another great, long-time friend.

This particular friend was one of three men at the gathering who were credited with shaping Jordan and me through sports, back when we were discovering our paths in life. In fact, two of them were also responsible for introducing Jordan and me, many years prior. Terry was my high school pole vault coach, and Todd was Jordan's coach. They brought us together and remained hugely important in our lives. The third coach was another Terry, who sat down to talk with me in between workouts about whether or not I should give a relationship with Jordan a chance.

Coaches who responsibly mentor their athletes tend to have large impacts, as these men did, and their commitment to Jordan and me made them family to us. As we spoke, I felt reaffirmed in my commitment to chauffeur the kids through their sports experience and told my friend that I hoped our kids would be lucky enough to find coaches who touch their lives as significantly as ours did.

We reminisced about years past. It felt like it had been a lifetime since Jordan and I were active pole-vaulters, but the memories flowed so easily, reminding me that I was more than just a caregiver to my five kids. Much more. I had an entire life before them, and my life would continue with them. There was more to me, and a stroll down memory lane was what I needed to unlock it all.

When the crowd was down to Reagan, Caisen and myself, Caisen asked, *"Can we take the shortcut to Grandma Roxie's house?"*

"Do you mean the greenway?" I asked, *"Because that isn't a shortcut, it's the actual way I go."*

He said, *"No mom, not the greenway. I'm talking about the redway. The shortcut way."*

I giggled at my son, who was certain he knew something I didn't. *"Nope,"* I said, *"because we aren't walking."* As we climbed in the truck with Reagan, I said, *"We're taking the roadway."*

The kids were hyper after the party, so bedtime didn't come together smoothly. It wasn't a problem, though, because I was excited, too. I might not have had my encourage-the-adoptive-mom-tank filled, but I did feel blessed to have chatted with so many friends, at one place, in such a short amount of time. And, I gained some new insights about myself and my situation.

The next morning, we had a few things to get done, like buying a birthday present for Jordan's mom for her birthday party later in the afternoon.

While we were getting ready to leave, Henry asked Jordan if he could play my mom's piano. Jordan said yes, and Henry attempted some nursery rhymes by following the key chart. He played independently until it was his turn in the bathroom.

As Henry got up, Brandon helped himself to the piano, without asking, and began pounding aggressively. He rocked enthusiastically, intending to make as much noise and ruckus as possible.

He was asked to be calm and gentle, and he repeatedly replied with, *"Yes mommy, I am."*

"No, you aren't," I said. *"But I need you to try. Please treat the piano better."*

When everyone had gone through the necessary steps of going potty, brushing their teeth, making their bed-space, getting dressed, and eating breakfast, it was finally time to leave. I thanked God, because I couldn't have taken another minute of Brandon, since he was still pounding away.

"All right everyone." I shouted, *"Get in the van, please."*

While most of my family headed out the front door, Brandon threw himself on the floor and screamed, *"Henry got to play longer!"*

I wasn't surprised he exploded, after several days without a full-fit. And it was better for him that he didn't have an audience and probably better for me, too.

"Henry's your favorite," he yelled. *"He always plays piano. You never let me. You're mean."* He emptied all of the boys' suitcases and threw the empty bags across the room. He took special care to throw each and every shoe he found. He also messed up beds and tossed stuffed animals, before moving to his bed-space, where he screamed into his pillow and kicked the wall beside him.

It was ridiculous, but also overdue.

Jordan quietly said, *"We still need to go shopping for my mom's gift, and we don't have any other time before the party to do it. Brandon clearly won't be ready any time soon, soooo..."*

We both knew what that meant. I was on Brandon duty. Not because I wanted to stay behind. Not because Jordan couldn't. We both knew Brandon needed me to absorb his rage. He threw rocks at me, and tipped beds on me, and yelled mean things at me, because he was testing me. I needed to pass his tests, so that Brandon could slowly develop an ability to trust, which would translate to others.

Jordan took the other four kids to pick out the birthday present, with an agreement that I'd text him when Brandon was calmed down and ready to go.

However, as soon as Brandon noticed that Jordan and the other kids had gone without him, he escalated into round two, and I thanked God for postponing the tantrum until after I'd had my epiphany about being more than just a caregiver. Just one day earlier, my soul would have struggled over being left behind to deal with another seemingly unnecessary meltdown.

Besides, I couldn't blame the kid. If I hadn't asked to play a piano before playing it obnoxiously for a bit and then was told it was time to go, I'd probably try to break a house too. Or not.

But, I wasn't Brandon. I hadn't experienced life the way that Brandon had. I wasn't in his shoes. And I didn't believe he wanted to be in his shoes either. He wasn't consciously deciding to ruin our days and his own. He just couldn't control himself, and when he lost control, he struggled to regain it. It was sadder than anything else, and he deserved the help needed to break the cycle.

Feeling creative, I considered how to redirect Brandon, thinking he must have a reset button. I'd already tried talking to him, guiding him, listening to him, and everything else that made sense, so I needed a new approach. I got a cup of water and splashed water in his face.

This did not work. At all. But it was worth a try, especially since I'd gained the rights to explore my own disciplinary tactics. And the shock in his eyes was priceless.

His yelling switched gears, and I had to work to keep myself from laughing.

"You got me wet! And you got Grandma Roxie's bed wet. I'm going to tell on you, and you're going to be in trouble. She's going to be mad at you for getting water on her bed. You're going to get a consequence! And you're going to have to say you're sorry. Because you made a bad choice. A really bad choice. Getting her bed wet. That was bad. And you got me wet. Why did you get me wet? You don't make any sense. You just got me wet for no reason. You're in trouble."

He went on and on. Each time he went through it, I found it funnier than the time before. And as I worked to hold back my giggles, I noticed his wording. It sounded like a combination of his words and mine, meaning I was rubbing off on him, even if only slightly. I wasn't proud of his fit, or of myself for throwing water in his face, which was ruled out as a solution, but I was proud of the baby step tucked in the meltdown.

I took a seat and made sure my energy was calm and quiet, so he couldn't draw anything fight-worthy off of me. I chimed in from time to time, and he gradually calmed out of it. He wasn't happy, and it took a while, but he got back in control. When he seemed to be feeling better, I asked him to clean up his mess, and he did, to the quality of a sloppy, pre-teen boy.

When I texted Jordan, he picked us up, and we headed over to join Jacob, Trish and Sophie at Nana Margaret and Papa Cliff's house for little bit, before heading over to Jamie and Jeff's house for the party. While visiting, Nana Margaret played songs on the piano for the kids, who were impressed by her talent. Of course, their attention spans didn't allow for a long show, but they all chimed things like *"Whoa, she knows all the keys,"* and *"Her fingers move so fast."*

When the kids got rambunctious, we walked them to the park near Margaret and Cliff's house. Jordan walked ahead with Brandon, Henry, and Clarence, and carried a basketball with him. I strolled behind them with Trish, Sophie, Faith, and Caisen. We got there a few minutes after the rushing kids, just in time to see Brandon was again frustrated.

Jordan said, *"Brandon, get off the court if you're going to complain."*

Brandon yelled, *"I'm not complaining, you are. You just don't want me to play."*

Jordan replied, *"You were invited to play, but you wouldn't let anyone else touch the ball."*

"Because I want to show them how good I am," he yelled, like that was reason to keep the ball from the other kids.

"Good at what?" Jordan asked. *"You just carried it around, refusing to dribble or share."*

"I don't want to play with you," Brandon screamed. *"I want to play basketball by myself."*

"That's not an option because the rest of us are playing. If you're just going to argue and complain, then you need to get off the court."

Jordan noticed I'd come walking up and gave me a very strong look, suggesting he was about to start pulling his hair out. It was hard to speak logic into such a close-minded kid. Jordan said to me, *"He won't do what I say, and he won't stop complaining about my directions."*

Brandon interrupted, *"Yeah, I'm complaining because Dad called me a complainer, so I'm complaining. If he didn't call me a complainer, I wouldn't complain. It's his fault, so he's in trouble."*

Jordan smirked, and said, *"Yeah, Jess, I'm in trouble."*

I bet Jordan would have loved a timeout. I know I would have. I'd probably prefer to use the time to nap, and he'd probably have other grown-up ideas. But we didn't have a timeout. We had Brandon.

Brandon didn't like that Jordan smiled and took it as Jordan making fun of him, so he crossed his arms over his face and yelled, *"It's his fault, he called me a complainer."*

It took some smooth talking, but I got Brandon off to the side, by placing my hand on his back, speaking gently, and guiding him toward the swings. I noticed Trish had Sophie on the play structure, and Caisen joined Jordan and the other boys. So, it was just Brandon and me, again.

I got myself situated in the swing, before pulling my big baby into my lap, somewhat sideways like the way a bride gets carried through a door, and got to work breaking things down.

"Dad wasn't calling you a complainer, he was saying that you were complaining. Were you complaining, or is there a different word that you would use to describe what you were doing?"

"I complained."

"So, was Dad wrong?"

"No."

"Then why are you upset?

"Because Dad called me a complainer!"

We did several rounds of the same dialogue. It drove me crazy that it took about thirty minutes sitting in the swing, holding my eleven-year-old, with the entire lower half of my body numb and tingling, before he realized he didn't have a reason to be offended. He needed the repetition, though I dreaded it.

"Ok," he said, *"I'll go play basketball now."*

"That's an interesting idea," I said. *"What do you plan on playing?"*

"I'm just going to shoot the ball so everyone can see how good I am at making baskets," he said, in a tone that had me convinced he really didn't see a problem with his idea.

I wanted to tell him that he shot like an old grandma, but I didn't. I asked, *"Would you enjoy standing there watching one of them shoot it over and over?"*

"No," he exclaimed, *"that'd be boring. I would never do that."*

"Well," I explained, *"it's not fair that they should stand to watch you, either. Your options are to play a game with them, or go play something else."*

"I don't want to play with them, so I'm going to the playground," he said.

"Sounds like a great idea, Brandon," I said. *"Maybe you should stop by Dad to apologize for hogging the ball and giving attitude?"*

Most kids would have dropped their heads at that idea, but not Brandon. He smiled and ran to Jordan and apologized. I saw Jordan nod and pull Brandon in for a hug, and then Brandon ran over to the monkey bars. Jordan then looked at me with an expression that we both knew meant, *"That kid is nuts."*

Trish commented about the efforts it took to resolve Brandon's fits, believing that's what she'd seen. I was glad she saw something happen with Brandon, and I let her know that it was only a basic frustration. There was no screaming, no violence, no alligator rolls, or anything else typical of fits. She saw him get stuck and the process for helping him get unstuck. The look on her face as she processed my information, now that she had some context to filter it through, showed understanding and compassion, which I'd been desperately seeking.

As we walked back to Nana Margaret and Papa Cliff's, Brandon strolled with us slower folk to hold Sophie's hand. I was pleased that Trish saw his softer, sweeter side, to balance everything out.

We quickly drove over to Jamie and Jeff's house and guided the kids to the backyard where their cousins, Jennifer and Justin, were on their big trampoline. The boys were told that the big kids and little kids would need to alternate turns, so that the smaller kids could also play. They could also play catch, play badminton, wander around the yard, or be social with the other people who were gathered, to include Uncle Jackson and Aunt Chelsea.

At dinnertime, four of my kids took a seat to wait for Jordan and me to dish their plates.

Henry did not. He was told to help himself, by someone that wasn't Jordan or me.

For a child with a history of neglect, hoarding tendencies and trust issues, this was not good.

He got himself two plates, piled high with enough food to last a week.

To be fair, he was a big eater. However, even just one of his two plates had more food on it than he could have possibly eaten. And it caused two separate problems.

First, my other kids became jealous and needy as they collectively decided that they needed to be able to get their own plates filled sky-high as well, otherwise, they weren't loved as much as Henry, and they would probably starve.

I tried to shut that down by saying, *"Wasting food isn't a sign of love. You feel love because you have parents who promise to always give you enough."* Bam.

The second problem was how defensive and possessive Henry got over the food, reverting back to his earlier days of being fearful that there wouldn't be enough. It was a major setback and brought a side of Henry out that we hadn't seen in a while.

I handled it as best I could. *"You four, eat your food and forget you saw anything. Henry, you come with me."*

I heard Clay complain as I turned my back, then Jordan readdressing them. He was great at damage control. We definitely needed each other in that moment because neither of us could diffuse both of our problems at once.

"Henry," I said, *"let's unload most of this onto one plate that I'll hold onto. Let's use the other plate to keep what you think you need. Your dad and I will responsibly eat off your big plate, so that the food doesn't go to waste, but we'll make sure to save some just in case you finish your appropriate plate, and want a few more bites."*

He looked at me with tears. It would have been so much easier if we only had one hurt child, but we couldn't give in, because it would teeter all of the other kids.

"Henry," I said, *"there's enough food on these plates for all seven of us and probably more. I promise, there's plenty for you, Dad, me, and a clown car of farm animals."*

He smirked, but quickly got back to his frown.

"Have you ever been denied enough food with us? Ever?" I asked.

He hesitantly answered, *"No."*

"I promise, Henry," I said, *"this is another time where you'll have plenty. Trust me."*

I know he wasn't comfortable, but he did as he was asked. He said nothing, but unloaded mounds of food and went to have a seat. My child chose trust, and I felt less sad over taking his extra food away. It was a good lesson for us.

While this was going on, I took notice of a side conversation in which people observed Jordan and me to be overprotective again. When Henry walked away, Jordan's sister said she'd told Henry it was ok for him to help himself to the food and assured me that there was plenty, so I shouldn't worry.

"I appreciate that there's enough food," I explained. *"But that doesn't mean he should get so much for himself. He's still a long way away from having a healthy relationship with food, and I don't want to go backwards on the work we're doing."*

It was a complicated situation because I understood most kids could fill their plates a mile high, without a problem. Emotionally healthy kids might eat a little too much before choosing to throw the rest away, but my kids would not throw any away. They'd eat until they hurt and then stash more in their cheeks and pockets, and I'd later find the rest under their beds or in their pillowcases.

It was hard feeling like I had to defend my actions, again, but it worked out. And, as before, everyone accepted my explanation of why we were doing things the way we were. They were learning more about our story through each bump in the road.

The kids got done eating and returned to playing. When cake came out, we all enjoyed a slice, before heading back to my mom's house. Jordan and I talked in the car and realized that Margaret's birthday was the first family event we'd been a part of in over four years. It was nice to be included.

It was nearly bedtime when some very dear family friends, who owned the daycare where Chris and I had spent much of our childhood, came by my mom's house to visit because they couldn't make it to the adoption party. They joined us for an evening stroll to the park.

I was giddy when I realized they'd come over, because laughter is guaranteed in the presence of Barb, and Bill's kind and gentle approach could sooth the most chaotic of minds.

As we walked, I paired off with Bill. He asked me about the details of our journey, which led into a conversation of parenting styles, and listened without any judgment or criticism. He was just genuinely interested in hearing our story.

As I shared how hard it was having to be so consistent and routine with discipline, Bill shared that his instincts would have been to essentially love the aches and pains away.

"I wish it was that simple," I said. *"But it isn't. Where they're at in their journey, consistency and routine is love. They aren't looking for a vacation family, or an over-correction to balance their past; they are unknowingly demanding a stable, constant, dependable home where they have control of their outcomes. We're teaching them that we love them enough to give*

them what they earn. It's a pattern they need to accept before we can build anything else."

"That makes sense," Bill said. *"I'd probably have a hard time being stern because I'd be thinking about what they've been through."*

"I feel that struggle, too," I said. *"But I've learned that a soft approach is challenging for kids who've developed manipulation skills for survival, because they take advantage. Henry in particular is always working an angle, and if he keeps getting away with his cons, he won't see a reason to change it, until the real world offers him a consequence to teach him a lesson we'd both wish I'd already taught. I owe it to him to be a strong example and a consistent platform."*

"It really is complicated, isn't it?" he asked.

"It's hard to balance playful love and structured love, but both are necessary," I said, *"And the structured side is the foundation to help them learn to receive all other aspects of love, in time."*

We arrived at the park, and Barb joined Jordan in playing with the kids. Bill stood with me and remained quiet, which I took as permission to continue.

"We want to give them the tools to build the lives they want. Therefore, there are times for crying with them, times for being direct and clear, times for 'Poor little kid, life isn't fair,' and times for 'You are responsible for your own decisions.' It's a constant struggle to know when to use each."

"Gosh, Jess," Bill said, *"I'm proud of you for what you're doing. They're lucky to have you."*

It happened. I received the validation and support. My heart was set on fire.

By the time our chat ended, our crew was ready to walk back to my mom's. We put the kids to bed, and I got a few minutes to visit with Barb and my mom, while Jordan chatted with Bill and my dad. As expected, we ladies filled the kitchen with laughter. Barb's sense of humor was good for my soul, as was Bill's unwavering support. It was a perfect night, which made me scared over what was to come. Good never stayed good for long with us.

The next morning, Caisen crawled in bed with Jordan and me, about two hours before it was time to get up. I was determined it would be a great day, so I didn't even ask why he was climbing in. I just snuggled him up and tried to doze back off.

Then, I smelled it. Pee. Strong pee. The little punk snuggled with me, covered in his own pee.

I asked what happened, and he stared at me. I asked if he knew he'd peed, and he frowned. I encouraged him to be honest, and he said, *"It was too dark, so I couldn't walk to the bathroom."*

That couldn't be true because he'd ask for help before peeing himself, wouldn't he? Then it dawned on me, the sun was already shining before he came in my room. He could see. Fibber.

Next, he said, *"But I couldn't remember the way,"* which was another lie.

Then, *"But the floor was cold,"* he said. But, his room was carpeted, and the house was warm. He kept digging the hole deeper and deeper over something that didn't require digging at all. Jordan and I took turns explaining why he didn't need to lie to us, but he wasn't having it.

I wanted to get over the whole thing, but the lying was an issue. Why did they all lie so much?

After getting Caisen changed and the sheets in the washing machine, I tried one last time to help him share the truth. Finally, he blurted, *"I was asleep, and I woke up in it."*

Why were they all so scared to just be up front? Oh yeah, because they didn't have a history of proper support.

"Caisen," I said, *"thank you for sharing the truth. I'm sure it was embarrassing to admit that you'd had an accident, but no matter the situation, the truth is always best. Don't be upset with yourself, bud, you didn't do anything wrong. You were exhausted and slept through needing to go potty. Next time, tell me, so I know what needs to be cleaned up."*

It always felt good to finish on a good note, but I also knew we'd have many more similar conversations before any changes were made. Honesty was hard for them, because of their stunted trust, skewed morality, and perceived reality that they weren't good enough. My poor kids. Not to mention that the extended time away from home, away from our routines, and filled with excitement, was taking its toll on my already fragile children, and on me. And we still had one mini-trip left.

CHAPTER 33

LIFE'S A BEACH

We'd already experienced plenty of highs, by working through obstacles, cultivating the kids' relationships and enjoying adventures, but we weren't done yet. I needed to pull it together for the final stretch of our family's meet-and-greet tour, which was another mini-trip, just two hours away at the Oregon Coast. We may have been exhausted, but I'd already RSVP'd *"yes"* to my niece's beach wedding, and I knew my mom deserved some quality time with us, after being our home base for two weeks. Besides, she invited some of my favorite people to join us.

Reagan and Jack got to my mom's house nice and early, ready to hit the road. My mom, dad, and sister were loaded up. My seven were buckled in, and we knew Chris and Laura would meet up with us later in the day.

It was go-time.

When we got to the coast, the salt-water smell filled the air. It brought back childhood memories for me, which I was glad to be facilitating for the kids. We couldn't replace their bad memories, but we sure could work to balance it out and eventually tip the scale with new memories, to include The Chowder Bowl, which was our favorite clam chowder place, followed by all the attractions my brother and I had visited every summer as kids.

When we finished our afternoon of being tourists, we made our way to the beach for two nights of fun. Chris and Laura got there just before us, and the kids sprinted from the cars to give them hugs.

While Jordan and my mom prepped dinner for the big group, Reagan got Jack a quick dinner to launch him into his nighttime routine, and the rest of us wandered out to the beach with the kids. It was windy and chilly, so the kids were in sweatshirts as they kicked sand around, looked for shells, and ran to-and-fro. I took pictures, reined them in when they wandered, and smiled at their discoveries.

Brandon had the most unique find of the group, a rock with the words, *"Let the sea set you free,"* painted on the front. On the back, it had a hashtag and directions to take a picture with it, share it on social media, and toss it back into the world. He was so proud of finding it.

As directed, we took his picture with it. Then, when he was asked to set it free, he cried.

"It's my treasure," he said. *"I don't want to give it back."*

"It wasn't ours to keep, Brandon." I explained. *"But I'll keep an eye out for it on Facebook and let you know where else it turns up. OK?"*

He nodded.

"Go find a special place to throw it," I said, *"then come catch up. It's time for dinner."*

Dinner was delicious, but I was more excited to push the kids through their bedtime routine, which happened just after eating.

Jack went to sleep first, in Reagan's room, followed by my four boys, who were put in a room together. There were only three beds in their room, so Henry and Brandon had the bunk beds, while Clay and Caisen shared a full-size bed, with their heads and feet at opposite ends.

Faith went to sleep on the floor of the room assigned to Jordan and me.

Though the rest of us weren't going to bed yet, we made sure everyone had their spaces assigned. Chris and Laura had a room. Reagan shared with Jack. My parents had a room. My sister had a couch. It was a full house!

Once the kids were all down for the count, a few of us climbed in the hot tub on the back deck. I powered down and enjoyed the sounds of the waves, the beauty of the stars, and the relief of some much-needed peace and quiet. This continued until Jordan whispered, *"You know the kids aren't going to sleep in, right?"*

Though I didn't love getting out of the tub, I knew his reminder meant it was time for bed. We snuck into our room so as to not wake Faith.

As expected, the younger kids woke earlier than any of the adults would have liked. While most of the youngsters happily played Go-Fish, Brandon let his attitude get the best of him. Since he wasn't playing well with the others, I pulled him aside to teach him Solitaire. The other kids enjoyed their game, Brandon enjoyed his one-on-one time, and everyone else enjoyed the reduction in arguing and yelling.

When Chris and Laura got up, they offered to go on a Starbucks run. Henry asked to join them, and I used my parental rights to personally authorize the ride with another adult. Parental rights rock.

They weren't gone long. And when they came back, Henry had a hot chocolate in hand. It was my suspicion that he intentionally saved it, because he immediately began flaunting the still-full cup, rubbing it in the faces of his siblings.

None of the kids handled it well, as they complained, *"That's not fair,"* and *"I want some."*

Of everyone who struggled, Brandon was the worst. And Henry got happier as Brandon got sadder. Showing off his treasured hot chocolate made him feel like someone's favorite, which was the only way he felt loved. If only he knew we had enough love for them all.

Chris and Laura felt bad, but it wasn't their fault. They were only being kind to their nephew, not knowing that Henry would brag about it, or how the other kids would respond.

Jordan thought it was worth pointing out that things worked best if either all the kids got something, or none of the kids. Or option three -- make sure that the one kid finishes his treat before rejoining the group. Solid advice.

My dad took Henry and Clarence down to the beach, which gave me space to address Brandon. It didn't take too long for him to settle down, since Henry and the cup were no longer in sight, but I still felt that my efforts earned me a break from Brandon, so I sent him down to join my dad's crew.

Of course, Caisen then got upset that he didn't go down to the beach when the rest of them did, but he was struggling to follow his morning directions of brushing his teeth and getting out of his jammies. *"When you finish your morning tasks, you can go down with your dad and uncle Chris,"* I said, which inspired him to pick up the pace, allowing the rest of the guys to leave.

We couldn't see exactly what they were up to from the house's beach view, but we could see that they were all going in and out of the very cold water. I thought it weird that my kids were ok with the cold ocean, after watching them freak out over the chilly lakes. Maybe they were adapting?

I didn't worry about the kids because whatever they were up to, they had three adults with them. Therefore, I joined the rest of the ladies in the kitchen, and we chatted for a good thirty minutes, before three of my boys abruptly barged into the house, looking purple and shivering uncontrollably.

They told me that their grandpa offered them each a dollar if they went into the cold ocean and submerged themselves. They hoped they could get extra dollars if they dunked multiple times, so they tried. The motivation was strong. Much stronger than their dislike of cold water.

I turned on the gas fireplace for the kids to stand in front of while they waited for their turn in the shower, and I looked up to see Jordan reach the deck with Caisen in his arms. However, instead of bringing Caisen into the house, I watched Jordan move to drop the frozen munchkin into the hot tub.

I rushed to stop him, but I wasn't fast enough. I got to the door just in time to hear Caisen scream at the top of his lungs, and I yelled at Jordan to get him out of the tub. My yelling wasn't necessary because Caisen's screaming was enough to let Jordan know something was wrong, but it was already out of my mouth.

Caisen continued screaming and crying as I snatched him from Jordan, wrapping him with a towel. As I carried him through the house, giving him cuts in line for the shower, Jordan was right behind me. I gave him a stern look and stated abruptly, *"A hot tub is too hot for kids and feels even hotter against cold skin."*

Jordan said, *"I'm sorry, Caisen. I didn't mean to hurt you. I just wanted to warm you up."*

Caisen wiped his eyes and nodded at Jordan.

Then, Jordan looked at me and said, *"I don't need to hear your 'what were you thinking?' tone. I'm not a child. I understand what happened, and I feel bad enough without you rubbing it in."*

As I turned the corner into the bathroom, I heard my brother, who had Jordan's back, call me the Scrooge, and the rest of the group laughed at it. It hurt, but I still had kids to tend to.

I handled the shower end of things, getting them shuffled through and into dry clothes, while my mom and Jordan kept the others a safe distance from the fireplace. It was a challenge to keep my tears tucked away, because I was replaying the words of Jordan and my brother in my mind.

When the task was done, and the kids were all warmed up and playing cards together in the living room, except for Brandon who was playing solitaire, I put myself in a time out.

As I shut the door behind me, I began sobbing. Once I started, I couldn't stop. I couldn't breathe, I couldn't collect myself and it took everything in me to keep quiet. I didn't want an audience, or a fight, or a pity-party. I just wanted to be left alone.

To be clear, my pain didn't come from being called out on my belittling tone, though I did feel bad over my reaction to Jordan, because I knew

Jordan didn't deserve it. And, I knew he would have pulled Caisen out and cared for him just fine if I wasn't there. I also wasn't upset over being called the Scrooge. Coming from my brother, it was no big deal. I typically would have rolled my eyes and responded to him with a joke or dig of my own.

The problem, however, was that I felt like Ebenezer. I was the Scrooge. I felt like I had been the bad guy for the entire trip. People were telling me my kids were doing great, and I couldn't agree. People said my journey was blessed, and I didn't feel it. And when I shared my feelings, people didn't understand, leaving me to just feel like a complainer or drama-queen. I felt I was disappointing everyone with my reality, which did not match the magical world they expected me to describe.

I had been defending myself, explaining myself, and responding to being undermined by people who seemed to think I needed their guidance, even though their guidance didn't apply to our situation. It was especially hard receiving the criticism, advice and undermining in front of the kids.

Though no one was poking at my parenting in that moment, my feelings were still triggered.

I was a special-needs mom, trying to accommodate my kids' special needs. I knew my kids needed my structure just as much as they needed my hugs and kisses, which was validated by their therapists. The kids were looking for predictable and dependable routines to define their new normal, which was threatened by the number of people who just wanted to spoil the kids into liking them.

Every time I tried to enforce routine or structure with the kids, someone had some version of, *"just have compassion"* advice, which felt both insulting and comical since compassion brought us to our five kids, who had been waiting for years for someone to step up. If they knew how much success we had already achieved as a family, or how many breakthroughs we'd already experienced, or where we'd started, then maybe they'd be praising me instead. But, they didn't.

That's when it all became clearer. I thought I'd be getting comments about my strong faith, impressive patience, or large heart. I was feeling wiped out before the trip, and I was expecting to use the time with loved ones to refill my love-tank. I needed support. I felt like I had been doing a great job for these kids, yet people weren't seeing the kids' baggage, so they weren't seeing my challenge, which meant they couldn't see cause for my wounded heart.

I was devastated to find there was no one to lift me up when I was feeling down. I needed God to stir something, because I was already too deflated after nearly a year with the kids to withstand so much loneliness on our vacation, with an expectation that I still had a commitment to fulfill.

Jordan came into the room to find me practically inconsolable. My hopelessness was swallowing me whole, and Jordan asked, *"Is something wrong?"*

Men.

My look told him his question was stupid, so he tried again. *"I mean, what's wrong, Jess?"*

I thought to say that I was tired and then I wanted to say that I felt misunderstood, but all I could actually say was, *"I want to go home,"* followed by louder crying.

I was so ready to go home, to our routine, our resources. Back to my cats and dogs. Back to reality, where we could get back to work without being under the microscope.

However, it wasn't time to go, yet.

Jordan was encouraging to me. He acknowledged that he was also ready to go home and that the length of our trip was getting to him, too. It was one thing raising our kids on our own turf, but raising them on the road was even harder.

We heard the door next to us close and assumed Reagan was coming or going. Jordan looked out our door and flagged her down, asking her to join us. Kudos to Jordan. If you don't know how to fix it, get a hold of the best friend.

I started my rant from the top and somewhere along the way I apparently spouted off something about not having the right kind of clothes for a cold beach wedding, which was happening in just a few short hours. *"Faith and I are going to freeze,"* I said, and then my problem-solving best friend stopped me to offer a solution to all my problems.

"All right, let's go shopping," she said. *"The outlets aren't far away, and it'll be good for both of us to get a parenting break. Jordan, Jack's napping in the next room. We'll be back later."*

Typically, I hated shopping. However, I didn't see another choice. Reagan was clear. Besides, it had been a long time since she and I had been able to hop in a car and take off. It felt so familiar and comfortable. Just a couple of ladies out on the town, like it was before we had kids.

We went to Old Navy and found a long dress for Faith and a dress with a jacket for me. It didn't take us long, but it was enough for me to clear my head and realize I wasn't in a hurry to return. When we were done shopping, we drove back to our children as slowly as possible.

When we returned to the house, my mom, dad, sister, daughter and I got gussied up for the special occasion. Everyone else planned to stay behind.

Upon getting to the venue, Faith got giddy. She said, *"I've never seen a real princess before,"* and I had to remind myself that even though she looked like a beautiful twelve-year-old on the outside, she was still a naïve little girl, somewhere around age four, on the inside. As she pointed out the flowers and all of the pretty ladies in dresses, I believed she had a fairytale moment. It was sweet to see.

When the music started, we took our seats amongst other friends and family. When my niece started down the aisle, Faith smiled with such excitement. I tried to see it through her eyes and found many special details to gawk over. I liked the way the groom looked at his bride and the way they were nervous while sharing their vows. I wasn't sharing the experience with my husband, but I reminisced over our special day and how the butterflies felt fluttering in my stomach. It was a beautiful wedding, and I felt lucky to have witnessed Faith's first exposure to something as lovely as a wedding.

At the conclusion of the ceremony, we mingled with the other guests in the intimate banquet room, until it was time for our group to split up. My dad was planning to stay for the entire event, however, my mom, sister and I needed to get back to the house. This left Faith with a choice to make.

I explained it to her clearly. *"You can either go back to the house with the rest of us, or stay to finish the wedding with your grandpa. There's no wrong answer. It's up to you."*

My dad, who was standing there with us, chimed in. *"We'll get to dance, and you can have a piece of the cake and a cup of hot chocolate. It'll be fun."*

She enthusiastically said, *"I'll stay with Grandpa. I've never had wedding cake before."*

Her answer surprised me, but I was excited at the idea that she was beginning to spread her wings. *"Ok,"* I said, *"listen to Grandpa because he's in charge. And when they ask for all the single ladies to come out for the bouquet toss, that includes you. Have fun, and I'll see you back at the house, later."*

She nodded enthusiastically.

As we walked out, I said to my mom, *"I'm so proud of Faith's decision to stay, as a balance for all of her regressions. Hard to believe that this is the same girl that just a few nights ago told me she didn't feel loved."*

Maybe it wasn't such a bad thing that our trip was so long?

As my mom, sister, and I were pulling out of the parking lot, my dad ran out to us, waving his arms in the air like a lunatic. My mom hit the brakes, giving each of us a strong slam against our seats. My mom rolled down her window, while I opened my door and got out.

"Jessie, Faith needs you," he said. *"She started crying and panicking as soon as you left."*

If it seems too good to be true, it might not be true.

As my dad and I approached the banquet room, Faith was being escorted outside, sobbing.

I asked, *"Faith, what's the matter?"*

"You left. I didn't know you were leaving," she said.

I was stunned. How was it possible she missed that detail? So much for progress.

We had a quick review of our earlier conversation, all the way up to the part where I'd said goodbye. Her response was, *"I knew my choices, but I thought I was picking if you and I were going or staying. I didn't know you were leaving."*

Baffled. Simply baffled. She ignored everything that was contrary to what she wanted to hear.

With a fresh platform, I again went over her options. *"Grandpa will happily keep you with him, and let you experience the rest of the wedding, or you come back to the house with us. There is no in-between or hybrid option."*

She chose to leave with me and glued herself to my side as she made her choice.

I apologized to my dad, who said his feelings weren't hurt. Like me, he was a little stunned, because it was hard to understand how she missed the details of what was happening. However, if there had been any doubts before this moment of Faith's special needs, they were no longer lingering.

We got back to the house to find that Chris and Laura had already left. We knew their time with us at the beach was going to be short, but that didn't make it any less sad that goodbyes were happening left and right.

After dinner, the remaining group wandered down to the beach. It was way after bedtime, but we wanted a few pictures of the kids with the sun setting behind them. We wrote our names and favorite phrases in the sand while we waited.

Faith wrote the words, *"Fight in Pink,"* with a breast cancer ribbon. I took her picture with it, as I teared up. *"What made you think to write that?"* I asked.

"Because it's on your keychain," she said.

I didn't know I was rubbing off on them, outside of the specific lessons I'd been working to help them learn. Seeing her crouching next to her phrase, indicating our bond was deepening, was refreshing. Not in the way I'd thought after I believed she was staying at the wedding, but in a better way. She was opening her eyes and heart toward me, giving me a platform of influence. She'd been calling me mom for a while because the title fit, but now she saw me as her mom, and I could feel it in that moment.

I accepted her gesture as a prompt to share with her why the fight against breast cancer was so important to me, and as I spoke of the devastating occurrences in our family, she appeared to take it in. I shared that I'd lost two grandmas to the disease, and a great-aunt, and that even my mom, her Grandma Roxie, had fought a battle. I hadn't seen many light bulbs flicker in Faith before that day, but for this talk, the bulb was strong. She and I had a real conversation, about a real topic, at an age-appropriate depth, and she both followed and participated.

No matter how steep the hill in front of her, this affirmed that there was hope. And hope was all the motivation we needed to keep working with her.

After our sunset pictures, we headed back up to the house. We quickly got all of the kids into bed. This time, instead of putting Faith on our bedroom floor, we put her in the room that had been Chris and Laura's. It was next to the living space, where she could hear the rest of us talking nearby.

Sitting around the kitchen table, my mom, dad, sister, best friend, husband and I shared stories, jokes, observations, and plans. It was a good time, but it would have been better if I weren't so burnt out on being social and engaged. Still, it was a best-case scenario for closing out the day.

Well, I thought the day had been closed.

However, while we were sitting there, feeling confident that we were done with kids for the night, my mom heard the floorboards creak. She then said to me, *"Jessie, she's back."*

I turned to see that Faith was lingering, not knowing how to ask for a goodnight chat to help her work through her discomfort of being in another new place, wondering if she was loved there too.

I joined Faith in her room, where we went over the details of where her room was in proximity to mine, to the bathroom, and to the kitchen where the adults were gathered. I reminded her that there was light from the kitchen, and she had her bear. We covered all of the details.

In addition, we also discussed the fact that she had just been standing there like a creeper, instead of approaching us. I inquired as to how long she would have stood there before speaking up.

Turns out, she would have stood there indefinitely.

I was irritated because she could have just asked for help. But she was too insecure and lost.

Anyhow, after our talk, she went to sleep. Well, she lay down, which I'm sure led to sleep.

I returned to the group and our conversation shifted back to the kids. I asked my mom for some of her thoughts, since this was her second time around the kids. My mom shared what improvements she recognized, what difficulties she noticed that she had missed during her visit a few months earlier, and some of the challenges she thought the trip brought out.

Our conversation certainly covered Brandon, but his troubles weren't new or surprising to anyone. In fact, I was impressed that we got through the trip with as few issues as we did. He was doing far better than I had expected him to.

Clarence had improved in so many ways leading up to the trip, that he was able to bond and enjoy himself for practically the entire trip. Of course, there were some bumps along the way, mostly about having to take showers, but that was such a small thing. He had been doing awesome.

Caisen also seemed to thrive. The extra attention coming at him really seemed to help him shed another onion layer. It was fun to see him smiling and laughing with so many people, getting piggyback rides, being tickled, and being snuggled. He was doing great!

Henry and Faith were harder topics.

Faith was shut down through the trip. Of course, she had been shut down in many ways all along, but this trip really highlighted for me that she was so much further from healthy than I had truly grasped. Especially when considering how confused she became at the wedding. She was far from being a typical, healthy twelve-year-old.

And Henry. Earlier in Henry's life, he had spent so much time flying under the radar that he was really able to hone in on his manipulation skills. He knew what he wanted, and he knew how to use his winning smile to get it. We had worked to redirect his lying and cheating tendencies, by over-appreciating honesty, and we felt great about the progress that had occurred. But, he reverted. Instead of feeling loved and accepted, he saw opportunities to gain special treatment and seized them.

Especially with my dad, who was just realizing he had been used a couple times during the trip.

The rest of us laughed as my dad shared some examples, including the fact the kids were told to leave my mom's dog alone, but Henry worked it out with my dad that he'd get to walk her, as soon as they got out of view of the rest of the group. And my dad had a couple of small wagers with Henry, in which Henry gained a total of five dollars. And he got seconds on desserts. And got to play on my dad's phone.

My dad wasn't sharing as a victim, but as a man who just realized his grandson had impressive game, and we all giggled at how well Henry read the scene and chose my dad as his ultimate sucker.

Henry was good at his craft. Very good. It was sad. He didn't see the value in relationships because he'd never had one worth investing in. And even sadder, we knew that our work was cut out for us, to re-do everything we had already worked through.

The final thought of the night was that even though the trip was tough for many reasons, it was worth it to get the extended relationships started. By plugging the kids into the family, they were gaining more stability, which would enable us to connect deeper with them, too. We just knew it.

Just like that, it was Sunday August 3rd. Our trip was practically over.

While we were packing, I found the painted rock that Brandon was supposed to throw back.

I asked, *"Why didn't you toss it like you were supposed to?"*

He covered his face and began to fit. *"It's my rock! I shouldn't have to give it away!"*

I reminded him that the rock was meant to change hands often, so we could watch its journey.

He abruptly shouted, *"It's mine. I found it fair and square. If they wanted it so badly, then they shouldn't have given it to me. But, they did, so it's mine now."*

Regardless of the compliments the adults exchanged about him the night before, he was still in need of help. Real help. And I was so anxious to get him home and into the newer form of therapy!

I gave him directions to go outside and toss it. He was upset, but he grabbed the rock and walked out of the room. I wasn't sure if he'd follow through or not, and I half expected I'd find the rock again, but there was always room to hope he did as he was told.

Once we were packed and ready, we took our seats in the cars. It was somber, because we knew that the conclusion of this mini-trip was also the ending to our overall trip, and while I was happy to go home, I was also sad to say goodbye.

Reagan drove Jack, Brandon, and myself.

Jordan and the other kids were split between my parents' cars.

I knew for certain that Reagan and I drew the short sticks, because Brandon wasn't having a good day. I knew, without a doubt, he was going to be a wreck, because there was something about the way he was muttering about the upcoming travel that didn't sound right.

He started with rounds of, *"I'm sad the trip is over,"* to which I agreed. Sad, but ready.

Then he asked, *"How long will it take us to get home?"*

"Two and a half hours to get back to Grandma Roxie's," I said. *"Then, a short drive to the airport early in the morning. Then, we'll fly most of the day. When we get to Georgia, we'll have a four-hour drive back to our house. We'll be home in time for bed tomorrow night."*

"I don't want to drive four hours," he said. *"That'll be boring."*

Then, he took it back from the top, with the same concerns and questions, at least ten times. I addressed each one like it was the first time, every time, and he seemed to be hearing it for the first time, too.

Reagan laughed, and I tried not to let Brandon see that I was laughing with her. The poor kid. He was super stuck. At least he had Baby Jack to distract him from time to time, before he remembered his concerns and started into the conversation again.

I couldn't decide if it was more funny or annoying, and I knew he wasn't going to turn off any time soon, so I focused on breathing. Anything to keep from dwelling on the never-ending drive.

We got to my mom's and worked on getting all of our things packed up and ready for our journey home. Packing made it all feel so final.

Chris and Laura came by to say goodbye, followed by Jackson and Chelsea. I was too exhausted for my goodbyes to be emotional, but I could see that the kids had plenty of emotion tucked in each of their goodbye hugs. I truly was glad we'd come, because the kids needed it, as did the rest of the family. Our two worlds had merged, which made our adoption story feel much more finalized.

We got the kids in bed as soon as we could, and got a few blinks of sleep, before our alarms went off at three thirty am on Tuesday, August 4th. We buckled our zombie-children into their seats, each holding their travel backpacks and teddy bears. My parents drove too because they'd need two drivers to take our vehicle back with them.

It was hard to say goodbye to my parents in front of the airport. I didn't think I had tears left in me, but I did. And I didn't think the trip would feel as long and as boring as Brandon anticipated, but it did. Probably because he made it that way, by complaining for the entire duration.

After twenty-five hours of travel, we finally pulled into our driveway. As we carried our bags inside, it felt both weird and amazing to be back within my own walls. I snuggled with my cats to cement the notion that I WAS HOME!

We emptied out the kids' backpacks after using them as carry-ons and slipped the pre-organized bundles of school supplies into each one.

The kids ran around for a bit while we started laundry. While emptying the pockets of the dirty clothes, I found that Brandon STILL had the rock. The little brat. I didn't feel like confronting him, so I took it to my room and placed it in the top drawer of my nightstand.

Thanks to the early start, the three-hour time difference, and short layovers, we were able to get the kids into bed close to bedtime. My quiet house felt perfect.

Jordan and I set our alarms for another early morning, knowing that the real world wasn't going to wait for us to recuperate. Jordan was headed back to work, and the kids were ready for their first day of school. I made sure it all happened smoothly and then I went to the pet boarder to pick up our dogs.

I could tell things were coming together for us. God was working in our lives. There was light.

CHAPTER 34

SEEING THE LIGHT

B eing back home felt great. The first day of school went great. Getting the kids registered for another round of sports was exciting. Most importantly, having the ability to change our kids' therapy routine was everything. God was taking care of our needs and walking along with us.

After giving the kids their options for the sports season, Brandon chose to play soccer again, which happened to be the only option for Caisen's age group. Henry picked tackle football. Clay also wanted to play tackle, but his age earned him a spot in flag football. Faith chose cheerleading.

I thought cheerleading was a great fit for Faith. She complained that she preferred volleyball, but volleyball wasn't available that season. I think she was just trying to align with me, not realizing that I had cheered myself, in between volleyball and track.

Based on the previous season, I knew it'd be challenging to balance our master schedule, but also well worth it for them to learn normal lessons like normal kids on sports teams. And, we could blend in with the other sports families and talk about sports stuff.

Once I had our sports plan penciled in, it was time to update our counseling schedule, including starting Brandon in his new form of therapy.

I wasn't thrilled to separate him from the other kids' routine, but I was happy to see if we could better help with his intense emotional responses, impulse control, under the surface rage, and processing skills. It wasn't ok that he'd try to jump out of moving vehicles with no regard for the person in his way. It wasn't ok that he'd hit, push, or throw things at people. It wasn't ok that he'd tip furniture over. He wasn't ok. The kid needed more help, and our safety required it.

So, as planned, we switched Brandon over to a new therapist who utilized Eye Movement Desensitization and Reprocessing (EMDR), which is a specific style of therapy that works to synch thoughts with instincts. As

I took Brandon to his first appointment, I prayed for the necessary break-throughs to spare us from having to take more drastic steps.

The new therapist helped me to better understand EMDR, which basi-cally boiled down to a style in which one works to merge the brain with the heart. Since many people know how they *"should"* respond in situations, but recognize that they don't respond that way, EMDR helps their reactions to be a better fit for their intentions, by using a machine that tells the brain it's in lesson-learning mode. It can't pick your thoughts or understanding for you, but if you're holding the vibrating modules, your brain understands that your thoughts are important to hold onto, sculpting better reactions.

She gave this example:

Let's say you were the first car at a red light. When the light turns green, let's say you touch the gas, and as you're passing through the intersection, you notice a car from your left is coming at you, running their red light. Let's say you hit the gas hard and get far enough ahead that you avoid the collision. At that point, you no-tice your heart racing.

There are a few options here. You could be the person who rec-ognizes it was a close call, and you make a mental note to look both ways before proceeding through future green lights. Or, you could continue to have a racing pulse all the way until you get to your destination, taking a little longer to work out the jitters. Or, you could notice your heart race every time you pass through that intersection in the future, or every time the same song comes on, or every time you get behind the wheel.

If you're the person in the third scenario, you might "know" it's silly to get so worried, but you can't help it. That's where EMDR comes in. As your brain is engaged, you are prompted to think through the notion that you don't need to be so worried and in-stead just need to look both ways before entering an intersection, and your brain absorbs it. You are storing the new lesson.

After hearing about the process, I asked if it would be a good option for my-self and for the other four kids, since we were all working on our emotional responses. Both the new therapist and the counselor we'd been working with confirmed it would be beneficial, so we all transitioned over.

Once all five kids were enrolled, my level of exhaustion went sky-high.

With our previous style, I had to endure two long in-home sessions per week where everyone played a part.

This new style required that I pull each kid out of school and deliver them to the office for their frequent appointments. Then, since that didn't eat up enough of my breathing-time, I also had to participate in each of the kids' sessions, in an overly empathetic way.

However, just like my view of sports, I knew that all of the challenge would be worth it.

My new master schedule was set. I had multiple counseling appointments every day and sports every night. I knew it would be challenging for me to maintain the load, more challenging than anything I'd ever done before, but I'd made a promise to my kids that I'd do what was best for them.

Week after week, I worked with the therapist to identify specific triggers, misunderstandings, missing skills or lessons, and anything else about each individual kid, so that we could work through it all, one topic at a time. At each session, I'd walk us through the minute details of a specific situation, pausing at every junction where a choice was made. The therapist would then hone in on that particular choice, and work with the kid to see the consistencies between how similar choices turned out and what other choices were available to them.

We focused on situations that related to a specific topic, trigger, or lesson, and stuck with it until that one lesson showed up. Then, we'd work to translate it to similar situations. And after a few sessions, you could see the impact in their lives, and we'd pick a new target to work through.

After working so closely with our therapist throughout the week, she quickly felt like part of the family. She was my battle-buddy. And though it was an exhausting phase, it was also rewarding.

Our therapist helped us to address Faith's impulse to shut down and hide when things got too real for her. This led us to look at her response to making mistakes, particularly her instinct to give Jordan the cold shoulder if he was the one to confront her about her mistakes. After working through several specific examples, we found the event that caused her to adopt this behavior.

Thanks to our therapist's setup, Faith was able to recall and share that her biological parents would fight in front of the kids. Faith said she found the fights interesting and watched often. Faith said that after yelling at each other, they'd stop talking to each other. They gave each other the silent treatment. Therefore, Faith hadn't witnessed the process of talking problems through. Therefore, Faith developed the belief that she was supposed to stop talking when she upset someone, using the silent treatment as a way of giving the other person space.

When we finally found the original lesson, Faith said, *"I didn't think I was supposed to talk to dad after messing up, because he wouldn't want to hear it."*

It was heart breaking. She wasn't giving Jordan the cold shoulder because she thought too little of him. Her silent treatment was due to an improperly stored lesson about how to handle those situations, specifically a thought that she wasn't worthy of a conversation to work out a problem.

Once this memory and improper lesson was opened, we were able to talk about a healthier approach to resolving conflicts. We talked about how healing can take place for both people when honest communication is used. Faith understood why talking would be better, allowing her to form a thought about the approach, while holding the vibrating EMDR tool. And just like that, Faith was able replace her inappropriate past lesson with her newer, healthier one.

And the next time she made a mistake with Jordan, she actually apologized to him. She was nervous, and he was surprised, and it ended in a hug. I felt I'd just witnessed a miracle.

However, targeting one lesson didn't inherently impact others. She was still confused about Jordan and continued undermining him with the boys, as well as getting lost on the way to the bathroom, forgetting her homework at school, and hiding both food and trash in her pillowcases and drawers.

But, she could at least apologize and talk it through. Lesson one.

Henry had a target of his own. He was focusing on his tendency to equate love with special treatment, which came back stronger than ever after he successfully pulled so many cons on our trip. But our therapist backed our play.

We worked through several specific examples where the therapist helped him to realize that his feelings of being unwanted, unloved, and unworthy were left over notions from a life he was no longer living. Things had changed, and his heart hadn't caught up yet.

As soon as he was able to logically see that his feelings hadn't taken his new situation into account, and that he actually had many reasons around him to feel loved, the handheld vibrating EMDR machine helped him to store the new lesson. In that moment, the feeling of being loved and safe became overwhelming for him. His tears of relief were so moving.

After a few sessions of focusing on his new lesson, it showed up at our dinner table. We were having pork chops with scalloped potatoes, applesauce, baked beans, and rolls. It was a big meal and happened to be one of Henry's favorites. He had a plateful. And when he finished his plate, he started to say something. However, he cut himself off. He tipped his head down and whispered, *"I am loved. I have enough."*

I felt my heart creep into my throat, and it was hard not to embarrass him by making a big deal out of it. I mean, he recognized in himself that he'd had enough and chose not to ask for more. Even though it was one of his favorites. I was so proud of him! His hard work was impacting his heart.

However, only one lesson at a time. Teamwork, honesty, and work ethic hadn't been addressed. So, just a few days later, Henry decided he didn't feel like going to football practice. Instead of sharing his feeling with me, he used his finger to wipe his practice off of my master dry-erase calendar.

Thankfully, I had already stored the day's events in my memory bank. So, when I noticed the subtle streak mark across the date, I was able to recall what used to be listed.

Upon talking to Henry about it, I received a lie.

Then another lie.

Then a story that contradicted both previous lies.

Eventually, the truth came out.

"I didn't feel like going," he said. *"So, I wiped it off the board."*

"Why didn't you just come talk to me?" I asked. *"I could have worked through it with you."*

"But," he said, *"I wanted it to be your mistake because then you'd have to make it up to me."*

Shot through the heart. I worded it back to him as, *"You wanted out of practice and thought that setting it up as my failure would be the most beneficial to you?"*

He agreed without seeing the problem.

My heart didn't just hurt over Henry's actions toward me, but also for the kid who had been living a life where those behaviors made sense. It was tragically sad.

Of course, that became the next EMDR target, and we got to work sorting through the mess.

And that's how life went on for about three months. We identified an inconsistent life-lesson, we worked on it, we nurtured a new lesson to take its place, and we observed the changes.

Then, we'd pick a new lesson and repeat the cycle.

We found some unique challenges in each child, as well as many similar ones.

Each kid needed help with understanding the purpose of a family, including the different roles, appropriate relationships, and team gains. We used sports analogies to help it make sense and talked about how family-teams win or lose together in this way:

If a team loses, even if your individual performance was outstanding, then you still record a loss. And, if your team wins, even on a day where you didn't perform so great, you still count the day as a victory. Because teams win and lose together. Therefore, teammates should encourage each other, instead of sabotaging people in order to feel better about themselves.

Just like a family. If we support our family members, we will all have a better chance at a good day, for the win.

The more comfortable they got on their sports teams, the easier it was to come up with analogies to help them see that our family was similar.

Brandon was learning a lot in soccer and was scoring goals, so we talked about the assists from teammates and the backup of having an efficient goalie on his team. *"We should count on our family and be accountable to our family, too,"* we explained.

Caisen was also developing his soccer skills, and we talked about working together and practicing at getting better, because things don't change themselves. You have to be willing to try something different.

Faith was having fun with bows and skirts, but was also working to learn cheers and moves. She wasn't remembering them very easily and was put to the test at a game where Faith was one of only two girls to show up. The coach didn't even come. Faith and one other girl had a choice to make. Sit and watch, or cheer by themselves. They cheered, showing courage and dedication, which is required to make changes at home, too.

We regularly referred back to the day where she chose to cheer, even with uncomfortable circumstances, to reinforce her pride over giving her best and remind her she possessed strength.

And then there was Clay. He was a monster on the field. He was diving for flags, getting filthy in every game, and even caught a touchdown pass, in the end zone, during the championship game, with his back to the quarterback because the pass was slightly overthrown and he had to run up under it. It was incredible. And our whole family praised him. Family praise was a new thing for us. Our teammate analogies were making an impact!

Another common concept the kids needed help with was understanding rewards and consequences. They seemed to believe that it didn't matter if they made good choices or not, because rewards and consequences were attached to an adult's mood, not their own choices.

We developed a recurring dialogue with the help of our therapist, for times of both consequences and rewards, to help them gain the knowledge. A typical conversation went like this:

Adult: If a mommy gave a spanking to a child who was being kind and sweet and well-behaved, would it be love?

Kid: No. That wouldn't be fair because they didn't earn it.

Adult: Well, if a mommy gave her kid a smile, high-five, hug, and kiss when he was misbehaving, would that be love?

Kid: No, because he didn't earn it.

Adult: So, does that mean that kids need to earn love?

Kid: No. Love isn't about getting what you want. Love is about getting everything you need and everything you earn, so that you can learn to make good choices.

Adult: So, is a mommy being mean if she gives her child a consequence for misbehaving?

Kid: No. That's love, because the mommy would be helping the kid to learn the lesson.

And with the aid of the small EMDR machine, the kids began to internalize this knowledge.

When it fully set in, the kids were able to feel more control in their lives. They could finally see that their choices mattered and were noticed.

It was incredible how positive the change was when the kids felt like they had the power to control an outcome. When they believed that they could both choose to avoid consequences, as well as earn rewards, they blossomed. And it felt like a miracle each time because it wasn't gradual. We'd work on a specific lesson for a bit, with no changes. Then, it would click; there was a noticeable change.

We had been praying and praying, and it felt like God was answering prayers faster than we could keep track of them. It was a beautiful phase!

It was compounded the first time I noticed the kids playing together, or at least in proximity to each other, without total emotional breakdowns. At one point, I was having a conversation with Caisen about his choice to shove a roll of toilet paper down the bathtub drain. It took a while because there were many lies to work through, but when I came back out into the living room, I found three kids sitting down drawing, sharing crayons, and a fourth kid doing a word search. I didn't think it was possible.

Next, the kids used better manners and responded to directions more appropriately. Then, they started telling the truth quicker. Many things were getting better. One at a time. And even though there was still a long way to go, we finally felt like the kids were hearing us and trusting us. The door of opportunity felt wide open.

Everyone was doing so great.

Everyone, except Brandon.

Sure, Brandon was doing well in his sessions, and it seemed like things were clicking, but it wasn't translating into his daily life. He was still falling apart too frequently, over things too small, and staying stuck for longer than was reasonable.

On the therapist's suggestion, we requested a medication change for Brandon, thinking maybe the cocktail was either aiding his irritability or preventing his newly learned lessons from showing up in his daily choices.

We knew that medications wouldn't cure his problems, but the hope was that a doorway could be opened for progress to take place. That hope was worth working through a few weeks of the worst we'd ever endured with Brandon, as his body adjusted to his new prescriptions.

While we waited for him to balance out, we were on high alert. All day. Every day.

One afternoon, he saw the preview for a movie he wanted to see. However, it was a day and time that didn't make sense for us to go to the theater.

"Why are you punishing me?" he screamed, while rolling on the floor. *"I didn't do anything wrong, so I don't deserve this consequence. You're a terrible parent!"*

"This isn't a consequence, Brandon," I said. *"In fact, we'd all like to see the movie. And we will, when the timing is better."*

He wasn't listening. He threw things, kicked things, and broke things, while screaming, *"You're a liar. You're the worst parent."*

When the weekend rolled around, we had many soccer and football games. Everyone worked hard. It was a good, sweaty day.

Their exhaustion translated into grumpy attitudes. By mid-afternoon, Caisen and Henry had each thrown good-sized tantrums, and Brandon had spent a lot of time whining and fussing.

While eating dinner, Brandon asked if we could go see the movie after we ate, and Jordan beat me to saying, *"No."* The kids were tired, so we chose to stay home and watch a movie instead.

Brandon lost it, again.

As a result, the backs of our couches got some new holes, and the neighbors were blessed with the echoes of the doors slamming. He was angry and loud and ruined the other kids' chances of enjoying their movie at home.

The following weekend, Jordan told me he hoped we could take the kids to the movie, but we didn't mention it to the kids, in case it didn't work out.

After everyone's games we ate lunch. Things seemed to be going well, so we loaded the kids up for the movie theater, without telling them the destination. We pulled into the Carmike parking lot, across from the Savannah Mall, and that's where it started.

Brandon lost it. He totally lost it. He was screaming, *"What? We have to go see a movie? That's boring! You're the worst parents ever!"* And so on and so forth. Hubby took the other four kids in to the theater, to experience the wonder.

I watched my husband as he walked through the parking lot: Tall, slender, military haircut, one kid on his back with a couple others walking close by. He was a sight for sore eyes.

I caught myself admiring him and felt proud of the progress I'd been making in my own thoughts as well. I felt I could breathe again. Well, I could breathe somewhat better, considering I was on Brandon-duty and relaxing deep breaths were hard to come by in the moment.

He screamed and yelled at me for a good forty-five minutes. During that time, I got out of the car to escape the echo of his screechy voice. He followed me.

It wasn't any less screechy outside the car, so I got back in the car to escape the embarrassment of the onlookers, and he followed me.

As he insisted that I was the worst parent ever, I realized that the closed quarters weren't good for my eardrums, so I got out again. Then I got in. Still, he followed me. It was no use trying to put space between us. I couldn't escape him because he knew not to shut the car door all the way, aware of the child safety locks.

And I knew not to force it shut unless we actually needed to be driving somewhere, because he would start working to dismantle the car from the inside. Scratch that. *"Dismantle"* sounds too gentle. He would detonate, attempting to blow the vehicle wide open. So, the cat-and-mouse game was my best option while I waited for the tantrum to run its course.

We both heard when a text came through from Jordan. We knew it was him because he had his own special alert tone.

As I worked to find my phone in my purse, Brandon sat behind me calling me a liar and a meanie, assuming I was telling Jordan that Brandon was still upset. But I wasn't. I hadn't even had a chance to read the text yet.

I got a hold of my phone and read the text aloud: Henry is in the lobby with tickets for you and Brandon.

As Brandon was yelling, I turned toward the back seat and said, *"I'm going in to get our tickets, in case you decide to calm down and watch the show. I know you'd be sad to miss it."*

Brandon screamed something about it all being my fault as I got out of the car. He didn't follow me because I had told him what I was doing. If I hadn't, he would have assumed I just wanted space again, and he would not have granted it. I had certainly learned the value of communication and appreciated that he believed me when I updated him, even though he often called me a liar.

As I made my way to the building, I could still hear him. I looked and saw our car shaking.

I thought to myself: *"It's sad that he can't even turn it off when he's alone."*

I quickly thanked Henry for waiting with the tickets and then walked back outside. What I saw shocked me, and I thought I had seen enough not to be shocked anymore. But, there it was.

Brandon had his hands on the back handle of our big-rig, with both feet squarely planted on the bumper. He was trying to break into the vehicle that he had apparently locked himself out of.

Instead of visibly walking towards him, I scooted over to the next aisle of cars and quietly approached. The cool breeze through the fallen leaves worked as cover noise for me.

When I got to our car, he had his watch off and was trying to pick the driver's door lock. Mind you, he was eleven. He was tiny for an eleven-year-old, but still eleven, and thought the best idea was to pick the lock to a newer model vehicle, which came stocked with an alarm, in broad daylight, in a public parking lot, with his watch. I assumed other eleven-year- olds would know that it was a failed idea to begin with, but Brandon looked determined.

I said, *"Brandon, that is enough. Someone is going to call the police on you!"*

He didn't even pause. The tantrum continued, and I didn't think there was anything I could do. I felt powerless. Eventually I just said, *"Do what you want, but I'm going in."*

Brandon followed.

Yes, he followed. But he still hadn't calmed down. I was hoping that he would be too embarrassed to continue whining and complaining in the actual theater, seeing how he was eleven and all. Boy, was I wrong. About five minutes after we entered, I wondered if the whole, *"Whose kid is this?"*

ruse would work. But he was in between me and another of our kids, locked in by my husband at the other end, obviously with us. Dang.

At about eight minutes in, he remembered that he wanted to watch the movie.

One might think this would be a good time to quiet down, but not this kid. Instead, he complained about having to miss the beginning, like it was someone else's fault. Then there was a funny scene, and he forgot he was mad. Then he remembered. Then he forgot. Then he remembered.

He was driving me insane, and I couldn't see any more options for working through it with him.

We finished the movie, and the complaining increased. *"It's not fair I couldn't see the whole movie,"* he said. *"They got to watch it, and I didn't."*

All I could think, and probably say, was, *"Right, poor Brandon. It's not fair."* followed by a silent prayer of, *"God, please help me."*

We got to the car, where things got interesting. Clarence reached to open the back door, and the handle came off in his hand, easily. No resistance of any kind. He actually tripped back a little because he was expecting the handle to hold on to the door. But it did not. He immediately began to cry, feeling sorry that he had broken the handle. Henry stared at the handle in Clay's hand with a dropped jaw.

Then it hit me.

I was gone for at least three minutes to get the tickets from Henry.

"OH MY GOSH! Brandon, you broke the handle off the car?"

"No, I didn't," he said, arms back over his face.

I gestured with my hands to silently communicate, *"Are you kidding me?"* to Brandon, who was peeking out between his arms.

It became obvious to him that there was no way around it. I mean, who else would have attempted to break into our car in a public place, in broad daylight, but instead of taking anything from inside, just put the handle back. Yeah. It was him, just before he moved to the back hatch, where I saw him.

The fit took off, because he was caught in a lie and had made a destructive choice, which left him scared of what the inevitable consequence would be.

It took some convincing before Brandon climbed in the car, where he punched and kicked the entire way home, while screaming, *"This car is stupid anyways!"*

The poor kid just couldn't control himself.

After getting the other kids in the house, I approached Brandon about his choices, reminding him that his feelings were allowed, but breaking things was not. I tried to initiate the scary consequence-conversation, saying he could pay me back for the damage by doing some basic chores for a week.

I thought it was a more than fair arrangement. I needed help with packing and cleaning because we were rapidly approaching our date for moving from Georgia to Missouri, only two months later. His chores would help me, while also teaching him a lesson about respect for property.

He wasn't happy and continued to whine and complain about it the rest of the day.

The following morning, Jordan took a couple of kids with him to a park, to include Brandon, who was still mad at me, like I was the one who misbehaved. I thought that giving him a break from me would be useful in calming him down.

I stayed at the house with Faith and Henry, who helped me clean out our china hutch.

Jordan thought Brandon had moved on, so we met up to grab lunch at Kentucky Fried Chicken.

Turns out, Brandon wasn't finished.

When we sat at the table, Brandon picked right back up in his anger towards me. I tried to de-escalate him, before realizing it was useless. In an attempt to smooth things out, I moved to a different table, thinking that he'd stop if he weren't looking at me.

Nope. He got louder.

He was going on and on about how terrible a parent I was. He said, *"You're mean and unfair, and you never do anything nice for me."*

It was embarrassing and hurtful. After all I'd done to prove myself to him, he still treated me as the enemy.

He went on, *"You only let me eat what you want to eat, and watch movies you want to watch, and go to the places that you want to go. You only care about yourself and not about me."*

He kept going and going and going, and there wasn't anything I could do. He was stuck, again.

I waited for him to burn out while hearing all of the hurtful things he had to say to me and about me.

Eventually, I couldn't handle it anymore. I had to stand up for myself. I found my opening and quickly made my points. *"You are being ridiculous. I need help getting ready for the move. I also have a bill to pay thanks to the broken door handle, because it's not fair that my kids should have to crawl in through the back hatch. You're the one that made the mistake, and your only consequence is being helpful to your mom, which is something you could also feel proud of. I'm not being unfair, you are."*

I'd like to say it was an automatic fix, but it wasn't.

I repeated myself, clearly and quickly, several times, and overloaded his system with my truth. When he uttered the words, *"I'll be your helper,"* we quickly tossed away everyone's trash and moved on. We didn't want to give him time to reconsider. I was too exhausted for another round, and Jordan was ready to escape the crowd of onlookers that I was ignoring completely.

It wasn't easy on our family. With Brandon around, it never was. But, I felt bad for him. He was in the way of his own happiness. Someone had hurt him in the past, but now he was hurting himself with his habits, tendencies, and inabilities. It was hard to watch and even harder feeling like I couldn't do much to help. I wanted to talk to him more about his choices and my feelings about him, but I knew it needed to wait until his session on Tuesday, where I'd have reinforcements.

In the meantime, Brandon helped me with chores that Monday, and it went terribly. He complained the entire time. *"I shouldn't have the consequence because I already served one. I missed the beginning of the movie, so I don't need another consequence."*

Round three commenced. I hated that his faulty, negative thoughts kept coming back, and our resolved conversations seemed to disappear.

When his Tuesday session came around, we focused on consequences. Our therapist wanted to help him with the concept, as well as reinforce that Jordan and I were more than fair, always.

She asked if he had ever earned money for a task.

He recalled that the other kids each got two dollars for an hour of weed pulling with the neighbor. He didn't help, so he didn't get paid. He was upset about that, but the therapist moved right past it, using Brandon's information to determine the hourly rate.

She helped him to do the math of how many hours it would take to pay back the three hundred dollars of car repair at two dollars per hour.

His math found that it would take one hundred and fifty hours.

She asked him what I was asking of him, and he said, *"One hour a day for five days."*

She again helped him with the math to determine that one hundred and forty-five hours of work, or two hundred and ninety dollars, was being absorbed by me. He was getting off easy.

She asked me to explain to Brandon why I was willing to accept such a soft consequence.

"Brandon, my focus isn't on the car. My focus is on you. I want you to learn a lesson that will help you in your life, more than I care about the handle on my car. I thought you'd be overwhelmed by one hundred and fifty days' worth of chores, which would hurt the lesson. I felt that five days would do. And five days of helping me would be good for us both."

He accepted the consequence, for the second time. However, we got home and Brandon worked maybe ten minutes a day before falling apart. It was an inconvenient daily struggle, when I was still looking for help. I had a huge project of packing ahead of me and a fear over what our lives would look like if Brandon never improved.

The next weekend, to fuel my fear, Brandon whacked Clay for getting too close to his puzzle. He served a two-minute time-out that took forty-five minutes.

Then, he got upset about having spaghetti for dinner, even though it was his favorite meal, and ended up breaking the glass out of the china hutch. It was especially obnoxious because I'd already emptied the hutch, with the help of Faith and Henry, and had listed the piece for sale on Craigslist.

Things were not going well.

At his next appointment, I left Brandon in the waiting room so that I could go in and have a chat with his therapist, where I reminded her that EMDR was our Hail Mary, and I was concerned it wasn't going to be enough for him.

Our therapist affirmed that we were doing all of the right things, and he wasn't getting better, and she didn't know the reason. It was hard to hear because it meant there wasn't anything else we could do. His journey wasn't in my control, and he didn't seem too concerned over the path he was on. We needed God to intervene, and I wondered what the lesson was for why He hadn't stirred things in Brandon's heart.

Our therapist told us that it might be time to move toward residential programs, where Brandon would go to a facility where they'd attempt to help him gain some control, so that he could come back to us and have a better chance at succeeding. She shared that he'd get around the clock treatment and care, to include safely tinkering with medications, so that they could help him through the tough stuff.

I fell apart, sitting there on her couch, holding the broken handle to my car. I was a sobbing, blubbery mess. I had worked so hard with Brandon, and I was scared that sending him away might turn him against us.

She reminded me that I had four other kids to also think about, because it wasn't safe for them to be near Brandon when he triggered, since he was unpredictable. His chances for living a successful, happy life were slim with the skills he had, and he was hurting the chances for the other kids, making their home unstable. Brandon deserved a better chance at life and so did the other kids, and I owed it to all of them, no matter how hard it was on me.

At the end of our talk, she said that she'd seek further information and told me not to worry about it until hearing back from her.

Easier said than done.

That night, I shared the talk with Jordan. We then did some preliminary research and found that there weren't any facilities near the Missouri Army installation we were moving to. We looked to see if there was one within a reasonable radius of my mom, thinking that it would be better for her to visit him than to have no one visit him.

As we negotiated priorities for picking facilities, I felt lousy. I worked hard to get over feeling like Ebenezer Scrooge, but it was coming back to me. I hated what I was looking into for Brandon.

Then it got worse. At the next session with our therapist, which happened to be my own session, she explained to me that, based on our insurance, Brandon would need to be hospitalized a couple of times before he would be considered for a residential treatment facility. Sadly, Reactive Attachment Disorder (RAD) didn't get a direct pass. However, in order to initiate a hospitalization, I'd have to call the police while he was in meltdown, reporting that he was a danger to himself or others, to justify the traumatizing procedure of having him taken away.

I couldn't do that. I wouldn't. I didn't feel comfortable calling the police during his fits because I needed him to see that I was working with him. Calling someone wouldn't translate as help for him.

While our therapist committed to researching other options, I focused on breathing and carrying out the routine of care we already had in place.

As I focused, and breathed, and focused some more, I reminded myself to take more breaths.

And before I knew it, it was Halloween. Our second Halloween. Our first repeat holiday.

Officially, from that moment, if the kids started a sentence with *"last year,"* they would finish with a memory shared with us. It was an exciting feeling.

To celebrate, Faith dressed as a pirate. A beautiful pirate. She even wore a pair of my hoop earrings and some makeup.

Brandon was Hulk. It was fitting.

Henry was Captain America.

Clay was the Red Power Ranger.

Caisen was Raphael. Cutest little Ninja Turtle I'd ever seen.

Our German Shepherd was a caterpillar.

Our Labradoodle was a bumblebee.

Jordan was a Ghost Buster.

I was a Witch, with a broom and everything. I couldn't find a Scrooge outfit, so I settled.

We were quite the crew walking down the street.

Though Brandon held true to his streak of pitching at least one big fit on each and every holiday, we were also able to note a subtle change. Nothing revolutionary, but I saw something.

While we were walking down the street together, going door-to-door, he kept stepping in people's grass. I continued to correct him, and instead of covering his face, he looked at me while I was talking. Of course, if I looked back at him, he'd shy away or cover one eye, but then he'd look back at me, while I was correcting. He'd only looked at me in correction-conversations when someone else was the enemy, like the therapist or caseworker. But, this time, I was the one correcting him, and he still looked at me.

Then, he looked at me through his arms in therapy, while I was describing the situations where he'd made bad choices, without grunting or saying, *"Nuh-uh."*

Next, he listened in therapy, without his arms. Still, if I looked at him, he'd cover back up. But it was progress. His arms were his protecting barrier, and he was slowly letting me in.

Then, he started responding to small requests during his fits. For example, there was a point where Brandon repeatedly slammed the door in a tantrum, and Jordan asked Brandon to stop. He moved away from the door and hit the walls instead. It was obnoxious, and I hated holes in the walls, but at least he abided a request.

It was subtle, but something was changing, which was proof that he could improve. It gave me hope that we'd survive without hospitalizing him. Those little adjustments were signs that he was learning to trust and depend on us. It may have been slow, but it was progress. Real progress. Thank God.

CHAPTER 35

BROUGHT TOGETHER BY GOD

M oving into our second year with the kids was truly remarkable. Yes, we were exhausted from so many days of intense work. Yes, we wondered what Brandon's potential was and if he'd ever reach it. Yes, we wondered if Faith was ever going to catch up to her peers. Yes, we wondered a lot of things, and yes, God was answering.

We had gotten through enough behavioral lessons with EMDR that we could finally look at the kids with fresh eyes. We found that some things went deeper than misguided lessons. Some examples were problems with memory, focus, organization, and impulsivity. And, in time, we'd have to look into additional options for continued impacts.

In the meantime, we were teaching the kids compensation skills for coping with their challenges. We learned that if they weren't learning a lesson one way, then we'd get creative, trying many approaches when necessary.

This wasn't only true for them. All people have to find the ways that they learn best.

One of the benefits of such an in-depth phase was the insight gained regarding their pasts. Each time they shared a memory, there was sadness. My heart broke for them regularly. But, there was also joy.

Every step backward was a setup for a couple of steps forward. Each time we identified a difficult memory, we were able to compare our current lives together against the circumstances of their past and help them safely let go of the fears and pain.

Though their healing journey was certain to be long, we helped them to know that they weren't alone. People may not have the same baggage, but all people are works in progress, including myself.

We had moments where things weren't falling apart. I could look around the room from time to time and see my kids playing, usually separately or in pairs, but looking content. And, when it was time to do homework, they stopped making up problems and questions in lame attempts to hog my attention. Instead, they made fun of each other's questions and tried to prove how smart they were by blurting out the answers.

We recognized we had more and more normal-family struggles. We noticed some normal-family conversations taking place. We even had moments where some of our kids responded to everyday challenges in ways considered age-appropriate. These moments weren't consistent, but they were happening.

And I realized that even in the moments when the thorns felt unbearable, there were still roses.

True, it can be a challenge to find the blooms. For instance, our second Thanksgiving together was terrible. Truthfully, it wasn't much better than the first, where Brandon dumped the bunk beds on me. Though he didn't pull the same stunt, there was again broken furniture, mean dialogue, and more questions about his potential, considering his lack of emotional restraint.

At the end of the day, a day meant for giving thanks, I found myself crying in my closet. Jordan and the kids were all tucked in bed properly, and I wasn't ready. And though I considered waking Jordan up to help me work through my feelings of disappointment, I didn't. I figured, God meant for us to share much of our faith-journey with each other, but He also intended for us to seek alone time with Him.

In my own quiet space, with tears in my eyes, I asked God some hard questions. I wasn't feeling strong enough to focus on faith alone, I wanted answers. *"God, why did you give me Brandon? And the others? Why did you ask this of me? What did I do to deserve such hardship? I understand that they're your children, and that you want all the best for them, but what about me? Where is my support?"*

As I sat there, overwhelmed with sadness at yet another holiday gone wrong, I waited for Him to answer. I didn't know how He'd reassure me, but I needed Him to. He could prompt Jordan to come find me, or a friend to call, or even a dog to come lick my tears. I wasn't picky. I just needed Him to do something. I'd been giving my best and on rough days like that one, it didn't feel like my best was good enough. I didn't think I was enough. The rocky road ahead was intimidating, and I was exhausted. I needed to feel God's presence.

I waited and heard no answer. No whispers, no phone calls, no slobbery kisses. Nothing.

I went to bed, believing that God cared about the rest of my family more than me. He asked too much of me, then ditched me to figure it out on my own. I'd felt lonely before, but never to that depth. And in response, all I could wonder was, *"Why did we sign up for this? This is too much."*

The next morning, I wasn't my chipper self. I struggled to find a reason to get out of bed, to get breakfast initiated, or to intervene when the kids bickered. I was struggling with my faith and disappointed in God. Where was He while I was struggling?

As I rolled through the morning, tearing up over each small task that came my way, Brandon approached me. I braced for the worst, before noticing his eyes were downward.

"Brandon, what's wrong, Bud?" I asked.

He answered, *"I'm sorry for pitching a fit yesterday and ruining Thanksgiving. I wanted it to be a special day."* And then, Brandon went on to have a very good day.

That was it. That was the message. God answered. God cared. God was with me, even when I questioned Him. I knew it, because Brandon's heart was showing, and he had interest in building something better and that could only be God's doing. And as I thought it through, it became easy to see that, even though Thanksgiving was a mess, the days surrounding Thanksgiving were pretty smooth. A victory. A God-sized victory. Not only had He answered me, in His way and with His timing, but He'd answered me every time before. I was not alone.

His timing for soothing my fears couldn't have been better, because we had a lot of things on our to-do list, including prepping for Christmas break, packing for our New Year's Day move to Missouri, obtaining new social security cards and birth certificates for each kid, and updating the kids' names in every database we could.

Those non-routine tasks had to happen in between keeping up with sports and school, nurturing our souls weekly at church, shuffling the kids through thirteen-to-eighteen appointments per week, trying to make the most of our time with our therapist, and fine-tuning the kids' medications with the psychiatrist before the move.

It was a busy, challenging time, and I was thankful that the kids had come far enough that we were actually accomplishing our tasks. We were actually doing a good job.

And while I tracked the family goals and movements, the kids had goals of their own.

Brandon was focusing on his response to conflict. He was learning to regain control of himself quicker and to offer apologies after. He was far from where he aimed to be, but the apologies helped.

Faith's instincts were dangerous, like the time she snuggled with a turned-on lamp for warmth, so she was working on checking in with me before acting on ideas. She was in pursuit of safer problem-solving skills.

Henry was working on self-love, as a precursor to feeling loved by others. It was tough hearing him talk about how he thought his past was his fault, or that he wasn't worthy of love. Hearing him argue with his internal voice gave me hope that he was on his way to a healthier ability to bond.

We were working with Clay on his mindfulness. He'd been bouncing around life so fast that he was missing many details. Initially, his speech was affected and his drawings were scribbles. He focused on slowing down to breathe, which was a long-term project. A sign of victory for him was drawing a gorilla he was proud of, enough that he wanted it displayed on the refrigerator.

Caisen was slowly working on bonding and connecting. It was a real challenge getting him to relax and engage, especially since his facial reads were so inaccurate. Our therapist had him practice copying facial expressions off of me. It's something that all babies go through with healthy parents, but he didn't.

At first, he was too embarrassed. He wouldn't even copy a smile.

After weeks of encouragements, he'd put his hands up as barriers so that only I could see, which was a sign of trust. The progress wasn't fast, but it was true progress. And as he focused on connecting with me, the bruises I'd gained through his tantrums began to fade. Instead of taking his anger out on me, he sought me for occasional hugs and kisses.

I was so proud of all of their progress, while also feeling the pressure of our timeline.

Christmas Break was a whirlwind. We offset the hours spent packing and cleaning by joining friends to watch a Christmas play at church, and visiting all of our favorite restaurants and local attractions one last time.

When Christmas Eve snuck up on us, we excitedly accepted an offer to eat at our friends' house. I don't know what we would have done without their invite, because our house was in boxes.

The night was better than I could have hoped for! Our friends arranged for the kids to decorate cookies, try new foods, and stay up to watch a

Christmas movie. The kids behaved better than I had expected. In fact, I felt they may have done better or as well as any other five kids of their ages.

Then, Christmas came.

Caisen pitched a fit, starting around six o'clock in the morning. Never found a logical reason to explain it, but holidays often had the effect. No matter the reason, he couldn't pull it together.

At seven o'clock in the morning, I apologized to the other kids who were waiting for Caisen to calm down.

Around eight o'clock in the morning, I told them that I appreciated how patient they were, and I understood if they wanted to open gifts without Caisen.

The kids voted, and they chose to continue waiting on Caisen.

My whole day was made in that moment.

It didn't matter that Caisen was still being a punk in my room. The other kids showed so many great qualities in their group decision that I felt proud.

And about forty minutes later, Caisen was ready.

He apologized to his siblings for holding them up, and thanked them for waiting. It was sweet.

The kids were prepared for their Christmas to be on a much smaller scale than the one before. Even though we had prepped the kids, I was still worried that they'd complain. Especially considering they complained the year prior, with many more gifts under the tree.

My mom was propped on the TV stand as we opened presents, thanks to video-chat.

Luckily, she wasn't with us in person, because she got hit in the video-head with a flying box. The kids thought it was so funny that unwrapping came to a halt as they laughed about it.

When it was all said and done, we found that the kids received less and responded with more. More happiness. More gratitude. More enthusiasm. More kindness.

My mom was in tears. The rest of us were laughing and smiling. It was a fun, chaotic morning.

While the kids began playing with their new things, Jordan and I got back to packing. We had less than a week before our big move, and still had plenty to do.

Busy or not, we all snuggled in to watch a nighttime movie to close out our Christmas Day, not knowing how it would turn out. If we expected it to go well, it didn't. But the reverse was also true.

As Jordan slid a DVD into the player, Clay got up from the spot he thought Brandon would want, choosing a space on the floor instead.

Clay's kindness earned him a compliment from me.

I immediately braced myself for Brandon's response, because Brandon regularly interpreted compliments given to other kids as backhanded ways for putting him down.

To my surprise, Brandon actually followed my lead and thanked Clay for moving. It was our own Christmas Miracle.

In fact, by the end of the day, I drew attention to the fact that we had just experienced our first full holiday where Brandon hadn't pitched any fits.

He pitched no fits.

Zero fits.

Less than one.

Yes, Caisen had pitched a fit. But not Brandon.

It was worthy of celebrating. I would have made his favorite breakfast the next morning or something, but my kitchen was in boxes. So, we went out to breakfast instead.

At breakfast, they all got pancakes with chocolate chips and whipped cream.

We knew how to make big deals over victories!

I hoped the celebratory breakfast would jumpstart another great day.

However, later while packing, I smelled something burning. It came from the kitchen.

I called for Jordan, and we frantically investigated. We opened the oven, checked the cupboards, and looked around all the surfaces. It took some serious effort before we discovered the source, a lighter tucked between some boxes on the kitchen table. It was still hot.

I had brought it out from my bathroom a little bit earlier, when I was packing up the candles and décor from my bathroom windowsill.

After some interrogations, we learned that Brandon first picked it up, which led to Henry playing with it. In the process, we also learned that Henry had burned down someone else's laundry room in the past. I'm not sure how we hadn't learned that before, but the kids brought us up to speed on the details.

I felt uncomfortable that he was playing with the lighter, and his explanation made it worse.

"No one likes me," he said.

After talking it through, I came to understand that since Brandon received praise for his holiday victory, Henry felt bad for himself. The fire made him feel better. A scary tendency, for sure.

However, we worked through it. We always worked through it. Whatever the obstacles were, we put the work in. And it was taking us less and less effort because they were able to navigate their feelings better and express them in conversations. Trust was growing stronger.

As scary as it was knowing that there were still some major struggles within each kid, we trusted that God would continue to guide us through the work that was still ahead of us.

As we looked back at what we had accomplished with the kids, we could also see that Jordan and I had a developed a stronger bond through living in the trenches together.

We had to count on each other to pick up the slack when things were heavy.

We had to count on each other for support in faith if one of us was questioning God.

We had to count on each other for emotional boosts when we were feeling burned out.

We had to count on each other, so that the kids couldn't divide us and conquer us.

We had to count on each other to talk us down if the other of us took offense to other people's inaccurate lingo or misguided assumptions about adoption, which happened often.

In fact, just days before the move, we had to nudge and kick each other quite a bit while applying for the kids' new social security cards, which is about a million times more challenging than you'd think.

The kids were with us as the teller was arguing that Jordan and I shouldn't be listed as the parents on the applications and that she'd need their *"other"* birth certificates to get their *"real"* parents' names.

Jordan kicked me, so I took a deep breath before saying, *"This here adoption decree names us as their 'real' parents and also voids any birth certificates printed before these here brand-new originals, which also happen to list us as the parents. The kids are adopted, which means that their birth parents are no longer legally responsible for them, or their social security cards. We are."*

Hey, I think I see another soapbox. I'm going to stand on it for a minute:

Mic-check. One-two-three. If you learn about an adoption, it is not ok to ask where the real parents are, because the adoptive parents really are the kids' parents. Also, you shouldn't ask if the parents would still like kids of their own, because their adopted kids are their own. If for some reason your curiosity is so great that you must ask some version of these questions, for the sake of all things good, DO NOT ask in front of the children. They don't need to hear you imply that they are not enough, or that there is any reason to question their parents' authority. The end.

Eventually, it all clicked for the social security clerk that we were the kids' parents. And with each conversation we engaged in, it got easier to address the wording details. In fact, many things got easier. We weren't pros, but we found our groove and continued to roll with it.

And just like that, we laid our heads down to rest, for the last time in Georgia, in sleeping bags. We had out our clothes for the next day, toothbrushes, and car games set aside, and everything else was packed and loaded in a twenty-six-foot Penske.

When the alarm went off, we got up and hit the road.

I drove my giant SUV, which pulled a twenty-foot flatbed trailer with Jordan's truck strapped on top. I had three kids, two dogs, and two cats in the SUV with me.

Jordan had the loaded Penske truck and two kids strapped in the front seat with him.

We had one thousand miles to go, in one day, with minimal stops. What could go wrong?

We were ready. We were set. Then we were gone. And even though I knew it would be a tough road ahead I also knew we'd be fine, because of what we'd already worked through. We had grown to be a family. A family brought together by God.

EPILOGUE

O ur family has been together nearly four years now, and it's hard to remember life before we brought our kids home. Truly, obstacles and all, it feels like we've always been together.

Over time, we have confronted more challenges, and found that some of what we thought we'd resolved came back. Isn't parenting like that... There's always another phase to go through!

However, it's been over six months since Brandon's last major-meltdown, where he kicked out a stairway baluster and set off the fire extinguisher inside our home. They say that time helps to heal old wounds. A few years were needed to help with the biggest of Brandon's hurts, and a few months were needed before I stopped flinching in anticipation of a fit that was no longer coming. As a result, I get to see Brandon differently. He is a teenager, he has an attitude, and he is stubborn. Also, he deeply loves art, reading and physical activity, and has intentions of being helpful and loving. I didn't feel lucky as I worked through his baggage with him, but I do feel blessed that he's developed the trust needed to drop much of it. Not all. But, much.

Faith has also come a long way. Her drawings show such light and care. She has a passion for fashion, loves sports, and loves offering an encouraging word to anyone who needs one. She has a long way to go in development, but she hasn't been stealing food and hiding it in her dresser drawers or floor vents for a while, which took great trust on her part that we'd always provide enough. Instead, she's been more forthcoming in conversations, and helpful in coordinating all the moving pieces at home. Watching her bloom has been deeply rewarding.

Henry is such a charmer. He is empathetic and intuitive. He can read people and situations with such ease. He is also clever and witty. Sometimes, his smarts get the best of him, and he has to be reminded to use his skills for good, but he always bounces back to show he truly cares for people, and wants to be a Soldier for Christ.

Clarence is our family clown. His lack of filter often gets him into trouble, but what he lacks in social restraint, he makes up with in personality! It only makes sense that so much passion contained in one body would result in a flop on the floor with rivers of tears... He loves to laugh, speaks his mind, and gives the best hugs.

Caisen is my challenge right now. I love the little man, and I am thankful that he's in my life. However, it makes me sad that he's expressing his anger much like Brandon used to. I'm hopeful that this phase will pass in months, instead of the years Brandon needed. And, I have reason to be hopeful. When Caisen isn't angry, he's my little lover-pants! He enjoys reading to me, and telling me stories. He's smart, engaging, and silly.

Jordan is doing very well. He is now a Company Commander, which keeps him busy. When he isn't working, he's watching our kids play whichever sport they are playing in a given season, or firing up the grill with whichever kid called dibs that day. He also likes to run with Brandon, ask Faith about boys, talk football with Henry and Clarence, and read with Caisen. He has a *"thing"* with each of them.

I stay busy as well. Between getting everyone to their ongoing appointments for continued growth and development, and carting them around to sporting events, and getting everyone out of the routine by seeking new hikes and outdoor adventures, I stay on the go. Not to mention, I just finished my memoir. About one-third of me thinks it's time to put the keyboard away... The other two-thirds is ready to start typing away on book number two...

Announcing our intention to adopt

*The first family picture we shared, without
breaking foster care rules. Easter, 2015*

*Signing the papers declaring we were ready to move
forward with our adoption. May, 2015*

One of many beach days. June, 2015

They each decorated their own bag-head so we could get a "real" family picture for my birthday. July, 2015

*So close to finalization, with one last
creative idea for sharing. July, 2015*

In front of the courthouse on Adoption Day, July 8th, 2015

THANK YOU

T hank you for reading my family's story. I pray you found it to be time well spent. If you believe this book was entertaining, or enlightening, or a blessing to you in any other way, please consider leaving a review with your favorite book distributor. For your convenience, a few direct links to reviewing sites are available to you at http://www.chasingkites.com/authors/Jessie-Gallaher/.

If you'd like to follow our story further, or get to know us better, please look for me at www.facebook.com/jgal814. I'd love to have you join me!

ACKNOWLEDGMENTS

I didn't always feel the desire to thank God on this journey, especially in the darkest moments. However, as I've watched His plan unfold, I am so thankful He chose me to be a part of it!

To those of you who answered late-night phone calls to help me recall details, consider word choice, or listen while I read you yet another version of the same chapter you'd heard six times, THANK YOU! I will forever cherish your involvement!

To Lorraine Anglemier: Your attention to detail and care for this project were crucial to its success! The many conversations we had along the way were divine! You were so much more than an editor for me, and I couldn't have done it without you! THANK YOU!

To Rachel McCracken with Chasing Kites Publishing: THANK YOU for holding my hand through the publishing process. It's been an absolute pleasure working with you, and I look forward to collaborating on future projects together!

To my Launch Team: For believing in me, encouraging me, giving feedback, and everything else, THANK YOU! Each of you means something special to me, and I couldn't have moved into launch day without you!

To my kids: Y'all are rock stars! I will forever cherish the memories of reading the chapters aloud to each of you, and listening to you laugh out loud at the chaos of our roots. You are the roses in my life. THANK YOU!

To my husband: You are an incredible rock! There is no one I'd rather walk through life with, and I'm thankful to have you!

ABOUT THE AUTHOR

Jessie is a wife, writer and an advocate for foster and adoptive families. She has a background in psychology and in working with adolescents. She maintains a Facebook page (www.facebook.com/jgal814) which seeks to inspire others to lean on their faith and improve their perspective. When it comes to outlook, she would love everyone to remember that *"It's a choice to focus on what is going wrong. It is a better choice to count your blessings."*

Jessie is a mom to five adopted kids. They have redefined what love means to her, as she now understands at a deeper level how much work love can require. Though life can be difficult at times, she maintains faith that all things are possible with God, and therefore continues giving her best effort to overcome each obstacle as it comes.

http://www.chasingkites.com/authors/Jessie-Gallaher/